Reclaiming Education

Renewing
Schools and Universities
in Contemporary
Western Culture

The Shard and Southwark Cathedral, London.

The cathedral is built on the site of 800 years of cathedrals from mid-19th century. The Shard by Renzo Piano built in 2009-2012.

Reclaiming Education

Renewing Schools and Universities in Contemporary Western Culture

Edited by

Catherine A. Runcie
&
David Brooks

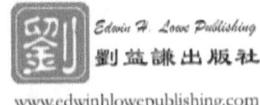

www.edwinhlowepublishing.com

Copyright © in this collection Catherine A. Runcie & David Brooks 2018.

Copyright © in the individual chapters remains with the individual authors.

All rights reserved. This book is copyright. Apart from any fair dealing for the purpose of private study, research, criticism or review, as permitted under the Copyright Act 1968, no part may be reproduced or stored by any process without prior written permission of the publisher.

Grateful acknowledgement is made to copyright holders of materials reproduced in this book. The publisher would be grateful to be informed of any inadvertent errors or omissions in the use of copyright material and would be pleased to correct them in any forthcoming editions

A catalogue record for this book is available from the National Library of Australia

ISBN 9780994168269

Edwin H. Lowe Publishing, Sydney.
www.edwinhlowepublishing.com
contact@edwinhlowepublishing.com
Edwin H. Lowe Publishing is the trading name of Edwin Hulme Lowe. ABN 60 901 995 995

Cover Image: Vincenzo Foppi, fresco 'The Young Cicero Reading', c.1464, The Wallace Collection, London.

Frontispiece Image: © I.F. Head, 2018, The Shard and Southwark Cathedral, London.

Tradition is not to preserve the ashes but to pass on the fire.

Gustav Mahler

Be a yardstick of quality. Some people aren't used to an environment where excellence is expected.

Steve Jobs

Universities should stand up for the preservation of learning, for the pursuit of Truth, and in so far as men are capable of it, the attainment of wisdom.

T.S. Eliot

An educated, enlightened and informed population is one of the surest ways of promoting the health of a democracy.

Nelson Mandela

The world would not be in such a snarl
Had Marx been Groucho, instead of Karl.

Irving Berlin to Groucho Marx on the occasion of his 75th birthday

In Memoriam

It is with the deepest regret that the editors inform our readers that the eminent musician, musicologist and music educator, Richard Gill AO (1941-2018), has passed away. During his last illness, Richard Gill volunteered to write for this book, so profound was his passion for music education, throughout all schooling, and in every walk of life. The editors are honoured indeed to have a paper from so great a musician and so beloved a man.

Contents

Foreword   1
   Catherine A. Runcie

Prologue: On Postmodernism   9
   David Brooks

PHILOSOPHY AND POLICY

The Centre Cannot Hold   20
   David Daintree

Reanimating the Liberal Arts in Australia: 32
A New Lease of Life for an Ancient Education
   Karl Schmude

Western Civilisation and All That   47
   Simon Haines

The Purpose of Education   54
   Kevin Donnelly

Australia's Decaying University: Identity Politics,   76
Psychology and Campus Intellectual Freedom
   Matthew Lesh

Britain and Western Civilisation in Australian   91
Undergraduate History Courses:
An Institutional Approach
   Chris Berg and Bella d'Abrera

Fostering "a rugged honesty of mind": The   100
Liberal Philosophy and Approach of Robert
Menzies to Education in Post-war Australia
    David Furse-Roberts

The Need for Discipline   119
    Greg Melleuish

The Concept of Equality in Education   131
    Steven Schwartz

Reclaiming Subsidiarity in School Funding   141
    Blaise Joseph

DISCIPLINES AND METHODS

Mathematics, Core of the Past and   149
Hope of the Future
    James Franklin

Art Teaching as Part of a Liberal Education   163
    Christopher Allen

Helping to Regain Lost Ground by Re-vitalizing   171
Music Education
    Richard Gill

A Plea for Narrowness   178
    Jeremy Bell

Reclaiming 'English'   189
    Barry Spurr

The Role of Appreciation in Literary Study: 202
its Centrality and Presuppositions
  David Brooks

The Cultivation of Memory: Developing Memory 229
Habits in the 21st Century Classroom
  Natalie Kennedy

The Spirituality of Time: Bridging the History 238
Gap in the Postmodern Classroom
  Sarah Williams

"Latin is for the Elite"...and other Zombie Myths 247
  Sarah Lawrence

Bridging the Wandering Islands: Education and 264
Connectivity. Some Personal Observations
  Ivan Francis Head

Contributors 281

Index 288

Foreword

Catherine A. Runcie

Hearth and health are deepest needs throughout all ages and among all peoples. They are the necessities that let us continue on this planet. Together they are our source of community, of love, joy, comfort, hope, and the need for our lost loved ones to prevail somehow, somewhere, beyond time. Evidence from long ago and all over shows that the needs of the hearth spill over, because the needs of the heart spill over, not just into survival practicalities, but into, as it were, the impracticalities too, art and song and the intricacies of faith, sometimes myth, sometimes magic, shoring mankind up before the mysteries of life and death and time. Mankind needed it all to survive.

In his famous TV series *The History of Britain*, historian Simon Schama says of the Neolithic household of Skara Brae, it had "style"; the actual interiors made "grand interior statements" with not just necessities but luxuries too, *objets d'art* of genuine houses of carved stone. The hearth is a precious place. In an even bleaker environment, the Inuit hearth defied the long dark winter by song accompanied by drumming. And the care of the dead, which goes back 100,000 years and beyond, shows mankind's deep and tender need to perpetuate someone precious. Think of the amphorae for babies at Banpo, Shaanxi—with the hole for the spirit to escape and hover somewhere and never end. And health—again evidence from long ago and all over—shows how mankind, often erroneously and needing especially to advance, kept trying to heal the sick and help the babe or the wounded warrior. Mankind is still trying.

But what secures them—hearth and health and all their needs? What obtains all their answers to their needs? Knowledge. Knowledge secures and obtains them—makes safe or tries to make safe hearth and health. And knowledge is efficiently harvested, remembered, tested, advanced and handed down from one generation to another by what has emerged as 'education'. Fortunately for mankind, education treats knowledge as treasure—as 'intergenerational treasure'. So it is.

Whether in a log cabin or under a palm tree or in an igloo or a cave or a fancy stone structure, now called a university—this latter becoming possible during the Christian and monastic era in Europe, starting with the University of Bologna in 1088, and in various forms crossing Europe, then the globe—education, wherever, maintained this pursuit of mankind's treasure, knowledge and its transmission. When a tunnel was built sloping upwards into an igloo and the cold air dropped at the low entrance, allowing warmth to stay in the igloo, and when a hole was finally made in the ceiling as a kind of flue, that was learning, learning which was sustaining. Indeed centuries later, that same knowledge helped to sustain American Arctic explorer Peary at the turn of the 20th century. He borrowed Inuit learning. Today we would call this Inuit lore "evidence-based science". It is knowledge. To use a woomera, as Australian Aboriginals did, to propel a spear to uncanny speeds not equalled until centuries later by a rifle, was "evidence-based science"—engineering, one has to say.

This is education over generations without the trimmings, no scholarships or accreditation but survival. Just survival. But it was shared, this knowledge, firming as 'education on the go'; and without it mankind might not have made it to the era of universities, or to today's schools, both primary and secondary, places where now we self-consciously understand the importance of education as shared treasure.

So, education protects this treasure knowledge, and knowledge protects hearth and health, as mankind traverses fickle history, as mankind comes upon plague or famine or a volcano or a tsunami—natural disasters. Or unnatural disasters—man's inhumanity to man, slavery, tyranny, brutality and war, times when to be merely human and to have human needs is perilous, or to meet human needs is dangerous.

But mankind's irrevocable dedication to truth is the protector of this existentially essential knowledge. And truth can only be maintained by never ceasing to debate and test available knowledge, by trying to clarify anomalies or seeming paradoxes through what one conceives as truth with brave honesty. I say brave, for is not honesty brave?

Throughout history, to veer from this dedication to truth has proved perilous. To traduce knowledge, to teach only half-truths, to create straw man arguments (which are rife in the various Movements for this and that today), to usurp debate and discovery by mandating thinking, is a betrayal of mankind. By way of patent contemporary examples: to treat Captain James Cook as if he were a conquistador is to deny his real role as an extraordinary explorer and mapmaker, precious to the whole world, and to deny a truth; or to ignore Leif Erikson in favour of Christopher Columbus, the Euro discoverer of 'America', when Erikson paddled around Newfoundland nearly 500 years previous to Columbus hitting the Bahamas, is to perpetuate diminishing the Vikings and their extraordinary achievements and to deny a truth. Or to ignore the earlier peoples who trekked thousands of kilometres across land bridges to get to, say, Canada, or trekked over land and paddled over treacherous water to reach Australia, is to perpetuate diminishing those peoples and to deny truth. It is simple and obvious to see that to perpetuate untruths or half-truths is a disservice to mankind, making its way through tricky history and its ever unpredictable threats and challenges. It is simple and obvious to see that to perpetuate untruths and half-truths is to proliferate harm.

I say proliferate, because when the harm that from time to time and too frequently takes hold, unknown and unforeseen consequences occur that shatter hearth and health, and mankind's very heart. Who would believe that the many interlocking falsehoods of Nazism, developing from the fake 'Aryan race', could lead in an unprecedented catastrophe to the deaths of millions of beating hearts?

Who today, staring at the frantic efforts of a Syrian child to breathe and the deaths of those who cannot, staring from the comfort of our sitting room and TV, is not witness to the horror and the falsehoods from Damascus that facilitate the crime of chemical warfare?

These brutalities, just taking those of our twentieth century and now the twenty-first century, have occurred incomprehensibly in the age of great universities and ready access to knowledge and the truth.

But universities, made up of mere mortals whose learning endows them with considerable power over the young, can have faults too, and can forsake truth for complacency or complicity with power; or—shamefully—with fashion, what the French call *des idées du jour*. Or, at its very nadir, a university or a privileged staff member can be totally complicit. Think of Heidegger, who, if he did not burn books, did sympathize with Nazism. He traduced truth.

In today's world, universities are more complicit with ideological fashion than with a specific political power, and thus may be given to half-truths and straw man arguments and sly sophisms. One has only to think of Auden's lines "Intellectual disgrace/ Stares from every human face," and one is tempted to say universities are disgracing themselves today.

A university has never had so much privilege and power as today, and thus has the obligation for all its teachers, learned and accredited, to protect existentially essential truth. In the past, universities created a way of doing so that seemed proof against *des idées du jour*—the university seminar—trailing its Latin origin in 'seed plot'. The seminar, so important now in universities, is the seed plot of truth, quite apart from the knowledgeable lecture. I quote, as an example of praise and gratitude for the seminar, from Professor Hu Zhuanglin, formerly of Peking University, who came out of Communist China in 1979-80, with a small group of scholars, affectionately called the Gang of Nine by those of us who taught them, to study English Language and English Literatures (British, American and Australian and Literary Theory). Without degrees themselves (in the name of egalitarian communism), these exceptional scholars went home with actual degrees from the University of Sydney, hard-earned and entirely valid, and they propelled learning among millions, learning English, who came to deserve accreditation at various levels throughout China. Professor Hu says:

We were ... greatly impressed by the methods of teaching and learning in Sydney University. Traditionally, in China, professors or lecturers dominated classes and did all the talking. But in Sydney University all the postgraduate courses were carried out in the form of a seminar. Though we had learnt the word 'seminar' through the Russian experts, it is our experience at Sydney University that taught us the essence of the word. Some participants volunteered to prepare topics by reading beforehand and presenting understanding ... in the classroom. Then the other participants raised questions or expressed their own views. Finally the lecturer made his or her summary, gave some comments, and clarified difficult points. ... Every participant had to hand in papers.[1]

Out of a seminar (not limited, I must add, as a mode of learning to graduates nor to English Studies, but which is provided to undergraduates, and in all disciplines), truth and not mandated half-truths, could prevail. In a seminar one could eschew Francis Bacon's famous perilous idols that arise from our human failings: idols of the tribe, idols of the cave, idols of the market-place, idols of the theatre. In his *Novum Organum* (1620), one will see how prescient Bacon was 400 years ago.[2] Today one might use different terms: the human tendency to hatred, associated with identity politics (idols of the tribe); narcissism, vanity, the perception of oneself as always a special case (idols of the cave); prejudices imputed to others such as sexism, racism, misogyny, elitism, and one's own never-to-go-unnoticed 'virtue-signalling' (idols of the market-place); not perceiving anew, or from first principles, the preying on ignorance or innocence, and asserting the constant pressure of copy-cat thinking, as if it were new—yet knowing that it is not persuasive but infectious—as contagious as the tattoos we see all around on the bodies of housewives to hoons to hoodlums (idols of the theatre).

Bacon would have no Uriah Heep, full of envy leading to deception and cruel crime; he would have no Caliban—not just Shakespeare's monster in *The Tempest*, trustingly taught language, only to use it spitefully in curses and falsehood, but Oscar Wilde's Caliban too. Wilde so shrewdly says:

> The 19th century dislike of Realism is the rage of Caliban seeing his own face in a glass. The 19th century dislike of Romanticism is the rage of Caliban not seeing his own face in a glass.[3]

---

[1] Hu Zhuanglin, *Crossing the Pacific* (Beijing: Peking University, 2016), 73.
[2] Idols of the tribe are tendencies inherent in the human mind which produce false cognitions. Idols of the cave are tendencies to error in each individual mind, whether from its natural constitution or from its education. Idols of the market-place are tendencies to error, founded in social intercourse with others. Idols of the theatre are tendencies to error, founded in the dogmas of existing philosophies. See Francis Bacon, Lord Verulam, *Novum Organum* (1620), Aphorisms xxxviii-xliv. There is an earlier version of the doctrine in Bacon's *The Advancement of Learning* (1605), Book II, Section XIV, §§ 9-11.
[3] Oscar Wilde, *The Picture of Dorian Gray* (London: Ward, Lock & Company, 1891), Preface.

So will we expect truth from Caliban—in his dealings with Miranda, or his devout following of two charlatans, Trinculo and Stephano? No. Bacon would have us eschew misplaced and tyrannical vanities and hatreds and their dire consequences.

Learning, knowledge, truth are for mankind's protection. They are survival necessities. To ignore truth, to give in to the idols, is to betray mankind, to lead us to the culling fields of war, and in our daily lives to the piteous self-deception and chronic discontent that we see all about us, and which make us vulnerable. The university of today, altered so much from when Hu Zhuanglin and his fellow scholars studied in the late 1970s, plus the school and high school of today, are obliged, more than at any other period of the recent past, to use their well-resourced extraordinary power with the wisdom of truth. They must eschew harbouring Caliban. I have heard of a university here that with no self-satire intended, advertised itself as the University of Unlearning. This is a sign of our times and should be resisted. Think if somewhere along mankind's path, learning was subverted, truth was subverted for a lust for power or out of malice. Had learning been betrayed or suppressed out of a power-lust or malice, say, under the palm tree, in the log cabin, or at a mother's knee, or from a warrior father, the canoe would tip; the igloo would give one black lung; the woomera would not propel. The season of sowing and reaping might be unknown. The long white cloud might not indicate land to the earliest seafarers of the Pacific. If truth had been falsified or falsity mandated, mankind would not have survived in all corners of the globe. Similarly, if today the necromancy of a Derrida or a Foucault or Lacan or Lyotard or Marcuse or Deleuze or Guattari, or of so many other intellectual carpetbaggers of the 'postmodern' era, were to prey uncontested on the vanity and the power of a university or any place of learning, then a student is likely to succumb to the wilderness of *anomie*.

Wittily and indelicately, Sir Roger Scruton calls what is peddled as truth by many French philosophers *metamerde*. What is peddled as feminist, egalitarianism and non-genderism, leaping to righteousness against 'sexism', is less than clear or logical, and lives in those institutions or minds where debate is throttled. One now can almost get away with saying that if a pebble were on a beach, and a woman stubbed her toe on it, that pebble would be sexist. Or one can get away with averring that the International Dateline proves Einstein's theory of time. Ludicrous? No. It merely takes ignorance and the suppression of truth, or the pressure of copy-cat thinking following *des idées du jour*. I hesitate to adduce an actual example. But after a recent episode of vandalism on a statue of Captain Cook (a graffito on the pediment which declared "No Pride in Genocide"), a well-qualified historian, who terms herself a "public historian", suggested the graffito might remain, as it is part of a debate that is a sign that:

social values associated with Australia's historical narrative and our ways of understanding and remembering the past are shifting....It demonstrates that Aboriginal people are demanding a voice and their rightful place in our history.[4]

The very credentialed historian rightly discards a view of Cook that is patently ignorant anyway—that Cook 'discovered' Australia, but backs a graffito that is equally ignorant. Surely here the answer to the Cook dilemma is to allow Cook to be known as a world-famous explorer and mapmaker whom even NASA praises for accuracy. Two wrongs don't make a right. Whatever happened subsequent to the Dutch, French, Portuguese or British making their way around a stunning new landmass (which the Ancients felt must exist as a counterweight to the Northern Hemisphere) is not the fault of these explorers. Should they not have come to Australia? Should it have been a forgotten landmass? The answers to these questions lie in a calm and more truthful education that yields a world view.

Another disservice to knowledge is in the teaching of sciences, subjects where distortion by Bacon's idols would matter a very great deal. Right now several university academics, such as Professor Leanne Rylands of the University of Western Sydney, and the Chief Scientist, Dr Alan Finkel, are concerned about the inadequate level of mathematics.[5] High schools are discouraging advanced sciences by not encouraging advanced mathematics.

In an article in *The Australian Financial Review*, the outstanding and modest Professor Michelle Simmons, who does not waste time prating about being a woman in a man's field, gets to the significant truth.[6] She says that Australia is losing out to the rest of the world in quantum physics, when it could lead. Very few of those sitting the NSW 2017 high school Higher School Certificate took physics—"a historical low". Why? Because there is not enough higher mathematics or physics in earlier schooling. This is a deprivation to a student, and is deplored by all quantum physicists, who could make Australia a Quantum Physics Hub.

No Australian can take this lightly. Australia is patently not the "lucky country". It is the plucky country. It is brainy and brave, and has achieved so much. Look at its pre-European and its European history. These histories should get together and sort themselves out; they should work interculturally. They should reclaim or create the most useful education for all. No Caliban, following the drunken Trinculo and Stephano.

---

[4] Andrew Taylor, 'Historian questions whether graffiti should have been left on Captain Cook statue', *The Sydney Morning Herald*, 18 April 2018, https://www.smh.com.au/national/new/historian-captain-cook-statue-graffiti-indigenous-20180418-p4zade.html

[5] Robert Bolton, '"Absolutely shocking" mathematics skills are being slammed by teachers', *Australian Financial Review*, 27/4/18, 3.

[6] Michael Bailey, ''Part physicist, part motor mechanic': quantum computer engineer shortage threatens hub hopes', *Australian Financial Review*, 12 March 2018, 12.

Now this deprivation in learning in the HSC curriculum to the student should be deplored by everyone, but by teachers especially. And teachers should also acknowledge that teachers' education needs to be reviewed in all subjects. They have been deprived too. They are rare professionals. They take up the task of transmitting truth with patience and care. This is a task that is both difficult and noble, as it is of vital importance for the whole of society. Professor Simmons mentioned in a TV interview recently that an HSC level question in "physics" was about having a nuclear reactor in your district and what would be the effect? She very kindly said she wished for more maths in physics. One might say one wanted more physics in physics as well.

I once, as an academic, had the experience of a high school student asking for help with an essay question as she sat across from me in the library. It went something like this: "Put yourself in Ophelia's place, and explain why she drowned herself." I was just not "educated" recently enough to know that the answer—mandated—was that Hamlet was part of the white male patriarchy (as was Shakespeare) and he showed her no respect nor understanding. I am waiting for a question on the HSC that asks, "Why did Portia need to dress up as a male in order to be defence in court for two white upper-class twits, Antonio and Bassanio?"

Anyone lamenting the school results that, we are told daily in the news, are poor in literacy and numeracy, wants students to be, say, as literate as can be for their age level, as they progress to the higher levels demanded in the HSC, where textual analysis, drawing on deep knowledge, is possible. Why should one be deprived of deep learning?

At the very least, in all our institutions, one must have the freedom to debate, to advance to deeper knowledge, and to eschew Bacon's idols. To persist with mandated thinking, to give in to vanities, to sneak in short-circuited arguments, to give in to Caliban's revenge, or to the ephemeral fashion of the times, to accept copy-cat thinking, instead of the honest, tough heuristic debate of the seminar, is to traduce the whole enterprise, won with such difficulty over so long—education that leads to truth.

Are we stalled at that stage right now? Mandated thinking that falsifies? Have we actually been in that stage for decades, and have not realised its consequences? Will we have, as Winston Smith is told in *Nineteen Eighty-Four*, a "boot on a human face – forever"? Are we in the Era of Caliban? Combine our *anomie* with "the cowardice of acquiescence", to use Simon Schama's phrase, and what have we? The loss of truth, and thus our moral agency? Or, are we stuck with the desire to use being a perceived victim in exchange for power? Are we misled into committing egregious present wrongs, thinking somehow that that eliminates past wrongs? This is an outrageous falsehood, so often committed, and much encouraged by those who do not wish any degree of content for anyone, or genuine righteousness. Or, are we stuck with the assumption that legal equality confers sameness—an error neither Thomas

Jefferson nor J.S. Mill committed. Is this today's learning, knowledge, education and seminar: mandated ideas in institutions, and in the symbiotic media, and even in some governmental instrumentalities—samples of proliferating harm—denying self-correction and refusing moral agency? Depriving the plucky country of that Quantum Physics Hub, and denying Australia literacy above the level of countries that spend much less than Australia on education, and also spend much less self-doubting argument about what to do?

We must never appease Caliban, as we are doing now. As a very lonely Winston Churchill warned in 1940: "An appeaser is one who feeds a crocodile, hoping it will eat him last."

During the editing of this book, which for a long while I did alone, I have felt overwhelmed by the generosity of serious scholars and thinkers, who gave such worthy papers, that were researched and written even during times of illness, when they were exceptionally busy, or under other forms of duress, and when they had to trust the editor, now two editors to my great pleasure, who were unknown to many of them. To be entrusted with papers so learned and so freely given was like being at an ideal university in an ideal society.

I thank these scholars and thinkers most deeply, and I thank David Menzies with whom the idea of this volume was hatched. I thank Professor Barry Spurr who gave us the title to this book, and much more over the years as colleague and friend, model teacher and scholar; Professor James Franklin, and Dr David Daintree, for their inspiring and unstinting help and knowledge just whenever needed; Karina Hepner, Professor Carole Cusack, Emeritus Professor Garry Trompf, Lyn Ashcroft, Professor Jennifer Gribble, Emeritus Professor Michael Wilding, Emeritus Professor Gerald Wilkes, the late Emeritus Professor Leonie Kramer, and my co-editor David Brooks. I am grateful, over decades in some instances, to friends and colleagues for their inspiration, learnedness, and the *sine qua non*, integrity. I thank Mary Wilson and Beverley Menzies. I thank the very patient publisher.

I thank my family, my beloved sister Jeanette, and my niece Lyn, Marlene and Harold, Huguette and Tom, beyond the vasty deep in Canada, and my family here, my beloved husband, ever inspiring, helpful and sustaining, and I thank my four children. I dedicate my small part in this book to my grandchildren—trusting the future.

Catherine A. Runcie
Sydney 2018

Prologue: On Postmodernism

David Brooks

Postmodernism is supposed to have been on the wane since the turn of the millennium. In a recent introduction to the subject it is claimed that postmodernism ended "on or about" 11 September 2001.[1] But, on the other hand, the author also suggests that what has followed postmodernism—what he calls "post-postmodernism"—is an "intensification and mutation of features and tendencies already present *within* postmodernism".[2] So, it would seem that we may be in just a new phase of postmodernism. At any rate, postmodernism is still taught in university courses, and its offspring, identity politics, is as vigorous as ever, both on university campuses and in national politics.[3]

Since postmodernism is clearly still a pervasive influence in intellectual life and education, and is to a great extent responsible for the problems in education addressed in this book, it may be desirable to make some observations on it here, to set the scene for some of the following essays.

Postmodernism can refer to a movement in the arts and literature, or to a world-view corresponding to the latest phase in the development of our society, postmodernity, or both. As a movement in the arts and literature, postmodernism must stand or fall on its own merits, and I shall say no more about it. It is postmodernism as a world-view that is the problem.[4] But this means considering the notion of postmodernity.

The "post-" in postmodernity implies that we have in some way got beyond modernity. Is this true? Cultural and philosophical terms can usually be defined in multiple ways, but some definitions are more useful than others,

---

[1] Brian McHale, *The Cambridge Introduction to Postmodernism* (Cambridge: Cambridge University Press, 2015), 175.
[2] *Ibid.*, 178. (Italics in original)
[3] Intellectual movements take about a generation to perform the tasks that they set themselves, but then hang on for another fifteen or twenty years, in decline, and with diminishing returns, while opposing forces gather. Since postmodernism in the English-speaking world began around 1980, one would expect that it would have done by now virtually everything that it intended to do—reviewing Western thought, art and literature from a postmodernist point of view. But, no doubt, it will persist for some time.
[4] Postmodern architecture, for example, is a kind of neo-eighteenth century art: polished, stylish, witty, self-reflexive, playful, amusing. The successful expression of this spirit in something as solid and fixed as architecture can be an artistic triumph. But the frivolity of postmodern theory is something altogether different, as we shall see.

because they open up a subject to clearer and fuller inquiry. The most useful definition of modernity involves coupling it with, and opposing it to tradition or traditional society. In traditional society, social and material change and development are either non-existent or so slow as to be imperceptible to members of the society. By contrast, in the modern society of the last two hundred years or so, industrialism and capitalism have brought about not only great change, but an ever-increasing rate of change, so that members of modern society experience constant change, and expect nothing else. We solve our problems by science and technology, but our solutions cause more problems, requiring solutions, which in turn produce more problems, and so on endlessly. The process is endless, because, short of a global catastrophe, we are never going to abandon science and technology. This surely is the essence of modernity, and we are stuck in it forever. Even if socialism were to replace capitalism, we would still be living in modernity. If all this is true, then there cannot be anything that might reasonably be called postmodernity. Postmodernity is an illusion. Where does this leave the postmodern world-view, and the theories about that world-view?

In the context of social theory, we owe the notions of postmodernism and postmodern society to the French philosopher Jean-François Lyotard, and his book *The Postmodern Condition: A Report on Knowledge*.[5] Although Lyotard writes of postmodern society, he is also willing to refer to post-industrial society, holding with others to the now common doctrine that in the latest phase of capitalism services have become more important in advanced economies than manufacturing.[6] Lyotard has no new economic analysis of this phase of capitalism to make. He refers to this phase of capitalist development as postmodern merely because he wishes to call nineteenth and early twentieth century capitalism modern. Thus, the terminology is merely a verbal matter, and of no theoretical significance.[7] What is of importance is the doctrine of social relations and of the alleged changing nature of knowledge in a post-industrial society, which Lyotard erects on the basis of the commonplace notion of post-industrial society.[8] Of even more importance are the fallacies and falsehoods by means of which Lyotard erects his doctrine.

Lyotard notes that in contemporary capitalism information in data banks accessed by computers has become a major "force of production". This has given corporations hegemonic control of knowledge, and subjected knowledge to a criterion of performativity, the most efficient ratio of inputs

---

[5] Jean-François Lyotard, *The Postmodern Condition: A Report on Knowledge*, Translation from the French by Geoff Bennington and Brian Massumi. Foreword by Fredric Jameson. Theory and History of Literature, Volume 10 (Minneapolis: University of Minnesota Press, 1984). Originally published as *La Condition postmoderne:rapport sur le savoir* (Paris: Les Editions de Minuit, 1979).
[6] *Ibid.*, 3 and n. 1, 85.
[7] *Ibid.*, xxiii, 3, 11.
[8] *Ibid.*, xxiii-xxv.

to outputs, for the sake of maximising profits. In this way, knowledge has, he alleges, become "political".⁹ But, the most advanced developments in natural science, he alleges, undermine the criterion of performativity, because those scientific developments call in question determinism and predictability.¹⁰ The implication is that science now has the potential to undermine capitalism.

All this is connected to postmodern "incredulity toward metanarratives", or, as we now usually say, the rejection of Grand Narratives.¹¹ The "narratives" of the emancipation of humanity, and of the unity of knowledge, which in "modern" society legitimated the pursuit of truth and the advancement of science have been subverted by nineteenth and twentieth century philosophy, and by twentieth century science.¹² It follows that we can no longer believe in the Enlightenment project of human emancipation by reason and science, the Hegelian systematisation of all knowledge, or in the offspring of these two, the Marxist project of communist revolution. We also have to abandon universalist notions of truth, objectivity, and humanism.¹³ All that remains is the subversion of discourses in the pursuit of justice for minorities and the marginalised.¹⁴

Is any of this true? First of all, the project of human emancipation and the ideal of the unity of all knowledge are not *narratives*.¹⁵ They are arguments or theories. They cannot be overthrown by "incredulity" or an arbitrary decision to "tell another tale". They can only be overthrown by arguments and evidence. Lyotard's efforts in this respect are feeble, and even absurd. He notes that scepticism and positivism in the nineteenth century already began to undermine metaphysical theories like Hegel's, but he does not elaborate

---

⁹ *Ibid.*, xxiv, 3-6.
¹⁰ *Ibid.*, 53-60.
¹¹ *Ibid.*, xxiv.
¹² *Ibid.*, xxiii-xxiv, 31-41, 41-47.
¹³ *Ibid*: on objectivity, see 39-41; on humanism, see 65-66; on truth, see 18-19, 23-24, 29. Lyotard is concerned with the legitimation of knowledge throughout this book, but he is continually sliding from epistemic legitimation (Is this true? Do we know it to be true?) to socio-political legitimation (Who decides if this is true? Who decides if this is knowledge?). Although continuing to talk about truth, he wants to take his final stand on the principle that truth is socially determined. See 6-9.
¹⁴ *Ibid.*, 65-67. See also Jean-François Lyotard, *The Differend: Phrases in Dispute,* Translated by Georges Van Den Abbeele. Theory and History of Literature, Volume 46 (Minneapolis: University of Minnesota Press, 1988). Originally published as *Le Différend* (Paris: Editions de Minuit, 1983).
¹⁵ Lyotard is the *fōns et orīgō* of our current fashion of declaring virtually anything to be a narrative. "Analysis reveals 2 main narratives: a 'crisis narrative' that views food insecurity as a 'production' crisis, common in the scientific and aid agency documents, and a 'chronic poverty narrative' that views food insecurity as fundamentally linked to poverty and low economic development, predominantly in the African policy documents. By identifying and describing these two distinct narratives, our goal is to initiate a debate around the hegemony of narratives, especially the production crisis narrative." Alexander F. Legwegoh and Evan D. G. Fraser, "Food Crisis or Chronic Poverty: Metanarratives of Food Insecurity in Sub-Saharan Africa", *Journal of Hunger & Environmental Nutrition*, Volume 10, Issue 3 (2015), 313-342 (from the Abstract). Lyotard classifies the "creation of wealth" as a grand narrative on page xxiii of *The Postmodern Condition*.

the argument.[16] He gives more importance to Gödel's Theorem, and to Wittgenstein's doctrine of language games. His argument is, first, that Gödel's Theorem makes impossible the ideal of the unity of all knowledge because the theorem proves that no system can be both consistent and complete[17]; second, that the incommensurability of language games fragments the project of human emancipation.[18] Neither of these arguments bears examination.

Gödel's Theorem belongs to mathematical logic. If it is to be extended to all systems of propositions, it only suggests that the principles needed to construct, say, a theory fall outside the theory. All this means is that the development of our knowledge involves systems within systems. The ongoing project of the unity of all knowledge is a process of totalizing, not the construction of a single totality. But we did not need Gödel in order to know that.[19]

In Lyotard's version of Wittgenstein's language games the different kinds of sentences—denotative, interrogative, prescriptive, evaluative, and so on—are held to be "incommensurable".[20] The project of human emancipation is a doctrine involving sentences of all kinds. But since these different kinds of sentences are incommensurable, they cannot form a coherent doctrine. So the project falls apart. This absurd conclusion is only possible on the basis of the positivist dogma that different kinds of sentences cannot be put together, but must always remain apart. It is a version of Hume's doctrine that "ought" cannot be derived from "is".[21] But this doctrine is not true. In the case of human emancipation, for example, facts bearing on human well-being have differential value. Some facts make for human well-being, and others do not. From this obvious distinction choices can be made. Such choices can be registered in sentences that are evaluative or prescriptive. Human well-being can be defined by physiology and psychology, because human beings are functioning organisms, and not inert matter.[22]

---

[16] *Ibid.*, 38-39.
[17] *Ibid.*, 42-44.
[18] *Ibid.*, 39-41.
[19] Aristotle's theory of the syllogism depends on the so-called Laws of Thought. But the Laws of Thought are not part of the theory of the syllogism. This does not invalidate either the theory of the syllogism or the Laws of Thought.
[20] For Wittgenstein's doctrine of language games, see Ludwig Wittgenstein, *Philosophical Investigations*, translated by G. E. M. Anscombe (Oxford: Basil Blackwell, 1972; originally published 1953). Ernest Gellner destructively criticised the doctrine of language games in his *Words and Things* (London: Victor Gollancz, 1959).
[21] David Hume, *A Treatise of Human Nature* [1739-40], Book III, Part I, Section I. Edited with an Introduction by Ernest C. Mossner (Harmondsworth: Penguin Books Ltd, 1969), 507-521.
[22] I am thinking of a social psychology such as Erich Fromm's. See his *The Fear of Freedom* (London: Routledge and Kegan Paul Ltd, 1942; *Man For Himself* (London: Routledge and Kegan Paul Ltd, 1949); *The Sane Society* (London: Routledge and Kegan Paul, 1956). Against the positivism of Hume we can set the Natural Law tradition of objective goods, which runs from Aristotle and the Stoics through St Thomas Aquinas to Hegel. Some will want to see objective good in terms of a union of human nature with some cosmic or divine good, as in the philosophies of Plato, Plotinus, St Augustine, St Thomas

The forays of Lyotard and other post-structuralists into natural science were destructively criticised by Sokal and Bricmont in the late 1990s.[23] Lyotard contends that new developments in science, such as quantum mechanics, fractals, and catastrophe theory, have called in question the "modern", i.e., nineteenth century, presuppositions of determinism and predictability, and replaced them with a search for "instabilities".[24] The criterion of performativity has been displaced by the postmodern criterion of "paralogy".[25] Paralogy (etymologically, 'beyond reason', and conventionally, 'false reasoning') is a "search for dissent", and the generation of new ideas for the sake of disruption.[26] Sokal and Bricmont, both practising scientists, have exposed the confusions and absurdities in Lyotard's account of contemporary science, and rebutted Lyotard's claims that science itself has changed. No such mutation from "modern" science to "postmodern" science has occurred. The validation of scientific theories remains what it was, "the comparison of theories with observations and experiments"[27]. It follows that Lyotard's claim that corporate hegemony over information is now threatened by the nature of science itself is baseless. It is just a grandiose but empty gesture.[28]

Lyotard, like other post-structuralists, is trapped within the "prison-house of language".[29] His version of this self-inflicted impotence is that in postmodern society the "social bond" consists only of Wittgensteinian language games, since all the Grand Narratives that previously held society together have faded away.[30] But, as we recall, what distinguishes language games for Lyotard is their incommensurability—which exists at multiple levels. Thus, not only are denotative sentences incommensurable with prescriptive sentences, but, at a higher level, the distinctive discourses of specific social groups, especially majorities and minorities, are also incommensurable. As a result, Lyotard sees human society as *agonistic*, as a contest or even a fight.[31] And yet, strangely, he is concerned for justice, especially—and yet for no obvious reason—for justice for minorities and the marginalized. However, this project is doomed to fail-

---

and Spinoza. See Charles Taylor, *Sources of the Self: The Making of Modern Identity* (Cambridge: Cambridge University Press, 1989).
[23] Alan Sokal and Jean Bricmont, *Intellectual Impostures: Postmodern Philosophers' Abuse of Science* (London: Profile Books Ltd, 1998). Originally published in French (Paris: Editions Odile Jacob, 1997).
[24] Lyotard, *The Postmodern Condition*, 53-60.
[25] *Ibid.*, 60-67.
[26] *Ibid.*, 64-66.
[27] Sokal and Bricmont, *Intellectual Impostures*, 125-128.
[28] Lyotard is prone to hyperbole. Thus, if scientists ignore a fellow-scientist's view, this is "terror". Lyotard, *The Postmodern Condition*, 63-64.
[29] This phrase was borrowed by Fredric Jameson from Nietzsche for his *The Prison-House of Language: A Critical Account of Structuralism and Russian Formalism* (Princeton, NJ: Princeton University Press, 1972).
[30] Lyotard, *The Postmodern Condition*, 14-17.
[31] *Ibid.*, 16-17, 64-67.

ure before it begins, precisely because of the incommensurability of language games. Because there are no rules whereby the language game of the majority and that of the minority can connect, consensus is impossible, and all the justice-seeking philosopher can do is to "bear witness" to the injustice to which a minority is being subjected.[32] From this we get our "culture of complaint" and status of victimhood. Lyotard thinks that it is only within minorities that there can be any discussion of common concerns with a view to seeking justice, as all members of the minority are playing the same language game.[33] For Lyotard "little narratives" are possible, even if Grand Narratives are not.[34] He takes no account of the possibility that there may be disagreement within minority groups. But, both in the case of majority-minority relations, and of intra-minority relations, the incommensurability of denotative sentences and prescriptive sentences means that participants cannot hope to arrive at a common truth. All that is possible is the irrational assertion of claims, either as the expression of desire, or as imposed on the basis of power. This can only be a politics of futility or a politics of violence.[35]

Like other post-structuralists, Lyotard regards "reality" (in quotation marks) as something constructed in discourse, as what people experience is determined by the discourses within which they live, i.e., by the language games that they play. There is no possibility of getting outside a language game. All one can do is to invent a new "move", and somehow persuade others to adopt the move.[36] There is no possibility of objectivity, and no possibility of truth. Even "truth" has to go into quotation marks, because even science, which consists only of denotative sentences, ultimately becomes something that is to be decided by "experts", the experts who are skilled in the language game of science.[37]

---

[32] *Ibid.*, 65-66. See also *The Differend*, in which Lyotard develops his theory of justice at length. Lyotard renounces all hope of social revolution. See *The Postmodern Condition*, 66.

[33] *Ibid.*, 66.

[34] *Ibid.*, 66. The possibility of "little narratives" for minority groups is derived by analogy with René Thom's catastrophe theory in physics, which proves, according to Lyotard, that "All that exist are 'islands of determinism'." *Ibid.*, 59. For Sokal and Bricmont's critique, see *Intellectual Impostures*, 127-128, 128-133.

[35] Lyotard wants to say that the rules of language games are established by "contract" between the players. Lyotard, *The Postmodern Condition*, 10, 66. But on his principles it is impossible for there to be any rational basis for such a contract. Similarly, Lyotard has no basis for criticising the language games of terrorists, pedophiles or common thieves. No doubt this is why some feel that postmodernism *ought* to have ended on 11 September 2001.

[36] *Ibid.*, 15-17, 43, 53, 63-64, 65-67.

[37] "It is recognized that the conditions of truth, in other words, the rules of the game of science, are immanent in that game, that they can only be established within the bonds of a debate that is already scientific in nature, *and that there is no other proof that the rules are good than the consensus extended to them by the experts.*" (my italics) *Ibid.*, 29. Science is "a pragmatic game—the acceptability of the 'moves' (new propositions) made in it depends on a contract drawn between the partners." *Ibid.*, 43.

Prologue: On Postmodernism

The distinction between science and myth, or between science and magic collapses, because science, myth and magic are all equally language games, each with its own rules. Since science has no intrinsic objectivity, it is just another language game.[38] This means that it can be dismissed by postmodernists as *Western* science, amid calls for a new African science or a new Asian science. We arrive at cultural relativism at its most irrational.

Since all universal notions are impossible, owing to the multiplicity of language games, it goes without saying that any notion of a common humanity is also impossible. Postmodernism, like other kinds of post-structuralism, is anti-humanist.[39] Thus, Lyotard's postmodernism embraces, and asserts defiantly irrationalism, anti-realism, and anti-humanism.

Why would anyone want to adopt these views? In Lyotard's case, the explanation is of the same kind as that which explains the motivation of other French post-structuralists, namely, the desire to get away as far as possible from Marxism, the hegemony on the Left of the French Communist Party, and the dominance of Jean-Paul Sartre. The young Lyotard belonged to the Marxist group *Socialisme ou Barbarie* (Socialism or Barbarism). For fifteen years or so he worked to promote Algerian independence from France, and hoped that the Algerian revolution would go over from a nationalist revolution into a socialist one. When this hope was disappointed, he became disillusioned with Marxism, and transformed himself into one of the leading philosophers of the post-structuralist reaction. This self-transformation was strengthened by the failure of the students-workers revolution of 1968.[40] It is hard to resist the view that the irrationalism of Lyotard's post-Marxist philosophy is a massive defence mechanism, a Reaction Formation, to protect himself from the seductions of totalizing Marxism and Hegelianism.

Given the trauma of the political upheavals of the 1960s in France and the French Empire, it is at least understandable that some French intellectuals on the Left might be tempted to take this irrationalist path. But this kind of explanation will not serve for the adoption of postmodernism in the English-speaking world.

In the English-speaking world postmodernism has become something much more formless than its French antecedents. It is a rag-bag that takes in not only Lyotard's philosophy but also the doctrines of the major post-structuralist thinkers, principally, the transmogrified psychoanalysis of Jacques Lacan, the deconstruction of Jacques Derrida, the discourse theory of Michel Foucault, and the philosophy/psychoanalysis of Gilles Deleuze and Félix

---

[38] *Ibid.*, 26-27, 40.
[39] *Ibid.*, 66.
[40] Ashley Woodward, 'Jean-François Lyotard (1924-1998)', *Internet Encyclopedia of Philosophy*. http://www.iep.utm.edu/lyotard/. www.utm.edu is the web address of the University of Tennessee at Martin.

Guattari.[41] Without wishing to seem overly paradoxical, I have to say that the irrationalism of Anglophone postmodernism exists at a lower intellectual level than that of the French originals. The French thinkers did at least take the trouble to construct their doctrines. In the English-speaking world, these doctrines have been taken over dogmatically, and lumped together, regardless of whether they are compatible with one another.[42] What has brought them together is not any objective connections between them, but rather the fact that they all tend towards having the same effect, namely, the rejection of totalizing theories, the rejection of reason as a power to know the world and to integrate the self, and the rejection of humanism. The Anglophone postmodernists take a shotgun approach to philosophical, social and political issues: if one part of the shotgun blast does not hit the target, perhaps another part will. The low-level irrationalism of Anglophone postmodernism has led to the elevation of the above thinkers to the level of *maîtres*, and the promulgation of various heresies: totalizing, essentialism, rationalism, historicism, humanism. These are marks of sin, and triggers to close down all discussion. The arguments of the French post-structuralists, like, say, Lyotard's invocation of Gödel and Wittgenstein, are merely taken for granted. The heresies have taken on the status of a creed.[43]

The explanation for the spread of Anglophone postmodernism, presumably, has something to do with the expansion of the university sector since the 1960s. But postmodernism did not really take off until about 1980. So, it is plausible to assume that its rise and flourishing have something to do with the onset of neoliberal economic management and globalisation in the 1980s.

---

[41] Lacan, Deleuze and Guattari are dealt with in Sokal and Bricmont, *Intellectual Impostures*, chs 2 and 9. Derrida and Foucault are examined from the standpoint of Critical Theory in Peter Dews, *Logics of Disintegration: Post-structuralist Thought and the Claims of Critical Theory* (London: Verso, 1987), and in Jürgen Habermas, *The Philosophical Discourse of Modernity: Twelve Lectures*, translated by Frederick G. Lawrence (Cambridge, MA: The MIT Press, 1987). Originally published in German as *Der philosophische Diskurs der Moderne: Zwölf Vorlesungen* (Frankfurt am Main: Suhrkamp Verlag, 1985).

[42] Anglophone postmodernism also lumps in Rorty's rejection of the correspondence theory of truth, Kuhn's theory of paradigms in the history of science, and Feyerabend's "anything goes" doctrine of scientific method. See Richard Rorty, *Contingency, irony, and solidarity* (Cambridge: Cambridge University Press, 1989); Thomas Kuhn, *The Structure of Scientific Revolutions*, 2nd edition, enlarged (Chicago: The University of Chicago Press, 1970; 1st edn, 1962); Paul Feyerabend, *Against Method*, 4th edn (London: Verso, 2010; 1st edn, New Left Books, 1975). It is worth noting that around the time that the views of Kuhn and Feyerabend were becoming fashionable, a realist philosophy of science was being developed by thinkers associated with the University of Oxford. See Rom Harré, *The Principles of Scientific Thinking* (London and Basingstoke: The Macmillan Press Ltd, 1970); Roy Bhaskar, *A Realist Theory of Science* (London and New York: Verso, 1997; originally published by Leeds Books Ltd, 1975). See also the magisterial study by the Oxford historian of science A. C. Crombie, *Styles of Scientific Thinking in the European Tradition: The history of argument and explanation especially in the mathematical and biomedical sciences and arts*, 3 vols (London: Gerald Duckworth & Co. Ltd, 1994).

[43] It is surely especially bizarre that Lyotard should import into France Wittgenstein's doctrine of language games, and then re-export it back to the English-speaking world, which had demolished it twenty years earlier (see note 20 above).

My explanation runs as follows. The expansion of the university sector had produced a new professional middle class, a mixture of an intelligentsia and an administrative class. A fraction (and only a fraction) of this class had radical or left-wing political sympathies, and was located mainly in the universities and the media. One subdivision of this fraction had a genuine desire to offer leadership to the non-class social movements—non-class, because class boundaries had been blurred by the long post-war economic boom, and because the traditional industrial working class suffered increasing political and economic defeats under the regimes of Margaret Thatcher and Ronald Reagan. This division was repelled by both Marxism and liberalism—by Marxism because of its working class connection, and by liberalism because of its association with the dominant social order. Postmodernism offered an ideology that was at least focussed on non-class social groups, including minorities and the marginalised, even though, as we have seen, postmodernism offered no practical way forward for such groups, providing only a futile politics of discourses and symbols, soon to be named "political correctness". A second division of this fraction (in my rather jaundiced view) wanted only the reputation of being radical, without being prepared to run any of the risks to career or status from any real political engagement. For them postmodernism has been mainly a matter of posturing and making paradoxical claims.[44] It was of this division that someone once remarked that postmodernists were the court jesters at the court of neoliberalism.[45]

As a kind of irrationalism postmodernism is subversive of the function of a university, and we need to leave it behind. In particular, the humanities cannot flourish without adequate foundations: rationalism generally, epistemological realism, and humanism. If these foundations are not present, it is difficult to see how the humanities can have any future. If they do not flourish, there will be little or no countervailing power against the degradation of the public domain by advertising agencies and public relations firms; students will not have adequate notions of the value of knowledge as an end in itself, and as the means to full human development; and the aesthetic and ethical dimensions of human experience will be permanently displaced by the "political", that is, by the reality of a stunted human nature that cannot get beyond ex-

---

[44] Right-of-centre commentators frequently assert that postmodernism is a front for Marxism ("cultural Marxism", "Neo-Marxism"). I think this is a mistake. The ideas of post-structuralism and postmodernism are quite different from, and in many cases opposed to the ideas of Marx, and even more Lenin. The antipathy felt by a genuine Marxist to postmodernism is apparent in Alex Callinicos's *Against Postmodernism: A Marxist Critique* (Cambridge: Polity Press in association with Basil Blackwell, 1989). In my experience, postmodernists would run a mile if anyone suggested that they had any connection to Marxism.

[45] I forget who. I apologize. I note that Owen Worth and Karen Buckley have published a criticism of the left-wing World Social Forum under the title "The World Social Forum: postmodern prince or court jester?" *Third World Quarterly*, vol. 30, issue 4 (2009), 649-661.

pressions of desire, and mindless assertions of power. Academics in the humanities should see it as part of their role to do what they can to restore these foundations.[46]

I must thank Dr Catherine Runcie for inviting me to contribute an essay to this volume, and then to act as co-editor. Sometimes one needs a prompt in order to clarify one's ideas, and I am very grateful to her for providing this one.

David Brooks
Goulburn 2018

---

[46] A personal note: when I began to study English at university level in the late 1960s, it was a prestigious subject. This was largely due to the poetry and criticism of T. S. Eliot, the critical theory and criticism of I. A. Richards and F. R. Leavis, and the scholarship of such as C. S. Lewis. Since then it has become a joke. Although philologists continue to do valuable work editing texts and collections of letters, writing biographies and so on, the critical side of the discipline has been degraded. 'Theory' (with a ridiculous capital 'T') has displaced its real intellectual foundations; deconstructive "criticism" has reduced it to absurdity; and Foucaldian studies have transformed it into a source of propaganda for social activists concerned only with the politics of desire and power. I cannot help feeling that this has been intellectual suicide. When all this stuff began to be imported in the 1970s and 1980s, sceptical academics faced a problem: it is difficult to tell a colleague that what he or she is teaching is intellectual rubbish. Long before political correctness, there was professional courtesy.

PHILOSOPHY AND POLICY

The Centre Cannot Hold

David Daintree

Turning and turning in the widening gyre
The falcon cannot hear the falconer;
Things fall apart; the centre cannot hold;
Mere anarchy is loosed upon the world,
The blood-dimmed tide is loosed, and everywhere
The ceremony of innocence is drowned;
The best lack all conviction, while the worst
Are full of passionate intensity…

…The darkness drops again; but now I know
That twenty centuries of stony sleep
Were vexed to nightmare by a rocking cradle,
And what rough beast, its hour come round at last,
Slouches towards Bethlehem to be born?[1]

Though we may have backed away from the ebullient Victorian belief in materialistic science-driven Progress, it is undeniable that the human race is far from static. Our life is much more complex than that of even our most recent predecessors, and the physical comforts and advantages now available to us have entirely outstripped, in their brilliance and variety, everything that went before. From a Christian perspective, we are advancing from the simplicity of a Garden to the City of God.

One of the indicators of the ineluctable movement in which we are all caught up is the mushrooming of the written record. Just 500 years ago libraries counted their books in the hundreds; now the size of the world's book stock is almost beyond reckoning. Until the High Middle Ages, and perhaps for a century or two afterwards, it was possible, at least in theory, for one man in his lifetime to read everything that had been written and preserved in the

---

[1] Excerpt from W B Yeats, *The Second Coming*.

libraries of the West.² Yet with the rise of the universities, and even before the general availability of printing, this point had been passed.

The effect of this growth on education has been cataclysmic, for the emphasis has necessarily shifted from gleaning facts to, effectively, culling them, from training memory to side-stepping mere recollection as a poor cousin to abstraction.³ My use of the word 'culling' may appear impolitic; certainly 'edit', 'select', or 'research' are kinder. But I prefer 'culling' as being closer to the somewhat unpalatable truth.⁴ Within every single subject of study, even within a particular speciality of that subject, it is now impossible for one scholar to read all the available material. Anglophone specialists may occasionally suggest that they have achieved a mastery of their subjects, but by and large we are poor linguists and the assumption, too often beneath the surface, that everything worth reading is available in English, is both impertinent and dangerous.

The apparent impossibility of coping with the growth of knowledge has been a major factor in the rise in our schools and universities of a nebula of petty and unrelated subjects, many of which are driven by the ephemeral fancies of the day. A secondary major factor has of course been the competitive commercialism of universities, about which more later.

Anatole France's character Abbé Coignard recounts an amusing tale about our thirst for knowledge—and our need to recognize and act upon the limitations of our minds:

> The young prince Zémire, having succeeded his father on the throne as Shah of Persia, sent for the wisest Academicians of the empire to find and prepare a Universal History. After twenty years, they came back with a string of twelve camels, each laden with 500 fat volumes. The Shah stared at the camels pessimistically. 'While you labored', he said, 'I have been growing old and am now half way through life. These books shall be stored in the Imperial Archives. Please prepare me an abridgement, more in keeping with the brevity of our existence here below.'

---

[2] Examples are Gilbert, Bishop of London 1128-34, called 'Universalis', because he was thought to have read everything, and his contemporary William of Malmesbury who had a reputation as the most learned man of his day.

[3] There is, I think, a discernible tendency in modern scholarship to despise memory. Lawyers seem to hold little law in their heads, though they doubtless know where to find it; historians often despise populist writers who are prodigiously well informed as to detail, but lack (it is claimed) analytical capacity. Ancient writers of porphyrian or acrostic verses, more difficult to compose than the most cryptic crossword puzzles, are dismissed as mere poetasters. Perhaps Medicine is the only modern discipline that requires its practitioners to hold in their memories at any one time a substantial amount of their subject. Many an emergency room patient must be thankful for that!

[4] I once knew a woman who was accepted as a PhD candidate in Middle Eastern studies by a distinguished Australian university. Her supervisor told her that it was 'not necessary' to learn Arabic.

> After another twenty years they turned up again with 1,500 volumes, piled on the humps of three camels. 'Cut it short', said the Shah, 'if you wish me to learn, ere I die, the history of mankind.'
> The leader of the group appeared after five years, walking painfully with the aid of crutches, and leading a small donkey with one fat volume on its back. As he entered the palace, a chamberlain said to him: 'Hurry, for the Shah is dying!' And indeed, the Shah lay on his death bed. With half-blind eyes, he gazed on the book that had been brought to him. And he groaned. 'I must die without knowing the history of men!' The leader, who was nearing his end no less than his Sovereign, answered: 'Sire, I can sum up, in a few words, all the books can teach us. Men are born, and they suffer, and they die!' And thus, late in life, the Shah learnt all there is in Universal History.[5]

Modern circumstances have presented us with challenges that would have been utterly beyond Anatole France's wildest imaginings. Everything that is now written, and very much of all that has ever been written, is now digitalized. Search engines can now discover in a trice what a researcher of just a few decades ago could struggle to unearth in days or weeks. Our corporate memory has increased a million-fold, but each individual's RAM, his 'onboard memory', is no greater than it was a thousand years ago, nor is there the slightest chance that it will increase. We may be sceptical about the possibility of artificial intelligences such as HAL, in Kubrick's *2001 A Space Odyssey*, evolving to the extent of having human feelings and ambitions, but the HALs of this world already run rings around the rest of us in their capacity for memory and calculation. Our problem is knowing what to ask them to do, and that is a problem that is becoming more, not less, difficult with every passing moment. No individual knows very much, in proportion to the world's knowledge; even panels of experts, to state an unwelcome truth, inevitably against such odds fall short of mastery.

Not only is our memory restricted and finite, but our capacity to make moral judgments is no greater than it ever was. Many wise people would argue that it becomes significantly diminished as we forget how to think for ourselves and rely increasingly on 'science' to solve our ethical dilemmas.

Where do we look for resolution, when the world's corporate knowledge is outstripping our individual personal intelligences almost literally at the speed of light? Here is a 'Big Bang' that impinges directly upon each one of us!

Because we are individuals trying to make sense of such overwhelming forces, an element of the personal has a necessary place in each man's response. I had the great good fortune to receive a more or less classical education. The reasons for that choice are unimportant and I claim no credit for

---

[5] The story, in this translation, is quoted by Daniele Varè, *Ghosts of the Rialto* (London, 1956).

them. Mine was not the full-on classical education that one would have experienced a hundred years earlier, exclusively devoted to the language and literature of Greece and Rome, but Latin and Greek were the major components of it, together with Comparative Philology and English, and some history and philosophy. By the time I arrived on the scene the great days of the Classics had already passed away. No longer might a British general announce his victory in a telegram, with a single Latin pun, in the certainty that it would be understood.[6] No English poet would dismiss the study of English literature as insufficiently weighty for inclusion in a university curriculum.[7] No more could a man like Prebendary Gaisford boast:

> The advantages of a classical education are twofold: it enables us to look down with contempt on those who have not shared its advantages, and also fits us for places of emolument not only in this world, but in the next.[8]

But for all that I am deeply and unrelentingly grateful to have had the opportunities that I happily stumbled upon, and greatly deplore the powerful trend in my own days to dismiss the classics as 'irrelevant', and Latin as a tedious, soul-destroying waste of time. That attitude was an over-reaction in favour of the 'new' scientific disciplines of Maths, Chemistry and Physics (which are valuable and necessary) as well as Sociology, Psychology, Geography (which, as undergraduate subjects, are perhaps less so).

A recovery of the great days of the Classics on anything like its former scale, even if that were desirable, is inconceivable. There will no doubt always be people who study the Classics for personal or scholarly reasons, at least so long as Western Civilisation endures, but such studies will never again be the bedrock of conventional education. Their strength as a discipline lay in their breadth of vision: they embraced the mental discipline of learning other languages, together with the psycho-social discipline of trying to get inside the heads of other cultures that shared our humanity yet were so utterly alien in their thinking. The classical world had long passed away, but its internal complexities were a world in microcosm, a closed laboratory, small enough to be studied at depth, whose subsequent effects upon our own culture were not only discernible but hugely inescapable. They shaped our world in ways so various and at depths so diverse that modern men (especially those who have

---

[6] General Napier was said to have announced his 1843 capture of Sindh - 'I have Sindh' – with the single word *peccavi* ('I have sinned'). In fact the story is apocryphal, but the fact that it first appeared in Punch illustrates exactly the same point about the wide public familiarity with Latin.
[7] A view that is at least implicit in T S Eliot's essay "Modern Education and the Classics", in *Selected Essays* (London: Faber and Faber Ltd, 1932), 507-16.
[8] This is very possibly apocryphal too, or, if genuine, was certainly intended ironically, but generations of classics students have delighted in it.

little awareness of history) struggle to retrace the steps they have taken. We are indeed dwarves on the shoulders of giants.[9]

There is evidence that some serious thinkers about education are reclaiming lost ground and positively re-evaluating much of what in our folly we once rejected out of hand, but unfortunately there are stronger forces at work.

During the 70s of last century the term 'Mickey Mouse subjects' was coined to describe certain arts and semi-scientific subjects that universities were at that time starting to make available to undergraduates in response to the rapidly growing number of enrolments in the post-World War II world. This trend was driven by the universities' fast emerging view of themselves as retailers of knowledge: to stock their shelves with an attractive range of pre-cooked and easy-care products made very good business sense. In this strategy they formed a not always easy but generally workable liaison with the political left that had as its own agenda a radical restructuring of society towards the advent of a Marxist and post-capitalist future.

Could anyone forty years ago have dreamed of the extent to which this trend would come to permeate the university sector as it does today? Arts faculties have become laughing stocks in some modern universities. There was a time when arts students were respected by their fellows in Law, Medicine or Science, as being engaged in worthwhile and demanding, if apparently impractical, intellectual exercises. Nerds and Geeks we might have been, but we were not negligible. When we enrolled in our courses, we knew that we would be expected to cover a range of material that may not have interested or pleased us in every one of its aspects, but was necessary in order to achieve a broad understanding of our subject. I recall very well that in English I in 1968 we were expected to learn the phonetic alphabet and read two of Chaucer's tales (untranslated, of course), four plays of Shakespeare, a wide selection of poetry from the eighteenth century to the present, and at least a dozen and a half novels from Richardson to E.M. Forster. It was a marvelous and intelligent selection carefully chosen to provide a background to further studies both in English—and for life.

It was inconceivable then that a person could complete an undergraduate degree in English, let alone a PhD, without being well read across the genres and the centuries. The same is true of History. Specialization in a particular area of literature or history without a broad-based training in the whole scope of the discipline would have once been unthinkable, but is now common. Of course my use of terms such as 'broad-based' is inevitably inexact and strongly subjective: I recognize that as an anglophone undergraduate my view of the world was scarcely comprehensive, nor even was that of my lecturers, but they tried to be. Women were very well represented among the novelists, but

---

[9] *quasi nanos gigantium humeris insidentes*: a remark ascribed by William of Malmesbury to Bernard of Chartres.

not so well among the poets, for the reason that relatively few women are reckoned among the great poets of our or any other literature. This may be a sad truth, but it is a truth nevertheless. It was not allowed to skew our judgments. The emphasis was on choosing the best, not righting perceived wrongs or applying with hindsight the moral principles currently in fashion. This does not mean that social justice is now or was then unimportant, but there has been a huge shift in thinking about how and when it is to be striven for. The Arts have suffered most in this reorientation, because they are by their very nature more open to interpretation, and none more so than the Disney-esque ones!

During a recent sojourn at the University of New England I was struck by the number of undergraduates I met who told me that they were studying criminology. Were they driven, I wondered, by zeal for the detection and punishment of crime? Or was their impulse merely one of curiosity about the psychology of criminals, or perhaps even the feasibility of themselves getting away with a career in the rackets? I have no idea, but I am certain that the nation has no need of the number of would-be criminologists it appears to be producing. It is of course understandable that criminology should be available to professionals at a postgraduate level, but surely only after first completing a sound training in the essentials of reading, writing and reasoning that are at the root of humane studies.

It is perhaps unfair to hammer criminology, for it is no worse an instance than dozens, even hundreds, of others 'specialisms' generally available in the varsity marketplace. What they all have in common, in contrast to more traditional academic programmes, is that they seek to narrow rather than broaden. Gender and Women's Studies may be acceptable at a postgraduate level, but they can have no integrity when erected on a base other than classical Sociology; polemical courses on racism and other such other causes are not the primary business of English or History departments, and will have no bottom unless well founded on broader studies. The awful truth is that young people are treating universities as cafeterias, choosing very unbalanced diets, and what is worse, the universities are pandering to them, meeting their needs and, of course, encouraging them. Business is business.

Literacy is in decline, but the greatest loss of all is history. Ignorance of history, even of comparatively recent events, or their submersion beneath various fatuous forms of identity politics, is a modern human tragedy. Evidence for this is not hard to find: ask any group of young graduates who were the major combatants in World War I, or why the Royal Arms are displayed in every little country courthouse, or whether tertiary education was available, at no cost, before Gough Whitlam, and you will get a less than complete answer. But they will all be able to tell you that 'equality' is a basic human right and assert any number of meaningless platitudes. G.K. Chesterton laments the modern habit of looking at the past 'only from the modern end'. Those brought up without awareness of history, he says, 'rebel against they know not what, because it arose they know not when; intent only on its ending, they are ignorant of its beginning; and therefore of its very being.'[10]

Postmodernism, with its aversion to the notion of objective truth, cringes before the enormity of the task of understanding the world. It masquerades as a kind of Socratic scepticism, which is what makes it attractive to so many. The well-known definition of pessimism as 'optimism with the facts' is clever and amusing, but it exposes the sad truth that for many people in our privileged western world life is cruel and meaningless, that the beauty and wonder have gone out of learning, and that in the end everything is hopeless. This has led, as inevitably as the needle turns to the pole, to a sense of frailty in the face of the universe. Correct vision perhaps, but wrong solution if it leads, as it almost always does, to premature specialization. Far too many children leave school never having learned to read, write and think straight, before going on to university to become criminologists, sports psychologists—or teachers! The introduction of continuous assessment from the 70s onwards to take the stress out of exams and, as student numbers soared, to make it easier for the less intelligent to get degrees (that of course was never admitted to be the reason) has greatly contributed to the gravity of the situation. Education can now be chopped up into even smaller units and modules for ease of digestion and subsequent oblivion.

Is there any escape from this frenzied abandonment of the objective aspirations of broad-based education?

At a meeting with IBM executives at Yorktown Heights, New York in January 1984, Dr Barry Jones (at that time Federal Minister for Science) asked, 'what type of people are you looking for?' Their reply surprised him: 'The same people we have always looked for—honours graduates in English or Philosophy who are good at playing chess'.[11] If a young person is taught well to communicate and to think, he can be trained, and re-trained, to do anything else. And to do it better than one who has had no basic training in humane skills. There is ample evidence to support this, and young people are themselves increasingly aware of the deficiencies in their own education. Anyone who has worked in an educational institution will have met intelligent students who realize that they have been short-changed.

So is there a workable solution?

Certainly there is no returning to the past—the only way is forward. Even if we could return to the past we would swiftly recognize that such educational advantages as existed, for all their quality, were available to far too few. Will the market-driven Mickey Mouse approach work for us? Not in the long

---

[10] *St Thomas Aquinas*, from chap. 3, "The Aristotelian Revolution", Kindle edition.
[11] This anecdote, which I had first heard many years ago, was confirmed for me by Prof Jones himself in an email in 2009.

term, for there is a void in the heart of mankind that needs to be filled with more substantial pabulum. Is there, then, a feasible alternative?

The conservative response will be to seek to look for those qualities in humanity that are universal, drill down into them with disciplined energy and extract the core material which is (or should be) the fundamental stuff of all education for work and for life. The notion of the *trivium,* the first stage of a liberal arts education that evolved in antiquity and continued through the Middle Ages to the very birth of modernity, is a reasonable focus deserving of reappraisal and even recovery. On the face of it, to the modern eye, the actual content of the *trivium*—grammar, logic and rhetoric—appears unexciting in the extreme. Why on earth would one commit to subjects of that kind when one could be doing 'relevant' things like rock music or tourism studies? Actually there should be no contest: you will be a better rock musician, or businessman, or doctor, or lawyer, or anything else, if you first prepare yourself as a fulfilled and integrated human being. The fundamental building blocks of these so-called liberal arts are clear thinking (twinned with efficient and accurate comprehension) and effective communication in speech and writing. To the modern eye the *trivium* looks absurdly naïve, but paradoxically its very simplicity and its open-endedness are its strengths: reading, writing, reasoning and persuasive eloquence constitute the foundation of rock on which everything else can be built. The *quadrivium* began the process of specialization—arithmetic, geometry, astronomy and music were its core subjects.[12] These represent a measured and orderly movement towards the detailed study of fundamentals. Do the hard yards first, so that criminology, journalism and marketing (for example) can reasonably follow in their due place.

It is often remarked that history, as such, formed no part of the classical *trivium* or *quadrivium*, yet I have argued that the neglect of history is perhaps the greatest disaster to have afflicted the contemporary educational world. Am I contradicting myself? In fact I think there is no conflict. Our modern tendency to specialise has made it harder to appreciate the whole picture and to recognize opinions, values and practices that are implicit but not stated. One example will suffice. English Literature, as a distinct subject, was not widely taught at all in schools or universities until the end of the nineteenth century.[13] That means, of course, that few writers in English before that time had ever studied English as a formal part of their education. Does that mean

---

[12] The *trivium* and *quadrivium* together constitute the so-called Liberal Arts, *Artes Liberales*, the studies deemed appropriate for a free man in a free society. The idea goes back to Cicero and Seneca, evolved gradually in the thought of such men as the pagan Martianus Capella and the Christian Cassiodorus Senator, until it became almost fossilized in the high Middle Ages. Nowadays in common parlance it can be applied to almost any selection of non-vocational studies.

[13] 'New' institutions such as the University of London were among the first to begin serious and formal teaching in English.

that Pope and Dryden, Byron and Shelley, Wordsworth and Tennyson were not well-read? Of course the reverse is true, which is the point exactly: the *trivium* and *quadrivium* as such had passed away by their time, but their essence remained, those foundations of rock had been firmly laid, and persons so well formed turned naturally and easily to the great writers of their own literature and history.

This chapter has concentrated on the Arts, so-called, because of the writer's own background and disposition. It might seem an impertinence to intrude into the world of science. And yet, why should that be so? Science, *scientia*, simply means knowledge. The gulf between Arts and Sciences, widening to breaking point within the past century and a half, has been a tragedy of modern education. That divorce, now almost absolute, has in my view greatly contributed to the crazy proliferation of arts courses, on the one hand, and narrowing of the scientific imagination on the other. Darwin would not have understood it, nor would Galileo or Newton, Mendel or Einstein.

In an ideal educational world one would hope for a rapprochement between what we now describe as the *arts* and the *sciences*. It is fair to say that people in the *arts* stream very often, as I have already argued, have a far too narrow experience of their cultural matrix as well as an ignorance of the sciences; but it is even truer to say that premature specialization in scientific and technical studies results in profound ignorance of the arts, especially history. If there were to be a rapprochement, what Arts courses ought a young student look for? It is not patronizing but simply realistic to recognize that school leavers, through no fault of their own, have limited discernment. If they have been forced into premature specialization in vocation-driven subjects, as almost all have, and fed on a supplementary diet of virtually content-free social justice dressed up as 'English' or 'History', they will be at a loss to make strategic choices that will lead them not only to an appropriate career but to a rich and fulfilled life. They will need guidance. Adults, whether parents or counsellors, who have the privilege of having their advice accepted should prioritize breadth of vision: will their choice of subjects lead them to seek connections between different cultures and customs? Will it assert the objective reality of truth and the distinction between good and evil? Will it help them to value the things of today in the context of history and tradition?

Some educators, at least, recognize that early specialization produces high achievers in specific areas who are less than competent outside their fields, even profoundly ignorant of whole areas of human knowledge that were once considered essential to human civility. How can a young man or woman be reasonably expected to make a life-long commitment to a career at 17 or 18, whose mind has never been properly exposed to the richness of human thought, in a world in which, as futurologists like to predict, many will need to re-train several times in the course of their lives? Surely we are asking too much (or too little) of the young people who are both the inheritors and shapers of the future? As one commentator observed, 'the idea that a 17-year-old should be expected to choose which vocationally focused degree they do is nothing short of ridiculous'. 'It's a recipe,' he went on to say, 'for a mid-life crisis'.[14] As a former president of a liberal arts college whose goal is to educate for life and not just for a job, I couldn't agree more.

In my admittedly fond view, Campion College addresses this problem well. All students take the same core subjects—History, Literature, Philosophy and Theology, all of which are integrated horizontally and vertically: in their first year students will study ancient authors such as Homer and Virgil, New Testament and patristic theology and ancient history, Plato and Aristotle. In their second and third years they move on chronologically, acquiring in three years a broad and expansive understanding of the flux of human thought and activity, a grasp of those basic and powerful ideas that have formed our actions, and a sense of the mutability and at the same time the universality of human life. As far as I am aware nothing as good as this is available at any other Australian university.

Is the Campion syllabus too narrow? It is true that Campion offers only a handful of subjects for the BA, while a conventional mega-university may offer 80 or 90. But the individual can select only a handful of those on offer. Moreover Campion's core subjects are exactly that—*core* subjects, subjects fundamental to humane studies—whereas some of the 80-90 alternatives fall far short of that, being offered either to extend their institution's marketability, or even (though this is never admitted) to present some easy options for less able students in a politically-correct world that increasingly insists on the 'right' of an increasingly large percentage of the population to a degree *of some kind*. We are in danger of selling ourselves short and wasting our most precious resources: young people of intellectual bent should be stretched and those whose talents are more practical should not be fobbed off with second-rate studies.

An alternative to the Campion approach is the notion of a literary 'canon' of Great Books that all should read.[15] Yet in a western culture that appears to be in terminal decline there can be no easy agreement on its content. To say so is not to be overly pessimistic, but merely observant: the time has long passed when we lived in a monoculture that agreed on the essential components of a sound education. Such a notion stems from a Judaeo-Christian matrix, in which the Bible and some of the classics of Christian literature hold unquestioned place. Some American institutions have adopted the Great Books as the basis of their undergraduate syllabus.[16] Even among like-minded

---

[14] Peter van Onselen, "Generalist degrees broaden young minds", *The Australian*, 27 April 2011.
[15] For a succinct survey see Mortimer Adler (Editor-in-Chief), *The Great Conversation: a Reader's Guide to the Great Books of the Western World*, University of Chicago/Encyclopaedia Britannica, 1992.
[16] For example Thomas Aquinas College, Santa Paula, California.

colleges, though, there may be variance between the lists, and the notion of such a 'canon' holds much less appeal for that growing sector of modern intellectual life whose members think sceptics such as Lucretius and Dawkins more deserving of a place in the literary hall of fame than an Augustine or a Chesterton. *Quot homines, tot sententiae*: in the post-Christian global village the notions of what constitutes the corpus of great books will be legion. An almost inevitable weakness of modern attempts at framing a canon is that they are usually heavily weighted towards modern authors and do not adequately reflect the diachronic and evolutionary character of human culture. They are in a sense two-dimensional: they expose the culture on top, but may tend to ignore the process by which it grew.

A solution may be to look at the manuscript tradition, to identify the books that shaped the western mind. Even sceptics would concede a place for the Bible, if only as a literary work, in the canon of western culture. There, and perhaps only there, is there some agreement. In secular letters, Virgil is a strong candidate. Manuscripts are very numerous.[17] And if Virgil earns inclusion, so must Dante and Milton, both heavily dependent on him. This is just one example, of course, but that same process can be used to trace other affinities and connections. I suspect that with the passage of time many of the works now being considered fit for inclusion in the canon will drop out of sight, and that if we are ever to have something approaching an agreed canon it will be a little more elongated in time, a little less mushroom-like in appearance, than any current model.

Several major Australian universities now try to oblige their students to broaden their education before commencing professional training by offering such courses as Medicine, for example, only in a postgraduate format. The intention behind this is excellent and laudable. But such a strategy too often fails to achieve its purpose, for many students enrol in undergraduate programmes such as Medical Sciences in the hope of improving their chances of gaining admission to Medicine later. All that is achieved is a lengthening of the period of training as a doctor. The lesson that IBM understood a generation ago has sadly eluded us.

Otherwise the universities will not change unless the market does. Only greater discernment among its 'customers' can drive change, but how can the community change its attitudes when its leaders and role models are leading it in another direction? Perhaps Canadian psychologist Jordan Peterson is right in asserting that the humanities should be taken out of the hands of the uni-

---

[17] B. Munk Olsen, *Catalogue des Manuscrits Classiques Latin copiés du IXe. au XIIe. Siècle* (CNRS Paris 1985) lists nine manuscripts from the eighth century or earlier, and two dozen from the ninth, exponentially more in each succeeding century, that contain all or substantial portions of Virgil's works.

versities altogether.[18] He makes a powerful argument, but it would be sad indeed if such were to happen.

The editors' purpose for this volume to which I have the honour to offer a chapter was a distinctly positive one. Contributors were asked to propose real solutions to the problems now besetting the educational scene. I am aware, however, that much of what I have said above might be construed as the mere maunderings of a grumpy pessimist nostalgically longing for a past that probably never was and certainly never will return. I plead in extenuation that the solution to a problem arises naturally from its recognition: if we know that most Arts students are wasting their time on quasi-academic fripperies, and that many people are getting into the sciences and professions with poor communication and reasoning skills; if we hear journalists and public figures talking nonsense about our own nation's history, whether through guile or ignorance; if signs such as these are there for all to see then we know we have a problem to which broader and truer education is the only real solution. But if the blind lead the blind, what hope is there for betterment?

I began this chapter with some profoundly pessimistic verses of the poet Yeats, but in fact I am an optimist. There is a discernible groundswell of opinion in favour of doing things better. It will not easily prevail, and there is no denying that we are close to the brink of a catastrophic collapse of the Western culture, but I think there is a good chance that we will squeak through. As a lecturer with the University of the Third Age I know well that many older people are conscious of important gaps in their education. But more importantly my work with students over the years has brought me into contact with students who feel acutely that they have wasted or are wasting their time and their potential in studies that contribute little to their career prospects, or to their enjoyment. There are also those, it is true, who have been so stifled that they have lost all interest in matters of the mind. And, grimmest of all, there are those driven by other agendas entirely who approve the radicalization of education and would welcome the collapse of existing institutions and a refashioning of human society along entirely different lines. The battle lines have been drawn up and we have strong allies in all those who now realise that they have been short-changed by the educational establishment. If we can fight our way back to a re-ordering of priorities, to a positive re-evaluation of the essential disciplines of reading, writing and reasoning, then the Great Books of human culture will self-select and we shall re-align ourselves to give due acknowledgement to 'the best that has been thought and said'.

---

[18] See him interviewed at https://www.youtube.com/watch?v=9-77NpxbE7k&feature=youtu.be for a forthright statement of his opinions.

Reanimating the Liberal Arts in Australia: A New Lease of Life for an Ancient Education

Karl Schmude

While mainstream university education in Australia has long been utilitarian in nature and governed by vocational demands, it has historically been combined with traditions of classical learning and intellectual cultivation. This balance has been gradually weakened by the proliferation of degrees in an array of career areas with little attention to any higher principles of inspiration and unity and the broader needs of cultural initiation and understanding. This essay will examine the need and feasibility of a liberal arts education as a cultural foundation for vocational training and an essential basis of democratic participation in society. It will discuss the development of Campion College as one model of educational revival in Australia, which focuses on the formative ideals and historical traditions of Western culture as a foundation of intelligent participation in society.

The traditional pattern of university education in Australia has been a blend of the utilitarian and the cultural. Students were prepared for a range of professions and other career paths, but the need was also recognized to provide an initiation into a culture; to expose young people, at a formative time in their lives, to the inheritance of ideas and ideals that formed the basis of their identity as a democratic people. This cultural objective was often unstated, and even unprogrammed, conveyed through subjects such as history, literature, philosophy and language. The humanities in particular, a vital part though by no means the complete form of the liberal arts emanating from the curriculum of the medieval universities, were a channel for appreciating and absorbing the beliefs and values of an historic culture. They imparted a sense of citizenship that prepared future graduates for intelligent participation in society.

In recent decades, this traditional model of university education has been supplanted by new elements and approaches. The immediately practical has attracted far greater emphasis, especially in response to career aspirations, and expressed in a rhetorical commitment to innovation and creativity. The American political scholar Peter Augustine Lawler has argued that modern higher education has become increasingly one-dimensional, functioning essentially as a servant of the marketplace. It steers clear of higher or deeper purposes and serves as an expensive trade school, offering students the technical and vocational competencies for making money and gaining power and status.¹

Reinforcing this powerful tendency has been what C. S. Lewis called "chronological snobbery", which reflects an uncritical acceptance of the intellectual fashions and assumptions of one's own time and disdains tradition as a gateway to accumulated wisdom.² It presumes that originality comes from ignoring and overcoming the past, rather than learning from its deep layers of distilled human experience. Yet originality is finally the fruit, not of abandonment but of adoption. It does not come out of a cultural vacuum, but from an immersion in the abundance of historical insight. We learn by imitation. As the American novelist John Steinbeck suggested, "only through imitation do we develop towards originality".³ It is by imitation that students are exposed, in Matthew Arnold's famous formulation, to "the best which has been thought and said in the world".⁴ At the same time, students can thereby be inoculated against the worst. They can be alerted to the possibility that the "new" ideas which might emerge from "innovation and creativity" may simply turn out to be the old mistakes, in different guises.

The traditional form of cultural education in Australia reflected the historical structure of the liberal arts in Western education. It was designed to prepare students for citizenship and community life, not just employment, for participation in a culture, not merely a workforce. The English historian Christopher Dawson analysed the intimate connection between educational practice and cultural transmission and survival:

> A common educational tradition creates a common world of thought with common moral and intellectual values and a common inheritance of knowledge, and these are the conditions which make a culture conscious of its identity and give it a common memory and a common past. Consequently any break in the continuity of the educational tradition involves a corresponding break in the continuity of the culture. If the break were a complete one, it would be far more revolutionary than any political or economic change, since it would mean the death of the civilization...⁵

Dawson believed that such an educational rupture had taken place in the West in recent centuries. A vacuum had arisen in universities from the disap-

---

[1] Peter Augustine Lawler, *American Heresies and Higher Education* (South Bend, Indiana: St Augustine's Press, 2016)
[2] C.S. Lewis, *Surprised by Joy* (London: Fontana, 1959), 167.
[3] John Steinbeck, *Travels with Charley In Search of America* (London: Heinemann, 1962), 130.
[4] Matthew Arnold, *Culture and Anarchy*, ed. R.H. Super (Ann Arbor, Michigan: University of Michigan Press, 1965), Volume V, 233, in *The Complete Prose Works of Matthew Arnold*, ed R.H. Super (Ann Arbor, Michigan: University of Michigan Press, 1960).
[5] Christopher Dawson, *The Crisis of Western Education; with Specific Programmes for the Study of Christian Culture by John J. Mulloy* (London: Sheed and Ward, 1961), 5.

pearance of "the classics", the study of Graeco-Roman language and culture that shaped the tradition of Western civilisation. This educational foundation was being replaced by a dual approach which intensified the collapse of a common culture of learning. In teaching, there was the utilitarian emphasis on vocational training, and in research as well as in teaching, an ever-growing subject specialisation and narrowing of focus. Modern education, in Dawson's judgment, was being reduced to "a disintegrated mass of specialisms and vocational courses".[6]

Yet the destruction of a common educational tradition was having a deeper cultural impact. It was contributing to a huge fragmentation of Western civilisation itself, the breaking up of a way of life which would, in time, empty out meaning and memory and disenfranchise the great mass of people, spiritually and socially, leaving them prey to the most profound evils—of spiritual emptiness, intellectual confusion, and moral uncertainty. In Dawson's words:

> Modern civilization in spite of its immense technical achievement is morally weak and spiritually divided. Science and technology in themselves are morally neutral and do not provide any guiding spiritual principle. . . . For modern society, like all societies, needs some higher spiritual principle of co-ordination to overcome the conflicts between power and morality, between reason and appetite, between technology and humanity, and between self-interest and the common good.[7]

For Christians, Dawson thought that the disintegration of Western civilisation was especially grave. It weakened the basic sense of cultural cohesion among ordinary people, and would finally destroy the very idea and possibility of a Christian people founded on shared beliefs and ideals. Dawson recognised that the cultural underpinning of the Christian faith—its philosophical outlook and legal framework, its literary and aesthetic expressions, its scientific energies—had long been supplied by this classical tradition, mediated as it was through the long night and creative dawning of the Middle Ages. The disappearance of these cultural influences would expose Christians in the West to the full force of secularist modernity, without the educational and cultural protection afforded by the old heritage of Christian humanism. In Dawson's eyes, only an historical steeping in Christian culture, in the spiritual springs of cultural expression throughout history, could anchor, and reanimate, a sense of Christian identity and understanding at the popular level.

---

[6] *Ibid*. 99.
[7] *Ibid*. 159.

Dawson proposed a systematic study of Christian culture in universities, which he believed would provide a channel for understanding Western civilisation from *within*. It would demonstrate the integration of natural reason and supernatural faith that underpins the Western tradition. This would give "the mind a unifying vision of the spiritual sources from which Western civilization flowed".[8] Such a process would call for a rediscovery of the tradition of liberal education, of the liberal arts as a coherent program across the major disciplines of study; in particular, history, philosophy, literature, science, language and theology. In the Middle Ages, these subjects formed the curriculum of the *trivium* and the *quadrivium*. The *trivium* corresponded roughly with the present-day humanities, consisting of the three subjects of grammar (writing), rhetoric (persuasion in word and speech), and dialectic (reasoning). The *quadrivium* comprised the sciences, embracing the four number-centred subjects of arithmetic (calculations and the connections between numbers), geometry (understanding and applying numbers, such as in geography and surveying), astronomy (study of the stars, and more broadly natural phenomena and the scientific principles governing them), and music (appreciation and application of harmonies). To an unrivalled extent, music epitomised the unifying potential of the liberal arts, bringing together the uplifting beauty of harmonies with the underlying mystery of transcendental meaning.

Do these programs in the traditional liberal arts offer anything of value to present-day higher education in Australia? The twenty-first century is shaped by globalisation, which renders cultural horizons less Western-centred, and by the pervasive impact of electronic technology, which obliterates boundaries and has given rise to a culture that is, at once, more individualistic and yet more subject to the conforming pressures of social media.

There are various signs of the continuing—perhaps even growing—value of the liberal arts in a vastly changed world. Recent studies, such as Randall Stross's *A Practical Education: Why Liberal Arts Majors Make Great Employees* (2017) and George Anders' *You Can Do Anything: The Surprising Power of a 'Useless' Liberal Arts Education* (2017), lay stress on the value of a broad undergraduate degree in preparing students for the workplace. Moreover, there is the corroboration of personal stories, such as the experience of Steve Jobs, founder of the Apple company, who recognised a close connection between the world of communications technology and the liberal arts. He believed that computer scientists should work together with artists and designers, and that the best ideas emerge from the intersection of technology and the humanities. When launching the iPad2 in 2011, Jobs commented: "It is in Apple's DNA that technology alone is not enough—it's technology married with liberal arts, married with the humanities, that yields us the results that make our hearts

---

[8] *Ibid.* 99.

sing".⁹ While Jobs himself dropped out of the liberal arts college he attended in Portland, Oregon, he continued to audit classes in calligraphy, learning about different typefaces that he thought were "beautiful, historical, artistically subtle in a way that science can't capture". He later incorporated these into the Macintosh, which he described as "the first computer with beautiful typography".[10]

A further testimony to the practical impact of a liberal arts education is the extent to which business leaders have benefitted from this form of foundational education. A third of the Fortune 500 chief executives, who lead America's largest companies, are liberal arts graduates.[11] The lack of a comparable opportunity and expectation in Australia—that corporate leaders could benefit from a broad education prior to training for a business career—has been highlighted by David Murray, the former CEO of the Commonwealth Bank and the Australian Government Future Fund:

> I would like to see a much bigger emphasis on liberal arts, philosophy and thinking skills followed by some specialisation, rather than the other way around. You have to question whether taking some of the best minds in the country through commerce/law so they can be better than you or I at interpreting 13,000 pages of tax legislation. Can we do something more with that mind?[12]

No doubt the liberal arts are especially conducive to certain professions, such as teaching, law and journalism, where a facility for language and communication is crucial, but they furnish a practical foundation for any career path, including categories of work which social and technological change have not yet created. They cultivate skills and understandings not readily developed in vocational degrees, which by their nature focus on employment imperatives and the acquisition of professional knowledge. The CEO of Walt Disney from 1984 to 2005, Michael Eisner, who completed a BA in English Literature and Theatre, has attested: "Literature is unbelievably helpful, because no matter what business you are in, you are dealing with interpersonal relationships. It gives you an appreciation of what makes people tick".[13]

---

[9] Jonah Lehrer, "Steve Jobs: Technology Alone Is Not Enough", *New Yorker*, October 7, 2011. Accessed 30 August 2017. https://www.newyorker.com/news/news-desk/steve-jobs-technology-alone-is-not-enough

[10] *Ibid.*

[11] Steve Sadove, "Employees Who Stand Out", *Forbes*, September 5, 2014. Accessed 9 September 2017. https://www.forbes.com/sites/realspin/2014/09/05/employees-who-stand-out/#6c53e8b969b0

[12] "Fillip for Liberal Arts, Philosophy from CBA Chief", *Campus Review*, October 19, 2005, 4.

[13] Jack Linshi, "10 CEOs Who Prove Your Liberal Arts Degree Isn't Worthless", *Time Magazine*, 23 July 2015. Accessed 29 September 2017 http://time.com/3964415/ceo-degree-liberal-arts/

A former CEO of the computer company Hewlett Packard, and a 2016 Republican Presidential candidate, Carly Fiorina, has recalled the long-term benefits of her first degree, a BA in Medieval History and Philosophy:

> While I joke that my medieval history and philosophy degree prepared me not for the job market, I must tell you it did prepare me for life. I learned how to condense a whole lot of information down to the essence. That thought process has served me my whole life... I'm one of those people who believes we should be teaching people music, philosophy, history, art.[14]

In addition to personal testimony, there continues to be, chiefly in the USA, an institutional commitment, not only to the educational value of the liberal arts, but to its cultural role in preparing citizens to take part in the life of a democratic society. A range of American tertiary colleges teaches a broad program at the undergraduate level. Some are of religious inspiration—for example, Thomas Aquinas College in California and Wheaton College in Illinois—while others are of secular origin, such as the long-established institutions of William and Mary College in Virginia and St John's College in Maryland and New Mexico. These institutions sprang from the initiative, not of governments but of independent bodies, especially Christian churches, as well as civic-minded individuals. Many of America's most prestigious institutions, such as Harvard, Yale and Princeton Universities, had religious origins, and began with programmes that constituted, in varying degrees, the liberal arts.

By contrast, universities in Australia were all founded by government, until the recent development of private universities, such as Bond University (established in 1997 for secular reasons by the entrepreneur Alan Bond) and the University of Notre Dame Australia (which was inspired by religious motives, initially in Fremantle, Western Australia, in 1989, and later in Sydney in 2006). The liberal arts have historically found a place in the arts faculties, chiefly of the older universities like Sydney and Melbourne. At times the newer institutions have developed a programme, if not precisely in the liberal arts, at least of a general education with cultural rather than vocational aims. One example was the University of New South Wales (UNSW), founded in 1958 from a technical college. In its early years, it introduced a General Studies programme of cross-cultural courses, offering science students an arts course, and arts students a science course, as a way of bridging the "two cultures" classified by the British scientist and novelist, C.P. Snow.[15] A popular course in the General Studies programme at UNSW was the history and philosophy

---

[14] *Ibid.*
[15] Since C.P. Snow's reflections on the "two cultures" of the natural sciences and the humanities, a third culture, the social sciences, has emerged for bridging with the other two, as analysed by Jerome Kagan in *The Three Cultures: Natural Sciences, Social Sciences, and the Humanities in the 21st Century* (Cambridge: Cambridge University Press, 2009).

of science, which familiarised students with the impact of science in the West, not only as a scientific phenomenon but as a development of cultural significance. A more recent example has been the University of Melbourne which, in 2005, streamlined the bulk of its undergraduate offerings to provide a handful of generalist degrees, as a broad preparation for specialist programmes at the post-graduate level in areas such as law, medicine, teaching and engineering.

It may not be realistic to expect, in the early decades of the twenty-first century, a large-scale preference for generalist degrees, but nor does emphasising employment paths and job qualifications guarantee practical results. A market survey of Australian graduates in 2014 revealed that, while getting a job was the main reason for choosing a course, a third believed that their education had failed them in the workplace.[16] The apparently practical education is proving in too many cases to be failing at the most practical moments.

Professional qualifications are important for accreditation purposes, though even this connection is now being questioned. The British advertising executive and magazine columnist Rory Sutherland contends that the utilitarian value of vocational courses is hugely overstated, and that such degrees should be shortened to one year. He cites a forthcoming book, *The Case Against Education*, in which the American economist Bryan Caplan reportedly argues:

> [M]ost education does not really add human capital or skills commensurate with its time or cost. It is instead a signalling mechanism where prospective employees must jump through hoops to advertise their innate intelligence and self-discipline to employers. Yes, graduates may make good employees, but they would have made good employees anyway without the three years and spiralling debt required to prove it.[17]

Apart from the employment benefits that have been presumed to flow from work-related degrees, the concentration on vocational knowledge does not fully equip students for the experience of life. It does not supply a cultural breadth and depth, nor does it nurture the intellectual flexibility needed in the workplace and beyond, in the way that an educational grounding in the liberal arts can do. A professional degree has no time or capacity to deal with the ultimate realities that affect human beings—love and beauty, adventure, struggle, suffering and death—which inspire or haunt their lives. It focuses on the "how" questions—how things came to be or could be—rather than the

---

[16] Natasha Bita, "Study 'Not up to the Job' of Readying Aussies for Work", *The Australian*, September 8, 2014, 5. See also the report of 27 July 2017. Accessed 28 September 2017. http://www.news.com.au/lifestyle/parenting/school-life/schools-and-universities-are-not-preparing-young-australians-for-the-workforce/news-story/9a62540dc50f160ba94d3b90b1092d07

[17] Rory Sutherland, "Universities Should Offer One-Year Courses", *The Spectator*, 17 June 2017, 49.

"why" questions—why things exist at all and what they mean.[18] As the historian of education, Diane Ravitch, noted rather sharply: "The person who knows 'how' will always have a job. The person who knows 'why' will always be his boss."[19] Nor does a simple reliance on the power of electronic communications meet this challenge. In Neil Postman's words: "The computer cannot provide an organizing moral framework. It cannot tell us what questions are worth asking".[20]

The vocational degree, particularly at the undergraduate level, is not in itself capable of producing well-rounded graduates. It confuses training with education, which the present-day university tends to promote as one and the same. A British student Carmody Grey has reflected on the challenge of justifying her recently completed doctorate in the humanities in the current university environment:

> Our universities are becoming training camps where students are invited to pay for a qualification that will, the theory goes (not that the theory is holding up very well), pay them back with interest in the future. Education is now an "investment" in the purely monetary sense. . . . Students are clients, universities are businesses. Thomas Merton wrote that the monastic life was "useless". It exists to demonstrate that life is not reducible to a utilitarian logic. Herbert McCabe wrote that the life of the Trinity is an eternal waste of time: like lovers simply spending time with one another. Study in the humanities should express the shattering mystery that the world, life, being itself, really have no point at all, except themselves. The painstaking labour of writing a thesis, which few people will ever read, in some way bears witness to the impossibility of measuring every human activity with the logic of the market.[21]

As the traditional vision of a liberal education has faded in mainstream schools and universities, its value has been recognized by a growing movement at the pre-school and primary level—namely, that of home education or

---

[18] Anthony T. Kronman addressed this need in *Education's End: Why Our Colleges and Universities Have Given Up on the Meaning of Life* (2008), in which he argued that the emphasis on a research ideal had removed from the classroom any consideration of the purpose and meaning of life, and the "blinding fog of political correctness" had weakened the confidence of teachers to explore such fundamental questions.

[19] Spoken at a Commencement Speech in 1985 at the independent liberal arts college, Reed College, Oregon. Quoted in *Here We Stand: 600 Inspiring Messages from the World's best Commencement Addresses* (Lyons NY: Lyons Press, 2009).

[20] Neil Postman, "Informing Ourselves to Death". Accessed 30 August 2017. https://w2.eff.org/Net_culture/Criticisms/informing_ourselves_to_death.paper

[21] Carmody Grey, "The Very Pointlessness of My Research Has Revealed to Me the Value of the Liberal Arts", *The Tablet* (London), 2 August 2017. Accessed 10 August 2017. http://www.thetablet.co.uk/columnists/3/10789/0//the-very-pointlessness-of-my-research-has-revealed-to-me-the-value-of-the-liberal-arts

home schooling.[22] Parents choose this form of education for various reasons, but one motive has been to give their children a more solid academic and religious grounding, especially in the fundamental subjects of the liberal arts, than is often available in the organized school systems. The curriculum allows for flexibility, but it is common to take account of the sixty volumes of "Great Books" of Western civilization, as well as the thousand "Good Books" highlighted by the American educator, John Senior, which have enriched the cultural mind and imagination.[23] The programme is taught in a personal and interactive manner, which encourages thinking and a grasp of content as well as communication skills. It can be provided online as well as on-campus, as the Angelicum Academy, a Catholic home school institution in America, has demonstrated, offering a broad program, initially at the high school level and, most recently, in philosophy and theology for university-level students.[24]

To a significant extent, Australian universities have replaced the study of the liberal arts—and its historical expressions in Western history—with programmes that respond to new social claims and ideological imperatives, especially in the areas of race, class, and gender. The cultural focus of the curriculum has shifted to the ancient life of Australia, as expressed in the history of Indigenous people; to non-Western cultures, chiefly Asian; and to gender studies. Insofar as there is a lingering attention to Western culture, it is commonly tinged with contempt rather than directed towards appreciation. An understanding of the Western tradition has dwindled, creating a condition of cultural amnesia that is difficult to challenge because of the predilection for novelty rather than restoration in educational policy-making and curricular design. Yet the deficiency of appreciation of Western culture is not new. As the medieval historian David Knowles noted in the 1960s about the study of history in British universities: "Those who plead for a wider study of the origins and characteristics of civilisations other than our own do not always remember how lamentably narrow is the knowledge that many undergraduates have of the foundations and content of our own culture."[25]

---

[22] Eg, Penny Travers, "Rising Number of Canberra Families Turn To Home Education, Self-directed Learning", ABC, 19 February 2016. Accessed 10 September 2017.
http://www.abc.net.au/news/2016-02-19/more-families-turning-to-home-education-in-canberra/7183834

[23] William Edmund Fahey, "Will Rascals Defend Our Civilization. . . And What Books Will They Read?", *Crisis Magazine*, 24 February 2012. Accessed 10 September 2017.
http://www.crisismagazine.com/2012/naughty-boys-and-the-defense-of-civilization-must-we-choose-between-great-or-good-books

[24] "The Liberal Arts Go Online", Catholic World Report.com, 2 August 2012. Accessed 30 August 2017.
http://www.catholicworldreport.com/2012/08/02/the-liberal-arts-go-online/

[25] M.D. Knowles, "Academic History", *History* 47, no.161 (1962), 227.

Apart from the occasional initiatives in mainstream institutions, the only concerted effort in Australia to offer a comprehensive program in the liberal arts at a tertiary level has been at Campion College. Established in 2006 in western Sydney as a private and independent college of Catholic inspiration, Campion has developed a single undergraduate degree, a Bachelor of Arts in the Liberal Arts. It consists of a core curriculum that studies the unfolding of Western civilisation—in history, philosophy, theology, and literature, with the additional subjects of language (Latin and Classical Greek), science, and mathematics offered for part of the programme. Students receive an integrated understanding of reality through various lenses—of history as the lived experience of a people, philosophy as the animating ideas of a culture, theology as a people's relationship with God and the transcendent, and literature as the imagination engaging with and illuminating truth. The aim is not primarily transmission of knowledge but rather immersion in a culture. The foundational subjects are studied for the purpose of learning how to think, how to bring together ideas and understandings to achieve an intelligible grasp of truth and reality. They are organised as far as possible in a chronological sequence so as to foster an integrated understanding of cultural experience and progression.

The first year of the Campion program addresses the ancient world, the second year, the Middle Ages, the third year, modern times. The individual subjects are studied against a common cultural background. The methodological norms of each discipline are respected—so that history is judged in the light of documentary evidence, philosophy in terms of the significance of ideas, and literature according to the imaginative penetration of various authors—but the College strives to teach the program as an integrated whole. It searches for the relationships between the different subjects, and seeks to bring together the insights that emerge, so as to cultivate the art of intellectual synthesis as a basis of intellectual maturity and cultural understanding. Thus in the second year course on Medieval Literature, Dante's *Divine Comedy* is studied as a supreme work of the poetic imagination, but it is also of relevance to the Philosophy programme as an expression of the philosophical synthesis commonly identified with Thomas Aquinas, and to History as revealing Dante's approach to the past as a mystical fusion of the ideas and figures of pagan antiquity and those of the Christian world. The parallels—and even the preludes and overtures—between these two cultures, the ancient and the medieval, the Roman Empire and the Church, Virgil and Beatrice, and nature and grace, can be drawn out to offer illuminating comparisons. They illustrate the connecting threads of historical and cultural and spiritual experience, which produce continuities as well as changes in the life of a people.

Similarly, in a compulsory science unit in third year, "The History, Philosophy and Social Study of Science", Campion students examine the emergence of modern science from a Western culture cradled in Christian ideas about the order of nature and the intelligence of created things. The roots of science and technology are seen to be not only material but also intellectual and religious. Only a liberal arts course that brings together philosophic thought, theological understanding, and literary intuitions, as well as the history of social conditions, can shed light on the scientific impulses that brought out the structure and laws of a rationally functioning universe, and laid the foundations of modern technological culture.

From its opening in 2006, Campion College has conceived of its purpose ambitiously, not as an additional component of higher education in Australia, providing a programme not available elsewhere, but as a different model of education. Such a vision has sought to offer a distinctive degree that would extend the institutional offerings available to Australian students, but its deeper inspiration has been intellectual and spiritual. Its programme of university-level study embodies the traditions of understanding that have formed the Western mind and sensibility—a dynamic blend of natural reason and supernatural faith, of rational thought and spiritual intuition. These traditions provide channels of access to the breadth of human existence, embracing not only the measurable and the containable, but also the impenetrable and the transcendental, thereby shedding light on spiritual as well as material realities. Campion's philosophical and cultural and religious life has been shaped by an openness to the broad sweep of human experience. The College believes that anything less is a narrow and inadequate education, because it does not take account of the fullness of human experience and aspiration, and confuses an education for life with training for employability. In the words of C.S. Lewis, "the task of the modern educator is not to cut down jungles but to irrigate deserts".[26] This led Campion College to establish in 2010 a Centre for the Study of Western Tradition, as a vehicle for encouraging scholarly discourse with other institutions, and attracting a wider academic and professional audience for the Liberal Arts.

A key sign of the transition from an education founded on cultural initiation, as represented by the liberal arts, to one governed by the shifting ideas of social relevance and political priorities, as well as by financial pressures, is the university library. The traditional notion of the library is that of a repository of learning, a centre for gathering and preserving the works of scholarship. The library has been an instrument of cultural continuity as well as stimulation, a bridge between the learning of the past and the scholarly promise of the future, captured in Isaac Newton's famous statement, attributed in an ear-

---

[26] C.S. Lewis, *The Abolition of Man* (London: Geoffrey Bles, 1967), 14.

lier form to Bernard of Chartres: "If I have seen further, it is by standing on the shoulders of giants".[27]

The contemporary university library is shaped by a different version of scholarship and educational service. It sees itself more as a process than a place, a vehicle of information retrieval rather than the centre and symbol of a university's intellectual infrastructure. The library's purpose and identity have diffused, and the role of collecting and preserving has given way to an emphasis on access and delivery. While the library survives as a physical centre, its building space has been reconfigured to accentuate digital access and accommodate modes of learning that are now social, not just solitary; conducted in informal groups that heighten discussion and the pooling of insights. At the same time, this emphasis can have an unintentional effect: it can devalue individual exploring and reading, which has often been the setting and inspiration for fresh ideas, and for the contemplation of their meaning in an individual's life and relationship with others.

Matthew Battles recounts the instructive history of a collection of fragments of ancient Hebrew manuscripts, which is "unparalleled among the libraries of the world". They were discarded but later rescued by a nineteenth century rabbinical scholar. The very fact of their presumed worthlessness, Battles argues, is what invests them with scholarly value. They now convey "a far more comprehensive message from their times than any vetted and authorized library collection ever could". The conventional library preserves what one generation believes at the time is worth preserving, and, in Battles' words, "regardless of the library's alleged political neutrality, its transparency, its seeming lack of roots, it contains the buried and often contradictory impulses of the princes, philanthropists, and academicians who are its authors". By contrast, the library of discarded manuscripts was "a simple refuse pile, unafraid of its own collected contradictions".[28]

Insofar as the modern academic library is much less a storehouse of scholarship than a functional instrument for accessing organized information, it is apt to play a diminishing role in the life of a university. It no longer signifies or underpins so unmistakably an educational culture, and is forfeiting its reputation as the custodian of a tradition of learning. Nor is it such a vital partner in the world of scholarly publishing and communication. It is ceasing to hold major resources, discarding low-use books for which there is no space and subscribing to journal literature on a rental rather than ownership basis. Journal cancellations and reduced book acquisitions will cause retrospective or cumulative material to be lost, not just current publications. The lack of a

---

[27] Isaac Newton, "Letter from Sir Isaac Newton to Robert Hooke", Historical Society of Pennsylvania. Accessed 26 September 2017. http://digitallibrary.hsp.org/index.php/Detail/Object/Show/object_id/9285
[28] Matthew Battles, *Library: An Unquiet History* (London: Heinemann, 2004), 196.

national storage facility in Australia for preserving scholarly materials withdrawn from individual libraries is reducing the long-term accessibility of materials for teaching and research.[29]

These changes have profound and lasting implications for the liberal arts. Digital access can be promoted to the point where it fosters the fallacy that all scholarly information of significance is available on the Internet, and that the printed book as a vessel of synthesized, consolidated knowledge is of receding importance in the world of learning.[30] Thus the scholarly memory of the library, and of the university it serves, risks being truncated, like a person whose brain is impaired by interference with the centres of memory.

In company with university presses and journals, academic libraries now struggle to function in this transformed environment. The immediate causes of their deteriorating place in universities, and in the broader culture, are well-known—financial cutbacks and the massive changes in communications technology. But the deeper reasons are cultural—that universities themselves have ceased, to a significant extent, to define themselves in intellectual or even educational terms. They no longer possess a clear understanding of their cultural purpose and identity. They envisage their role—or accept it as an assigned justification by government—as engines of economic development and earners of export income. They are understood as fulfilling an economic and political purpose, even more than an educational and cultural one.[31]

A senior university press editor in America has pointed to the difficulty of sustaining the intellectual infrastructure of universities, particularly in support of the liberal arts, at a time of financial cuts and changing social and political imperatives:

---

[29] As the print collections of academic libraries in Australia are dispersed to maintain "steady state" libraries, there has not emerged a national strategy for the comprehensive preservation of material, underpinned by discovery and delivery services. Some university libraries have individual storage arrangements or, in Victoria and South Australia, cooperative facilities, but in contrast to their counterparts in areas of North America and such European countries as Scotland, France and Finland, there is no national storage centre to provide continuing access to discarded collections. Cathie Jilovsky and Paul Genoni, "Changing Library Spaces: Finding a Place for print". Accessed 29 September 2017.https://www.caval.edu.au/assets/files/Research_and_Advocacy/VALA2008_Paper_Jilovsky_&_Genoni.pdf

[30] Michelle M. Wu, "Why Print and Electronic Resources are Essential to the Academic Law Library", [Georgetown] *Law Library Journal* 97, 2005, 235-256. Accessed September 28, 2017. http://scholarship.law.georgetown.edu/cgi/viewcontent.cgi?article=1784&context=facpub

[31] In November 2016, the Universities Australia website highlighted the increasing importance of universities in generating export income. The education of international students, a worthy aim in itself, was chiefly presented as an investment in education for economic gains. It has been Australia's third largest export, behind only iron ore and coal. Universities Australia. Accessed 30 August 2017. https://www.universitiesaustralia.edu.au/Media-and-Events/media-releases/International-education-generates-a-record--20-3-billion-for-Australia#.WcwzD9MjHIs

> Universities encourage venture-capital thinking. That means it's easier to get money for projects that don't exist. . . . There's less concern about what upholds the institutions that we depend on. . . .
>
> A lot of things that underpin the academy weren't made to be evaluated on a cost-benefit basis independently as if they were part of a corporation.[32]

The university library can hardly resist being recast as a cog—admittedly, an expensive cog—in a machine that is geared, not so much to the promotion of intellectual penetration and cultural appreciation that inform citizenship in a democracy, but to financial goals and the measurable outputs of material development. The change has reflected a reversion—from the ordering of knowledge and the nurturing of wisdom, which should be the overarching goal of education, to dealing with data, the raw material of information, which can only have meaning if it has been absorbed sufficiently to shed light on human reality.

Yet the library can still serve the role of educational midwife, introducing students to a world of accumulated knowledge that fosters a richer understanding of reality. The availability of a large library collection, assembled over a long period, has traditionally provided the setting for serendipity, of importance to both the humanities and the sciences. The opportunity for undirected browsing enables scholars to traverse the literature and make discoveries that cannot be predicted. Online journals have been a boon in many ways, enhancing access to periodical literature in various fields, and repositioning study and research activities to the convenience of the individual office rather than the communal space of a library. They serve, in the words of the American university leader Vartan Gregorian as "profoundly integrative tools", acting as a technological reinforcement of the naturally unifying effects of the liberal arts.[33] They can be an instrument that brings together findings and insights, and cultivates intellectual growth, helping the scholar and student to grasp the relationships between various fields of knowledge.

Yet online journals are not a simple equivalent to printed journals in another form, for they operate in different ways. Printed journals lack the sophistication of keyword searching, but they offer a freedom to roam and a flexibility of enquiry that are especially conducive to the liberal arts, and cannot easily be replicated by the search engines of a programmed environment. By their nature, printed journals can yield valuable ideas and discoveries unexpectedly, immersing the enquiring scholar or student in a broad pool of

---

[32] Scott Smallwood, "The Crumbling Intellectual Foundation", *Chronicle of Higher Education*, 20 September 2002, A10-11.

[33] Vartan Gregorian, "Colleges Must Reconstruct the Unity of Knowledge", *Chronicle of Higher Education*, June 4, 2004, B13.

learning opportunities. Perusing a substantial journal run in a particular discipline can be of decisive value at an early point in a scholarly enquiry. It can sharpen and clarify the questions a researcher is wrestling with, well before he begins to formulate clear answers or conclusions. Above all is this true of the intellectual life of the liberal arts, which is founded on a different principle of progress from that of the pure and applied sciences. The liberal arts work by means of a deepening of discernment and the discovery—or rediscovery—of insights, as when historical events and figures or literary works stimulate fresh interpretations; whereas the principle governing progress in the sciences is linear, based on proving or disproving theories, and retaining or discarding interpretations, according to the emergence of new evidence.

In the 2014 survey of Australian graduates, a quarter indicated that they had enrolled in their university courses for non-vocational reasons, to gain "a broad and varied knowledge".[34] Such an opportunity provides a point of re-entry for the liberal arts, a means of achieving a new connection with the heritage of Western civilisation, and countering the cultural amnesia that school and university programmes in Australia have visited upon successive generations of students.

Given the vocational and other pressures on present-day students and their families, the practical possibilities of a resurgence of liberal arts education may seem remote; but the perspective of hopeful realism captured by Christopher Dawson is worth recalling: "The soil must be broken—the plough and the harrow must do their work before the seed can produce a good harvest. But this is the age of the plough and the harrow, not the time of harvest".[35]

Higher education itself is a season for the plough and the harrow. It calls for a clarity and conviction of purpose, and a patient postponement of results. The harvest comes later.

---

[34] "Study 'Not Up To the Job' of Readying Aussies for Work", *The Australian*, 8 September 2014.
[35] Christopher Dawson, *The Movement of World Revolution*. (London: Sheed and Ward, 1959), 179.

Western Civilisation and All That

Simon Haines [1]

"Western civilisation" shouldn't be a contentious concept. If "civilisation" refers to the communal arrangements of relatively large or dense populations, widely distributed in time and space, but broadly affiliated by enduring practices, rules and beliefs, and embellished and facilitated by characteristic arts, techniques and individuals, then that term seems uncontroversial. No-one objects to the study of Chinese, Persian, Mesopotamian, Arab, Indian, Aztec, Inca or classical Greek civilisations.

As for "Western", we are happy to speak of western Australia, or the western isles of Scotland. Something being west of something else doesn't seem intrinsically objectionable. We all have to be west of somewhere. Europe is west of Asia and the Middle East (although north of Africa). It has a civilisation with distinctive features and inheritances (although some of these derive from its closest neighbours). The Americas are west of Europe and in turn inherited many of these features, and "Euro-American civilisation" is a bit of a mouthful, as well as incomplete seen from New Zealand and points west.

Furthermore, many of these distinctive features are recognised worldwide as uncontroversially "Western", as opposed to Chinese, Aztec and so on. Homer and Dante, Shakespeare and Goethe, Jane Austen and Joan of Arc, Plato and NATO, Beethoven and Bartok, Leonardo and Picasso, the Parthenon and the Pantheon, Napoleon and Julius Caesar, Botticelli's Venus and the Mona Lisa, the Roman Empire and Christianity, the Enlightenment and its revolutionary American, French, industrial and scientific heirs, democracy and human rights—most educated Chinese people, for example, would recognise much of this bucket list as "Western", are interested in its features, and where feasible would want to photograph themselves standing in front of one.

"Civilisation" is an unremarkable concept, then, and so is "Western". But there's a nuclear reaction when the two are put together. The idea of "Western civilisation" *is* contentious. Criticism of it is constant, and is of two kinds. The first comes mainly from scholars and intellectuals, who offer some version of the argument that the *concept* is empty or meaningless. The second

---

[1] First published as Simon Haines, "An Education Manifesto for Western Civilisation", *Quadrant* No. 542, December 2017, vol. LXI, No. 12, 14-17

criticism (censure, really) is of the *thing*, "The West" and all its works. In its domestic or endogenous form this also comes mainly from intellectuals, less scholarly ones on the whole, including especially students. But there is also an exogenous form, from people all over the world with radical non-western or anti-western attitudes and agendas, either covert or overt. Some of these are genuinely dangerous, even murderous—but they still think of the West as a real thing. Taking the two broader types of criticism together: either western civilisation is nothing, or it is wicked. Either it doesn't exist, or it shouldn't.

The denial of its existence is an example of a common intellectual propensity to scrutinise some familiar object more and more closely until the object itself disappears, as under a microscope. Max Planck and Erwin Schrödinger led quantum physics into seeing the visible world as fundamentally made of invisible energy. The harder scholars look at "Western civilisation", the more fine-grained their analysis becomes, the less aware they are of the larger entity. Instead, they see its important sources and analogues in the Middle East or Africa (if Egypt is Africa), or the Arab scholars of the so-called "early middle ages" (a Golden Age for them) who were such vital (though not the only) transmitters of Greek thought to Europe. They see "Europe" and "the West" as concepts with identifiable provenance, so that almost by definition they once "didn't exist". They see the concept as embracing so many dissimilar or conflicting elements that it has no real meaning any more. They have difficulties with calling its essential elements "western", properly speaking (Christianity arose in the Middle East and so many of its adherents are now African or Asian). Above all, they can't see "Western civilisation" as having any single, essential defining feature.

These are all valuable arguments, taken separately. They derive from a peculiarly modern hybrid of philosophical scepticism and scientific empiricism, both immensely helpful—and distinctively "Western"—ways of scrutinising received opinion: so long as they are used with discrimination. Unfortunately both are prone to extremism in the form of a denial of ordinary experience. To adapt Dr Johnson's rebuttal of Bishop Berkeley: George of the Quantum Jungle may know that the tree is really a wave-function, or even suspect sometimes (as a lapsed idealist) that it does not exist when he's not there to see it; but he'd better watch out for it all the same.

The other major type of criticism, on the contrary, argues that Western civilisation is not only real, but liable to mug your grandmother. A recent column in *The Stanford Daily* warned that reviving the university's western civilisation course, now moribund like most such courses in the United States, would mean "upholding white supremacy, capitalism and colonialism, and all other oppressive systems that flow from Western civilisations". The list of distinctive western features mentioned above, from this point of view, would include Hitler not Goethe; genocidal imperialism not democracy; racism not multiculturalism; the burning of the Summer Palace not the building of the

Winter Palace; slavery not abolition; misogyny not *amour courtois*; crusades not cathedrals; narcissistic consumerism not rational choice; capitalist greed not free markets; environmental destruction not green activism; vested interests not inclusiveness: and so on. The West is the *real* "evil empire". According to the endogenous or Western critics mentioned above, it is a place of barbarism; according to the exogenous or non-Western ones, it is a place of decadence, and the endogenous critics are themselves symptoms of this condition, which is contagious. Taken together, these two views resemble Oscar Wilde's of America: that it had passed straight from barbarism to decadence without any intervening period of civilisation.

The non-Western critics aren't entirely wrong in seeing that strain of Western self-criticism (or self-censure) as contagiously decadent. It has mutated out of a more generalised anti-civilisation attitude, with ancient roots in both classical misanthropy and the Christian doctrine of original sin. It derives in its modern distorted form from Rousseau via Nietzsche (and indeed Wilde, who was a bit of a Nietzschean in his own quiet way). From this perspective any civilisation at all is necessarily built on hypocrisy and oppression. *Homo homini lupus est*; and the larger the pack the more lupine its behaviour. So says the misanthropist, and he has a point. Without faith we are fallen creatures, savage wolves. So say St Paul and Augustine, and they have a point too. But the modern anti-civilisation view sees only the wolf and never the lamb: never the good shepherd.

Sometimes the circle closes, and those who deny "Western civilisation" merge with those who hate it. It is unreal *and* it is evil. Now cognitive dissonance is not an unusual disorder. Like Alice's White Queen, many people are quite capable of believing six impossible things before breakfast. But in some cases, as Humpty Dumpty points out soon after, it's no longer a question of the absurd things people can do with words or ideas—only of "who is to be master". This is not logical or ontological any more: it's ideological. Even pathological. This dissonant cross-breed is the most implacable form of all hostile criticism of "Western civilisation" because the true ideologue cannot see that the enemy even exists other than as an ideological construct. All politics is ideological, all ideology is political, and there is nothing else—no private space or identity at all (Orwell's central insight in *1984*).

There is also a sophisticated, declinist variant of the barbaric-decadent position: call it the Spenglerian gambit. Instead of saying that western civilisation exists but it shouldn't, this variant says that it should but it doesn't, or at any rate soon won't. For Oswald Spengler, writing his *Decline of the West* at the time of World War I, civilisation is what happens when a culture loses its vitality, as had already happened, he thought, in the tragic, Faustian West. Just as "decadent" and "declining" mean "falling down" and "sloping down", so World War I marked an epochal decline in Western self-belief and ushered in a celebrated era of decadence. This is an Hegelian attitude to history, except that where Hegel thought humanity had found its apotheosis in the Prussian state providentially inhabited by Hegel (Francis Fukuyama also thought he stood at such a point, although he doesn't think so any more), Spengler and his heirs think they live *after* some imaginary noontime, in the twilight of the gods, the *Abendland* of their civilisation—or at least, of their culture. These critics have no objection to cultural studies, by the way. Just as long as you don't call it a civilisation. Or carry on about its "values".

So there's a huge market for views that "Western civilisation", far from being uncontentious, is a contradiction, a monster, a nonentity or an anachronism. If you wanted to design courses on this subject, you could easily devote half a dozen to pointing out that it wasn't a real or proper subject for a course. There will always be ignorant people who persist in thinking that there is a thing called "Western civilisation", and that it has been a Good Thing, on the whole: so they will always need to be told that there isn't, and it hasn't. Impossible not to think of John Cleese in *The Life of Brian* irritably dismissing the objections of his fellow-activists in the Judaean People's Revolutionary Front: "*apart from* .... antibiotics, antiseptics, disinfectants and indeed all modern medicine; eradication or reduction of ancient endemic diseases and perinatal mortality; rule of and equality before the law; electricity; the internet; unprecedented equality between the sexes; representative democracy and separation of powers; two industrial revolutions; worldwide transport and telecommunications systems; religious tolerance and separation of church and state; the abolition of slavery; liberal individualism; open markets; vastly increased average prosperity, health and longevity: and of course all the aforementioned artists and thinkers......*what has Western civilisation ever done for us?*"

If you were establishing a Centre for Western Civilisation, or a BA in the subject, those awkward JPRF cadres might give you grounds for hope, despite all the criticism. Returning to Alice, you might think of the disappearing American "Western civ" courses as a kind of Cheshire Cat: the body may vanish, but the smile lingers on. Or perhaps as Schrödinger's Cat: Western civ is dead in a box, but also at the same time very much alive. Yes, there have been terrible crimes and abuses—as with any civilisation, any large scale human enterprise at all. Man *is* a wolf to man. There *are* evil people. But we've heard about all that *ad nauseam*: let's also remember the other side. The concept of Western civilisation *is* a bit nebulous, as you'd expect with such a vast geographical and chronological range of languages, cultures, religious denominations and value systems. But there's still a family resemblance. We recognise its features, its "cloud-capped towers and gorgeous palaces", as well as its sewers and dark alleys. As Augustine said about time, we all know what it is, we all live with it, even if we can't *say* what it is.

And in this case we do all live with it, including in Australia: but we can and should say quite a lot. This is no "insubstantial pageant fading". The very terms its critics use to attack "Western civilisation", sceptical, empirical, political, are the terms it has taught them. The chambers and spaces they march and protest in, the institutions they condemn, are the ones it has built and opened and maintained for them. The liberal tolerance they sneer at is what tolerates their sneers, where other civilisations would have imprisoned them, and do. Its openness to the whole world, to new experience, its adventurous spirit of discovery and curiosity, its desire "to strive, to seek, to find", and yes, its capacity to criticise itself, is what has distinguished this civilisation from others. Its very variety of cultures and values, so often incompatible and conflicted, has also given it a hybrid toughness, a capacity to adapt and assimilate, to tolerate and include. Millions of non-Westerners (including some who think it is wicked) want nothing more than to live in it, while Westerners lucky enough to have it as a birthright take it for granted. How we would miss it if it really didn't exist! It may not be a perfect model for a fully inclusive or genuinely liberal human civilisation, one neither repressive nor prodigal, but truly magnanimous. Still, it may be the closest we've yet come, as a species.

No doubt you noticed that the words "it" and "its" appeared many times in the previous paragraphs. Aha, cry the sceptical-empirical crowd: there's the rub. There is no "it", no essence. And as for the political crowd, any mention of an "It" will horrify them: here is the Stephen King monster. That grin…surely not a cat but an evil clown…oh God, *it's getting out of the box!*

The same answer works in both cases: "it" isn't an It. There is no essence and there is no monster: only grammar. "It" is a *pronoun*; "Western civilisation" is a handy phrase referring to a very large and dynamic collection of multifarious but still associated practices, artefacts and ideas. Taking a BA in Western Civilisation would be like exploring the world's most interactive museum, a tour opening out towards an almost infinite variety of affiliated models for living together or alone, more or less successfully. No monsters, except those bred by the sleep of reason. No essence, any more than a long piece of rope has a single thread running all the way through it: but it may have long sequences or patterns of threads of the same colour, and still it's one rope, and when it takes you all the way to the summit, you will find that the whole point, the meaning, was in the climb.

All of which is to say that by its very nature an educational enterprise or space should not be a political or ideological one. Clamouring about "upholding white supremacy" is as overwrought and anachronistic as asking whether classicists ran the British Empire along Roman models, or whether conversely imperialist attitudes ran the classics (yes, this controversy is currently a hot topic in some academic circles). How many angels can you persuade to dance on the head of your pin? All the noise prevents a generation of young people from hearing the "music of humanity" as played by one of its great orchestras—and from themselves learning to play (yes, of course, there are other orchestras: by all means listen to those too: but how many can one person actually belong to?).

Over 2,500 years of philosophy and literature, of buildings, paintings and music: the value-dissolving dilemmas of tragedy, the formal resolutions of architecture, the clarifying scrutiny of logic, the agonies, ecstasies and quiet reassurances of religious faith (and doubt), the competing claims of social obligation and individual fulfilment: why should a few current, crude political obsessions (almost fantasies: "the heart's grown brutal from the fare") deny school leavers, or indeed older students, access to this vast centuries-long conversation about the meaning of life—of their own lives? Let them find the values they need for themselves, induce them from the texts, ideas, arts and institutions they study. That induction is an education: a leading in and a leading forth: a finding within a text which is at the same time a finding within oneself. Let the students find out whether there is or isn't a thread, or a pattern of threads, running from Pericles' funeral oration to Justinian's *Corpus* to Magna Carta to the Bill of Rights to the *Declaration of the Rights of Man*: or for that matter from *Lysistrata* to the *Declaration of the Rights of Woman*: or from Helen of Troy to Dido to Héloïse to Anna Karenina: or from Milton's Satan to Anakin Skywalker: or right through the Old and New Testaments and out into much of our literature and art. In doing so, in encountering so many other voices emphatically unlike theirs and yet still able to speak to their common condition, they will also be finding out what their own values are and where they have come from, including as Australians: and that a shallow fixation on the present and its irritable discontents doesn't even begin to scratch the surface of all that has been thought about value and meaning, courage and wisdom, anger and revenge, prudence and judgement, hope and despair, freedom and serfdom, remorse and forgiveness, gratitude and envy, democrats and aristocrats, oligarchs and monarchs, revolution and restoration, beauty and truth and love, in the many constituent cultures of our civilisation across the ages and across the world.

This isn't the kind of education Australian arts faculties have been able to offer for quite some time, if ever. Our single-discipline-with-outside-major model is British, indeed Scottish, not American. But it isn't working any more for undergraduates in the humanities. The research- and rankings-driven, relentlessly vocational agendas of our universities mean that arts academics are forced to teach their research in order to justify their existence. This makes it hard to create integrated teaching degrees with coherent, overarching disciplinary perspectives, as opposed to an assemblage of research programmes with teaching spinoffs (however fine the research or teaching). At the same time the inspiring big picture and great ideas curricula which have changed so many lives in liberal arts colleges are out of the question. These massified post-Dawkins institutions can't afford the small, intensive, high-quality classes which alone make such integration and inspiration possible: the kind of close attention to a complex pattern of thought which alone enables genuine critical judgement. Imagine if a university had the funding to enable classes of just half a dozen top-flight students, many of them on scholarships, embarking on the kind of education described above. Now if only someone could make *that* kind of learning possible . . .

The Purpose of Education

Kevin Donnelly

What does it mean to be educated and what is the purpose of education? How such questions are answered is crucial, as education, in addition to being essential for the wellbeing and continuation of one's community and society, distinguishes civilised cultures from those that are primitive and less advanced.

Education also deals with the physical, moral, emotional, intellectual and spiritual aspects of each individual and how she or he finds happiness and fulfilment. To be educated is to appreciate what constitutes the good life and to be able to identify right from wrong and true from false. Education, in addition to providing entry to employment, also addresses existential questions about the meaning of life and the nature of the universe in which we live.

No approach to education is neutral or value-free, as all curriculum frameworks, syllabuses and pedagogy, to a greater or lesser degree, reflect the beliefs and values of their designers and other curriculum theorists and practitioners. As argued by Neil Postman:

> ... by definition, there can be no education philosophy that does not address what learning is for. Confucius, Plato, Quintilian, Cicero, Comenius, Erasmus, Locke, Rousseau, Jefferson, Russell, Montessori, Whitehead and Dewey—each believed that there was some transcendent political, spiritual or social ideal that must be advanced through education.[1]

One approach to education centres on what Australia's Brian Crittenden describes as a liberal education. An education involving:

> ... a systematic and sustained introduction to those public forms of meaning in which the standards of human excellence in the intellectual, moral and aesthetic domains are expressed and critically investigated.[2]

As noted by Alan Barcan, and by Geoffrey Sherrington and Hannah Forsyth, for most of the 20th century curriculums across state and territory schools,

---

[1] N. Postman, *Technopoly The Surrender of Culture to Technology*, (New York: Vintage Books, 1993), 171.
[2] B. Crittenden, *Cultural Pluralism and Common Curriculum* (Parkville: Melbourne University Press, 1982), 88.

and universities for that matter, were closely associated with a liberal view of education, a view of education associated with the educational philosophy of Matthew Arnold and John Henry Newman, and that can be traced back via the Enlightenment, the Reformation and Renaissance to the ancient Greek philosophers and sophists.[3]

Drawing heavily on the new sociology of education movement, a second approach to the question of the nature and purpose of education involves a rainbow alliance of theories, including classical Marxism, neo-Marxism and feminist, gender, queer and postcolonial theories, as well as postmodernism and deconstructionism. While often in disagreement, what such theories hold in common is a radical critique of a liberal view of education and education's relationship to society and the world at large.

A third approach involves adopting a child-centred, inquiry-based approach to education and the curriculum, where a student's interests and motivations are centre-stage, and essential content is secondary to the process of learning. More recently, child-centred learning has been renamed as personalised learning, where teachers, instead of being masters of their subject, are described as 'facilitators' and 'guides by the side', and students are described as 'knowledge navigators' and 'digital natives'.

A fourth approach to deciding what constitutes a worthwhile education, based on the belief that we have entered a post-industrial, digital age where the new technologies dominate, is to champion 21st century learning. Advocates argue that as it is impossible to know the future, especially in relation to the changing nature of employment and the impact of the new technologies on society and the world at large, that education must focus on generic competencies and skills such as: learning how to learn, working in teams, communicating ideas, solving problems and collecting and analysing information. As a result, an argument is put that any curriculum based on the established disciplines is inflexible, irrelevant and obsolete.

Closely associated with 21st century learning is a utilitarian approach that defines education in terms of the types of technical knowledge and skills needed to strengthen the economy, improve productivity and to make Australia more internationally competitive in what is an increasingly globalised world. Instead of being committed to the search for wisdom and truth, universities, with a few exceptions, are more like corporate organisations focused on increasing market share and responding to government-initiated policies and initiatives.

---

[3] A. Barcan, "Ideology and the Curriculum", in *Education and the Ideal*, ed. N. Smith, (Epping, New South Wales: New Frontier Publishing, 2004), 16; G. Sherrington, and H. Forsyth, 2012. "Ideas of a Liberal Education, an Essay on Elite and Mass Higher Education", in *On the Purpose of a University Education*, ed. L.Boschiero, (North Melbourne: Australian Scholarly Publishing, 2012), 48-66.

While the four different approaches to defining the nature and purpose of education have an important role to play in the school curriculum and an individual's education, not all are of equal value or worth in terms of what it means to be educated in its fullest and most enriching sense. In the following I shall argue for the preeminent place of a liberal education and the need to ensure that all students have the right to be introduced to and become familiar with what Matthew Arnold, when detailing the nature and significance of culture, describes as:

> ... a pursuit of our total perfection by means of getting to know, on all matters that most concern us, the best which has been thought and said in the world; and through this knowledge, turning a fresh and free thought upon our stock notions and habits.[4]

An argument will also be put, notwithstanding the vital importance of a liberal education, that since the mid-to-late 60s its place in the school curriculum has been undermined and weakened and, as a result, increasing numbers of students are completing their school education culturally impoverished and morally and spiritually adrift.

A Liberal Education

If then we recognize education as an initiation into a civilization, we may regard it as beginning to learn our way about a material, emotional, moral and intellectual inheritance, and as learning to recognize the varieties of human utterance and to participate in the conversation they compose.[5]

Contained in the above quotation is a definition of the purpose of education that centres on the need to initiate each generation into what Oakeshott describes as a 'conversation'. To be educated, by definition, requires becoming familiar with and able to participate in a conversation "begun in the primeval forests and extended and made more articulate in the course of the centuries".[6]

Neil Postman, when arguing against what he sees as the destructive effects of the new technologies, also refers to the idea of education involving a conversation, when describing what he refers to as a broader, more enriching view of the curriculum. One where:

> ... to become educated means to become aware of the origins and growth of knowledge and knowledge systems; to be familiar with the intellectual and crea-

---

[4] M. Arnold, *Culture and Anarchy*, 1968 Edition (Cambridge: Cambridge University Press, 1968), 6.
[5] M. Oakeshott, "The study of 'politics' in a university" in *Rationalism in politics and other essays*, ed. M. Oakeshott, (Indianapolis: Liberty Press 1991), 188.
[6] See M. Oakeshott, "The voice of poetry in the conversation of mankind" in ed. M, Oakeshott, *Ibid.*, 490.

tive processes by which the best that has been thought and said has been produced; to learn how to participate, even if as a listener, in what Robert Maynard Hutchins once called The Great Conversation.[7]

This view of education is based on the premise that education does not arise spontaneously or by accident, and that it requires a prolonged and sustained initiation into the major forms of knowledge, understanding, dispositions and habits of mind traditionally associated with the academic disciplines that have, since the time of the ancient Greeks, evolved and changed over some hundreds of years. While drawing on other cultures over an extended period of time, it is also the case that a liberal view of education is intimately associated with Western culture and Western civilisation.

Such a view of education, unlike vocational education and training, is not immediately practical or utilitarian. As suggested by John Henry Newman when detailing the nature of a university education, it involves a:

> … process of training, by which the intellect, instead of being formed or sacrificed for some particular or accidental purpose, some specific trade or profession, or study of science, is disciplined for its own sake, for the perception of its higher object, and for its highest culture.[8]

T.S. Eliot, when defining the nature and importance of culture and the place of universities within the context of Western civilisation, makes a similar point when he argues that universities should be independent of government and not centred on training. Instead, Eliot argues universities "should stand for the preservation of learning, for the pursuit of truth, and in so far as men are capable of it, the attainment of wisdom".[9]

A liberal view of education, in addition to being centred on the pursuit of truth and wisdom, is also committed to objectivity and balance. Instead of education succumbing to short-term political expediency or a particular ideological view of the world the ideal is one where education is concerned with critical inquiry, reason and impartiality. As such the purpose of education is to:

> … facilitate independent evaluation of social practice… as instruments of insight and criticism, standing apart from current social conceptions and serving autonomous ideals of inquiry and truth.[10]

---

[7] N. Postman, *Technopoly The Surrender of Culture to Technology*, (New York: Vintage Books, 1993), 188.
[8] John Henry Newman, *The idea of a university defined and illustrated* (1852). Retrieved 22 May, 2017 Accessed http://www.gutenberg.org/files/24526/24526-h/24526-h.html
[9] T. S. Eliot, *Notes towards the Definition of Culture* (London: Faber and Faber, 1948), 123.
[10] I. Scheffler, "Reflections on Educational Relevance", in *The Philosophy of Education*, ed. RS Peters (Oxford: Oxford University Press, 1973), 75-84.

Critical in this regard is that a liberal education is not one where what counts as accepted truth is moribund or ossified. As noted by Arnold, the ideal is one where education, and culture more generally, turns "a fresh and free thought upon our stock notions and habits". Especially in disciplines like mathematics and science, once accepted theories and beliefs are always open to contestation and, if found wanting, are reviewed and changed. In relation to science James Anthony Gibbons makes the point:

> "Proposed explanations are tested against the physical world and, depending on their success in accounting for that physical world, may be accepted as a step in the search for truth".[11]

At a time when schools are being pressured to define educational success in terms of literacy and numeracy results as measured by the National Assessment Program Literacy and Numeracy at years 3, 5, 7 and 9, it is also important to recognise that a liberal education embraces a broader view of education. One that deals with what a Victorian Ministry of Education report describes as our "best validated knowledge and artistic achievements".[12] Subjects like mathematics, science, history, music, art, language and literature form the basis of such an education and are vital if students, to use an expression associated with E.D. Hirsch Jr, are to be culturally literate.[13]

A liberal view of education is also based on the premise that to understand the present and to be in a better position to shape the future one must acknowledge and learn about the past. Disciplines and subjects like mathematics, science, philosophy, music, poetry, drama and ethics can be traced back to the ancient Romans and Greeks and, as a result and as argued by Bloom:

> Such an education is largely dedicated to the study of the deepest thinkers of the past, because their works constitute a body of learning which we must preserve in order to remain civilized and because anything new that is serious must be based on, and take account of, them.[14]

---

[11] J A. Gibbons, *On Reflection* (Adelaide: Flinders University Institute of International Education, 2004), 29.
[12] Victorian Ministry of Education, *The Ministerial Review of Postcompulsory Schooling. Report Volume One* (Ministry of Education: Melbourne, 1985), 16.
[13] E D. Hirsch, Jr. *Cultural Literacy: What Every American Needs To Know* (New York: Vintage Books, 1988).
[14] A. Bloom, "The Democratization of the University" in *Giants and Dwarfs Essays 1960-1990* (New York: Simon and Shuster, 1990), 374.

In addressing the question "What is the point of education?", David Albert Jones and Stephen Barrie touch on another significant aspect of a liberal education—the central importance of education dealing with ethical and moral beliefs and values.[15] Education in its fullest and most rewarding sense deals with the "integral formation of the person through cultivating the virtues", especially the "cultivation of moral and intellectual virtues, for the good of the person and for the common good of society". In exploring this aspect of a liberal education the authors refer to the works of Aristotle, Plato, Cicero, Ambrose and Augustine. Also acknowledged is the influence of Christianity on Western civilisation's concept of a liberal education and the importance of introducing students to a transcendent and spiritual sense of one's self and the wider world.

As previously mentioned, notwithstanding the strengths and benefits of a liberal education, since the mid-to-late 60s it has been replaced by a number of curriculum innovations and theories that have acted to undermine its legitimacy and central place in the school curriculum.

The New Sociology of Education Movement and the Impact of Theory
As argued by Roger Kimball, Allan Bloom and Alan Barcan, the late 60s to mid-70s was a time of dramatic and far-reaching change across Europe and the English-speaking world, symbolised by: the rise of the counter-culture movement, Woodstock, Vietnam moratoriums and a revolt against the status quo and established authority.[16]

Kimball, citing the Italian Marxist Antonio Gramsci and the German cultural-left radical Rudi Dutschke, argues this was a time when student radicals and sympathetic academics decided that the most effective way to undermine the status quo, and transform society was to take 'the long march through the institutions', especially schools and universities. If Western style capitalism could not be overthrown by the revolution, then the strategy would be to take control of key institutions and continue the fight for change from within. As argued by Michael Gove:

> The thinkers of the Frankfurt School revised Marxism as primarily a cultural rather than an economic movement. In place of anger at traditional capitalism, scorn was directed at the reigning values of the West.[17]

---

[15] D A. Jones and S. Barrie, *Thinking Christian Ethos: The Meaning of Catholic Education* (London: Incorporated Catholic Truth Society, 2015), 53.

[16] R. Kimball, *The Long March* (San Francisco: Encounter Books, 2000); A. Bloom, *The Closing of the American Mind* (New York: Simon and Schuster, 1987); A. Barcan, *Sociological Theory and Educational Reality Education and Society in Australia since 1949* (Kensington: New South Wales University Press, 1993), 104.

[17] M. Gove, *Celsius 7/7*, (London: Weidenfield & Nicolson, 2006), 64

Such was the dramatic and far reaching impact of the cultural-left's long march through America's higher education system that Allan Bloom described what was happening as a "dismantling of the structure of rational inquiry"[18]. Universities, instead of being committed to the liberal ideals of objectivity and the search for wisdom and truth, become politicised, as subjects like history, literature and political science were attacked as uncritically accepting the strengths and benefits of Western civilisation—a civilisation, supposedly, guilty of imperialism, colonialism, misogyny, racism, classism, homophobia and ignoring the plight of the disadvantaged and dispossessed. According to Barcan what became known as the cultural revolution:

> ... favoured relativism; (where) absolute beliefs, based on Christianity or liberal humanism, became unfashionable. Politically, a new radicalism and a new concern for minorities emerged.[19]

As a result the American academic Christopher Lasch argues that instead of the university curriculum embodying a universal, transcendent truth, cultural-left critics condemned it as disguising the self-serving power of "white Eurocentric males".[20] Lasch also makes the point that if knowledge is not inherently worthwhile or based on rationality and reason then:

> ... it is no longer necessary to argue with opponents on intellectual grounds or to enter into their point of view. It is enough to dismiss them as Eurocentric, racist, sexist, homophobic - in other words, as politically suspect.[21]

Education, especially the school curriculum and the relationship between schooling and society, became a prime target for those on the cultural-left committed to radically reshaping Western society. The new sociology of education movement, drawing extensively on a range of Marxist and Neo-Marxist theories, argued against a liberal view of education based on the belief that it is conservative, inequitable and elitist. As argued in the introduction to the 1976 publication *Schooling and Capitalism: A Sociological Reader*:

> Schooling is not just one among many of the social institutions which contribute to the perpetuation of the capitalist mode of production, it is arguably the most important... the education system has been credited with the power to aid economic progress, to alleviate social ills, and develop and push forward our cultural heritage while providing for the fulfilment of the individual. The rationale for

---

[18] Bloom, *Op Cit*, 313
[19] *Ibid.* 104.
[20] C. Lasch, *The Revolt of the Elites and the Betrayal of Democracy* (New York: W. W. Norton & Company, 1996), 12.
[21] *Ibid.* 13.

this collection of articles takes as its central purpose a critique of this liberal ideology and its practice.[22]

Contributors to the collection of essays included a number of influential cultural-left authors including: Herbert Gintis, Samuel Bowles, Pierre Bourdieu, Michael W. Apple, Raymond Williams, Antonio Gramsci and Paulo Freire. A common theme, drawing on Althusser's concept of 'the ideological state apparatus', is that education is central in reproducing and reinforcing the values and ideology that underpin capitalism. The reason why so many are not committed to radical change is because a liberal education, supposedly, normalises the status quo and is instrumental in spreading what Friedrich Engels describes as "false consciousness".[23]

As a result, the English sociologist M.F.D. Young argues that the type of academic curricula associated with a liberal education, instead of having an intrinsic value or worth, is a socio-historical construct reinforcing the dominance of those already privileged and in control of society. He argues what constitute academic curricula:

> …can be seen as social definitions of educational value, and thus become problematic in the sense that if they persist it is not because knowledge is in any way best made available according to the criteria they represent, but because they are conscious or unconscious cultural choices which accord with the values and beliefs of dominant groups at particular times.[24]

Lasch makes a similar point to M.F.D. Young, when referring to the cultural-left's argument that "knowledge equates with power", and the belief that the more traditional view of education is responsible for keeping "women, homosexuals and 'people of color' in their place".[25]

In Australia during the 70s and 80s the new sociology of education movement had a significant influence on teacher education courses, and on what constituted a valid and worthwhile curriculum. One textbook widely set for education courses, *Making the Difference,* argued "schooling reproduces the structure of inequality itself"[26]. As a result, the authors argue teachers "had to decide whose side they are on", especially given that:

---

[22] R. Dale, G. Esland and M. MacDonald, *Schooling and capitalism: A Sociological Reader* (London: Routledge and Kegan Paul,1976), 1.
[23] F. Engels, "Engels to Franz Mehring", (1893). Retrieved 6 June 2017 from https://www.marxists.org/archive/marx/works/1893/letters/93_07_14.htm
[24] M. F. D. Young, ed., *Knowledge and Control New Directions for the Sociology of Education* (London: Collier Macmillan, 1971), 38.
[25] C. Lasch, *Op Cit.,* 12.
[26] R W. Connell, D J. Ashenden, S. Kessler and GW. Dowsett, *Making the Difference: Schools, Families and Social Division* (North Sydney: George Allen & Unwin, 1982), 27.

Education has a fundamental connection with the idea of human emancipation, though it is constantly in danger of being captured for other interests. In a society disfigured by class exploitation, sexual and racial oppression, and in chronic danger of war and environmental destruction, the only education worth the name is one that forms people capable of taking part in their own liberation.[27]

Another text widely used in education courses, also critiquing what was seen as a more traditional and conservative view of education, was titled *Undemocratic Schooling: Equity and Quality in Mass Secondary Education in Australia*, where the argument is put that, notwithstanding some changes leading to greater diversity and increased equality, certain kinds of knowledge are still privileged, leading the authors to conclude:

> ... this hierarchy acts as a machine, translating social power into academic merit and thus conserving the wider social structure itself.[28]

According to cultural-left critics, a liberal view of education based on meritocracy, competitive examinations, streaming and an academic curriculum that acknowledges the importance of Western civilisation is inequitable, and guilty of reproducing disadvantage. As a result, the school curriculum, in the words of the Australian Teachers' Federation, must be re-designed to take into account:

> 2.2.2 The pronounced inequality of the distribution of social, economic, cultural and political resources and power between social groups, which restricts the life development of many, and
> 2.2.3 The role of the economy, the sexual division of labour, the dominant culture and the education system in reinforcing inequality.[29]

In Victoria, the Year 12 Higher School Certificate (HSC) was targeted by the Education Minister and later Premier, Joan Kirner, and the Victorian Secondary Teachers Association as epitomising all that was wrong with the education system. In arguing that the HSC should be replaced by the Victorian Certificate of Education critics condemned the HSC for favouring elite non-government school students (who generally outperformed government school students in relation to academic results and tertiary entry) and for being overly academic and competitive. Such was the opposition to Year 12 competitive examinations that one of Victoria's more influential educationalists, Bill Han-

---

[27] *Ibid*, 208.
[28] Teese, R & Polesel, J. 2003. *Undemocratic Schooling: Equity and Quality in Mass Secondary Education in Australia*. Carlton, Victoria. Melbourne University Press, 18
[29] Australian Teachers' Federation. 1988. *1988 ATF Curriculum Policy*. Canberra, 1.

nan, argued that tertiary selection should be by ballot, as ability was decided by "social distinctions, such as wealth, educational background, ethnic grouping and so on".[30] When arguing for what he described as "educational socialism", Hannan also argued:

> I believe that income, status, privileges and so forth should be levelled as quickly as we can... We don't have to wait for society to change before education can change. By changing it, we help to change society.[31]

Underpinning the argument for change was the belief that the Year 12 curriculum and examination system needed to be radically overhauled on the basis that education, according to Joan Kirner, had to be redesigned to be "Part of the socialist struggle for equality, participation and social change, rather than an instrument of the capitalist system".[32]

While the new sociology of education movement's critique of a liberal education embraced a Marxist view of society and the role of education in reproducing capitalism, a more recent attack is represented by a rainbow alliance of cultural-left theories including: postmodernism, deconstruction and feminist, post-colonial and lesbian, gay, bisexual, transgender, queer and intersex (LGBTQI) theories. While reflecting a range of viewpoints and assumptions about the nature and purpose of education and the relationship between schools and society, what all hold in common is a far-reaching and radical attack on a liberal view of education and Western civilisation. The Italian philosopher, Marcello Pera describes the argument put forward by the cultural-left as follows:

> The notion that the judgement of cultures or civilizations constitutes an invalid mode of inquiry has been put forward, most notoriously, by the school of thought known as relativism. Various names have been given to this school today: post-enlightenment thinking, post-modernism, "weak thought", deconstructionism. The labels have changed, but the target is always the same: to proclaim that there are no grounds for our values and no solid proof or argument establishing that any one thing is better or more valid that another.[33]

One of the central tenets of a liberal view of education is the belief that while it is not always possible to identify what is true and what is false, it is at

---

[30] B. Hannan, *Democratic Curriculum*, (North Sydney: George Allen & Unwin, 1985) 58.
[31] *Ibid*, 61
[32] J. Kirner, "Choice, Privilege and Equality – The Socialist Dilemma?" in Victorian Fabian Society Pamphlet 41, *Education – Where From? Where To?* (Melbourne: The Victorian Fabian Society, 1984), 11 – 18.
[33] M. Pera, "Relativism, Christianity, and the West" in J. Ratzinger and M, Pera, *Without Roots The West Relativism Christianity Islam* (Basic Books: New York, 2006), 11.

least possible to recognise what more closely approximates the truth in an objective and impartial way. Frank Furedi, as a result of postmodernism, suggests such is no longer the case when he writes:

> It is frequently argued that there is no such thing as the truth. Instead of the truth, people are exhorted to accept different opinions as representing many truths. Michael Foucault's claim that there is 'no truly universal truth' has gained widespread influence in academic circles. Truth is rarely represented as objective facts; it is frequently portrayed as the product of subjective insight, which is in competition with other equally valid perspectives.[34]

Whether denying the referential quality of language, or putting forward the argument that how one responds to literary texts is subjective, or arguing a belief in cultural relativism, and that Western science cannot be privileged as it is simply one science among many, postmodernism and deconstruction have had a profound impact on education and the curriculum. Gary Marks offers a similar critique as Furedi when arguing that postmodernism "explicitly rejects Western and scientific ways of acquiring knowledge".[35] After briefly describing the theories put forward by advocates of postmodernism, including Jacques Derrida, Michael Foucault, Jean-François Lyotard and Jean Baudrillard, in relation to education, Brian Crittenden concludes:

> If we were to accept the doctrines of postmodernism and its interpretation of contemporary society, anything like a systematic education would be impossible. Although the details vary, the fundamental problems with all versions of postmodernism are the advocacy of a radical form of relativism and the dissolution of the self in a montage of 'discourses' or 'language games' by which we happen to be shaped at any given time.[36]

In relation to the school curriculum, while not as dramatic as what has occurred at the tertiary level, the impact of cultural-left theory has been significant and far-reaching.[37] Literary texts, instead of being valued for their moral and aesthetic character, are deconstructed in terms of power relationships; especially the new trinity of 'gender, ethnicity and class'. The definition of what represents a worthwhile text for study has been exploded to include: popular magazines, SMS texts, cartoons, videos, films, graffiti and students' own writing. Drawing on the more extreme elements of reader-response the-

---

[34] F. Furedi, *Where Have All The Intellectuals Gone?* (London: Continuum, 2004), 4.
[35] G. N. Marks, *Education, Social Background and Cognitive Ability* (Oxford: Routledge, 2014), 7.
[36] B. Crittenden, *Thinking about Education* (South Melbourne: Longman Australia, 1996) 41
[37] See K. Donnelly, *Why our schools are failing?* (Sydney: Duffy and Snellgrove, 2004); and K. Donnelly, *Dumbing Down* (Prahran: Hardie Grant Victoria, 2007) for a detailed analysis of the impact of Neo-Marxism and theory on the school curriculum.

ory and deconstruction, students are also taught that how one interprets a text is subjective and that texts are socio-cultural constructs. This leads to a situation where there is a:

> ... turning away from literature as literature and an eagerness to transmogrify it into a cultural artefact (or "signifying practise") to be used in waging an always anti-establishment ideological political struggle.[38]

The Western Australia Curriculum Council's Years 11 and 12 'Texts, Traditions and Cultures' syllabus provides a clear example of the impact of 'theory' on the school curriculum when it argues:

> The concept of the literary is socially and historically constructed, rather than objective or self-evident. Constructions of literacy are embedded in social contexts, reflecting particular knowledge, values, assumptions and power relationships... Constructions of the literary are subject to dispute and can privilege certain groups and ideas and exclude or marginalise others.[39]

Drawing on the works of the Brazilian Marxist Paulo Freire, the concept of literacy, instead of being conceived as teaching the ability to read and write, based on learning the alphabet and a phonics and phonemic awareness approach, also became radicalised. Freire, who toured Australia in 1974, condemns the more traditional approach to education for disempowering individuals by treating them as passive receivers of knowledge and failing to teach 'critical literacy'. Freire made famous the idea that traditional learning was based on a 'banking concept, one where:

> Our traditional curriculum, disconnected from life, centered on words emptied of the reality they are meant to represent, lacking in concrete activity, could never develop a critical consciousness. Indeed, its own naive dependence on high-sounding phrases, reliance on rote, and tendency towards abstractness actually intensified our naiveté.[40]

Even though Freire worked mostly with illiterate peasants in South America a number of cultural-left education academics and the Australian Association for the Teaching of English (AATE) argued his theories should also apply to Australian classrooms. At a national conference in Brisbane organised by the

---

[38] D. Patai, and W.H. Correll (eds), *Theory's Empire: An Anthology of Dissent* (New York: Columbia University Press), 8
[39] Curriculum Council, *Texts, Traditions and Cultures* (Western Australia: Curriculum Council, 2005), 13.
[40] P. Freire, *Education: The Practice of Freedom* (London: Writers and Readers Publishing Cooperative, 1974), 37.

AATE the argument was put that there needed to be a greater focus on teaching 'critical literacy', especially concentrating on "the need to critique and rework Freirian approaches to critical literacy in the light of feminist, poststructuralist and socially-based linguistics".[41]

As a result of cultural-left theory, history teaching, instead of dealing with the grand narrative associated with Western civilisation, presents students with a fragmented, politically correct interpretation, where the focus is on marginalised and disadvantaged groups and issues and topics considered contemporary and immediately relevant. Stuart Macintyre and Anna Clark describe the more radical approach to history as "history from below", that is, history as "no longer an authoritative account of decision-making written from the official record but as the lived experience of ordinary people".[42]

In his submission to the 1999 national inquiry into history teaching Mark Peel describes the new history as involving:

> ... themes and concepts rather than supposedly desiccated chronologies (one that) emphasises the wider value of problem-based learning especially suited to historical investigation, privileges the study of representations and methods of textual analysis, highlights the problems of perspective and evidence, insists upon sensitivity to cultural differences and the inclusion of different perspectives silenced by 'grand narratives'... [43]

The Australian National Curriculum, developed by the Australian Curriculum, Assessment and Reporting Authority (ACARA) also represents an illustration of the impact of cultural-left theory on the curriculum. Subjects like history and literature are interpreted through a politically correct prism involving Aboriginal and Torres Strait Islander, Asian and sustainability cross-curriculum priorities. Early drafts of the history curriculum left out any reference to Magna Carta and as argued by Greg Melleuish in his analysis of how Western Civilisation is treated: "... we get a quasi-Marxist view *and* the exclusion of the most important modern political philosophy, liberalism".[44]

Child-centred and Process Driven

Curriculum documents are now much more likely to be talking about 'learning' than 'knowledge'. There has been a movement towards emphasising stu-

---

[41] C. Walton, and A. Luke, "Conferencing critique: progress on teaching for cultural literacy", *Education Australia*, Issue 18, 1992, 24-25.

[42] S. Macintyre and A. Clark, *The History Wars* (Melbourne: Melbourne University Press), 41.

[43] M. Peel, "A submission to the National Inquiry Into School History", in *The Future of the Past. The Final Report of the National Inquiry into School History* (Churchill: Faculty of Education, Monash University, 2000), i – ix.

[44] G. Melleuish, "History in the national curriculum" in *The National Curriculum: A Critique,* ed. C. Berg, (Melbourne: Institute of Public Affairs, 2010), 1–22.

dents rather than teachers; to prioritising process over content; to wanting subject–learning to be thought of in terms of what the learner should be able to do as a result of that teaching.[45]

While Oakeshott's metaphor of education as a conversation implies an interaction and dialogue between the student and teacher, since the late 60s and early 70s critics have characterised a liberal view of education as being too subject-centred, guilty of being delivered *ex cathedra* and for undervaluing the world and interests of the child. One Australian publication criticises the more traditional approach for treating the student as a "receiver of transmitted knowledge" while the more progressive model allows the student to be an "active constructor of knowledge".[46] Another publication written by the Victorian Committee for English in Technical Schools[47] also privileges a child-centred view of education, when it refers approvingly to an Ontario report that argues:

> Never lose sight of the fact that the child, as the learner, is not only the centre of the school system but the only reason for its existence.[48]

Associated with the argument that education should be child-centred is the belief that the process of learning (often described as inquiry-based or discovery learning) is more important than teaching what Jerome S Bruner describes as "the structure of the discipline".[49] In their account of developments in the school curriculum during the years 1975-2005, Lyn Yates and Cherry Collins describe the period as one where:

> ... there was a strong shift over the period we are examining from an emphasis on knowing things to being able to do things. In the interviews we conducted with senior curriculum actors we also noted how rarely 'knowledge' came into the frame of their talk about curriculum, compared with a focus on outcomes, politics and management of resources; or compared with a focus on the developing child (from a cognitive developmental perspective).[50]

---

[45] L. Yates, C. Collins and K. O'Connor, *Australia's Curriculum Dilemmas: state cultures and the big issues* (Melbourne: Melbourne University Press, 2011), 34.
[46] S. Kemmis, P. Cole, D. Suggett, *Towards The Socially Critical School* (Melbourne: Victorian Institute of Secondary Education, 1983), 11.
[47] Standing Committee for English in Technical Schools, *Use Your Own Words* (Melboune: Education Department of Victoria, 1982), 14.
[48] Report of the Royal Commission of Teaching School Enrolments in Ontario. Undated and quoted in Standing Committee for English in Technical Schools, 1982.
[49] J.S. Bruner, *The Process of Education* (New York: Vintage Books, 1960), quoted in B. Crittenden, *Content With Process In Education: A Place For Cultural Literacy* (Bundoora: La Trobe University, 1987), 7.
[50] L. Yates and C. Collins, "The Absence of Knowledge in Australian Curriculum Reforms", *European Journal of Education*, Volume 45, Issue 1, 2010, 89-102.

Developments in Australia reflect progressive education in England where the 1967 Plowden Report into primary school education also adopts a child-centred view of education, when suggesting teachers should emphasise learning through "individual discovery", and "first-hand experience", and "that knowledge does not fall into neatly separate compartments".[51] As a result, many primary schools, and secondary schools for that matter, both in England and Australia, introduced innovations like: general studies, electives, open classrooms and learning being immediately contemporary and relevant to the student.

A.S. Neil, the founder of the English school Summerhill, provides a clear illustration of what is meant by a child-centred view of education. Neil justifies establishing Summerhill on the following basis:

> Well, we set out to make a school in which we should allow children to be themselves. In order to do this, we had to renounce all discipline, all direction, all suggestion, all moral training, all religious instruction... My view is that a child is innately wise and realistic. If left to himself without adult suggestion of any kind he will develop as far as he is capable of developing.[52]

As noted in the above quotation, the assumption is that children, left to their own devices, learn naturally, and that teachers and a formal, subject-based curriculum are unnecessary. Drawing on a Rousseauian, romantic view of childhood, the belief is that children are inherently good, and display a willingness and ability to learn, unsupervised by adults or constrained by a subject-based, more formal curriculum.

The American educationalist John Holt argues in a similar vein, when he argues "children have a style of learning that fits their condition, and which they use naturally and well until we train them out of it".[53] Both Neil and Holt oppose the more formal approach to education based on discrete subjects and areas of learning taught by teachers in a formal and explicit way. More recently, the New Zealand Curriculum Framework published in 1993 provides another illustration of what is meant by a child-centred view of education, when it states that the curriculum is based on the belief "that the individual student is at the centre of all teaching and learning".[54] A publication by the Australian Council of Deans of Education, published in 2001, also pro-

---

[51] Plowden Report, *Children and their Primary Schools*. Central Advisory Council for Education. London. H.M.S.O, 1967, 187-8, quoted in *Perspectives on Plowden* ed. R.S. Peters (London: Routledge & Kegan Paul), 3.
[52] A.S. Neil, *Summerhill* (Middlesex: Penguin Books,1968) 20.
[53] J. Holt, *How Children Learn* (New York: Dell Publishing Company, 1970), 1.
[54] Ministry of Education, *The New Zealand Curriculum Framework* (Wellington: Learning Media Limited, 1993).

motes a child-centred view of learning when it argues that the curriculum must allow students to "move from assisted learning to autonomous and self-directed learning".[55] The ACDE justifies the need for what is described as 'New Learning' by characterising the more traditional subject-based approach to the curriculum as "learning by rote and knowing the 'correct answers'", and as an approach in which what was taught was "too often narrow, decontextualised, abstract and fragmented into subject areas artificially created by the education system".[56]

A critique is also made of what is described as "knowledge for its own sake", and education privileging "received bodies of knowledge and fixed skills sets"[57], on the basis that it is more important to emphasise "self-awareness, problem solving and intercultural skills—strategies, in other words, for dealing with diverse settings and rapid change".[58]

Closely associated with a child-centred, process model of education is what is known as 'constructivism'—a style of teaching and learning where students negotiate what they want to learn, learn at their own pace and are not taught in a structured, teacher-controlled classroom. During the 1990s what was described as Outcomes Based Education (OBE), as noted by the one-time head of Australia's Curriculum Corporation, Bruce Wilson, became the dominant curriculum model across Australia's states and territories.[59] Central to OBE was constructivism, a theory based on the belief that:

> … the classroom is no longer a place where the teacher ('expert') pours knowledge into passive students, who wait like empty vessels to be filled. In the constructivist model the students are urged to be actively involved in their own process of learning. The teacher functions more as a facilitator who coaches, mediates, prompts, and helps students develop and assess their understanding.

A more recent interpretation of child-centred learning relates to what is described as personalised learning. A 2007 Victorian Department of Education publication, under the heading "Learners are central", describes personalised learning as an approach to education that involves:

- a highly structured approach that places the needs, interests and learning styles of students at the centre;

---

[55] Australian Council of Deans of Education, *New Learning: A Charter for Australian Education* (ACDE, 2001).
[56] *Ibid*, 85.
[57] *Ibid*, 86.
[58] *Ibid*
[59] B. Wilson, *Current Educational Priorities, Future Directions and Initiatives*, IARTV Occasional Paper, (Melbourne: IARTV, 1996), 5.

- engaged learners who are informed and empowered through student voice and choice;
- assessment that is related to meaningful tasks and includes assessment for and from students; and
- a focus on improving student outcomes for all and a commitment to reduce the achievement gap.[60]

Associated with personalised learning is a heavy reliance on information and communications technology (ICT) on the premise that the new technologies provide a flexible, dynamic, interactive and resource-rich approach to education. Students are described as 'digital natives' and 'knowledge navigators' and teachers, instead of teaching in a more formal and explicit way, are described as 'facilitators' and 'guides by the side'.

While there is much of value in adopting a child-centred, process approach to the curriculum, there are also significant flaws. Ignored is that information is not knowledge and understanding is not wisdom. To be educated in its most enriching sense is to be introduced to and appreciate Arnold's "the best that has been thought and said" and such an initiation requires teachers and human interaction.

Critics of the more traditional approach associated with a liberal education are often guilty of setting up a 'straw man' that misrepresents and simplifies what is being critiqued. As previously mentioned, Arnold is clear when discussing culture that equally as important as learning about the "best that has been thought and said' is the need to turn "a fresh and free thought upon our stock notions and habits".[61] T.S. Eliot makes a similar point when arguing that the need is "to maintain the continuity of our culture—and neither continuity, nor respect for the past, implies standing still".[62]

Oakeshott's metaphor of education involving a conversation also implies that there is a dialogue and an interaction between the student and the teacher that is more than simply one-sided. Bruner, while acknowledging the importance of the learner, signals a further danger in adopting a child-centred approach where what is learned relies on the child's interests, motivations and local environment. Bruner argues:

> A generation ago, the progressive movement urged that knowledge be related to the child's own experience and brought out of the realm of empty abstractions.

---

[60] Victorian Department of Education, *Personalising Education: from Research to Policy and Practice* (Melbourne: Department of Education, 2007).
[61] M. Arnold, *op. cit.*
[62] T. S. Eliot, "The Aims of Education" in *To Criticise the Critic* (1965), quoted in G. H. Bantick, *T S Eliot and Education* (London: Faber and Faber, 1970).

A good idea was translated into banalities about the home, then the friendly postman and trashman, then the community and so on.[63]

Competency Based and 21st Century Learning

Research suggests that to cope with the demands of the 21st century, students need more than core subject knowledge.[64] Students also need some different skills from those learned by students in the 20th century, and skills identified as 21st century skills are those needed to succeed in a complex, competitive, knowledge-based, information-age, technology driven economy and society.[65]

The fourth approach to addressing the purpose of education involves a utilitarian approach focusing on preparing students for the world of work and what are described as 21st century capabilities and skills. According to this approach the so-called traditional curriculum, drawing primarily on a liberal view of education, is obsolete, irrelevant and incapable of preparing students for a digital age dominated by the new technologies. As argued by a media release published by Victoria University's Mitchell Institute, detailing a report titled *Preparing Young People for the Future of Work*:

> Our education system was formed in the manufacturing era… Young people need different skill sets to what is taught in the traditional curriculum if they are to thrive in high-tech, global, competitive job markets.[66]

While a liberal view of education draws largely on the established disciplines, on the assumption that to be educated is to be familiar with an evolving corpus of knowledge that has stood the test of time, the competency-based movement looks to the future where the new technologies have radically changed how we perceive ourselves, interact with others, and what constitutes both leisure and work. The Mitchell Institute justifies its focus on 21st century learning on the basis that:

> Education systems have not been designed to foster the types of capabilities needed to navigate complex environments and multiple careers… Future genera-

---

[63] J.S. Bruner, *The Relevance of Education* (New York: W.W. Norton & Company, 1971), 63.
[64] M. Bruniges, *21st Century Skills for Australian Students* (report from 21st Century Skills Forum Tokyo, Japan, 14 Nov 2012), NSW Education and Communities, Sydney, accessed Aug 2015, http://www.dec.nsw.gov.au/documents/15060385/15385042/21C_skills_for_Australian_students_141112.pdf.
[65] Queensland Curriculum & Assessment Authority, *21st cCentury Skills for Senior Education. An Analysis of Educational Trends*, (Queensland Curriculum & Assessment Authority, 2015). Retrieved 22 August, 2017 from https://www.qcaa.qld.edu.au/downloads/publications/paper_snr_21c_skills.pdf
[66] Victoria University, "Experts agree: schools not preparing students for twenty-first century", 27 March 2017. Retrieved 10 August, 2017 from http://www.mitchellinstitute.org.au/media-releases/experts-agree-schools-not-preparing-students-for-twenty-first-century/

tions will navigate a vastly different world of work to that of their predecessors. Technology is rapidly disrupting how we live and work".[67]

In the Australian context the advent of the competency movement, one where knowledge of specific disciplines is secondary to allowing students to develop work-related competencies, is best illustrated by the Finn and Mayer reports released during the early 1990s.[68] While including aspects of the more traditional curriculum in competencies such as Language and Communication, Mathematics and Scientific and Technological Understanding, the Finn report also sought to include Cultural Understanding, Problem-Solving and Personal and Interpersonal Characteristics. Such competencies are presented as generic in nature and not grounded in any particular subject or discipline.

The Mayer report represents a purer form of the competency movement with its argument that if young people are to "participate effectively in the emerging forms of work and work organisation" they need to be familiar with the following key competencies: Collecting, Analysing and Organising Information; Communicating Ideas and Information; Planning and Organising Activities; Working with Others and in Teams; Using Mathematical Ideas and Techniques; Solving Problems and Using Technology. Once again the assumption is that such competencies can be taught without reference to particular disciplines and that essential knowledge is secondary to developing work-related transferable competencies and skills. Clearly, the purpose of education is not knowledge and understanding for their own sake, but to ensure a more productive, flexible and adaptive workforce.

The more recent example of the competency movement relates to what are termed 'general capabilities' that form a critical part of the Australian National Curriculum. These are listed as: literacy, numeracy, information and communication technology capability, critical and creative thinking, personal and social capability, ethical understanding and intercultural understanding. The capabilities are described as "an integrated and interconnected set of knowledge skills, behaviours and dispositions that can be developed and applied across the curriculum".[69] As with the argument used to justify the Finn and Mayer competencies, ACARA argues that the capabilities are essential if the curriculum is to meet the "changing expectations of society and to contribute to the creation of a more productive, sustainable and just society".

---

[67] K. Toril and M. O'Connell, *Preparing Young People for the Future of Work*, Mitchell Institute Working Paper No. 01/2017 (Melbourne: Mitchell Institute).

[68] B. Finn, *Young People's Participation in Post-Compulsory Education and Training* (Australian Education Council Committee, 1991); E. Mayer, *Competencies* (Australian Education Council and Ministers of Vocational Education, Employment and Training, 1992).

[69] Australian Curriculum Assessment and Reporting Authority. *General Capabilities*. Retrieved 22 August, 2017 from https://acaraweb.blob.core.windows.net/resources/General_Capabilities_2011.pdf

While there is no doubt that Western society, as a result of the new technologies and the increasingly interconnected nature of the global environment, is ever changing, the principal fault with the competency and capabilities movements is that both confuse education with training and acquiring work-related dispositions and skills. While such dispositions and skills are important, equally, if not more important, is the need for students to be educated in the word's fullest and most enriching sense. Being familiar with and appreciating the significance and value of what the Blackburn Report describes "as our best validated knowledge and artistic achievements", while not directly contributing to a more efficient and productive workforce, is essential for one's sense of what it means to be human and what it means to be fully alive.[70]

As argued by Hirsch, it is also the case that so-called generic skills and competencies do not arise in a vacuum—the reality is that as they are domain-specific, they can only be effectively taught in the context of particular subjects and disciplines. Hirsch argues:

> The real-life competencies that people need, such as the abilities to read, to write, to communicate, to learn, to analyze, and to grasp and manipulate mathematical symbols, have major components that psychologists have found to be "domain-specific". This means that an ability to think critically about chess does not translate into an ability to think critically about sailing.[71]

The ability to be critical and creative when analysing a literary work such as a poem is very different from analysing and evaluating the significance of an important historical movement or event. Similarly, the way one communicates ideas and information varies according to the subject matter and what constitutes the relevant concepts, language and ideas. The NSW educational psychologist John Sweller puts the same argument as Hirsch when he states that "We should be teaching domain-specific knowledge, not generic skills" and that "Initial instruction when dealing with new information should be explicit and direct"[72]. In his submission to the Review of the Australian National Curriculum Sweller goes on to argue:

> There is little more useless than attempting to teach generic thinking skills and expecting students to be better thinkers or problem solvers as a result. Despite decades of work, there is no body of evidence supporting the teaching of thinking or other generic skills.[73]

---

[70] J. Blackburn, *Principal Recommendations of the Ministerial Review of Post-Compulsory Schooling*, (Education Department of Victoria, 1985), 16.
[71] E.D. Hirsch, Jr., *The Schools We Need and Why We Don't Have Them* (New York: Double Day, 1996).
[72] J. Sweller, Submission to the Review of the Australian Curriculum (2014), 1.
[73] *Ibid.* 3.

It is also the case that a number of what are listed as work-related competencies, such as ethical understanding and Personal and Interpersonal Characteristics, are essential aspects of a liberal view of education, and are best taught in the context of established subjects. Studying literature and history, for example, involves ethical values and judgements, and the development of character, and how best to relate to and interact with others.

Conclusion

As previously argued, no approach to the curriculum or pedagogy is ever value-free or neutral, and over the last 30 to 40 years it is possible to identify four major educational theories that have impacted on state and territory schools. The four approaches to defining what it means to be educated and the purpose of education include: a liberal education; one based on the new sociology of education and theory; one that is child-centred and process-driven; and the fourth that is competency-based and focused on 21st century learning.

While an argument can be put that each approach has a place in the school curriculum, not all are equally beneficial or worthwhile. Defining education in terms of power relationships, where the belief is that Western civilisation is riven with injustice and inequality and that the status quo must be overthrown, confuses education with indoctrination and what is politically correct. The argument that there are no absolutes or self-evident truths, as knowledge is a social construct, and how one perceives the world is subjective and relative, leads to either silence or epistemological suicide.

The danger in restricting learning to the world of the child and his or her local environment is that such an educational experience is superficial, patchy and limited. To be properly educated is to be introduced to a corpus of knowledge that is often foreign and not immediately relevant or useful to the world of the child. Education in its broadest and richest sense challenges and enlarges the child's understanding and allows the individual to encounter and appreciate what was previously unknown and unimagined.

Basing the curriculum on competencies and 21st century learning ignores the fact that generic skills and dispositions do not exist in a vacuum as they are domain-specific. Bruner's admonition to teach "the structure of the discipline" reinforces the point that particular competencies are best taught when they are embedded in particular subjects. Overemphasising 21st century learning is not only unduly utilitarian in its approach, it also ignores the reality that there is much about human nature and the world in which we live that is unchanging and best taught by acknowledging the past.

Human nature and emotions like love, hate, jealousy, ambition, pride, self-sacrifice and loyalty have not changed since the time of the ancient Greek playwrights like Sophocles and Euripides. In the same way, much of current philosophy can only be fully appreciated and understood by recognising the contributions made by Socrates, Plato and Aristotle.

In opposition to the three approaches to education briefly detailed above, it is a liberal education that best addresses what it means to be educated and the purpose of education. Education in its fullest and most enriching sense is not concerned with practical skills and training, but addresses fundamental questions about the nature of reality and one's significance and place in the wider universe. As noted by T.S. Eliot, a liberal education stands "for the preservation of learning, for the pursuit of truth, and in so far as men are capable of it, the attainment of wisdom".[74]

Closely associated with a liberal education is a commitment to rationality and the ability to more closely approximate the truth of things, and to identify what constitutes right and wrong reason. A liberal education is also based on the established disciplines of knowledge that are an essential part of a conversation that predates the individual and that is on-going. A liberal education is also inherently ethical and moral as it deals with what constitutes good and bad behaviour and how best to contribute to the common good.

---

[74] T. S. Eliot, *Notes towards the Definition of Culture*, op cit.

Australia's Decaying University: Identity Politics, Psychology and Campus Intellectual Freedom

Matthew Lesh

Australian taxpayers spend billions of dollars on higher education with the expectation that universities provide a positive contribution to society. An essential purpose of universities is to provide a place where people are free to explore ideas. A liberal society depends on this competition of ideas to strive for truth and understanding of the world. Today's universities, however, are at the forefront of cultural attack on the core foundations of the Enlightenment. Identity politics pits groups against each other rather than respecting individuality; the anti-fragility movement is infantilising students using speech codes, trigger warnings, and safe spaces; all intermixed with postmodernism's rejection of truth. The psychological elements are working symbiotically with the identity politics paradigm. Meanwhile, university administrators are succumbing to small numbers of organised students at the forefront of these damaging ideas. But not all is lost—students are increasingly realising the absurdities and pushing back. We are potentially on the horizon of a new campus free speech movement, but sadly things might have to get worse before they get better.

Thirteen years of schooling under your belt and you've finally made it. It's results day, and after waiting for the excruciatingly slow website to load, your ATAR finally appears. '94.5' pops up on the screen. You're jubilant. You'll be the first person in your family to make it to university, and you have done well enough to get into one of Australia's most prestigious universities. You will be faced with student debt for years, but, you know it'll be worthwhile. You'll be in the academic big leagues, with the opportunity to *learn* among Australia's best.

A few months later, in the final days of summer, you arrive at campus for the first day of orientation. As you walk into campus you witness a kerfuffle. Curiosity gets the better of you and you stop for a moment. "You can't display that poster, it's racist and disgusting," you overhear a middle-aged woman say to a student wearing a 'Liberal' t-shirt.[1] To your surprise, the woman

---

[1] This series of events happened at the University of Melbourne in 2013. See John Slater, "The Academics Who Hate Free Speech," *Quadrant Opinion* (blog), April 16, 2013,

who looks like an academic is pointing to a poster of someone you recognise, former Prime Minister John Howard. The poster says "we will decide who comes to this country and the circumstances in which they come". Campus security speaks next, instructing the Liberal students to leave campus. Strange, you think, why aren't they allowed? One of the reasons you wanted to go to university was to hear from lots of different viewpoints.

A week later it's time for your first lecture for a compulsory politics major subject called *Authority*. "I'm a revolutionary Marxist, and if you're not one by the end of the semester I haven't done my job properly," the lecturer quips.[2] You're not sure if he's joking, and even if he is, you wonder if there is some truth to it. After the lecture you hurriedly walk to your first tutorial. You get chatting to another student on the way. He tells you that he hasn't bothered with this week's reading material.[3] "J.S. Mill is just an old dead white guy, why would I bother reading him?" he says. This all seems a bit strange to you. Didn't people come to university to learn?

From the Age of Enlightenment, humanity has hunted truth and progress through learning. Universities, which taxpayers spend billions funding, serve a key role in this process. They research, and teach the next generation to increase the sum of human understanding and knowledge.

This process, which is essential to discover truth, requires the freedom to explore ideas. It is only through debate and contest, including exploring uncomfortable ideas from a range of competing perspectives, that understanding can be increased. "Both teachers and learners go to sleep at their posts as soon as there is no enemy in the field," wrote J.S. Mill in *On Liberty*.[4] It is under the disinfectant of sunlight that good and bad ideas can be separated, and we can strive to improve society.

President Abraham Lincoln is often attributed with the saying that the "philosophy of the school room in one generation will be the philosophy of government in the next".[5] The culture on campus today will define the future

---

https://quadrant.org.au/opinion/qed/2013/04/the-academics-who-hate-free-speech/.

[2] I personally attended the lecture where this happened, and have been told by other students that the same lecturer has made this 'joke' in subsequent years.

[3] Senior Lecturer Lauren Rosewarne notes the increasing tendency of students to show up to class unwilling to do readings that disagree with their pre-existing ideas. "This year for example, I had a slew of students arrive having already decided that radical feminism – not my political bent, no, but essential to cover – is oppressive devilry. Which means that when they're in tutorials, they are politically opposed to engagement. That they didn't do the assigned reading in some kind of bizarre (and lazy) protest." See Lauren Rosewarne, "Warning Sign: Trigger Warnings and Externalities," *The Conversation* (blog), June 24, 2016, http://theconversation.com/warning-sign-trigger-warnings-and-externalities-61592.

[4] John Stuart Mill, *On Liberty* (Project Gutenberg, 2011), http://www.gutenberg.org/ebooks/34901.

[5] As with many quotations, this may not have been said by Lincoln. Nevertheless, the sentiment stands, no matter the author.

of Australian society. Today's students are tomorrow's voters, politicians, judges, bureaucrats and educators.

If universities teach students to explore ideas with which they disagree, to challenge their beliefs, and to keep an open yet critical mind, then this will be the future of public debate. If the opposite is taught—that some ideas are too dangerous to be heard, that you should judge a person's opinion on the basis of their gender, skin colour or sexuality, and that using violence to shut down debate is acceptable—then we can expect that to be the future.

Universities are increasingly doing more of the latter than the former. There is a growing censorious culture on campus that is endangering the very purpose of higher education and the future of Australian society. The illustrative story which opened this chapter is based on true events in recent years at Australia's universities. And these incidents are becoming more common. The experience on Australian campuses is part of a growing censorious culture at universities across the Anglosphere.[6] The incidents that receive attention, the most ridiculous or psychically violent, are the tip of the iceberg, with much more happening that does not get reported. The incidents themselves are also symptoms of a deeper ideology and institutional issues within universities that are vital to grasp in order to understand the state of the modern university.

This essay explores the two underlying causes of the growing censorious culture on campus. Firstly, the growth of postmodernism intermixed with identity politics that establishes victimhood, feeds psychological issues, and is used to justify censorship. Secondly, the serious institutional failings of universities that enable the shutting down of ideas.

The End of Class, the Birth of Identity

Historically, the political left, following the 19th century writings of Marx, was driven by class conflict. Leftists sought to drive divisions between the working class (the proletariat) and the ruling class (the bourgeoisie). Their ultimate aim was to foment a revolution, socialise the means of production, and install a 'dictatorship of the proletariat'. Marx's grand theory of history presupposed that the internal contradictions in capitalism made communism an inevitability.[7]

This logic has, however, fallen apart. Those societies that have followed the communist path, be it the Soviet Union historically or Venezuela and

---

[6] See audits of free speech in Britain, Canada and the United States: FIRE, "Spotlight on Speech Codes 2016," *Foundation for Individual Rights in Education* (blog), 2016, https://www.thefire.org/spotlight-on-speech-codes-2016/; Tom Slater, "Free Speech University Rankings! - A Spiked Campaign," *Spiked! Online*, 2016, http://www.spiked-online.com/free-speech-university-rankings/; Justice Centre for Constitutional Freedoms, "Campus Freedom Index," Campus Free Speech Index: Measuring the state of free speech at Canadian public universities, 2017, http://campusfreedomindex.ca/.

[7] Karl Marx and Frederick Engels, *Manifesto of the Communist Party* (Marxists Internet Archive, 1848), https://www.marxists.org/archive/marx/works/download/pdf/Manifesto.pdf.

North Korea today, have been abject failures economically and socially. In the West, the revolutions never came, and everyone is a lot richer, thanks to the free market system. In the 20th century, incomes rapidly increased, life expectancy improved, and technology revolutionised the nature of work, diminishing the capital-labour distinction.[8] By 2000, 93 per cent of Australians identified as middle class, with similar numbers in other Western countries.[9] The effort to raise class consciousness and divide by income levels failed. Economic freedom was too successful.

The Left, however, has found a new ideology. Rather than traditional Marxists, from the mid to late 20th century postmodernists began to dominate the humanities. At their core, postmodernists reject the Enlightenment notions of generalised progress and truth. Instead, postmodernists argue, reality is constructed by individual experience.[10] They reject the liberal notion of the universality of certain ideals—like the rule of law or democracy—and focus on how actors use language and power, what they call 'discourse', to oppress others.[11]

Building on Marxist ideas, postmodernists claim dominant norms are embodied in a 'superstructure'—which includes everything from art and culture to law, media and politics. The 'superstructure' is controlled by powerful forces in society to limit the opportunities for thought and prevent change. Postmodernists, dismissing the existence of universal truth, claim that the language of powerful social actors, which they call 'discourse', creates reality and advances the oppressive 'superstructure'.

In the past, Marxist class politics sought to achieve equality. They were misguided in their direction and methods. However, at least they sought a form of progress. A postmodernist, in contrast, has no such optimistic vision of a better future. Instead, the world is in constant power flux between different groups. Postmodernists aim to dismantle the superstructure by challenging the norm, which necessitates dictating the language and discourse that society can use.

We should of course always be prepared to be critical when analysing society. However, the aims of postmodernists, to completely change how society functions, go much further. The University of Sydney's slick 'Unlearn' marketing campaign outlined these goals and how they can relate to a univer-

---

[8] See Human Progress for a range of statistics: Cato Institute, "Human Progress," 2017, http://humanprogress.org/.

[9] Peter Saunders, Cathy Thomson, and Ceri Evans, *Social Change and Social Policy: Results from a National Survey of Public Opinion*, Social Policy Research Centre Discussion Papers 106 (Kensington, NSW: Social Policy Research Centre, University of New South Wales, 2000), https://www.sprc.unsw.edu.au/media/SPRCFile/dp106.pdf.

[10] Peter L. Berger and Thomas Luckmann, *The Social Construction of Reality: A Treatise in the Sociology of Knowledge* (London: Allen Lane, 1967).

[11] Sara Mills, *Discourse*, 2nd ed. (London: Routledge, 2004).

sity. The campaign synopsis states that the University of Sydney aspires to "demolish social norms and build new ones in their place".[12] This is not a healthy critical disposition, it is an effort to change society by revolution, to dismantle the superstructure.

Identity politics gives postmodernism practical political meaning. Identity politics defines the oppressed and oppressor. It is not just economic, like the Marxists claimed. It is now based on personal identity categories, typically race, gender, and sexuality. The owner of the means of production is no longer the enemy, it is the white straight male who, through the language he uses, exercises power and dominates society to the detriment of minorities. Identity politics is not necessarily wicked. It is not necessarily wrong to consider class, race, gender and sexuality, or to examine power relationships. It can be helpful to fight genuine discrimination in the name of treating all individuals equally, which is the goal of liberal humanism. The early feminists sought for women to be treated equally, including the ability to vote and work rather than being in the control of men. Martin Luther King Jr similarly pursued a classical liberal agenda. He wanted to live in a nation where people will "not be judged by the colour of their skin but by the content of their character".[13]

Modern identity politics reverses this principle. It seeks to treat people *differently* based upon gender, skin colour and sexuality. Because certain groups are oppressed, they must be promoted *above* others. This addresses 'structural' power imbalances. Identity politics follows the postmodernist doctrine, that truth is subjective and what matters is the individual experience and discourse, and applies this to oppressed identity groups. That is, the worth of an opinion is assessed on who is speaking, and not what is being said. A white man's opinion, who is inherently racist because he benefits from power imbalances, is worth less than a woman's.

Ideas and people are no longer judged on their individual merit, but rather linked to their group identity. The original goals of the anti-racists, feminists and gay rights activists, for everyone to be treated equally no matter their skin colour, gender and whom they love, are lost in contemporary identity politics. This is combined with 'intersectionality', which establishes a hierarchy of intermingled victimhood, connecting together racism, sexism, and homophobia. This amounts to a complete abandonment of individuality. You cannot exist separately from your identity.

In just one ridiculous example, a student at an Australian university told me that he was reprimanded for self-describing as 'wholesome,' because that was furthering white supremacy and racism. The logic underlying this bizarre

---

[12] The University of Sydney, "Unlearn - Home," The University of Sydney, 2017, http://sydney.edu.au/unlearn/home.html.
[13] Martin Luther King, "I Have a Dream" (Lincoln Memorial, Washington D.C., August 28, 1963), http://www.americanrhetoric.com/speeches/mlkihaveadream.htm.

assertion is that a black or brown person would not be described as wholesome and therefore he, as a white male, was being racist to describe himself that way. This identity politics paradigm seeks to *find race* where it otherwise does not exist, and assumes racism where it does not exist. Colour blindness is no longer the aim.

The impact of identity politics on campus life is extremely problematic. In a world where there is no truth, where all that matters are experiences defined by identity, and language furthers oppression, it is justifiable to silence certain voices and ideas. In the identity politics paradigm, universities become indoctrination factories, in which identity-based truth is pursued, rather than being places of exploration and learning.

A South African student campaign takes this logic to the extreme. University of Cape Town student activists have established a campaign called '#ScienceMustFall'. They argue for the abandonment of all existing scientific knowledge. 'Science as a whole is a product of western modernity, and the whole thing should be scratched off,' one of the students on a panel said.[14] She then went on to call for a 're-starting' of science from an 'African perspective', and used the example of 'witchcraft' as an alternative science. This campaign is the logical extension of abandoning truth and asserting that *who is speaking* matters more than *what is being said*. This is not an isolated incident. In another case, students at Pomona College in California, from the campus Black Lives Matter group, claimed that "the idea that there is a single truth…is a myth and white supremacy".[15] In another case, students disrupted an event about free speech, with a speaker from the American Civil Liberties Union, because, as they chanted, "liberalism is white supremacy".[16]

Leftist Australian students are also judging the value of a perspective by the speaker's identity, rather than what is being said. The National Union of Students, the representatives of Australian students, holds an annual conference in Melbourne. The conference organisers split policy into chapters. Some of these are typical student issues, including welfare, education, and administration. Others are defined by identity, such as ethnocultural, women's, and queer. In debate about the latter set of policies, delegates can only speak on the category if they identify as part of the group. You have to be a woman to speak on women's policy, 'ethnocultural' (non-white) to speak on ethnocultural policy, or queer to speak on queer policy. The logic of limiting

---

[14] praag, *Science Must Be Abolished: UCT Students*, 2016, https://www.youtube.com/watch?v=ZUPsGDFZzVM.

[15] Matthew Reade, "Students Demand Administrators 'Take Action' Against Conservative Journalists," *The Claremont Independent* (blog), April 17, 2017, http://claremontindependent.com/students-demand-administrators-take-action-against-conservative-journalists/.

[16] Robby Soave, "Black Lives Matter Students Shut Down the ACLU's Campus Free Speech Event Because 'Liberalism Is White Supremacy,'" *Reason.Com* (blog), October 4, 2017, http://reason.com/blog/2017/10/04/black-lives-matter-students-shut-down-th.

speakers to an identity asserts that what matters is not ideas, but, rather, subjective experience. Meanwhile, the University of Melbourne Student Union ran a workshop in which men were encouraged to speak less and be less manly in class.[17] This is premised on the same logic: that it is identity, not ideas, that matter.

Identity politics is also deeply engrained in what students are being taught. The Institute of Public Affairs' Dr Bella d'Abrera found, from a systematic review of Australia's 746 history subjects across 35 Australian universities in 2017, an overwhelming bias towards subjects related to class, gender and race.[18] These are no doubt important elements of historic analysis, however d'Abrera finds that the focus on identity has detracted from teaching traditional historic subjects from Australia's western heritage.

The Silencing of Debate and the Rise of Victimhood

By not separating ideas from personal characteristics, there is a rapid progression towards the feeling of offence. Expressing a contrary view is taken as a personal attack on an identity—rather than a useful way to explore ideas—and offence is immediately caused. Ideas are not merely wrong, they're immoral and indicative of an oppressive power structure. The only way to fight back against the superstructure, the dominant cultural values, is to silence its proponents. In other words, free speech is simply a tool of the elites, a tool of the privileged class, to oppress minorities.

This logic of oppression and victimhood is being used to argue for the silencing of debate in Australia. Brittney Rigby, the "Human Rights Defender Student Editor" at the University of New South Wales' Australian Human Rights Centre, writes that free speech "isn't always free" because "society [is] still plagued by discrimination (gendered, racial, hetero-normative, class-based structures still underpin public discourse)".[19] "One person's free speech is another's oppression," she writes.

In practice this has meant silencing speakers. Liberal student delegates were prevented from speaking at the National Union of Students' (NUS) national conference in late 2015.[20] The University of Sydney Union initially

---

[17] Rebecca Urban, "Don't Act the Man, Students Told," *The Australian*, May 18, 2017, http://www.theaustralian.com.au/higher-education/university-holds-workshops-on-male-privilege/news-story/11beb4c070b5f975926066bd729551a6.

[18] Bella d'Abrera, "The Rise Of Identity Politics History In Australian Universities" (Melbourne, VIC: Institute of Public Affairs, October 17, 2017), http://ipa.org.au/publications-ipa/media-releases/rise-identity-politics-audit-history-teaching-australian-universities-2017.

[19] Brittney Rigby, "Freedom of Speech, s 18c and Yassmin Abdel-Maggied," Australian Human Rights Centre, *Human Rights Defender* (blog), June 6, 2017, http://www.ahrcentre.org/news/2017/06/06/920.

[20] Honi Soit, "NUS NatCon Live Blog," *Honi Soit* (blog), December 6, 2015, http://honisoit.com/2015/12/nus-natcon-live-blog/.

blocked a men's mental health group, the Brotherhood, Recreation and Outreach Society (BroSoc), from affiliating on the basis that it promoted "traditional masculinity".[21]

The University of New South Wales' Diversity Toolkit exemplifies how identity politics can detract from academic pursuits.[22] The 'Indigenous Terminology' section contains 'More appropriate' and 'Less appropriate' statements. The guide is, in effect, a speech code. In the name of sensitivity, it is not appropriate to say that Dreamtime stories are 'myths' and 'folklore'. It also instructs against saying that "Aboriginal people have lived in Australia for 40,000 years", because this supports "migration theories and anthropological assumptions". In the name of identity politics, simply expressing a scientifically established fact—that Aboriginal Australians arrived on the Australian land mass at a historic point— is discouraged.[23]

In the latest concerning twist, it is asserted that speech which offends an identity group is violence. Psychology Professor Lisa Barrett, writing in the *New York Times*, claims that because language *can* cause stress and that "prolonged stress can cause physical harm," speech "can be a form of violence".[24] Professor Jonathan Haidt and Greg Lukianoff responded in *The Atlantic*, by arguing that while it is true stress can be physically damaging, this does not mean that words are themselves violence.[25] A lot of activities, such as setting difficult work tasks or homework, can cause stress. However, they, like words, are not violence because there is no intention to cause physical damage to a person.[26]

The danger inherent in this logic is that if *words are violence,* then it is justifiable to use violence, and threats thereof, to censor certain words. This chills free speech. In one case, a peer-reviewed journal article was withdrawn by *Taylor & Francis* following "serious and credible threats of personal violence"

---

[21] Justin Pen, "Board Blocks BroSoc," *Honi Soit* (blog), September 26, 2014, http://honisoit.com/2014/09/board-blocks-brosoc/.

[22] University of New South Wales, "Diversity Toolkit," n.d., https://teaching.unsw.edu.au/diversity-toolkit.

[23] It should be a point of pride for all Australians that we were likely the first land mass outside of Eurasia and Africa to be occupied. The latest evidence suggests Aboriginal Australians arrived between 65,000 and 80,000 years ago, see Genelle Weule, "Ancient Indigenous Rock Shelter Rewrites Australia's Human History," *ABC News* (blog), July 20, 2017, http://www.abc.net.au/news/science/2017-07-20/aboriginal-shelter-pushes-human-history-back-to-65,000-years/8719314.

[24] Lisa Feldman Barrett, "When Is Speech Violence?," *The New York Times*, July 14, 2017, sec. Opinion, https://www.nytimes.com/2017/07/14/opinion/sunday/when-is-speech-violence.html.

[25] Jonathan Haidt and Greg Lukianoff, "Why It's a Bad Idea to Tell Students Words Are Violence," *The Atlantic*, July 18, 2017, https://www.theatlantic.com/education/archive/2017/07/why-its-a-bad-idea-to-tell-students-words-are-violence/533970/.

[26] This, of course, does not include speech that *incites* violence. For example, a speech to an angry mob that instructs them to physically attack an individual is speech that is, and should be, prohibited under the law.

directed at the journal editor.[27] A *Brookings Institution* survey found 51 per cent of American students think it is acceptable to interrupt a speaker to prevent them from being heard, and even more frightening, almost 1 in 5 students thinks it is acceptable to use violence to shut down a speaker.[28]

This has been the experience on American university campuses. At Middlebury College, libertarian author Charles Murray and his progressive host, Professor Allison Stanger, were physically attacked when they were leaving campus.[29] Conservative provocateur Milo Yiannopoulos was forced to evacuate University of California, Berkeley—ironically the historic home of the campus free speech movement—because of violent protesters. Professor Bret Weinstein, at Evergreen State College, was confronted by 50 students in class who demanded he resign following an email in which he rejected the demand that all white students and faculty leave campus for a day.[30] He was subsequently advised by campus police to stay off campus due to threats to his physical safety.

The use of violence to censor ideas has reached Australian campuses as well. Protests against Liberal Party politicians have often turned physical. At the University of Sydney, Foreign Minister Julie Bishop was interrupted during a speech and assaulted by students when she exited the venue.[31] Former federal parliamentarian, Sophie Mirabella, was shouted down and physically confronted during a guest lecture at the University of Melbourne.[32] Students justified the interruption against Mirabella, whose family heritage is Greek, on the basis that "racists are not welcome here". During the same-sex marriage postal survey debate, a stall set up by 'No' campaigners at the University of Sydney was surrounded by a counter-protest. This rapidly turned physical,

---

[27] Justin W, "'Credible Threats Of Personal Violence' Lead To Retraction of Colonialism Paper," *Daily Nous* (blog), October 9, 2017, http://dailynous.com/2017/10/09/credible-threats-personal-violence-lead-retraction-colonialism-paper/.

[28] John Villasenor, "Views among College Students Regarding the First Amendment: Results from a New Survey," *Brookings* (blog), September 18, 2017,
https://www.brookings.edu/blog/fixgov/2017/09/18/views-among-college-students-regarding-the-first-amendment-results-from-a-new-survey/.

[29] Charles Murray, "Fecklessness at Middlebury," American Enterprise Institute, *AEIdeas* (blog), June 12, 2017, http://www.aei.org/publication/fecklessness-at-middlebury/.

[30] VICE News, *Evergreen State College Controversy (HBO)*, accessed October 2, 2017, https://www.youtube.com/watch?v=2cMYfxOFBBM.

[31] Australian Associated Press, "Student Protesters Guilty of Assault on Julie Bishop, Claims Christopher Pyne," *The Guardian*, May 17, 2014, sec. Australia news,
http://www.theguardian.com/world/2014/may/17/protesters-guilty-of-assault-on-julie-bishop-claims-pyne.

[32] Benjamin Preiss, "Student Protesters Disrupt Lecture by Former Federal Liberal MP Sophie Mirabella at Melbourne University," *The Sydney Morning Herald*, May 19, 2014,
http://www.smh.com.au/federal-politics/political-news/student-protesters-disrupt-lecture-by-former-federal-liberal-mp-sophie-mirabella-at-melbourne-university-20140519-38ix3.html.

'No' posters were stolen, a table up-ended and police attended.[33] It is shocking that simply voicing a contrary opinion on campus attracted a mass violent response.

The Rise of Feelings
There is an important psychological element to calls for censorship.[34] Demands for censorship are typically put in terms of feelings, to protect mental health from supposedly dangerous ideas. During my time studying at the London School of Economics, I attended a Free Speech Society event with two comedian guest speakers. Ironically, the society was almost banned when it was first proposed in early 2016.[35] A small group of students, office-bearers in the LSE Student Union, attended the event to oppose the speakers—a challenge that should be welcomed. A female student asked "Why are your arbitrary principles more important than other people's emotions?" The postmodernist logic, that nothing is sacred, combines closely with the need to protect feelings. One of the comedians appropriately responded that "They're not arbitrary principles, they're fundamental to a democratic society". This did not convince the students who left the room shortly thereafter.

Psychologists have written, with much concern, about the growth of over-parenting that, with the benign aim to protect young people from harm, can have unintended side-effects.[36] For example, research has found that not allowing kids to roam without parental oversight is linked to weaker and less resilient children.[37] Similarly, parents and teachers who refuse to explicitly criticise young people may be making them less willing to hear ideas that diverge from their own. Like a muscle, we must be stretched by uncomfortable scenarios to make us strong. Adversity builds resilience.

---

[33] Pallavi Singhal, "Police Called as Hundreds of Protesters Surround Sydney University 'Vote No' Rally," *The Sydney Morning Herald*, September 14, 2017, http://www.smh.com.au/national/education/police-called-as-hundreds-of-protesters-surround-sydney-university-vote-no-rally-20170914-gyhca1.html.

[34] For further discussion, see Greg Lukianoff and Jonathan Haidt, "The Coddling of the American Mind," *The Atlantic*, September 2015, http://www.theatlantic.com/magazine/archive/2015/09/the-coddling-of-the-american-mind/399356/.

[35] Lucy Sherriff, "A University's Free Speech Society Might Be Banned - Because It Spoke Out Against Banning Societies," *HuffPost UK* (blog), May 2, 2016, http://www.huffingtonpost.co.uk/2016/02/05/lse-free-speech-society-speakeasy-calls-for-ban_n_9166228.html.

[36] Jean M. Twenge, *IGen: Why Today's Super-Connected Kids Are Growing Up Less Rebellious, More Tolerant, Less Happy--and Completely Unprepared for Adulthood--and What That Means for the Rest of Us* (New York City: Atria Books, 2017); Lenore Skenazy, *Free-Range Kids, How to Raise Safe, Self-Reliant Children* (San Francisco: Jossey-Bass, 2010).

[37] Peter Gray, "The Decline of Play and the Rise of Psychopathology in Children and Adolescents," *American Journal of Play* 3, no. 4 (2011): 443–63; Richard G. Tedeschi and Lawrence G. Calhoun, "TARGET ARTICLE: 'Posttraumatic Growth: Conceptual Foundations and Empirical Evidence,'" *Psychological Inquiry* 15, no. 1 (January 1, 2004): 1–18, https://doi.org/10.1207/s15327965pli1501_01.

An article in *Farrago*, the University of Melbourne's student magazine, about mental health issues displays how far this has spread. The article opens by discussing the curious case of Natalie, a Bachelor of Arts student who spirals from receiving disappointing marks to anxiety and depression. "Helpless. All I felt was helpless", she says.[38] We should of course have sympathy for students who are struggling with mental health. However, it is concerning that something so routine for any student—suboptimal marks—caused such an extreme reaction.

A survey, by Mission Australia, has identified a growth of mental health issues for young Australians, with the level of probable serious mental illness increasing from 18.7% in 2012 to 22.8% in 2016, and as high as 27.4% among 18-19 year olds, the age at which people enter university. Young people, who grew up in the safety-before-criticism paradigm, have growing mental health issues, and are incapable of coping with challenging situations. Individuals who are unable to deal with being challenged are unsuited for academia, which requires a willingness to explore ideas, even uncomfortable ones.

The University of Melbourne's Lauren Rosewarne has warned that "many students are now far more likely to come to class with their views fully formed before I even open my mouth".[39] Rosewarne, who teaches gender studies, which is at the forefront of these issues, notes the swift changes in just the past five years. She says students refuse to do assigned readings because of their pre-existing prejudice against the content, and interrupt her in lectures to correct language.

There has also been a proliferation of trigger warnings, and content disclaimers to stop students from feeling uncomfortable, and safe spaces, physical locations designed to prevent certain ideas from being expressed.[40] Trigger warnings have been used for issues such as racism, homophobia, disability, colonialism, torture, and, at Melbourne's La Trobe University Student Union, trigger warnings can be used for body image, eye contact, food, and insects.[41] The warnings change understanding, damage student mental health, and contradict the entire purpose of higher education: to challenge, not coddle, students.[42]

---

[38] Jessica Tsin Ti, "Poor Counsel: When Special Consideration Doesn't Cut It," *Farrago, Edition 4,* 2017.
[39] Rosewarne, "Warning Sign."
[40] See Matthew Lesh, "Triggering Censorship," *Institute of Public Affairs Review: A Quarterly Review of Politics and Public Affairs, The* 68, no. 2 (August 2016): 16. for a full discussion of the methods used to censor on Australian campuses.
[41] "Students Refuse to Learn Tolerance," October 9, 2016, http://www.heraldsun.com.au/news/opinion/rita-panahi/too-many-modern-students-refuse-to-learn-tolerance-and-respect-for-diversity-of-opinion/news-story/6f60755f738a13cca87291148798a5bb.
[42] Matthew Lesh, "WARNING: This Article Contains Ideas That Offend," *The Spectator Australia,* August 20, 2016, https://www.spectator.co.uk/2016/08/warning-article-contains-ideas-offend/.

The psychological elements work symbiotically with the identity politics paradigm. They fuel each other. Identity politics provides the ideological justification, that discourse must be silenced to fight oppression, and the mental health side makes students particularly receptive to censoring speech that hurts their feelings. This establishes a cross-section of support for censorship of ideas.[43] If universities are to function, students and academics must be able and willing to explore a wide cross-section of ideas, play them up against each other, and be free to come to their own conclusions.

The Universities' Response
Ideally, universities would be fighting back against these trends, trying to impart to students and academics that censorship is unacceptable and that they must explore a variety of ideas. Some universities have chosen to fight back against the trend. The University of Chicago has declared that "it is not the proper role of the University to attempt to shield individuals from ideas and opinions they find unwelcome, disagreeable, or even deeply offensive… fostering the ability of members of the University community to engage in such debate and deliberation in an effective and responsible manner is an essential part of the University's educational mission".[44] Chicago, however, is in the minority of American colleges, and there is yet to be such an emphatic defence of freedom of expression by an Australian university.

Australian universities have widely supported the limiting of free speech. The Institute of Public Affairs' *Free Speech on Campus Audit 2016* found eight-in-ten Australian universities have taken action or maintain speech codes that stifle freedom of expression on campus. Just one university, the University of New England, received a Green ranking for no threats.

Universities, often in the name of diversity and tolerance, have explicit policies that forbid "insulting" and "unwelcome" comments, "offensive" language, and, in some cases, "sarcasm" and hurt "feelings". It is practically impossible to have an open debate in which you cannot hurt someone's feeling––particularly considering how easily people's feelings can be hurt in the modern age. Universities have, in effect, institutionalised the identity politics paradigm. Australian universities are increasingly operating like businesses, responding to consumer (student) demands. However, the vast majority of students do not engage in the demand for changes. This gives disproportionate weight to a small number of radical and vocal students.

The University of Western Australia rejected, and no other university was willing to accept, the establishment of an Australia Consensus Centre led by

---

[43] Frank Furedi, *What's Happened To The University?* (London: Routledge, 2016).
[44] Committee on Freedom of Expression at the University of Chicago, "Report of the Committee on Freedom of Expression," n.d., https://provost.uchicago.edu/FOECommitteeReport.pdf.

Danish author and environmentalist Bjørn Lomborg.[45] The rejection came following protests by students, academics, and sections of the media. UWA Student Guild president Lizzy O'Shea argued against the centre because of Lomborg's "controversial trackrecord".[46] Monash University has become the first university to introduce trigger warnings on university course guides.[47] The introduction of these warnings came after years of student demands led by the Monash Student Association's Women's department.[48]

The weakness of university defence for freedom of expression is epitomised by their response to a spate of demands for censorship by Chinese international students. In four known instances during 2017, Chinese students have complained that lecture material does not align with Chinese government foreign policy.[49] In some of these cases the universities capitulated to student demands. The University of Sydney has apologised and committed to not using a map that displays disputed territory as part of India and Bhutan rather than China.[50] Monash University withdrew a textbook following criticism of a question in a quiz.[51] The Group of Eight, the representative body of Australia's top universities, has responded to the issue by saying they are more concerned about losing the Chinese student market, which amounts to 130,000 students, than protecting academic freedom.[52]

---

[45] Calla Wahlquist, "University of WA Academics Demand End to Deal with Climate Change Contrarian," *The Guardian*, April 24, 2015, sec. World news, http://www.theguardian.com/australia-news/2015/apr/24/university-of-wa-academics-demand-end-to-deal-with-climate-change-contrarian; Oliver Milman, "Bjørn Lomborg's $4m Centre Rejected by Flinders University Academics," *The Guardian*, July 28, 2015, sec. World news, http://www.theguardian.com/world/2015/jul/28/bjrn-lomborgs-4m-centre-rejected-by-flinders-university-academics.

[46] Australian Associated Press, "WA Students Call for Bjørn Lomborg's $4m for Climate Research to Be Rejected," *The Guardian*, April 21, 2015, sec. Environment, http://www.theguardian.com/environment/2015/apr/21/wa-students-call-for-bjrn-lomborgs-4m-for-climate-research-to-be-rejected.

[47] Lesh, "WARNING: This Article Contains Ideas That Offend."

[48] Monash Student Association, "Monash Student Council: Confirmed Minutes, MSC 13/16" (Monash University: Monash Student Association, December 7, 2016), http://msa.monash.edu.au/app/uploads/2017/03/MSC-Confirmed-Minutes-13-16.pdf.

[49] Emma Reynolds, "Chinese Students in Australia: Tensions Rise as Students Turn on Australian Professors," *news.com.au*, September 1, 2017, http://www.news.com.au/finance/economy/australian-economy/tensions-rise-as-chinese-governments-influence-infiltrates-aussie-universities/news-story/e7768b0bb1f5953a7608884527387372.

[50] Primrose Riordan, "Wrong Map Ignites Uni Fury," *The Australian*, August 21, 2017, http://www.theaustralian.com.au/national-affairs/sydney-lecturer-apologises-for-use-of-map-offending-chinese-students/news-story/2b1cccbe438d1c680fcbff60f8e7d97e.

[51] Primrose Riordan, "Chinese Get Book Removed," *The Australian*, May 29, 2017, http://www.theaustralian.com.au/higher-education/monash-throws-out-the-textbook-over-chinese-student-complaints/news-story/3453651355ed61ab28989e7623c8dd9d.

[52] Primrose Riordan, "Top Unis Admit China Influence, Go8 Fears Backlash," *The Australian*, September 23, 2017, http://www.theaustralian.com.au/higher-education/top-unis-admit-china-influence-go8-fears-backlash/news-story/c3286cf68d58f03b849d85b22bbd5b96.

Conclusion

The plague of postmodernist identity politics has infected the culture of Australia's universities, threatening a key purpose of higher education: to explore ideas. Universities cannot function without a need to strive for the truth. This is their core mission. Identity politics prioritises hurt feelings above facts, logic and challenging ideas.

Proponents of identity politics claim racism, sexism and homophobia are everywhere on the modern day university campus. This is ironic, of course, since universities are some of the most progressive places in Australia. Nevertheless, their misguided claims have a very real chilling effect. It is becoming impossible to undertake constructive discussion in class.

Conservative, classical liberal and libertarian students often feel too uncomfortable to express their political opinion for fear of abuse and potential bad marks. This hurts the education of all students, who are exposed to fewer ideas as a consequence. This creates a 'snowflake' generation, lacking resilience and unprepared for the real world.

Freedom of speech is fundamental to humanity. It allows us to express who we are as people. This derives from our equal moral worth.[53] The more we censor, the more we endanger ourselves and our own freedom in the process. Moreover, attempts to limit freedom of speech are condescending. The idea that you have a right to restrict someone from hearing an idea presumes that they are unable to hear a bad idea and decide for themselves that it is bad. This is a moralizing view now adopted by the modern left with an unforeseen vengeance in the name of their chosen identity groups. They simply assume that they have the moral authority to censor certain ideas.

The state of higher education in Australia is of concern. It is, nevertheless, important to put this in perspective. Most of Australia's academics are professional, knowledgeable and do their best to teach a variety of ideas. Meanwhile, the vast majority of students are there to learn, and are uninterested in the nonsense of student activists. However, it remains the case that an aggressive minority, steeped in certain theories about the functioning of society, are having a damaging impact.

The current situation necessitates relentless vigilance by those who wish to protect universities. The worst absurdities of censorship must be highlighted, and there must be advocacy for cultural change. There is some good news on this front. Australia's university regulator, the Tertiary Education Quality and Standard Agency, backed down on instructions to universities that threaten academic freedom, and has explicitly stated that "Measures taken to ac-

---

[53] Chris Berg, *In Defence of Free Speech From Ancient Greece to Andrew Bolt* (Melbourne, Victoria: Institute of Public Affairs and Mannkal Economic Education Foundation, 2012).

commodate diversity should also not contravene the pursuit of free intellectual inquiry, and more generally, freedom of expression."[54]

Despite limited publicity, there are now 17 Australian members of Heterodox Academy, who promote a diversity of viewpoints in academia.[55] They join over 1,250 academic members across the Anglosphere. In the United States, there are a number of state legislators enacting law to protect free expression on campus.[56] There is also a growing student-led free speech movement forming on American, British, Canadian and Australian campuses. The situation may get worse before it gets better. Nevertheless, the active resistance to efforts that undermine the functioning of universities has begun.

---

[54] Matthew Lesh, "University Regulator Backs down on Free Intellectual Inquiry Attack," *Freedom-Watch, Institute of Public Affairs* (blog), May 31, 2017, https://ipa.org.au/publications-ipa/freedomwatch/university-regulator-backs-free-intellectual-inquiry-attack.
[55] Heterodox Academy, "About Us," Heterodox Academy, accessed October 2, 2017, https://heterodoxacademy.org/about-us/.
[56] Chris Quintana and Andy Thomason, "The States Where Campus Free-Speech Bills Are Being Born: A Rundown," *The Chronicle of Higher Education*, May 15, 2017, http://www.chronicle.com/article/The-States-Where-Campus/240073.

Britain and Western Civilisation in Australian Undergraduate History Courses: An Institutional Approach

Chris Berg and Bella d'Abrera

This essay explores the results of a major empirical research program into the content of undergraduate history courses in Australian universities. It finds that subjects covering Britain and some of the key themes of Western Civilisation are conspicuously absent. The essay explores why this absence is significant. In an 'institutional' approach to history education, history courses should focus on exploring with students the institutional origins of their own society. The institutional approach suggests a normative history education canon which, for Australia, would be directed towards the history of Britain and Western Civilisation.

"Study history, study history. In history lie all the secrets of statecraft", said Winston Churchill.[1] He could have added that in history lies a guide to many of our most important contemporary questions: national identity, human freedom, our shared democratic stake in society, and the relationship between individual and community. In Australia, as in every other country, history is a battleground on which politics is fought. But Churchill's advice is incomplete. What history should be studied? In this essay we explore this question in relation to the teaching of history in Australia in undergraduate history courses.

The content and composition of Australian undergraduate degrees in history have been the subject of a number of reports and surveys since the early 1990s. Between 1992 and 2002, the Australian Historical Association (AHA) conducted three 'State of History' surveys which reviewed the history curricula in Australian universities. In 2004, it commissioned Carly Millar and Mark Peel to survey every history program in universities in Australia, and in New Zealand, Papua New Guinea and Fiji. The request had been made to the AHA by various heads of history departments in response to the downsizing of history departments during the 1980s, as well as 'anxieties' about a crisis within the discipline at Australian universities. According to the AHA, the aim of the curriculum reviewer was to 'gather comparable information on the

---

[1] Attributed to Winston Churchill.

changing shape and content of a 'history major' or similar sequences in different institutions.'[2] Millar and Peel looked at the history programs of 57 different institutions in Australia, New Zealand, Fiji and Papua New Guinea. In 2015, the Institute of Public Affairs published a systematic review of all 739 history subjects offered to undergraduates across 34 Australian tertiary institutions. The 2015 report surveyed a total of 35 history programs, along with a further additional 10 separate ancient history programs. A follow-up report, published in 2017, looked at 746 history subjects taught across 35 institutions of higher learning in 2017.[3]

Why should we be concerned about undergraduate history teaching? Directly, history students become the next generation of historians and history teachers at the secondary and tertiary level. What is taught today will be the body of knowledge for future students of history. Even for students that do not go on to use their knowledge of history in a professional setting, their knowledge becomes the common stock of historical understanding in Australian society. Indirectly, undergraduate history courses are a proxy to view the state of professional academic history, subject to the limitations of student demand (discussed below).

This essay first makes a normative case for a history canon that focuses on the origins of Australia's institutions. Then it outlines how undergraduate history subjects deviate from that canon. Finally, it concludes with some thoughts about the significance of history in Australian politics and culture.

Institutions as the Carriers of History

The most important question in social science is why some individuals, communities, and societies are better off—in the sense that they are wealthier, happier, healthier, freer, more generally prosperous—than others. At this extreme level of abstraction, social science is not a dispassionate accounting of the state of the world. It is a search for the mechanisms of human betterment, with the hope that this knowledge can be used to raise living standards. In history, as in a number of other social science domains, this pushes us towards a few key questions.

We are much richer than our ancestors. But the path to prosperity has not been linear. As Gregory Clark wrote in his 2007 book *A Farewell to Alms*, the economic history of the world is simply described.[4] Between 1000 BC and 1800 AD incomes varied across time and place but were relatively stagnant—

---

[2] Carly Millar and Mark Peel, "Australian Historical Association 2003-4 History Curriculum Review: Final Report to the Aha Executive," (Australian Historical Association, 2004).
[3] Stephanie Forrest, Chris Berg and Hannah Pandel, "The End of History...in Australian universities", (Institute of Public Affairs, 2015); Bella d'Abrera, "The Rise of Identity Politics: An Audit of History Teaching at Australian Universities in 2017", (Institute of Public Affairs, 2017).
[4] G. Clark, *A Farewell to Alms: A Brief Economic History of the World* (Princeton University Press, 2008).

the data show no long term upward trend. In 1800 something happened. We can observe a sharp increase in aggregate incomes in the developed world after 1800, and a modest decline in the least developed countries. So what caused the dramatic take-off in global income? What accounts for the "great divergence" in incomes between the rich and the poor world?

The framework of new institutional economics provides a guide through these questions. Institutional economics allows us to focus on the historical paths and processes which create the societies we observe. New institutional economics was developed in the second half of the twentieth century as a framework to study the emergence and evolution of institutions which coordinate economic activity. Institutional economics, in both its 'original' and 'new' variations, differs from neoclassical economics in that it focuses not on the tendency of markets to move towards a static equilibrium but on process and evolution.[5] The original institutionalists like Theodore Veblen and John R. Commons were interested in the role of law and Darwinian change in structuring human behaviour outside the neoclassical strictures of *homo economicus*. The founding documents of new institutional economics were Ronald Coase's 1937 paper "The Nature of the Firm" and his 1960 paper "The Problem of Social Cost".[6] For Coase, institutions exist to manage the transaction costs of coordinating activity between individuals with diverse preferences.

The abstract simplicity of this approach has turned out to provide substantial explanatory power for long-run development and change in human societies. Institutions include formal structures like legal frameworks, constitutions, the strength and form of property rights, political structures such as representative democracy or autocracy, but also informal structures such as norms, beliefs, ideologies and conventions. These institutions provide individuals with expectations about how they believe others will act, reducing the costs of exchange. As Douglass North, one of the central founders of the new institutional economics school wrote, "Throughout history institutions have been devised by human beings to create order and reduce uncertainty in exchanges".[7]

Central to the institutional worldview is the notion of path dependency. Institutional choices made in the past help determine the spread of choices available in the present. For Mancur Olson, path dependencies can lead to the build-up of social rigidities and sclerosis as special interest groups protect the

---

[5] Gonzalo Caballero and David Soto-Oñate, "The Diversity and Rapprochement of Theories of Institutional Change: Original Institutionalism and New Institutional Economics," *Journal of Economic Issues* 49, no. 4 (2015), 947-977.
[6] Ronald H Coase, "The Problem of Social Cost," *The Journal of Law and Economics* vol. 3 (Oct.,1960), 1-44; "The Nature of the Firm," *economica* 4, no. 16 (1937), 386-405.
[7] Douglass C. North, "Institutions," *Journal of Economic Perspectives* 5, no. 1 (1991), 97.

privileges they have obtained through the political process.⁸ For Daron Acemoglu and James A. Robinson, path dependencies can prevent innovative change.⁹ Institutional analyses give causal, semi-deterministic credit to the origins of the status quo. In this sense, institutions are the 'carriers of history'. While some institutional economists have been vague about exactly how history relates to the present, Paul A. David outlines the connection between path dependency—which suggests a deterministic relationship to the past—and evolution—which suggests that new institutional forms can be experimentally developed.¹⁰ As David argues, historical choices 'attract' present day decision-makers to certain paths, in order to exploit: a) mutually consistent expectations about the range of possible outcomes; b) existing information channels that have been developed for the efficiency of the status quo; and c) the complementary relationships between institutions. He concludes that:

> Yes, institutions do 'evolve' in a manner that shares important attributes with biological processes of evolution. But, affirming this to be true makes it all the more apposite for economists to grasp the implications of the view that biological mechanisms of selection are very much bounded by the material that they find already on hand.¹¹

This approach gives us a highly present-centric focus on the task of historical understanding. The process of discovering historical knowledge is often seen as subordinate to two opposed aims. On the one hand it forms part of what is seen as 'generalisable education'—the forging of conceptual connections that can be used in different fields.¹² To learn history is to learn something about the character of human societies but also the methods by which we can understand that character. The historian's craft is both a toolset and a philosophy of knowledge. On the other hand, historical knowledge is seen as valuable in and of itself—not because of the lessons we might draw from the past for today, but because it has intrinsic worth, both as a source of interest and as a reflection of a deeply embedded human desire for discovery.¹³ Institutional economics provides a third instrumental purpose of history education:

---

[8] Mancur Olson, *The Rise and Decline of Nations: Economic Growth, Stagflation, and Social Rigidities* (Yale University Press, 1982).
[9] Daron Acemoglu and James A. Robinson, *Why Nations Fail: The Origins of Power, Prosperity and Poverty* (Profile Books, 2012).
[10] Paul A. David, "Why Are Institutions the 'Carriers of History'?: Path Dependence and the Evolution of Conventions, Organizations and Institutions," *Structural change and economic dynamics* 5, no. 2 (1994), 205-20.
[11] *Ibid.*, 217.
[12] Gardner Campbell, "Integrative Learning and the Gift of New Media: General Education for the 21st Century," Presentation delivered at Benedictine University, March 19 2010.
[13] On the value of knowledge more generally see J.L. Kvanvig, *The Value of Knowledge and the Pursuit of Understanding* (Cambridge University Press, 2003).

an understanding about the shape of future choices and paths available. This is not simply an expansion of the idea that 'if we don't know where we came from, we will not know where we are going'. Rather, history education provides instrumental knowledge of limits and constraints that future choices are going to face.

An Institutional History 'Canon'?

The institutional philosophy of the value of history education is not value-free: it provides as much a guide to the purpose of history education as to the content of that education. History educators and those who develop history curricula at the secondary and tertiary level are not faced with an undifferentiated space from which to select topics, areas, eras, and themes. Millar and Peel emphasised two major factors behind what was offered: student demand and staff expertise or interest.[14] Funding is closely tied to enrolment, and subjects which fail to attract students are unlikely to survive. Universities reported that their students tended to be more interested in dramatic subjects like war and the Holocaust. Trevor Burnard, head of the school at the University of Melbourne's School of Historical and Philosophical Studies, has written that "The realities of our parlous funding… mean that we have to be responsive to student interest and student demand. The reason British history is less taught now than it once was has little to do with politics, and everything to do with student preferences".[15] Likewise, having conducted an (as yet unpublished) update to Millar and Peel for the Australian Historical Association in 2017, Paul Sendziuk and Martin Crotty argue that "Academics and their managers are acutely aware of areas of student interest, and tend to respond to student demand rather than shaping it".[16]

Staff expertise also limits the range of subjects that can be offered. As Millar and Peel write, "teaching programs in history are driven by the changing enthusiasms, expertise and capacity of their staff, with formal review, hiring policies and program planning shaping but not determining the overall curriculum".[17] Smaller universities with fewer teaching staff mean that single staffing changes can significantly affect course offerings. Curriculum and course designers find themselves having to balance the *importance* of a set of courses for the history field and the attractiveness of that same set of courses for students who are both sovereign consumers of their education and subject to the paternal responsibilities of their educators.

---

[14] Millar and Peel (2004).
[15] Trevor Burnard, "Memo to the Ipa: History Teaching Is Driven by Student Demand, Not 'Identity Politics'," *The Conversation*, 18 October, 2017.
[16] Paul Sendziuk and Martin Crotty, "'Identity Politics' Have Not Taken over University History Courses," *Ibid.*, 19 October, 2017.
[17] Millar and Peel (2004), 6.

Australian history courses are shaped for relevance in a way that goes further than just a simple demand model: they cluster around the recent past rather than taking the longer perspective; they focus on Australia, and nations and regions in which Australia has had a historical interest; and they privilege themes (such as gender and race) that have direct relevance to today. Additional 'significant' historical moments and themes which have less direct relationship to Australian students studying in Australian universities also receive a reasonable showing: the French and Russian Revolutions, for example, clearly form part of a general historical education. Fundamentally, students are not born with a lack of interest in certain historical periods and areas of study. They are acculturated over time—by their schooling, for instance—into believing that Australian or British history is less interesting than other fields. Student demand for history subjects does not emerge out of nowhere. History educators at all levels are part of the process of creating interest in the students themselves. While demand is obviously a large and important factor in shaping what universities can offer, the profession helps create that demand.

Millar and Peel describe the 'canon' of Australian history teaching as a positive description of what is taught, or in the light of limited resources, sampled.[18] By contrast, the institutional approach offers a normative perspective on what the history canon ought to be: *the subjects, themes, and areas which have given us our prevailing institutions and shape our present choices.* The institutional approach is not meant to be exclusive. It is not controversial to say that history programs are and ought to be balanced between staff expertise, student interest and other measures of relevance. But as our survey of Australian history courses has shown, they are significantly deficient according to this institutional model.

What would an institutional canon look like in Australia? Our contention is that it would privilege the history of Britain and Western Civilisation more generally. Other histories are of intrinsic interest, of social, economic and political relevance, and can provide insights into historical and epistemological method. But institutional history would be, for Australia, dominated by the societies from which the country drew its institutional framework, and the civilisation which that framework in turn developed.

Undergraduate History in Australia: An Audit

So how does Australian undergraduate history teaching perform in relation to this vision of an institutional canon? As Millar and Peel have shown, the 'canon' of large-scale, comparative and global histories, organized around themes and specializations, began to appear in the 1970s and 1980s. This included

---

[18] Mark Peel and Carly Millar, "Canons Old and New: The Undergraduate History Curriculum in 2004," *History Australia* 2, no. 1 (2004), 14.

subjects on all periods of Western history: British history, Ancient Greece and Rome, U.S history, and Australian national history. Millar and Peel noted that there was an increasing tendency for departments to cancel subjects in these areas and to replace them with the new histories in order to 'capture the interest of students'. The authors concluded that 'in the larger institutions, and compared to programs of ten or twenty years ago, it would now seem more difficult for a student to construct a history sequence that was one nation or continent, but less difficult to focus upon a particular period….'[19] In other words, in 2004, very few Australian institutions of higher learning were offering undergraduates the opportunity to approach history sequentially rather than thematically.

The IPA's 2015 report drew attention to a number of trends occurring in Australian history programs since Millar and Peel's report.[20] These changes reflected changes in the history profession, student demand, university and department resources, and broader social attitudes towards history. General and national history subjects were giving way to thematic and specialized subjects based on narrow topics such as imperialism, gender studies and film studies. Many institutions offered only Australian history and the twentieth century whilst completely neglecting to offer subjects on other geographical regions and other significant areas of history.

Unfortunately, this phenomenon is not confined to Australia, but is found in the humanities across the Anglosphere. In a speech to the American Council of Trustees and Alumni, Professor Niall Ferguson lamented the fact that history at American colleges is 'suffering a decline and fall, and faster than Gibbon's Roman Empire.'[21] To understand exactly why, Ferguson investigated the history courses currently available at Yale, Harvard and Stanford. Although the concept of the significant historical event has in recent years become rather unfashionable, for fear of privileging the history of elites, and thus has been virtually proscribed by the academy, Ferguson devised an historical canon comprising 20 topics which he believed should be the basis for any undergraduate modern history degree in the United States.[22] He then investigated the frequency with which those topics appeared amongst the courses. He discovered that just 7 out of the 20 were generally available to undergraduates, while 'gender' had become the most important subfield in the academy. 'History', he concluded, 'is in trouble.'[23]

---

[19] *Ibid.*, 5.
[20] Stephanie Forrest, Chris Berg and Hanna Pandel, "The end of History…in Australian Universities" (The Institute of Public Affairs, 2015), 2.
[21] N. Ferguson, "The Decline and Fall of History", *American Council of Trustees and Alumni,* October 28, 2016, Washington DC, 11.
[22] *Ibid.*, 13.
[23] *Ibid.*, 17.

The 2015 and 2017 audits confirm similar trends in history teaching in Australia.[24] The fear of singling out some historical events to the exclusion of others, with a move away from a standard 'core' curriculum, has changed the structure and composition of history in Australian universities. In 2017 there were 746 history courses available to undergraduates in Australia. Of these 241 could be said to cover the history of Western Civilisation. They included topics such as Ancient Greece and Ancient Rome, the Middle Ages, the History of Christianity, the Enlightenment, the French Revolution, the Industrial Revolution, the Russian Revolution, and the Cold War. These are topics which contribute towards an understanding of the unique and essential contributions that Western Civilisation has made to the world, and which should be the essential core of an undergraduate history degree in Australia.

However, a breakdown of the 241 courses reveals that there was a predominance of some core topics over others, specifically those which concern ancient and modern history. The ancient world, for example, was extremely well represented in Australian universities, with 57 and 53 courses, covering Ancient Greece and Ancient Rome respectively. At the other end of the historical timeline, there was a plethora of courses on the Twentieth century, with Nazism/Fascism and Communism (48), World War I (42) and World War II (51) being the most commonly offered units. In comparison, there were noticeably fewer courses offered to students which covered the historical periods and events of the intervening two millennia, with just 23 courses which touched on the Reformation, and 19 each on the Enlightenment and the Industrial Revolution.

Only two universities offer specific courses based on the concept of Western Civilisation: Notre Dame University's 'Western Civilisation to 1500' and Federation University's 'Western Civilisation in World History'. Perhaps more indicatively, the audits reveal that there is a paucity of British history subjects available to students in Australia. Of 739 subjects in the 2015 audit, only 15 surveyed British history, while 6 of these were principally concerned with the twentieth century, that is, the history of Britain after the establishment of Australia.

Table 1: British History Subjects, 2015
Jane Austen History and Fiction (Australian National University)
Tudor-Stuart England, c.1485-1714: Politics, Society and Culture (Australian National University)
Literature and Society (Charles Sturt University)
The Rise of Britannia's Empire and the Colonial Experience (Flinders University)

---

[24] Stephanie Forrest, Chris Berg and Hannah Pandel, "The End of History...in Australian universities", (Institute of Public Affairs, 2015); B. d'Abrera, "The Rise of Identity Politics: An Audit of History Teaching at Australian Universities in 2017", (Institute of Public Affairs, 2017).

The Fall of Britannia's Empire and the Postcolonial Experience (Flinders University)
Myth, Legend and History (La Trobe University)
Little Britain: Culture, Society and the end of the Empire (La Trobe University)
Twentieth-century Britain: Rule Britannia to cool Britannia (Monash University)
Britain 1700-1830: Power, Sex and Money (University of Adelaide)
The Swinging Sixties: The 1960s in America, Britain and Australia (University of New England)
Churchill's Britain: Crisis and Conflict (1875-1945) (University of Queensland)
Roman Britain (University of Western Australia)
Twentieth-century Britain (University of Western Australia)
Crime and Punishment in Britain 1600-1900 (University of Western Australia)
Britain in the Age of Botany Bay, 1760-1815 (Western Sydney University)

Since 2014, there have been two valuable additions from Melbourne and Monash Universities. Second year students at Melbourne taking 'Britain in the Wider World 1603-1815' will cover major events in British history such as the Civil War, the Glorious Revolution and the Industrial Revolution, while students at Monash taking 'Medieval and Early Modern Britain' study the political change in the British Isles from the arrival of the Normans to the restoration of the monarchy in 1660. In general, however, the trend towards fragmented and parochial subjects continues, with many of the British history subjects as specialty subjects focusing on gender or crime and punishment.

Conclusion

How we understand our history is how we understand ourselves. Australia's historical memory has gone through waves of debate in the last few decades, but those debates have accelerated in recent years. For example, the 'change the date' campaign seeks to move Australia Day from January 26, which commemorates the anniversary of the 1788 arrival of the First Fleet at Port Jackson, as to "continue to celebrate Australia Day on January 26 is to participate in [a] cult of forgetfulness" about indigenous dispossession.[25] This campaign, and its embrace by a number of local governments that are moving or seeking to move official ceremonies from that day, speak to unresolved and disputed understandings of the foundations of the country and its future direction. The historical profession has taken up the challenge of integrating deep understanding of the indigenous history of the Australia that met Arthur Phillip's fleet. This is necessary and important. However, as this essay has shown, the history of the British institutions which were imported with that fleet is being unfortunately neglected.

---

[25] The Greens, "Petition: Change the Date," https://greens.org.au/change-the-date.

Fostering "a rugged honesty of mind": The Liberal Philosophy and Approach of Robert Menzies to Education in Post-war Australia

David Furse-Roberts

As Robert Menzies delivered his landmark "Forgotten People" broadcast on 22 May 1942, with the Second World War raging in the jungles and on the high seas of the Pacific, he waxed lyrical about his ancestral home and its zest for learning:

> If Scotland has made a great contribution to the theory and practice of education, it is because of the tradition of Scottish homes...The Scottish farmer ponders upon the future of his son, and sees it most assured not by the inheritance of money but by the acquisition of that knowledge which will give him power; and so the sons of many Scottish farmers find their way to Edinburgh and a university degree.[1]

In a country that, for the best part of three centuries, had boasted twice the number of universities as its much more populous southern neighbour, Menzies revered the Scottish contribution to Education and he desired post-war Australia to tread a similar path as it progressed and modernised as a Pacific power.[2]

Whilst Menzies is justifiably remembered most as a champion of liberal capitalism and free enterprise who shepherded Australia through an unprecedented period of economic growth and prosperity, he also warrants the reputation as one of Australia's preeminent education prime ministers. Indeed education was one of Menzies' chief policy preoccupations whilst Prime Minister. As Andrew Carr and Benjamin Jones appreciate, it was Menzies who not only resolved one of the most acrimonious debates in Australian history on government aid to church schools, but was Australia's longest serving

---

[1] Robert Menzies, "The Forgotten People", Broadcast, 22 May 1942 in Robert Menzies, *The Forgotten People and other Studies in Democracy* (Sydney: Angus and Robertson, 1943), 4.
[2] After the founding of the University of Oxford (c 1096) and the University of Cambridge (c 1209) in England, four universities were established in Scotland; St Andrews (1413), Glasgow (1451), Aberdeen (1495) and Edinburgh (1583). The next universities in England, London and Durham, were not established until the 1830s.

prime minister who significantly expanded the nation's university system after World War II.[3] His contribution to education was such, that it has since been acknowledged even by his successors on the opposite side of the political divide. Former Labor Prime Minister Julia Gillard credited Menzies for demonstrating that "he understood the power of education as a force for good, a force for equity and a force for change".[4]

While the contribution of Prime Minister Menzies to education is appreciated, it is less widely understood what that contribution actually entailed in terms of both his input into Australia's burgeoning higher education sector after World War II and his support for school education, particularly in the private sector. To date, there have been some welcome studies on the contribution of Menzies to education, most notably his role behind the 1957 Murray Committee on universities and his 1963 decision to grant state aid to Catholic and independent schools.[5] While this existing literature has provided important insights into the administrative steps and legislative reforms taken by the Menzies Government in education policy, the underlying philosophy and approach of Menzies to education remain largely unexplored as has the crucial impact of his own formative years in shaping his outlook on education.

Accordingly, this essay begins by outlining the education of the young Menzies and how his personal experiences of home life, school and university gave rise to the guiding principles and objectives he brought to education policy as a young parliamentarian in Victorian politics, and finally as prime minister of Australia. The essay goes on to discuss the extent to which Menzies' educational ideals were grounded in liberalism, a philosophy he had effectively helped re-establish in Australian politics with the founding of the Liberal Party in 1944. Turning to the fields of university and school education, it discusses how Menzies' approaches to these respective sectors was guided by his liberal instincts and penchant for "pure learning" in the humanities. Finally, the piece examines Menzies' much-noted support of independent schools and probes the reasons why the Prime Minister and his government vested so heavily in the private school sector. Thus by drawing from a range of original sources, not least Menzies' own speeches, this essay aims to furnish readers

---

[3] Andrew Carr and Benjamin T Jones, "Civic Republicanism and Sir Robert Menzies: the non-Liberal side of the Liberal leader", *Journal of Australian Studies*, 2013, Vol 37, No 4, 495.

[4] Julia Gillard, "The Sir Robert Menzies Oration 2008", (The University of Melbourne, 6 November 2008), 2.

[5] See for example, A.W. Martin, "R G Menzies and the Murray Committee", in F.B. Smith and P Crichton (eds), *Ideas for Histories of Universities in Australia*, (Division of Historical Studies, Research School of Social Sciences, Australian National University, 1990), 94-115; Grant Harman, "Development of Higher Education", in Scott Prasser, J.R. Nethercote and John Warhurst, *The Menzies Era: A Reappraisal of Government, Politics and Policy* (Sydney: Hale and Iremonger, 1995), 243; and Bob Bessant, "Robert Gordon Menzies and Education in Australia", *Melbourne Studies in Education* 47: 1-2 (2006), 163-187.

with a more complete understanding of the personal and philosophical driving forces behind his support for all levels of Australian education in the post-war period of growth and prosperity.

Menzies' Own Educational Background

Born in the small north-west Victorian town Jeparit on 20 December 1894, the son of a store keeper and dressmaker, Menzies imbibed his love of learning from an early age. Whilst his parents, James and Kate Menzies, had received little formal education, they were both "great readers" and said to have spoken "educated English". In his boyhood, Menzies grew up on what he described as a "fascinating melange of books" that included Henry Drummond for evangelistic theology, Jerome K Jerome for humour, and *The Scottish Chiefs* for historical fervour.[6] This diet of reading no doubt furnished the young Menzies with his lifelong interest in English literature, theology, history and humour which frequently coloured the speeches he gave during his long public career. In addition to instilling their son with a penchant for reading and learning, James and Kate firmly believed in the value of formal education and were resolved to provide young Robert with the educational opportunities they had not enjoyed themselves.[7] Accordingly, they looked further afield from their small district of Jeparit to the regional city of Ballarat to enrol Robert in the Humffray Street State School, an establishment with a State-wide reputation for academic excellence.[8] Excelling academically himself, Menzies won scholarships to Ballarat's Grenville College and Melbourne's Wesley College where his love of learning and English literature continued to flourish.

In an age when Australian universities were still the preserve of a tiny minority, chiefly of free scholarship awardees and students from prosperous families, Menzies entered the University of Melbourne on a scholarship in 1913 to study Law. As Greg Melleuish points out, Menzies was the first Australian Prime Minister since Alfred Deakin to attend and graduate from an Australian University.[9] At Melbourne, Menzies appreciated first-hand, both the vocational and civilising value of a university education as he shone in his studies and extra-curricular activities on campus. His academic record reflect-

---

[6] Henry Drummond (1851-1897) was a Scottish Presbyterian evangelist, biologist, writer and lecturer; Jerome K. Jerome (1859-1927) was an English writer and humourist, known for his works including *Three Men in a Boat* and *Idle Thoughts of an Idle Fellow*.; *The Scottish Chiefs* (1810) was a historical novel about William Wallace, the thirteenth-century Scottish knight, authored by the Scottish historical novelist Jane Porter (1776-1850).
[7] Robert Menzies, *Afternoon Light: Some Memories of Men and Events* (Melbourne: Cassell Australia, 1967), 10.
[8] Allan W Martin, *Robert Menzies: A Life* (Vol 1) (Melbourne: Melbourne University Press, 1996), 12.
[9] Greg Melleuish, "Sir Robert Menzies and Higher Education", in J.R. Nethercote (ed), *Menzies: The Shaping of Modern Australia* (Brisbane: Connor Court Publishing, 2016), 259.

ed not only his dedication to mastering his chosen profession of law but also his love of what he would call "pure learning' in the humanities, most notably history and English literature. In addition to achieving first-class honours in law, Menzies won the Dwight Prize in British History and Constitutional History, the John Madden Exhibition in Jurisprudence and the Jesse Leggatt scholarship in Roman law, the law of contract and the law of property, as well as the highly-sought after Bowen prize for an English essay.[10] Far from being detractions from his study of law, Menzies regarded his studies in history and English literature as an adornment to his vocational training. They not only helped place the discipline of law in its broader cultural context but ultimately equipped him to be a more rounded lawyer with a deeper understanding of human nature.

Menzies' Early Approach to Education
From his own university experience of studying English literature and history in conjunction with Law, Menzies maintained throughout his public life that the purpose of education was to inculcate in every student a "general knowledge of the world" as well as the "specialist knowledge" of their chosen vocation. In the early stages of his political career, as a Member of the Victorian state parliament from 1928-34, Menzies supported the vision and efforts of the Education director, M.P. Hansen, to provide a broad, liberal education rather than a specialised, vocational training for students up to the ages of fourteen or fifteen years.[11] In 1929 he told the Victorian Legislative Council that, "if we regard education as a preparation for life, as a preparation for citizenship, then I am all in favour of an unspecialised education to the age of fifteen years, and, if we can afford it, to the age of sixteen years".[12] As with education at the tertiary level, Menzies regarded the function of schooling as not merely to inculcate "a technical efficiency that will enable them to earn a living", but to produce in every citizen "some kind of a broad and enlightened intelligence".[13]

Even after the austerity of the depression years, with lingering public concerns about education costs, Menzies' emphasis on both the vocational and civilising mission of education remained unshaken and he brought this outlook to the Federal realm of politics following his election to the seat of Kooyong in 1936. Speaking on a motion in 1945 debating the future reform of education, Menzies told the House of Representatives that "The first function of education is to produce a 'good man and a good citizen'. Its second

---

[10] Martin, *Robert Menzies*, 19.
[11] Bessant, "Robert Gordon Menzies", 167.
[12] Robert Menzies, *Parliamentary Debates* [Victoria], (Legislative Council, 11 September 1929), 1517-18, quoted in Bessant, "Robert Gordon Menzies", 167
[13] Bessant, "Robert Gordon Menzies", 167.

function is to produce a 'good carpenter or a good lawyer'.[14] The then Leader of the Opposition went on to say that the 'good carpenter' and 'good lawyer' would be all the better at their respective crafts if a humanities education could furnish them with a "civilised point of view".[15] According to Menzies, this would help such tradespeople or professionals to "become aware of the problems of the world, acquire some quality of intellectual criticism, and develop that comparative sense which produces detachment of judgment and tends always to moderate passion and prejudice".[16] Whilst conceding that the old classical notion of education had its shortcomings, most notably its neglect of modern factors, Menzies rejected the notion that disciplines such as English literature, history or philosophy could be discarded as "useless learning". On the contrary, they were indispensable to building more well-rounded and cultured citizens if such disciplines could complement the necessary training for the modern trades and professions.

Education and Liberalism

In adulthood, his faith in education was augmented by a liberal philosophy that esteemed education as one of the great driving forces of modern civilisation. In one of his early speeches, Menzies explained how education and learning could act as a catalyst for greater human freedom in that "No society can confer the benefit of mental or spiritual freedom upon its members unless at the same time it encourages the search for truth and the fearless facing of the problems of the intellect".[17] Appraising the progress of human civilisation over the past century, Menzies had welcomed all the tremendous advances in science, technology and nutrition "directed towards the attainment of a higher degree of bodily wellbeing", but at the same time, reminded his audience that the modern "conception of a liberated body inhabited by a stunted mind and a poor spirit is not a noble one".[18] Accordingly, Menzies believed that future investment in education was essential if human civilisation was truly to flourish with free minds inhabiting free bodies. For Menzies, palpable improvements to standards of living and physical health needed to be accompanied by educated minds, restless in their quest for truth and beauty in whatever discipline.

For Menzies and other liberals, the power of education lay in its capacity to improve individuals, thereby allowing them to bring a better world into being.[19] Liberals saw education as having the potential to furnish individuals

---

[14] Robert Menzies, "Motion on Education", *Commonwealth Parliamentary Debates*, (House of Representatives, 26 July 1945), 4617.
[15] Menzies, "Motion on Education", 4617.
[16] Menzies, "Motion on Education", 4617.
[17] Robert Menzies, *Freedom in Modern Society*, (1935) 4.
[18] Menzies, *Freedom in Modern Society*, 4.
[19] Melleuish, "Sir Robert Menzies and Higher Education", 259

with the great faculties of reasoning, wisdom, sound judgment, moral character and religious faith which would equip them to become eminently better citizens. With his fondness of law, history and English literature, Menzies extolled the merits, especially, of a humanities-based education which provided the indispensable intellectual foundation for the liberal ideal of human freedom to flourish. In a 1959 address to students at a university in Indonesia, then a newly independent nation looking to expand higher education for its citizens, Menzies told his audience why universities continued to invest in the humanities:

> The greatest point about a University is the quality of the mind and spirits that it produces. That is what counts in a University, that is why you have Faculties of Arts, that is why you study literature, or study history. Not because you are all going to be lecturers in English, lecturers in history, but because these studies broaden the mind, extend the horizons of the mind, and give a new freedom to the spirit of the student.[20]

For Menzies, an education steeped in the humanities disciplines would ultimately ensure the survival of democracy in Australia.[21] The humanities would help inculcate the virtues of moderation, decency and selflessness amongst Australia's citizenry, providing a healthy counter-weight to the vices of greed, selfishness and prejudice that could all too readily stem from an emphasis on material progress alone.

Menzies' affirmation of learning in the humanities stemmed from his commitment to a liberal, humanist philosophy that affirmed the primacy of human dignity and human understanding. Not so much of a secular humanism, in the contemporary sense, but more of a theistic, Christian-derived humanism that emphasised the relationship of people to each other as well as their relationship to their God. In a 1961 address to the Australian College of Education, Menzies articulated his humanist philosophy when he told his audience that "I have stressed the point of ethics because I believe that the most important thing to consider and learn in this world is the nature of man, his duties and rights, his place in society, his relationship to his Creator".[22] Quoting approvingly from the British educationist Sir Richard Livingstone (1880-1960) in *The Rainbow Bridge* (1959), Menzies affirmed that "history and literature must enter into any education; for they are our chief record of man and his ways". With their focus on the human condition, it was disciplines such as

---

[20] Robert Menzies, "Address to Students at Gadjah Mada University", (Jogjakarta, Indonesia, 3 December 1959), 4.
[21] Melleuish, "Sir Robert Menzies and Higher Education", 260.
[22] Robert Menzies, "The Challenge to Education", Inaugural Address to the Australian College of Education, (19 May 1961), 5.

history, literature, sociology, philosophy and religious studies that provided students with essential insights into human character and human relationships.

Against the backdrop of a conflict-ridden twentieth century that had witnessed the most egregious incidents of human misunderstanding, Menzies believed that a humanist dimension to education was more important than ever as Australia braced for the complexities of the space age. In one of his signature radio broadcasts of the 1950s, "Australia Today – Man to Man", the Prime Minister reminded his listeners that the scientific age had not rendered the humanities redundant: "Let us by all means have scientists, and the best we can find. But let us also have people of humane letters, who can remind us that the most important thing in the world is not the machine, but man".[23] Returning to the contemporary challenge of education, he declared, "We must recapture our desire to know more, and feel more, about our fellowmen; to have a philosophy of living; to elevate the dignity of man, a dignity which, in our Christian concept, arises from our belief that he is made in the image of his Maker".[24] Affirming both the human and the divine, the humanist philosophy Menzies brought to education was informed by both his Scottish Presbyterian upbringing and his reverence for the liberal Enlightenment stemming from John Locke (1632-1704). In essence, Menzies' liberalism was not just a narrow pecuniary creed about the freedom for individuals to accrue as much wealth as they desired, but one that also affirmed the intrinsic worth and dignity of human beings, and this was no more evident than in his philosophy of education.

In contemporary times, the indebtedness of Menzies' educational philosophy to the liberal ideals of freedom, human dignity and equality is widely recognised. As David Kemp appreciated in a recent essay, Prime Minister Menzies' reforms to both school and university education were guided by the vision that better education would lift the whole of society and the quality of every institution in it. It would improve leadership, it would improve public debate, and it would produce greater equality.[25] Ever mindful of its far-ranging benefits, Menzies saw education as a means of promoting citizenship, personal development and social mobility, as well as boosting the national economy. According to Menzies, the better educated a nation's citizenry could be, the greater its capacity for self-government, an outcome the liberal standard-bearer regarded as critical to neutralising any future overreach of the state. Speaking on "The Future of Education" in 1943, Menzies observed that:

---

[23] Robert Menzies, "Australia Today – Man to Man" (Broadcast, 17 March 1954), 1.
[24] Menzies, "Challenge to Education", (1961), 9.
[25] David Kemp, "The Political Philosophy of Robert Menzies", in J R Nethercote, *Menzies: The Shaping of Modern Australia* (Brisbane: Conner Court, 2016), 19

> ...the greater the facilities for post-school education, and the more continuous the interest of the citizen in the cultivation of the resources of his own mind, the more successful and intelligent will self-government become.[26]

Thus, with the expansion of universities in the post-war era serving to equip more Australians with the wisdom and wherewithal to think for themselves and make their own decisions, the less need there would be for government to intervene and prescribe how citizens should run their lives.

Similarly, the Australian educationist Professor Dame Leonie Kramer (1924-2016) recognised the inescapable nexus between the political philosophy of Menzies and his approach to education, remarking that "nowhere were Menzies' liberal-conservative principles better expressed than in his views about, and exceptional contributions to, education in Australia".[27] Kramer noted that 'so far as Menzies is concerned, education is the indispensable instrument in the promotion and protection of democracy'.[28] Kramer was evidently alluding to Menzies' conviction that education and democracy were synergic, a notion he gave expression to in a wartime address to the Camberwell Town Hall in his own electorate of Kooyong:

> Democracy cannot succeed merely by grace of a few leaders or a few thinkers. It must develop its citizens to the limit of their individual intelligence. It can never rest on its laurels while any boy or girl lacks the opportunity to become a trained and qualified citizen [29]

In accordance with liberal thought, Menzies saw education as furnishing individuals with the capacity to bring a better world into being that was freer and more democratic. As Melleuish perceives, "the power of education to effect progress has been a crucial element of liberalism since the nineteenth-century in Australia" and it was indeed Menzies who brought this outlook to bear on his government's approach to education.[30]

Menzies and Higher Education

The educational focus of Menzies was chiefly on universities with their long tradition of cultivating civilised minds. In his landmark 1942 "Forgotten People" speech, widely interpreted as the blueprint to the resurgent liberal movement he would eventually lead back to power in 1949, Menzies articulated his post-war vision for Australian higher education:

---

[26] Robert Menzies, "The Future of Education", (Broadcast, Melbourne, 19 February 1943), 2.
[27] Dame Leonie Kramer, "Education Politics and Democracy", *The 1987 Sir Robert Menzies Lecture* (Melbourne: Sir Robert Menzies Lecture Trust, 1999), 164.
[28] Kramer, "Education Politics and Democracy", 167.
[29] Robert Menzies, "Opening Speech", (Camberwell Town Hall, Camberwell [Victoria], 23 July 1943), 8.
[30] Melleuish, "Sir Robert Menzies and Australian Education", 258.

> Are the universities mere technical schools, or have they as one of their functions the preservation of pure learning, bringing in its train not merely riches for the imagination but a comparative sense for the mind, and leading to what we need so badly – the recognition of values which are other than pecuniary?[31]

Far from functioning merely as utilitarian 'degree factories' to churn out the greatest volume of graduates, Menzies saw universities as the great incubators of civilisation. Together with the British institutions of parliament and the courts, the Universities of Oxford and Cambridge represented the highest form of British civilisation to Menzies. As Bob Bessant observes, "the university was the ultimate expression of Menzies' faith in education as a civilising agent".[32] In addition to merely equipping undergraduates with essential training and vocational skills, the university would serve to cultivate the character of their students and encourage them to seek truth and beauty in their chosen discipline. Rather than standing aloof from the world, the university would bridge the gulf between the 'academician' and the 'good practical man'. In so doing, it would be in a position to contribute to the common good by producing an educated generation who understood the practicalities, values and aspirations of ordinary citizens.

In a 1939 address delivered at the Annual Commencement of the Canberra University College,[33] Menzies outlined what he saw as the sevenfold mission of the university. First, the university was to be the "home of pure culture and learning" which was indeed its "original medieval function".[34] As such, a university education would serve as a check on utilitarianism with its tendency to undervalue the classical disciplines for want of profitability. Second, a university would fulfil its vocational function as a 'training school for the professions', in what Menzies identified as the academy's "great and relatively modern function".[35] Third, the university would "serve as a liaison between the academician and the good practical man", by fostering the "mutuality between the theory and the practice" of one's vocation.[36] Fourth, the "University must be the home of research" where its pursuit required "infinite patience, precise observation, an objective mind, and unclouded honesty".[37] Fifth, the university needed to "be a trainer of character" where the

---

[31] Menzies, "Forgotten People", (1942), 7.
[32] Bessant, "Robert Gordon Menzies", 166.
[33] Founded in 1930, Canberra University College was originally a Canberra campus of the University of Melbourne that eventually merged with the Australian National University (ANU) in 1960.
[34] Robert Menzies, *The Place of a University in the Modern Community*, An Address Delivered at the Annual Commencement of the Canberra University College 1939 (Melbourne: Melbourne University Press, 1939), 11.
[35] Menzies, *Place of a University*, 19.
[36] Menzies, *Place of a University*, 22.
[37] Menzies, *Place of a University*, 25.

quest for higher learning would not only enlarge the mind but enrich the character of the individual.[38] Sixth, the university had to "be a training ground for leaders" where the riches of a higher education imbued students with an obligation to serve the public.[39] Finally, a university needed to be the "custodian of mental liberty, and the unfettered search for truth".[40] For Menzies, "a rugged honesty of mind" that did not shrink from the truth when it came upon it in its path was one of the "noblest of virtues".[41]

Menzies as Prime Minister was committed to advancing both the stature and scope of Australia's universities in the 1950s. In the post-war world, he envisaged these institutions as playing an ever more important role in raising educated individuals to become the future leaders of Australian democracy. To facilitate the greater participation of Australian citizens in higher education, Menzies took steps towards the Commonwealth funding of universities beginning with a scheme of undergraduate university scholarships inaugurated from the early 1950s. This initiative was followed by his instigation in 1956 of the Prime Minister's Committee on Australian Universities chaired by the British academic, Sir Keith Murray. To be sure, the post-war Chifley Labor Government in 1949 had set up an investigation into the funding of universities and the need for a permanent and comprehensive scholarship scheme, but it was the Menzies Government that modified its terms of reference leading to the establishment of the Murray Committee.[42] Like that of the Prime Minister, Murray's philosophy of university education was essentially traditional, broad and non-utilitarian. He saw the universities as guardians of the received intellectual standards and intellectual integrity of the community, intent on the discovery of new knowledge and the training of future professionals who were to have "a wide general education as a background to their professional knowledge".[43] Like Menzies, he affirmed that the need for education in the humanities was as great, if not greater, than ever before.

Reporting on the state of universities in Australia, the Murray Committee tabled a Report in 1957 that recommended a tripling of Federal government funding for universities, emergency grants, significant increases in academic salaries, extra funding for buildings, and the establishment from 1959 of a permanent committee, the Australian Universities Commission, to oversee and make recommendations concerning higher education.[44] Within days of the Report's release, Menzies announced that he would implement virtually all

---

[38] Menzies, *Place of a University*, 26.
[39] Menzies, *Place of a University*, 27.
[40] Menzies, *Place of a University*, 30.
[41] Menzies, *Place of a University*, 32.
[42] Harman, "Development of Higher Education", 243.
[43] Sir Keith Murray, "Guest of Honour talk", (Australian Broadcasting Commission, 2FC, Sydney, 22 September 1957), quoted in Bessant, "Robert Gordon Menzies", 179.
[44] Harman, "Development of Higher Education", 246.

of its recommendations.⁴⁵ Under his leadership, the government inspired and supported an unprecedented expansion of education in areas that had traditionally been the preserve of state governments. New universities including the University of New England (1954), Monash University (1958), Macquarie University (1964), La Trobe University (1964), the University of Newcastle (1965) and Flinders University (1966) were established placing tertiary education within reach of those who could not otherwise have had ready access.⁴⁶ The expansion of universities in Australia was matched by sharp increases in student enrolments from 53,700 in 1960 to well over 88,230 in 1966.⁴⁷ In the press conference immediately after his retirement as Prime Minister on 20 January 1966, Menzies cited his support for universities as one of his government's greatest achievements in domestic affairs.⁴⁸

Given that Menzies envisaged the university as "the home of research" in his sevenfold rationale for its place in the community, he had a vision for modern Australian universities to be not only centres of vocational training for the professions but research-intensive hubs. By nurturing postgraduate students of the highest calibre, Australian universities could aspire to be at the cutting-edge of research excellence in the developed world. Indeed Menzies regarded postgraduate students and researchers as critical to the whole future of university education. As Chancellor of the University of Melbourne, Menzies told a 1967 assembly of graduands at his *alma mater* that he hoped many of them would go on to post-graduate and research work. Remarking that there was "nothing more terrible than a second-rate university" and "nothing more inspiring than a first-rate university", the Chancellor recognised that institutions such as Melbourne had to invest in future research to maintain their reputation:

> If this is to continue to be a first-rate university, then more and more we will have to produce our own teachers, our own experts in the field of research, because we have reached the stage in history where we can't import them with the ease with which they were available 40 years ago.⁴⁹

For Menzies, it was no longer acceptable, or indeed viable, for modern Australian universities to look to either "Oxbridge" or American Ivy League insti-

---

[45] John Howard, *The Menzies Era: The Years that Shaped Modern Australia* (Sydney: HarperCollins Publishers, 2014), 246.
[46] Petro Georgiou, "Menzies, Liberalism and Social Justice", *The 1999 Sir Robert Menzies Lecture* (Melbourne: Sir Robert Menzies Lecture Trust, 1999), 3.
[47] Harman, "Development of Higher Education", 248.
[48] Robert Menzies, "Press, Radio and Television Conference Given by Sir Robert Menzies at Parliament House", (Canberra, 20 January 1966), 7.
[49] Robert Menzies, "Speech by Chancellor to Graduates at Degree Ceremony", (University of Melbourne, 26 April 1967), 4.

tutions for the recruitment of their experts. As part of an advanced and forward-looking nation, it was high time for Australian universities to invest in cultivating their own crop of home-grown researchers and experts. As an Australian patriot, Menzies desired Australian universities and Australian academics to be comparable to the best of the academy overseas.

Conscious of Australia's place in the Asia-Pacific, Menzies also maintained that strong Australian universities with Australian-trained academics would enable the nation to be a major hub and provider of higher education in its own region. With the Colombo Plan having brought many promising students from Asian countries to study at Australian universities since the early 1950s, it was critical that these universities continue to have the wherewithal to provide such opportunities into the future. In his memoirs, Menzies wrote that Australia has:

> so great a duty to our neighbours, particularly our Asian neighbours, to assist them in the raising of their own educational, medical, scientific and technological development that we must take our part in finding or training our share of expert minds that they need.[50]

Far from Australian universities simply fulfilling a paternalist role of providing education and training for its regional neighbours, however, Menzies' vision was for Australia's institutions to play a part in helping the nations of the Asia-Pacific, such as Indonesia, Malaysia, Singapore and Thailand, to develop their own centres of learning and professional excellence.

While Menzies' conception of a university education remained avowedly traditional, particularly with its emphasis on "pure learning" and character formation, his attitude about the availability and access of such an education was progressive and gender-inclusive. Eschewing the old notion that universities were the preserve of society's elite, he told parliament in 1957 that "it is not yet adequately understood that a university education is not, and certainly should not be, the perquisite of a privileged few". Recognising the need for the academy to adapt to the complexities of modern life, Menzies affirmed his vision to broaden the reach of higher education:

> The social, scientific, economic and industrial complexities of Australia to-day are largely beyond the imagination of forty years ago. Great skill achieved after high training is no longer to be regarded as something to be admired in a few....Viewed in this way, our universities are to be regarded not as a home of

---

[50] Robert Menzies, *The Measure of the Years* (Melbourne: Cassell Australia, 1970), 89-90.

privilege for a few, but as something essential to the lives of millions of people who may never enter their doors.[51]

From the very outset, it was Menzies' vision that the greater number of Australians engaged in higher education would include a higher percentage of women. In a 1942 wartime broadcast on education, he had insisted that "Higher education for women must come to be regarded as normal, and not as the eccentricity of a potential 'blue stocking'".[52] He argued that the equality of the sexes could not be maintained "if a slapdash training in a few minor ornamental accomplishments is considered an adequate education for the daughter of the house."[53] During Menzies' prime ministership, the number of female students enrolled at Australian universities increased from 19.7% in 1952 to 25.9% by 1964.[54]

Menzies and School Education

In addition to supporting the consolidation of Australian higher education, the other educational priority for Menzies was Commonwealth support for secondary, primary and even preschool education. In October 1942, at a time when Australia was engaged in the immediate war effort, Menzies turned his attention to the vital role of schools in building up a future generation of more enlightened and civilised citizens after the war. In his radio broadcast to the nation, Menzies firstly urged schools to retain the services of their teachers, both male and female, and second, for schools to better prepare boys and girls for the opportunity of higher education with politics, business and the civil service requiring better educated recruits.[55] Beginning, however, with kindergarten, Menzies acknowledged that this early phase of education could no longer be regarded as merely a family responsibility, or as something left to the community efforts of mainly female volunteers. On the contrary, the community needed to invest more in formal preschool education to ensure that children before the age of five were adequately equipped for primary school.[56] Turning to primary and secondary education, Menzies held that the role of schools was not simply to impart knowledge, develop discipline and

---

[51] Robert Menzies, "Universities Committee Report Speech", *Commonwealth Parliamentary Debates*, (House of Representatives, 28 November 1957), 2702.
[52] Robert Menzies, "Schools and the War", Broadcast, 16 October 1942 in Menzies, *Forgotten People*, 159.
[53] Menzies, "Schools and the War" in Menzies, *Forgotten People*, 159.
[54] "Table 1. Higher Education Students by Selected Characteristics, 1949-2000", in The Department of Education, Training and Youth Affairs, *Higher Education Students Time Series Tables: Selected Higher Education Statistics*, (Canberra: Commonwealth of Australia, 2001), 5.
[55] Menzies, "Schools and the War", in Menzies, *Forgotten People*, 159.
[56] Menzies, "Future of Education", (1943), 1.

train character in the narrow sense, but to "be places where the mind is enriched by the right visions and where the ends of life are learned".[57]

In his vision for school education at all levels, Menzies envisaged an extremely important role for teachers, not as indoctrinators nor as mere childminders, but as professional educators responsible for moulding the mind and character of the rising generation. Despite the fact that the teaching profession, in recent decades, has tended to lean more towards the progressive side of politics, it found a firm advocate and ally in Menzies as the Second World War came to an end. In his July 1945 education motion, he had called for attention to be directed to "the problem of the qualifications, status and remuneration of teachers". Menzies told the House of Representatives:

> The task of the teacher is one which brings him for hours every day, for many days, and for a number of years, into close contact with his pupils during their most formative years. It is a task which, if well performed, can do more to produce good citizens than all the acts of Parliament ever passed.[58]

Together with parents, teachers played a major role in determining the character of the next generation. According to Menzies, their potential power of influence surpassed that of other leading professionals:

> The teacher does the work of making men. The physician and the surgeon can, at best, repair them; the lawyer can, at best, adjust their differences; and the engineer can, at best, provide them with the means of physical community association; yet, of all these professions, that of teaching is the worst paid, and, broadly speaking, enjoys the least recognition in a social sense.[59]

In an age where society insisted on higher teacher qualifications, Menzies lamented the fact that teachers were paid only a fraction of what was awarded to other trained professionals such as doctors. The Opposition Leader concluded that "A community which was aware of the supreme importance of its educational system would insist upon the highest qualifications for teaching, and would reward those qualifications with adequate remuneration and proper recognition".[60]

Support for Independent Schools
While he was committed to both a strong public and private education sector, Menzies had a special commitment to Commonwealth support for non-government schools which he esteemed as the great incubators of personal

---

[57] Menzies, "Motion on Education", 4617.
[58] Menzies," Motion on Education", 4617
[59] Menzies, "Motion on Education", 4617
[60] Menzies, "Motion on Education", 4618.

individuality, moral character and classic liberal values more broadly. As Bessant appreciates, the private schools epitomised the liberal creed of Menzies with the Liberal Party founder esteeming them for nurturing the qualities of initiative, independence, free-enterprise, self-sacrifice and citizenship.[61] Far from private schools merely representing exclusive bastions of upper-middle class privilege drawn from inherited wealth, Menzies appreciated that these institutions often had humble beginnings where the enterprise, industry and self-sacrifice of parents made it eventually possible for children to receive an alternative education to that provided by the state. The private school therefore epitomised that "independence of spirit" which typified the outlook of Menzies' "Forgotten People".[62] For Menzies, the establishment of independent schools could also provide parents with a degree of variety and choice for their children's education. In contrast to the homogeneity of the socialist state, this free exercise of educational choice was part of the free, liberal society Menzies envisioned.

Eschewing a homogeneous, one-size-fits-all approach to school education, Menzies maintained that a diversity of independent schools was necessary to tailor education to the individual needs of different children and their families. While believing very sincerely in the equality of all human beings, with their souls standing "equal in the sight of God", it was manifest to Menzies that individual pupils varied in their interests, personalities and intellectual capacities, and the approach of teachers needed to reflect this:

> The good teacher is not the one who sees a class as a mass or his own work as a job controlled by routine or rules, but the one who sees his pupils as individuals. They are not to be forced into one mould, but to be encouraged to expand and grow.[63]

Indeed, one of Menzies' chief objections to the socialist philosophy was its insistence on uniformity and the stifling of human individuality. Just as it was wrongheaded for the state to conform its citizens to one mould, Menzies saw the school as having no business to do likewise with its own pupils. Thus, while the objective of school education was to equalise opportunity for all boys and girls, it could not guarantee a uniform pathway and outcome for all, given the natural disparity in individual talents and abilities. In an address to the Federation of Parents and Citizens Associations of NSW, Menzies stated:

> Our great function when we approach the problem of education is to equalise opportunity to see that every boy and girl has a chance to develop whatever fac-

---

[61] Bessant, "Robert Gordon Menzies", 173.
[62] Bessant, "Robert Gordon Menzies", 174.
[63] Robert Menzies, "Sydney Grammar School Appeal", (13 June 1970), 2.

ulties he or she may have, because this will be a tremendous contribution to the good life for the nation, and to their own good life, because there's an immense personal satisfaction in accumulating some of the treasures of the mind. But we're never to fall into the error of thinking that we are all equal in talents, in aptitudes, in industry, in ambition, in energy, because if we are obviously not all identical, one or the other, in this way, it follows that what may be a very proper course of education for one may be inadequate for another, or inappropriate to a third.[64]

Menzies thus saw a vibrant private education sector, supporting a diversity of denominational and specialist schools, as providing the optimal climate for the varying aptitudes, interests and needs of pupils to be individually catered for.

The other attribute of independent schools that Menzies valued was the religious dimension they typically brought to education, given that the vast majority of these had a church foundation. Historically, most private schools in Australia were founded by the churches of Christian denominations, most notably, Catholic, Anglican, Presbyterian and Methodist, together with a small number of schools founded in the Jewish tradition. Menzies viewed religious education, of whatever background, as conducive to good character and good citizenship and was therefore keen for his government to support financially these institutions. In his address to the House of Representatives on the Education motion, Menzies argued that the religious element to education was indispensable:

> I have no hesitation in saying, and I have said it many times before in the course of my life, that I believe that religion gives to people a sensitive understanding of their obligations, and that is something which the world sadly needs at the present time....Nobody can suppose that we are educating our children, except for disaster, by turning them out of purely secular establishments at the age of fourteen, fifteen or sixteen, merely educated to a point at which they think that there is nothing for them to learn, aggressively conscious of what they suppose to be their rights, and oblivious of that penetrating feeling of moral obligations to others, which alone can make a community of men successful.[65]

Having witnessed the barbarism of two world wars in the first half of the twentieth-century, coupled with what he perceived to be a decline of traditional moral standards in the second half, Menzies maintained a steadfast faith in the value of a religiously-informed education.[66] In an address to an assem-

---

[64] Robert Menzies, "Address to Federation of Parents and Citizens' Associations of NSW", (1964 Annual Conference, 14 August 1964), 3.
[65] Menzies, "Motion on Education", 4616.
[66] Menzies, *Measure of the Years*, 93.

bly of students at Sydney's Newington College, he told his audience that the standards of faith and the impulses of the spirit, that church schools such as Newington provided, would "enable them to avoid the bitter wretched paganism that has beset the world in the last 50 years".[67]

Appreciating the need to substantiate his support for independent schools with concrete government assistance, Menzies as Prime Minister took the first initiative to provide state aid to independent schools, particularly those in the Catholic system. His understanding of the dire funding needs for independent schools, however, was evident long before the 1963 state aid decision of his government. As early as 1943, six years before his return to the prime ministership, Menzies had opined that "it is unlikely that the church schools can in the post-war period efficiently survive unless there is some measure of State assistance to them". Foreshadowing the assistance package his government would eventually provide for such schools, Menzies concluded his 1943 address with this appeal:

> My own belief is that…we must all be prepared to come together in the post-war world to devise ways and means of ensuring that those who are content with a purely secular education should be able to get it while those whom such an education will never satisfy should be able to get the kind of training they want for their children without absolutely bankrupting themselves in the process.[68]

The point Menzies made was that under existing arrangements, the parents of private school-educated children unfairly had to pay twice—once as taxpayers for the maintenance of the state schools, and again as parents for the maintenance of their children at church schools.[69] Accordingly, Menzies believed that some state aid for the private sector would relieve the financial burden for parents to pay high fees to send their children to independent schools.

After returning to the prime ministership in December 1949, the first practical measure Menzies introduced to assist independent schools was a 1952 amendment to income tax laws to allow a parent to claim up to £60 for school tuition fees as an allowable deduction. Given that the parents of state school pupils paid little in school fees, the tax concession was of most benefit to private school parents.[70] A further concession Menzies made to the private school sector was a change to the tax laws in 1954 to enable donations made to schools for building purposes to be claimed as tax deductions. The Prime Minister held that this would give a considerable boost to the private school councils which could now more readily obtain gifts from individuals for

---

[67] Robert Menzies, "Speech at Newington College", (Sydney, 29 April 1961), 3.
[68] Menzies, "Future of Education", (1943), 2.
[69] Menzies, "Future of Education", (1943). 2.
[70] Bessant, "Robert Gordon Menzies", 175.

school buildings.[71] In 1956, the Menzies government gave the first direct aid to private schools in Canberra, whereby the Commonwealth undertook to reimburse the interest (up to 5% per annum) paid on loans raised to finance new schools or extensions.[72] Indeed, Menzies regarded this last decision as the precursor to what he would describe as "a quite revolutionary change in Government education policy" with the announcement of state aid in November 1963.[73]

Announcing an assistance package in his policy speech for the 1963 election, the Menzies government pledged to fund science blocks for all schools to the tune of £5 million, and similar amounts of £5 million annually for state technical education. In addition, the government launched a Commonwealth Scholarship scheme offering an annual grant of 10,000 scholarships to secondary school students. Like the funding for science and technical education, the two-year scholarships would be open to students of all secondary schools, both state and independent, without discrimination. The funding for science would accomplish the material goal of aiding technological progress and national development while the scholarships would advance Menzies' objective of raising an educated generation of future leaders to run the country. The extra funding measures were particularly welcomed by Australia's Catholic community that had been long aggrieved by the lack of financial help from governments. As a mark of appreciation, the Catholic Church hosted the Presbyterian Menzies as guest of honour at its 1964 Cardinal's Dinner.[74] According to John Howard, the historic decision of Menzies on state aid not only rectified the injustice felt by Australia's Catholics for over a century, but helped to reduce the sectarian divisions in Australian society still raw in the early 1960s.[75]

As Melleuish observed, there was a consistency in Menzies' philosophy and approach to education from his days as a young Victorian state MP in the late 1920s to his retirement years as an elder statesman in the 1970s.[76] The consistency of his thought on the essential character-building role of education, the primacy of "pure learning" in the humanities, the importance of both humanist and religious values, and the mission of education to produce good citizens could be attributed to a sustained liberal philosophy that affirmed human dignity and the mutual obligations of citizens in civil society. Indeed Menzies regarded education and an authentic liberalism as symbiotic whereby an education, particularly in the humanities, would serve to inculcate

---

[71] Bessant, "Robert Gordon Menzies", 175.
[72] Bessant, "Robert Gordon Menzies", 175.
[73] Menzies, *Measure of the Years*, 92.
[74] Robert Menzies, Speech by the Prime Minister, The Cardinal's Dinner, (Sydney, 30 July 1964), 1-6.
[75] Howard, *The Menzies Era*, 314.
[76] Melleuish, "Sir Robert Menzies and Australian Education", 264.

in citizens the liberal values of individual enterprise, free inquiry, moral character and human understanding that, in turn, provided the optimal climate for education to flourish.

Certainly, this was Menzies' vision and the reforms inspired by the Murray Report led to a burgeoning higher education sector of new public universities, while state aid to Catholic and private schools opened the gate to the proliferation of new independent schools in Australian towns and suburbs. Although Menzies would have no doubt been gratified by this ensuing growth of education, the evolution of the universities, especially, into large vocational training centres reliant on revenue would have been at odds with his vision for universities as seats of humane learning and civilised ideals. The approach of Menzies to education reveals that he was both a traditionalist and a moderniser who strove to make education accessible to more citizens, especially women, yet at the same time, desired educational establishments to remain true to their founding character and purpose. The Australia in which Menzies brought his philosophy and approach to education was a vastly different society from that of today, nevertheless, the educational vision of Menzies for institutions to produce erudite, cultured and well-rounded graduates, with a humane understanding of their obligations, is a salutary reminder to the academy that the education business is infinitely more than just a commercial enterprise.

The Need for Discipline

Greg Melleuish

The biggest problem of education in Australia has been the decline of standards in literacy and numeracy which can be seen in the decline of Australian students in international rankings in these areas. A modern society in which technology plays such a crucial role needs to have a citizenry which is not just proficient in its capacity to read, write and do mathematics but who have a high level of rational and logical thought. Such capacities are required not just for reasons relating to technology but also because democracy assumes a citizenry which is capable of discussing public affairs in an intelligent fashion. In any case, individuals benefit from having their intellectual capacities developed and expanded.

The big problem is that current educational practices do not deliver in this regard. I believe that there is a correlation between the decline in public debate, and the capacity of the wider population to conduct rational debate, and the decline of rigour and discipline in educational practices. Modern educational practices have produced a population which is more highly educated in terms of credentials than any in history but which lacks the genuine capacity for rational and critical thought. This can be seen in the rhetorical devices designed to appeal to the emotions used by the advocates of Anthropogenic climate change and the recent campaign in favour of same sex marriage.

It is extraordinary that the leading articles of nineteenth century Australian newspapers were far more rational and cogently argued than those found today in so-called quality newspapers. This was in colonies which did not possess a high level of education in formal terms. In his memoirs, Billy Hughes describes the papers delivered at Leigh House, a working person's educational institution in Sydney, in the early 1890s which offered lectures on Marx, Spencer, Henry George and Kant, writers many graduates would struggle with today.[1] Closer to the present, Ben Chifley, Prime Minister of Australia from 1945 to 1949, filled his speeches with economic detail, assuming that his listeners could follow such expositions.[2] Chifley had been an engine driver and a self-taught economist.

---

[1] W.M. Hughes, *Crusts and Crusades: Tales of Bygone Days* (Sydney: Angus & Robertson, 1948), 73.
[2] A.W. Stargardt, ed., *Things Worth Fighting For: Speeches by Joseph Benedict Chifley* (Melbourne: Melbourne University Press, 1952).

One does not need to read editorials in the newspapers of the twenty-first century carefully to absorb their arguments and to see if such arguments are justified by evidence. They are exercises in rhetoric which aim to strike an emotional chord with the reader.

There has been a failure in contemporary Australian democracy to produce an educated rational citizenry. The development of democratic government in Australia is closely linked to the birth and subsequent growth of educational institutions in this country. Universal primary education was introduced in the various colonies in the 1870s; in the wake of a second education revolution in the 1950s there was a massive increase in both secondary and tertiary education. Perversely there seems to be a relationship between the growth of institutional education and the quality of public debate in Australia. Why should this be? Can it be reversed? These are the questions which this essay pursues. It argues that the real problem with modern education lies with liberalism and its belief that individuals can pursue any activity so long as they do not harm others. This leads to two conclusions. The first is that utility is the best tool for evaluating a course of action. The second is that there is no real difference between a vocation and an avocation; pushpin really is as good as poetry.

Under the reign of liberalism what is lost is the pre-liberal emphasis on discipline as the basis of educational practice, on the idea that in order to achieve mastery in an area of human activity it is necessary to make demands on individuals that limit their autonomy and freedom. In its place education in a liberal age emphasises that one should simply pursue those things which one finds interesting, those things which will lead to the maximum amount of pleasure. The consequence is that human beings under liberalism fail to meet their full potential. While human beings may be plastic entities in that they are capable of doing a variety of things, to mould that plasticity in a particular direction requires considerable effort. It does not come naturally; it requires discipline.

The connection between learning and discipline has long been recognised. The word *shastra* in Sanskrit, meaning science, is derived from the verb *shas* which means to teach or punish.[3] This connection between punishment and learning is also found in the Indo-European languages of the West. Discipline, an area of study, also means to chastise or punish to bring about correct behaviour. Discipline derives from the Latin *discipulus* which is also the source of the word disciple. *Discipulus* and *shastra* are etymologically distinct (Doniger links *shas* to chastise) but both demonstrate a linkage between two areas which to the modern mind would seem to be distinct. This linkage reflects a long held belief, that properly conducted learning requires discipline in

---

[3] Wendy Doniger, *Hindus: an alternative history* (Oxford: Oxford University Press, 2009), 309.

the sense that to master an area of study requires dedication, hard work and a willingness to forgo other activities in the pursuit of that goal. In the nineteenth century, it was recognised that liberal education meant the mastering of quite difficult subject areas including classical languages and mathematics. It was the mastery of these disciplines which enabled a student to have the necessary tools to engage in intellectual life. Now it seems to mean sitting around and discussing topics without any real knowledge of them. Modern education seems to believe that learning does not require any discipline, only the unleashing of a student's 'natural' capacity to learn. The student does not need to become a 'disciple'.

Whether we like it or not, the reality is that to master any kind of skill requires hard work and discipline so that the body, and the mind develop the capacity to do what is required in an apparently natural fashion. But, of course, there is nothing natural about the skill which even a gifted athlete or musician demonstrates, no matter how gifted they may be. The gift needs to be cultivated and nourished so that it can flourish. Human beings, and their plastic natures, need to be moulded, and then to mould themselves, if they are to achieve a high level of expertise in any particular domain.

This is reflected in traditional forms of education. For example, in the Roman world the desired excellence was in rhetoric. Students were attached to a particular teacher and would become part of his 'family'. Beginning with grammar, they would immerse themselves in the important texts, including memorising significant passages, as well as learning the art of rhetoric. This was demanding and required the total absorption of the student into its world.[4]

Liberal education as it emerged in the nineteenth century did not consist in sitting around and discussing the nature of the world and human existence. It involved discipline. Again it required absorption in classical texts and a high level of skill in philology and/or mathematics.

What has changed in the modern world? I think that the answer is liberalism, especially the liberalism which emphasised the need to unleash the human personality from the chains in which it had been placed by the world or society or even educational practices. It assumes the goodness of human nature and the innate capacity for human beings to learn and to know. The real problem for a liberal is that human beings refuse to follow the path which God and nature have established for them:

> GOD makes all things good; man meddles with them and they become evil. He forces one soil to yield the products of another, one tree to bear another's fruit. He confuses and confounds time, place, and natural conditions. He mutilates his dog, his horse, and his slave. He destroys and defaces all things; he loves all that

---

[4] Edward J Watts, *The Final Pagan Generation* (Oakland: University of California Press, 2015), 51-58.

is deformed and monstrous; he will have nothing as nature made it, not even man himself, who must learn his paces like a saddle-horse, and be shaped to his master's taste like the trees in his garden.[5]

Liberalism was a reaction to the restraints of ancien regime Europe which embodied principles of hierarchy, aristocracy and privilege. Such a society could be understood as being founded on artifice as opposed to nature. To follow nature was to discover the true self as opposed to the artificial self which society constructed. Hence true liberty exists when the state takes the shackles off individuals, thereby allowing them the space not only to flourish but also to develop their capacities as a fully rounded individual, as can be seen in the following quotation from Humboldt:

> This individual vigour, then, and manifold diversity, combine themselves in *originality;* and hence, that on which the consummate grandeur of our nature ultimately depends,—that towards which every human being must ceaselessly direct his efforts, and on which especially those who design to influence their fellow men must ever keep their eyes, is the *Individuality of Power and Development.* Just as this individuality springs naturally from the perfect freedom of action, and the greatest diversity in the agents, it tends immediately to produce them in turn. Even inanimate nature, which, proceeding in accordance with unchangeable laws, advances by regular grades of progression, appears more individual to the man who has been developed in his individuality. He transports himself, as it were, into the very centre of nature; and it is true, in the highest sense, that each still perceives the beauty and rich abundance of the outer world, in the exact measure in which he is conscious of their existence in his own soul. How much sweeter and closer must this correspondence become between effect and cause,—this reaction between internal feeling and outward perception,—when man is not only passively open to external sensations and impressions, but is himself also an agent![6]

Notice the emphasis on originality, as if one can only be original if one is free from restraint. Traditionally, one is only able to be free from restraint, as for example in Plotinus and most forms of mysticism, if one has undergone a long period of preparation. It is hard work moving beyond the darkness of the cave. In the modern liberal world all one has to do to be free is to cast off the limitations of society. Fulfilment is through limiting those restraints and allowing human nature its full capacity to develop. It can be achieved in an easy and comfortable fashion.

---

[5] J J Rousseau, *Emile,* http://oll.libertyfund.org/titles/rousseau-emile-or-education, accessed 23/9/2017.
[6] W von Humboldt, *The Spheres and Duties of Government,* http://oll.libertyfund.org/titles/humboldt-the-sphere-and-duties-of-government-1792-1854, accessed 23/9/2017.

A similar view can be found expressed by John Stuart Mill. Mill saw convention as the great enemy and tradition as something which prevented dynamic and energetic human beings from fulfilling their potential by looking for ever new ways of doing things.

> This question really depends upon a still more fundamental one, viz., which of two common types of character, for the general good of humanity, it is most desirable should predominate—the active, or the passive type; that which struggles against evils, or that which endures them; that which bends to circumstances, or that which endeavours to make circumstances bend to itself.

> In proportion as success in life is seen or believed to be the fruit of fatality or accident, and not of exertion, in that same ratio does envy develop itself as a point of national character. The most envious of all mankind are the Orientals.[7]

On this basis, he held India in very low regard as a place which lacked energy and vitality. Hence Indians were not worthy of self-government; he was incapable of seeing the extraordinary achievements of Indian civilisation because they were traditional. Modern linguistics would not exist without Sanskrit.[8] But all Mill could see was a people who had a so-called static civilisation.

This, of course, is the problem. Humboldt and Mill wished to break free of the restraints which tradition had supposedly placed on individuals. But this meant breaking free of the constraints which have long been the foundation of a good and thorough education.

Pierre Manent has also argued that modern liberalism is an attempt to escape from the restraints which both republicanism/classicism and Christianity had placed on human beings. In both cases pursuit of the ideals involved placing restraints on the human personality. The pursuit of magnanimity and civic virtue and the pursuit of humility both limit human beings and force them to pursue practices which do not allow the soul to flourish as it could. It is painful to follow the discipline required to achieve virtue, a pain which chafes because it reminds people that the attainment of virtue requires great effort which may go against the inclination to do as one pleases. Modern humans simply wish to escape from the demands which the pursuit of virtue makes and to be left alone.[9]

Human beings are naturally plastic. That plasticity is what enables them to adapt to changing circumstances. In this sense, there is no fixed ideal of

---

[7] John Stuart Mill, *On Liberty, Representative Government, The Subjection of Women* (London: Oxford University Press, 1971), 190, 192.
[8] Sheldon Pollock, *The Language of the Gods in the World of Men: Sanskrit, Culture and Power in Premodern India* (Berkeley: University of California press, 2006), 164.
[9] Pierre Manent, *The City of Man*, Trans. Marc A Lepain (Princeton: Princeton University Press, 1997), 181.

'nature' to which human beings can aspire. There are paths down which human beings travel; those paths require that human beings have their natures shaped and moulded appropriately.[10] To pursue a particular path of virtue means shaping human nature in a particular way and this cannot be done without individual human beings submitting to discipline.

Liberalism has a universal model of human nature which essentially pours scorn on those sorts of activities which do not fit its model. Liberalism sees only one way to 'enlightenment' and that way displacing practices which require discipline in the 'primitive' past. In their place it advocates protean individuals who can express their true nature once restraints are removed. In reality, given that the ways of discipline constitute most of human culture prior to the age of liberalism, this means that the 'free' individual is left with a fairly empty model of human nature. That empty space comes to be occupied by utilitarianism.

Utilitarianism as the modern ideal replaces restraint in the name of an ideal with a way of life which is devoted to comfort and the avoidance of pain.[11] This model of human nature has considerable implications for education and for what is seen to be required for someone to acquire a competence in a particular area. If human beings are understood to possess an unlimited potential by nature, then the way to unleash that potential is by creating the appropriate conditions under which it will flourish. Individuals can be left to pursue what particular activity catches their fancy. It becomes a matter of following one's path because it is pleasurable and provides one with the maximum amount of utility. If an activity is painful then it should be avoided. The pathway to acquiring knowledge and skill is the one which affords the maximum amount of pleasure.

In part, this is a consequence of living in an age of comfort where the objective is to live a life which is as comfortable as possible and in which such things as struggle, competition and pain are reduced to a minimum; life is indeed meant to be easy. This can be seen in a number of areas.

One is in the technology of sporting goods. Traditional tennis racquets were made of wood and required considerable skill in their use if one was to hit the ball in the 'sweet spot'. Today, much larger racquets have increased the ease with which one can make a good shot. Much the same is true of developments in the manufacture of golf clubs.

Technology is utilised to make things easier; when things are made easier, the level of skill required to carry out a task is reduced accordingly. The same is true in the training of the mind. It is well known that a fairly basic technol-

---

[10] See G Melleuish & S Rizzo, "Limits of naturalism: Plasticity, Finitude and the Imagination", *Cosmos & History*. 2015, Vol. 11 Issue 1, 221-238.
[11] G Melleuish, "Living in an age of comfort: understanding religion in the twenty first century", *Telos*, 166, Spring 2014, 9-24.

ogy, writing, has the effect of reducing the human capacity to remember things. Illiterate people have much better memories than literate ones because literate people have acquired an aid to their memory. Even then, it is worth noting that much of traditional education was taken up with memorising long slabs of literature, especially poetry. This is true in non-Western cultures; it is considered a great thing in the Islamic world to be able to recite the whole of the Quran.

It could be argued that writing both diminished human capacities and enhanced them, and there is truth in this assertion as human beings used writing to develop capacities that only come with the skill of writing. It allows human beings to develop their ideas, and learning how to write instils both discipline and a training of the mind, especially in terms of hand-eye coordination. There is a certain joy in putting pen and ink to paper and good handwriting very easily becomes a form of artistic expression. There is a trade-off between written and oral expression. Writing might lessen the capacity of the human mind to remember large amounts of text, but it also develops a whole range of other skills, particularly with regard to particular modes of rationality, as A.D. Luria demonstrates.[12] Similar observations could be made regarding the use of written numerals and musical notation, which both reduce certain skills and enhance others.

My mother left school at the age of fourteen to work in a department store, which meant that she had to sell lengths of cloth in imperial measurements which were bought in pounds, shillings and pence. Whether that is done mentally or on a piece of paper, it still requires considerable mental acuity. Now consider the case of the introduction of calculators. When I was at school I used the most advanced device for mathematicians, the slide rule. The introduction of the calculator has certainly made life easier for all concerned; it has also reduced the need for individuals to be precise in their mathematical calculations, as a machine does it for them. The effect is somewhat similar for the tennis or golf player. Near enough is now good enough. One does not need to hone one's skills, to be precise. Having calculators and decimal coinage and modes of measurement certainly has made life easier.

Traditional educational practices assumed that the attainment of a high level of skill required considerable dedication and sacrifice; it could not be done without some pain. There was equally an expectation that students undergoing such training would be occasionally riotous and needed opportunities to let off steam. It had to be rigorous because even with writing and a simple number system which included zero, there was a lack of mechanical devices to make life easy.

---

[12] A.D. Luria, *Cognitive Development: Its Cultural and Social Foundations*, Trans. Martin Lopez-Morillas and Lynn Solotaroff (Cambridge Mass.: Harvard University Press, 1976), especially Chapter 5.

The question must now be asked: if writing conferred considerable advantages on individuals even if it lessened their capacity to memorise material, then what advantages does the use of calculators and other kinds of computing assistance, such as spell checkers, confer on those who use them? The answer invariably given is that it allows students to tap into their creative and their critical powers because they no longer have to devote their talents to learning what are considered to be lower level skills and a form of drudgery.

This might seem quite sensible, except one might ask: what is the basis of these 'creative powers'? The assumption would seem to be that everyone possesses such powers as a gift from nature and the objective of education is to provide the conditions under which they can be unleashed. Apparently, they do not require careful cultivation of human capacities; they do not require discipline. That one can be creative without possessing any real skills is a liberal fallacy.

Part of the problem is that human beings have a natural inclination to take the path of least resistance. Human beings have a plastic nature but, as has been argued, that plasticity does not enable them to acquire new skills and capabilities without a considerable amount of effort. A small minority does possess both the capacity and the energy to master skills in what looks like an effortless fashion. But that is not true of the great majority of human beings. If they are to attain a skill they must endure what is required to obtain that mastery. When that mastery comes, it can lead to great pride in having achieved something which initially appeared to be out of reach.

The problem, as has been argued, is that modern liberalism began in the belief human nature was being limited and restricted by the institutions and structures of society. To flourish it should have those restrictions on it removed. But what if the consequence of lifting those restrictions and limitations is to discourage the pursuit of difficult and arduous activities? Benjamin Constant, at the very birth of modern liberalism, recognised that modern liberty could not compel individuals to use their talents to work with others for the common good.[13] Modern individuals are free to cultivate their gardens and to do as they please. Compulsion becomes a dirty word and individuals are free to waste their talents if that is what they wish to do. The only liberal principle which applies is that their actions should not bring harm to others.

In a similar vein Alexis de Tocqueville argued that one of the characteristics of modern democracy is its fondness for comfort:

> The love of well-being is there displayed as a tenacious, exclusive, universal passion; but its range is confined. To build enormous palaces, to conquer or to

---

[13] Benjamin Constant, "The Liberty of the Ancients compared with that of the Moderns", in *Benjamin Constant Political Writings*, ed. and trans. Biancamaria Fontana (Cambridge University Press, Cambridge, 1988), 310–11.

mimic nature, to ransack the world in order to gratify the passions of a man, is not thought of: but to add a few roods of land to your field, to plant an orchard, to enlarge a dwelling, to be always making life more comfortable and convenient, to avoid trouble, and to satisfy the smallest wants without effort and almost without cost. These are small objects, but the soul clings to them; it dwells upon them closely and day by day, till they at last shut out the rest of the world, and sometimes intervene between itself and heaven.[14]

Now it is true that many individuals follow pursuits which interest them with a vigour and energy which can be quite astonishing. Modern liberalism encourages them to follow their avocations primarily because it makes no judgements regarding their value. And this is the problem; while it is very pleasant to have an avocation it is not necessarily the case that many of these avocations have any real value beyond providing a degree of pleasure and satisfaction for those who pursue them. In a liberal view of the world this is justification enough; such avocations have utility in that they bring pleasure. They may even be justified on the grounds that they provide an economic benefit. Avocations can be both pleasurable and profitable.

What liberalism cannot justify is the pursuit of virtue. Virtues may not be either profitable or pleasurable. They might very easily make demands on the individual which require him or her to abandon their avocations in favour of more serious activities. Despite the best efforts of Seneca, Nero preferred to cultivate his artistic avocation rather than undergo the discipline required to pursue the vocation of ruling the Roman Empire. By way of contrast, in our own age, one can only admire the considerable discipline which the Queen exercises as she carries out her public duties. The fact that the behaviour of Her Majesty stands out is an indication of the character of our age. It is an age of avocation because it is also an age of comfort. It is not an age in which individuals struggle to achieve great things.

The idea that an avocation is as worthwhile as a vocation has considerable consequences for education, especially the type of education which is practised in an age of comfort. If the desire is to pursue those forms of activity which one finds easy and pleasurable, then a student is able to avoid studying those subject areas which are hard and difficult and might therefore cause pain. There is no overall ideal of what an educated person might look like as has previously been the case, only a desire that they should be able to fulfil their talents, whatever they might be. Or, that they have the 'skills' required by a society for whom the only justification for anything is utility.

The natural consequence of such a view of education is that students tend to avoid those subjects which make a demand on them and pursue those

---

[14] Alexis de Tocqueville, *Democracy in America*, trans. Henry Reeve, http://www.bostonleadershipbuilders.com/tocqueville/book2-2.htm, accessed 23/9/2017.

which are easier. To take one example, there has been a flight from difficult subjects in the New South Wales HSC over the past fifty years. In 1967 there were a little over 18,000 candidates. Of these 16, 497 did Mathematics, 1538 did Latin, 6709 did French and 7976 did Economics. In 2016 there were 67000 HSCs awarded. 8671 did 2 unit Maths, the equivalent of Maths in 1967, 164 did Latin, 779 did Continuers French and 5196 did Economics.[15] Even with the cohort five times the size of that of 1967 the numbers of students doing the level of Mathematics which taught calculus halved!

Given the emphasis which is now placed on STEM subjects in contemporary society, the decline in the number of students who have studied the foundations of modern mathematics is astonishing. And this is matched by the number of students who study languages. Things which are difficult are off the table for large portions of Generation Snowflake and are replaced by things which are easy. Too many of them fancy themselves as modern day Neros who have creative artistic gifts to share with the world. The decline of 'hard subjects' at school is explained by the unholy alliance of utility and avocation, and both are an expression of the failure of liberalism to provide any guidance regarding the nature and purpose of education.

The decline has another side which is the demonization of those cultures, largely from East Asia and India, which continue to impose discipline on their children. Consequently, students from these backgrounds perform very well in subjects such as mathematics because they are encouraged to put in a lot of extra work. This may well mean sacrificing other activities in the pursuit of academic success. It also means having coaching to ensure that they are successful in winning entry to selective schools, thereby leading to claims that they are 'gaming the system' by those who are unwilling to impose such discipline on their children.

This is essentially the cry of those wedded to a culture of comfort against those who insist on a more traditional disciplined approach. Children should be allowed to be children and play and enjoy themselves. Its advocates fail to see that this vision of childhood is far from being 'natural' and represents a particular modern cultural pattern. For much of history the life of most children was nasty, brutish and short. Moreover, this vision of childhood as fun is buttressed by a view that those who follow the path of discipline lack genuine creativity but are only highly proficient technicians.

Apart from being highly racist, this view flies in the face of the history of the West. The creative thinkers of the West until the twentieth century enjoyed a rigorous disciplined education, either classical or mathematical/ scientific in nature. Certainly, they were not captive to that education, but it formed the basis on which they were able to develop their ideas. One does

---

[15] These figures can be found at http://www.boardofstudies.nsw.edu.au/ebos/static/ebos_stats.html and http://www.boardofstudies.nsw.edu.au/bos_stats/, accessed 23/9/2017.

not become creative if one's mind has been emptied of its furniture. One just floats empty and vacuous ideas. Being creative without some sort of disciplined training is very much like building the house on the sand.

The decline of such disciplined education may very well explain why as more and more individuals achieve higher and higher levels of credentialed education the capacity for critical and creative thinking in the wider culture has declined. It would appear to be the case that logical and rational argument based on empirical evidence is increasingly being replaced by rhetoric and appeals to the emotions in public debate. Governments routinely fail to provide detailed evidence to justify their actions. Advocates for radical change routinely twist and distort their arguments and, even, tell lies. This is what happens when 'creativity' without discipline becomes the focus of education.

It may be argued that the development of mass education in a democratic society necessarily leads to a dilution of rigour in its educational practices. I do not believe this to be the case. The evidence seems to indicate that an increase in formal education is related to a lower standard of rationality in the society, i.e., individuals with a lower level of formal education in the past had a greater capacity for rational argument than equivalent individuals today with a higher level of formal education.

The real culprit is liberalism and its accompanying philosophy of self-expression, creativity and individual development. Much as liberalism is desirable in its respect for individual autonomy, one of the consequences of that autonomy is to encourage educational practices which lack rigour and discipline. At the same time, a liberal society assumes individuals who possess a certain type of personality, one which is capable of disinterested rational thought, even though its educational practices might militate against the development of such a personality.

There is an unwillingness to face up to this fairly fundamental contradiction of a liberal society, which requires disciplined individuals if it is to function properly, yet encourages education practices which discourage the development of such individuals. At an intellectual level, this means that the principles underpinning liberalism need to be reconsidered and the whole issue of autonomy re-evaluated. To become an individual may require that one lose one's autonomy for a period so that it can be reclaimed at a later stage. There is also a need to recognise that the nature of liberalism is such that it cannot provide answers to a whole range of questions regarding the nature of the good life.

The real question is how one is to reinstitute a regime of discipline in a culture which is so addicted to comfort and which panders to the quest for ease and self-indulgence. It is like reforming addicts in a society which is largely composed of addicts and which views non-addicts as weird. It is an indication of how peculiar the current situation is when those who lose out to the more disciplined seek not to emulate them but to find ways of undermining them.

And yet it is definitely the case that those who are willing to submit to discipline will outperform those who do not. The real issue is to find the means whereby young people are encouraged to study subjects which are difficult so that when they perform well they are rewarded. There are two possible routes one could propose to encourage much more disciplined educational practices.

The first is top down. The Commonwealth government recognises that educational standards have declined in Australia. Australia's place in the international pecking order regarding proficiency in English and mathematics has declined over the years. There needs to be an attempt to remedy this situation by the encouragement of teaching practices which are both vigorous and rigorous. Just how far governments can change teaching practices is questionable. The problem is that the liberal way is entrenched in the culture and influences teaching practices and the way in which teachers are trained.

The second is bottom up. Parents must make choices which enable their children to develop their capacities. As it stands most parents accept the liberal myth and believe that the key to education is to unlock the creative potential of their children. Parents also tend to think in liberal, that is to say utilitarian, terms. The evidence would seem to indicate that education based on liberalism does not work. A common response is to deny the evidence and seek ways to undermine those who are successful, a common postmodernist practice; or one can accept the reality, a utilitarian reality, that educational practices based on liberalism are self-defeating.

The big hope is that both parents and government will see the reality which is before their eyes; that educational practices which have their origins in liberalism promise liberal autonomy even as they fail to deliver the capacities which make that autonomy possible. One suspects, unfortunately, that only a major crisis will force the hand of both governments and parents. Human beings have a remarkable capacity for pretending that all is well and problems will correct themselves. And an educational system which increasingly fails to develop capacities for rational thought only makes the situation worse.

The Concept of Equality in Education

Steven Schwartz

Bewilder'd in the maze of schools

Alexander Pope, *An Essay on Criticism* (1709)

As Socrates discovered when he challenged the teachers' union of his time, education is political, and dissenters pay a heavy price. Education disputes are less lethal today; rebels no longer pay with their lives. It's only their careers that die.

Each day brings another skirmish in a seemingly endless education war. Some battles concern technical issues such as how children should be taught to read. Other fights are about the content of the school curriculum. What should students learn about history, religion and culture? Teachers' unions campaign against national assessments while employers want more vocational training to prepare graduates for work. Conservatives worry that identity politics is destroying social cohesion while progressive educators seek a curriculum that respects "difference". The most intractable quarrels are about money—how much is needed, how it is distributed and how it is spent.

Whatever their backgrounds, when it comes to education, even sworn enemies agree that all children deserve equal treatment. Who could disagree? There is one small problem. Opponents disagree about what they mean by equal. Resolving these disputes is difficult because they are clashes of values, cultural crusades, in which each side considers the other immoral.

Private schooling is a prime example. In an article titled, "If You Send Your Kid to Private School, You Are a Bad Person", Allison Benedikt calls parents who send their children to private schools "morally bankrupt".[1] Alan Bennett, author of the widely admired play, *The History Boys*, claims private education is "unfair" and "not Christian either". He says that "souls ... are equal in the sight of God and thus deserving of ... a level playing field".[2] Omitting the part about God, the Australian Broadcasting Corporation takes

---

[1] Allison Benedikt, "If You Send Your Kid to Private School, You are a Bad Person," *Slate*. 29 Aug 2013. http://www.slate.com/articles/double_x/doublex/2013/08/private_school_vs_public_school_only_bad_people_send_their_kids_to_private.html

[2] Alan Bennett, "Fair Play," *London Review of Books*, 36, no. 12 (2014): 29-30.

a similar view. In a website purportedly designed to help parents decide whether to choose public or private schooling for their children, the ABC urges parents to eschew private schooling and "bring back some balance".[3]

Ad hominem name-calling (bad person, morally corrupt, not Christian) obscures substantive issues. Instead of focussing on the character of commentators, it is more illuminating to examine the logic and values underlying their rhetoric. Using the debate about private schooling as an example, this essay aims to clarify what is meant by equality in education and to consider ways to achieve it.

First, A Few Facts About "Private" Schools

As noted, debates about schooling are about values, and we are each entitled to our own, but there exists only one set of facts. So, let's get those straight from the outset.

Around one-third of Australian students are enrolled in non-government (independent and Catholic) schools.[4] Critics commonly refer to these schools as "private", a label intended to make them sound exclusive and perhaps to imply that they are profit-making organisations. Because the term is in wide use, especially in respect of the best-known schools, this essay will also refer to non-government schools as "private". However, it is important to note that virtually all of these schools are non-profit charitable institutions and only a small number deserve to be called elite.

Critics often assume otherwise. They portray private schools as privileged and exclusive, their students the scions of wealthy families. This description certainly applies to some private schools and their students, but not the majority. The non-government sector also includes schools catering to families of average income, remote indigenous schools run by local communities, special needs schools for children with disabilities and schools for students who have been excluded from public schools.[5] Some do not even charge tuition fees. Counting fees, gifts and government subsidies, the resources available to independent and Catholic schools are remarkably similar to the funding available to public schools.[6]

---

[3] Cristen Tilley, Ben Spraggon and Nathan Hoad, "You Decide: Should You Send Your Kids to Public or Private School." Australian Broadcasting Corporation. 30 January 2018. http://www.abc.net.au/news/2018-01-31/public-vs-private-school-you-decide/8380290
[4] "Schools, Australia 2017," Australian Bureau of Statistics. 2 Feb 2018. http://www.abs.gov.au/ausstats/abs@.nsf/mf/4221.0
[5] Colette Coleman, "We Hear the Same Lazy Myths About 'Private Schools', But the Term is Meaningless," ABC News. 14 February 2018. http://www.abc.net.au/news/2018-02-14/independent-schools-not-private-and-not-always-rich/9421584
[6] Jennifer Buckingham, "Debate About Independent Schools Must Move Beyond Stereotypes," *Sydney Morning Herald*, 1 Feb 2016. http://www.smh.com.au/comment/debate-about-independent-schools-must-move-beyond-stereotypes-20160131-gmhwbj.html; Jennifer Buckingham, "The Truth About

With these facts in mind, let's turn to the concept of equality. As applied to education, equality may refer to the resources available to schools, their admissions policies (open to all students or just a select few) or how much their students learn (as measured by scores on standardised tests). These features of the education landscape are observable, quantifiable and objective. However, equality may also allude to philosophical concepts that are not so easily measured such as justice, impartiality and a "fair go". The next section focuses on easily measurable indicators of equality; abstract ideas about equality are covered later in the essay.

Objective Measures of Equality

Opponents of private education say that forcing all students to attend public schools will create a "level playing field". This phrase could be taken to mean that public schools provide an equal education to all their students but, when looked at empirically, schools turn out to be far from equal.

It is true that all schools teach some version of the Australian Curriculum, but those with superior resources may supplement their teaching with additional subjects, provide more elaborate facilities (swimming pools, sporting grounds) and offer a greater range of extra-curricular activities. The differences between schools are extreme. Rural and remote schools (private as well as public) may lack basic internet connectivity while selective metropolitan schools (public and private) offer state-of-the-art computing facilities. Class sizes and teacher qualifications also vary widely across both public and private schools. When it comes to resources, neither the private nor the public sector can claim their schools are all equal.

Student selection policies also vary. Unlike most public schools, which accept all local students, private schools usually get to choose the students they admit. Critics of private education believe that sharing classes with other selected students confers an advantage on private school students. They often neglect to mention that some public schools are also selective, and their students experience the same advantage.

Learning, as measured by standardised tests such as the National Assessment Program—Literacy and Numeracy (NAPLAN) also differs widely among schools. Some differences are the result of exceptional teaching, but most of the variability in performance relates to social status. That is, students from wealthy families perform better on standardised tests than those from disadvantaged families. This relationship holds true for both private and public schools.[7]

Private Schools," *Issue Analysis*, no. 13, 1 Aug 2000. https://www.cis.org.au/app/uploads/2015/07/ia13.pdf
[7] Trever Cobbold, "Thirty Studies and 15 Years Later: Review Shows Public Schools Produce Same Results," *Sydney Morning Herald*, 20 April 2015. http://www.smh.com.au/national/education/thirty-

In summary, objective equality is not a feature of Australian education. Within both the private and the public sector, schools differ in their resources, admissions policies and learning outcomes. Since public schools are not all equal, why do critics believe that forcing all students to attend them will produce a level playing field? To answer this question, we must move from objective measures of equality to consider more abstract ideas such as "equality of opportunity".

Equality of Opportunity

Although the critics of private education rarely mention it, parents' right to choose private education is enshrined in international agreements as well as in state and territory acts. These legal instruments have been adopted by various Australian governments and promulgated by the Australian Human Rights Commission.[8] An example is the United Nations' *International Covenant on Economic, Social and Cultural Rights* (ICESCR), which states:

> Parties ... undertake to have respect for the liberty of parents and, when applicable, legal guardians, to choose for their children schools, other than those established by the public authorities, which conform to such minimum educational standards as may be laid down or approved by the State. (Article 13, Paragraph 3).[9]

It could not be clearer. The ICESCR, which holds the force of law, confirms that Australian parents and guardians are free to enrol their children in government-approved private schools if they wish. This right has been reaffirmed by a more recent agreement (the United Nations' *Convention on the Rights of the Child*), which affirms "the liberty of individuals and bodies to establish and direct educational institutions".[10]

The United Nations and the Australian Human Rights Commission are not dominated by snobby right-wing reactionaries dedicated to protecting the privileges of the wealthy. Quite the contrary. Yet, both organisations uphold the right of parents to send their children to private schools. Why do critics judge parents immoral for exercising an internationally respected legal right?

---

studies-and-15--years-later-review-shows-public-schools-produce-same-results-20150415-1mlrvg.html

[8] "Right to Education," Australian Human Rights Commission. Accessed 1 Feb 2018.
https://www.humanrights.gov.au/right-education

[9] Office of the High Commissioner for Human Rights. "International Covenant on Economic, Social and Cultural Rights," United Nations. (1976).
http://www.ohchr.org/EN/ProfessionalInterest/Pages/CESCR.aspx

[10] United Nations Convention on the Rights of the Child. (1990).
http://www.ohchr.org/EN/ProfessionalInterest/Pages/CRC.aspx

The answer lies in the existence of other rights that critics believe should take precedence.

Rights inflation is a well-known problem for policymakers. Once governments get in the business of specifying them, rights tend to multiply, get tangled and even conflict. For example, the ICESCR, which acknowledges the right to private schooling also guarantees every child the right to an "equal opportunity for education". As critics point out, not everyone has the chance to attend a private school; some families cannot afford the fees. Thus, private schooling violates the right to equal opportunity; closing private schools will level the educational playing field. Note that equal opportunity, at least in this form, does nothing to ensure that public schools provide all students with an equal education; it merely compels everyone to attend them.[11]

Stephen Pinker illustrates the moral problem with such a "levelling down" approach to equality with an old Russian joke from the communist era.[12] Igor and Boris are peasants who can barely afford to feed their families. They have few possessions and little money, but Boris owns a scrawny old goat. One day a magic fairy appears to Igor and grants him one wish. Igor wishes for Boris's goat to die. The fairy grants Igor's request. As a result, Igor is no longer envious of Boris' goat, but he is not any better off. Similarly, forbidding parents to exercise their right to private schooling, by itself, does nothing to improve public schooling. If equality is the goal, then education policy must be based on something more positive than spite, it must guarantee every child an equal right to education. The next section discusses what such a guarantee involves.

An Equal Right to Education

Carving a lamb roast for a family dinner is not typically considered to present a moral dilemma, but the carver does face a principled decision—how big a portion should each family member receive? One possibility is to serve everyone an equal share. Equal sharing is egalitarian; every family member has a right to meat, and each receives the same amount. However, children usually eat less than adults. An equal allocation would leave the adults hungry and the children with left-overs or tummy aches. Because family members have different appetites, the server decides to allocate the roast proportionally; adults will receive bigger portions than children. Other allocation rules are possible. For example, larger portions could go to those who helped prepare the dinner

---

[11] Providing low income families with tuition vouchers that could be used to send their children to private schools (if they choose) would achieve equality by adding an opportunity rather than subtracting one. This is not a policy favoured by the critics of private schooling.

[12] Stephen Pinker, "Why Income Inequality is not the Injustice We Perceive it to be," The Big Think. 13 Feb 2018. http://bigthink.com/big-think-books/steven-pinker-enlightenment-now-inequality-happiness

or to those who are most fond of lamb and derive the most pleasure from eating it.[13]

Well-meaning people differ in which rule they prefer. Egalitarians would most likely opt for equal portions; libertarians might say that those who made the meal are entitled to bigger servings and utilitarians would probably support giving more meat to those who derive the most pleasure from eating lamb. They may receive different amounts of meat, but, in every case, family members have an equal right *according to the allocation rule*.[14]

What does a lamb roast have to do with education? Like the family members at the dinner table who have an equal right to lamb, students should have an equal right to education according to the policies governing the allocation of education. One possible rule is to allocate education equally to all children. This is consistent with Australia's historical egalitarianism; everyone deserves a fair go. Ideally, egalitarianism is best achieved by levelling up—offering every child a high quality, well-resourced education even if this requires an increase in educational expenditure. However, penurious governments may find it easier to achieve equality by levelling-down—providing every child with the same mediocre education.

As noted earlier, strict egalitarians believe that equality should be pursued even if it requires levelling down. For example, Benedikt, the writer who called parents bad for choosing private schooling, admits that forcing all parents to send their children to public schools could mean that some receive "mediocre educations". Nevertheless, she is certain that "it will be worth it, for the … common good."[15]

Is equal education—even if it is mediocre—unquestionably fair? Benedikt thinks so. But David Gonski, the Chair of the federal government's Review of Funding for Schooling, disagrees.[16] Equal education is only fair if all children start from the same place and have the same educational needs. In practice, this is rarely true. For a variety of reasons (disability, social disadvantage, remoteness, poor English, historical injustice), some children start from behind.

---

[13] Mary Warnock, "The Concept of Equality in Education", *Oxford Review of Education* 1, no. 1 (1975): 3-8.

[14] As in the sense that all people are equal before the law. This example comes from Joseph Levitan, "The Difference Between Educational Equality, Equity and Justice—and Why it Matters." *American Educational Forum*, 2 May 2016, http://www.ajeforum.com/the-difference-between-educational-equality-equity-and-justice-and-why-it-matters-by-joseph-levitan/; See also, Richard Wollheim and Isaiah Berlin, "Equality," *Proceedings of the Aristotelian Society, New Series*, 56 (1955 - 1956), 281-326. (Published by: Oxford University Press on behalf of The Aristotelian Society.); Mary Warnock, *op cit*.

[15] Allison Benedikt, *op cit*.

[16] David Gonski (Chair). "Review of Funding for Schooling." Department of Education, Employment and Workplace Relations. (2011). Canberra. https://docs.education.gov.au/system/files/doc/other/review-of-funding-for-schooling-final-report-dec-2011.pdf

They require specially tailored educations to catch up. Even if it means providing education unequally, Gonski believes that equity demands giving each child the education he or she requires to reach an acceptable level of educational achievement. Many educators, ethicists and philosophers agree.[17] Like the carver of the lamb, they believe a proportional allocation is preferable to equality because the former is sensitive to each child's individual needs.[18] All children have an equal right to education, but equity demands that those who are disadvantaged receive special assistance. Gonski recommends that equity applies to all schools—only the degree of disadvantage matters in determining where extra educational resources go, not whether a school is private or public.

The success of a proportional allocation policy is usually assessed by how much it closes the gaps in achievement between advantaged and disadvantaged students. Following Gonski's recommendations, government funding for public schools is becoming more equitable.[19] This should reduce the gaps among schools and students, but gaps will never completely disappear because equity is not the only rule determining the distribution of education. Superior students with exceptional skills or talents, who are expected to derive significant benefit from enhanced education, receive enhanced education in a selective public school (or a scholarship to a private school). This is similar to giving larger servings of lamb to those who would derive the most pleasure from eating it.

Special treatment for bright students is justified by utilitarian appeals to the greater good. The whole society benefits from cultivating high academic achievers. They become leaders, create inventions, start businesses and make exceptional contributions to the general welfare. Unlike equity, a policy designed to help children make up for disadvantage, a utilitarian policy aims to raise the achievement of bright students. If it succeeds, the gaps between children may widen rather than shrink. However, by combining utilitarianism with equity, the remaining achievement gaps should reflect students' willingness to work hard and devotion to learning rather than their social class, gender or disability.

In addition to equity and utilitarianism, there is a third allocation rule operating in education; it is libertarian. Parents who wish to spend their money on educating their children should be permitted to do so. As we have seen, this right is enshrined in law. Unlike equity or utilitarianism, the success of the

---

[17] Hugh Lazenby, "What is Equality of Opportunity in Education?" *Theory and Research in Education,* 14, no. 1 (2016): 65–76.

[18] Although they are often used interchangeably, equality and equity are different policies. The former treats all students equally whereas the latter requires a proportional allocation rule.

[19] As this essay is being written, the government is awaiting receipt of an updated Gonski report. New recommendations are likely, but the idea that resources should be distributed proportionally is unlikely to change.

libertarian rule cannot be evaluated using scores on standardised tests or benefits to society. The libertarian policy is not aimed at closing or increasing performance gaps among students or at any other specific learning outcome; it is a derivative of liberty which is viewed by libertarians as an intrinsic good. People should be able to use their honestly earned assets as they see fit.

Let's stop here for a moment and summarise the discussion thus far. Australian schools differ in resources, teacher quality and the breadth of the subjects they teach. So, what does it mean to speak about equality in education when, in objective terms, schools are far from equal? One possibility is to reduce opportunity by eliminating the option of private schooling but, apart from reducing envy, this does not ensure all students an equal right to education.

Currently, there are three policies governing access to education. To compensate for disadvantage, equity demands that some students receive more or, at any rate, a different education from others. Exceptionally bright students are also treated differently from other students; they are offered places in selective public schools (and scholarships to private ones) because a highly educated population provides significant social benefits. Finally, parents are permitted to spend their money on private education if they desire (a libertarian ideal).

Under each policy, all students have an equal right to education although it is clear that they will not all receive the same education. Would closing private schools make any difference? This topic is considered next.

What If Everyone Attended a Public School?

Closing private schools and compelling their students to attend a public one would change some things. For example, the cost to the taxpayer would increase dramatically. Non-government schools enrol one-third of all children; forcing them into public schools would increase their numbers by 50%. Public funding for education would not increase by 50% because the public subsidies currently received by private schools would follow students to the public sector. Nevertheless, educating all children in public schools would cost taxpayers billions of extra dollars to house and teach them.[20]

What would these billions buy? The answer is not very much. All children would retain an equal right to education under the accepted allocation rules. Those who suffer from disadvantage would still require additional resources while especially gifted students would continue to receive an enhanced educa-

---

[20] Rodney Nillsen, "Do Private Schools Save the Taxpayer Money?" Undated. https://www.uow.edu.au/~nillsen/schoolsfundingpiece.pdf

tion in selective schools.[21] Educational outcomes, which are now roughly the same for public and private schools (once social class is taken into account), will remain unchanged. In a few areas, learning may go backward. For example, country students currently in private city boarding schools would be required to attend typically smaller and less well equipped local schools while remote communities that established their own schools because they were not satisfied with their former public ones, would be forced to go back to accepting whatever education the public system provides.

Why do the critics of private schooling advocate spending so much extra money for no extra gain? Benedikt says that forcing children into public schools would give wealthy influential parents a stake in the public system. If their children were forced to enrol in public schools, wealthy parents would be motivated to use their influence to ensure these schools offered a high-quality education.[22] Perhaps they would if they had to. But, wealthy families tend to live in salubrious suburbs. Their children would attend their neighbourhood public school along with those of their equally wealthy neighbours. Their high socioeconomic status would ensure that their neighbourhood school performs well on tests such as NAPLAN. Housing patterns would also ensure that children from middle and lower-socio-economic households study with children from similar backgrounds to themselves. In effect, the same social class distributions that exist today would be present after the influx of private school students.

The only way to get around the clustering of children from wealthy backgrounds in neighbourhood schools would be to compel students from higher income families to attend schools in low-income neighbourhoods (or vice versa).[23] In the 1960s and 1970s, American children were "bused" to other neighbourhoods to encourage the racial integration of schools. Busing was not a successful strategy; wealthy parents simply moved to more distant suburbs too far for a daily commute.[24] An alternative way to mix students is to offer all families education "vouchers" that could be used to pay private school fees. The Netherlands adopted this strategy with some success.[25] Without forced mixing, closing all the private schools in Australia would have no effect on who studies with whom.

---

[21] Many critics of private schooling do not like selective public schools either. They believe that selection confers an "unfair" advantage on their students. In their ideal world, there would be no private or selective public schools.
[22] Allison Benedikt, *op cit*.
[23] Matthew F. Delmont, *Why Busing Failed: Race, Media, and the National Resistance to School Desegregation* (Oakland, CA: University of California Press, 2016).
[24] Matthew F. Delmont, *op. cit.*
[25] Henry M. Levin, Ilja Cornelisz & Barbara Hanisch-Cerda, "Does Educational Privatisation Promote Social Justice?" *Oxford Review of Education* 39, no. 4 (2013): 514-532.

Given that closing private schools would cost taxpayers a great deal of money and produce little or no change in educational outcomes, what is motivating those who continue to oppose private education? Like Igor, the Russian peasant, is their opposition solely based on spite and envy?

Not entirely. Some critics believe that wealthy private schools are receiving too much financial support from the Commonwealth government.[26] These schools use their government subsidies to finance excellent facilities (swimming pools, climbing walls, elaborate dining halls) when this money could be better used to help poorer schools. This criticism has merit. School funding rules are opaque; they represent decisions taken at many different times by many different people, mostly for reasons of political expediency. However, an objection to school funding policies is not an argument for closing private schools; it is a reason for changing the rules that govern school funding—which is what the government (and the opposition) is pledged to do.

Coda

Education is a battleground in which warriors hone ideas into weapons. Equality is one of those ideas.

Everyone agrees that all children have an equal right to education. The question is how to ensure this right when the resources available to schools and families are not equal. It is unfortunately true, misery loves company, but spending billions to prevent parents from exercising their legal right to send their children to private school is misguided. It will reduce opportunities and, unless we are prepared to force children to mix in schools, it will not change who studies with whom. Most important of all, ending private schooling will not raise educational outcomes.

A school system made up entirely of state-of-the-art institutions staffed by master teachers offering all children a high-quality education tailored to their needs is a noble vision. However, this does not describe the world in which we live. Although it is far from perfect, our current mixed system of public and private provision provides choice for parents, encourages high performers and compensates for disadvantage. It is equitable and fair. Funding formulae should be rationalised, and resources should go where they are most needed. New initiatives should be aimed at improving learning rather than fostering mediocrity in the name of equality.

---

[26] Laura Perry and Emma Rowe, "Yes, Some Australian Private Schools Are Overfunded – Here's Why," *The Conversation*, 3 Oct 2016. https://theconversation.com/yes-some-australian-private-schools-are-overfunded-heres-why-66212

Reclaiming Subsidiarity in School Funding

Blaise Joseph

The economics law known as the low-hanging fruit principle states that fruit pickers are most productive when they first start as they can easily reach fruit on the lowest branches, but later on they become less productive as they need to climb higher to pick the remaining fruit. The amount of fruit gathered, therefore, isn't just a question of how many fruit pickers there are, but also of whether or not the low-hanging fruit has already been picked. This gives rise to the concept of diminishing marginal returns; that is, the more extra funding you put into something, the smaller the extra returns for the additional funding.

That has to be the starting point for any rational discussion about school spending. Too often, politicians and education stakeholders immediately jump to the conclusion that more fruit pickers are needed, without first determining if the low-hanging fruit has already been picked, or if they have been busy picking the wrong fruit.

Hence the perennial spectacle of political parties promising significantly more funding to improve the school system, without providing any evidence that a lack of funds is the problem in the first place. Governments have a duty to both students and taxpayers to ensure school funding is spent efficiently and effectively; more money can be a means to an end, but not an end in itself.

School Spending and Student Outcomes

School funding is an important factor in the quality of an education system. Adequate resources are necessary for a decent education, but not sufficient. There is no clear positive relationship between school spending and student achievement.

The Organization for Economic Cooperation and Development (OECD) recently concluded that beyond a certain point of school funding, extra money does not positively influence student results, as measured by the international standardised test, Programme for International Student Assessment (PISA). According to the OECD:

> Among the countries and economies whose cumulative expenditure per student is under USD 50,000, higher expenditure on education is strongly associated with higher PISA science scores. But this is not the case among high-income coun-

tries and economies, which include most OECD countries. It seems that for this latter group of countries and economies, factors other than the level of investment in education are better predictors of student performance.

> ...although countries and economies might have similar levels of expenditure on education, they can perform very differently...Whatever the reason for the lack of a relationship between spending per student and learning outcomes, at least in the countries and economies with larger education budgets, excellence in education requires more than money.[1]

This confirms there are diminishing marginal returns to school spending, and in most OECD countries funding is not a strong predictor of student performance.

Other factors besides school funding are more significant in determining student results. For example, a recent study examined the influence of education investment and school discipline on education performance. It found that school discipline is actually much more important than school funding in affecting education performance—school funding explained only 12 per cent of the variation in school results, while classroom discipline explained the other 88 per cent.[2] This is an example of how a focus on funding can be misplaced. Sound, evidence-based school discipline policies and practices do not necessarily cost any more than ineffective ones, but in contrast can have a significant positive impact on student learning.

There is some conflicting evidence on the question of school funding. Six recent studies have been cited to suggest that increased school funding improves student results, especially for disadvantaged students.[3] Each study found evidence of positive effects of increased school funding on student outcomes. However, all of these studies either did not consider the marginal effects of increased school funding off high bases of existing funding, or else

---

[1] OECD, *PISA 2015 Results, Policies and Practices for Successful Schools: Volume II* (Paris: OECD Publishing, 2016), 42.

[2] Hana Krskova and Chris Baumann, "School discipline, investment, competitiveness, and mediating educational performance", *International Journal of Educational Management*, 31, no. 3, 2017, 293-319.

[3] Bruce Baker, *Does Money Matter in Education?* (Albert Shanker Institute, 2016); Kirabo Jackson, Rucker Johnson, and Claudia Persico, "The Effects of School Spending on Educational and Economic Outcomes: Evidence from School Finance Reforms", *The Quarterly Journal of Economics*, 131, no. 1, 2016, 157–218; Julien Lafortune, Jesse Rothstein, and Diane Schanzenbach, *School Finance Reform and the Distribution of Student Achievement* (No. 22011, National Bureau of Economic Research, 2016); Christopher Candelaria and Kenneth Shores, *The Sensitivity of Causal Estimates from Court-Ordered Finance Reform on Spending and Graduation Rates* (Centre for Education Policy Analysis, 2015); Joshua Hyman, "Does money matter in the long run? The effects of school spending on educational attainment", *Economic Policy*, forthcoming, 2017; Rucker Johnson and Kirabo Jackson, *Reducing Inequality Through Dynamic Complementarity: Evidence from Head Start and Public School Spending* (No. 23489, National Bureau of Economic Research, 2017).

related to specific situations in the United States where the funding increases were coming off significantly lower bases of per student funding compared to current average OECD levels. Therefore, these studies do not undermine the argument that extra money for schools beyond a certain point is not effective.

There is even some evidence to suggest that extra money can potentially have negative effects on student achievement, if used poorly. For instance, classroom technology is a common school investment, but does not necessarily lead to better outcomes. In fact, beyond a certain level of education technology use, it can be detrimental to student learning. The OECD's comprehensive report on technology and schools in 2015 concluded:

> Resources invested in ICT for education are not linked to improved student achievement, in reading, mathematics or science.
>
> In countries where it is less common for students to use the Internet at school for schoolwork, students' performance in reading improved more rapidly than in countries where such use is more common, on average.
>
> Overall, the relationship between computer use at school and performance is graphically illustrated by a hill shape, which suggests that limited use of computers at school may be better than no use at all, but levels of computer use above the current OECD average are associated with significantly poorer results.[4]

This means investing more funding in the wrong areas can actually be counterproductive, reaffirming the basic principle that school funding should not just be a question of how much money is spent, but rather *how* it is spent. The inescapable conclusion is that attempts to improve education by simply spending more money are doomed to fail.

Decentralising School Funding Responsibilities

The key to ensuring school funding is well-spent is to empower schools and authorities at a more local level, and avoid one-size-fits-all approaches from federal governments. Naturally, this should come with the expectation of increased school accountability and transparency at the local level. In many countries—especially those with federalist systems such as the US and Australia—it would be desirable for the federal government to have little or no involvement in school funding allocation. The benefits of this approach include greater accountability by avoiding the 'blame game' between federal and state governments, a more efficient funding allocation that better caters for

---

[4] OECD, *Students, Computers and Learning: Making the connection* (Paris: OECD Publishing, 2015), 146.

local considerations, and a reduced or abolished federal department of education with a smaller cost to the taxpayer.

The main objection to this policy is that it creates a lack of uniformity across a country's schools system. But this is actually one of the strongest arguments in favour: lower levels of government are better able to understand and cater for the needs of their schools than the federal government. Due to demographics and geography, there will generally be different educational needs across different parts of a nation, and hence school funding systems have to be substantially different by area for them to provide for the needs of their local populations.

Furthermore, transferring all school funding responsibilities to lower levels of government allows for more competition between governments to offer the best education system. This would be beneficial for students in the long-term, as governments would be under more pressure to ensure their school funding systems maximise student performance. There would also be greater accountability for school outcomes, as local governments would have to justify their own school funding systems and educational performance, without being able to blame the national government.

There are several examples in the OECD of decentralised school funding systems, where the federal government does not allocate money directly to schools, and lower levels of government manage distribution of school funding. For example, in Canada there is no federal department of education, and provinces have full responsibility for school funding allocation. Spain and Japan also have very decentralised systems where most school funding and policy responsibilities belong to provincial governments.

This means forgoing nation-wide consistency in schooling, and would limit the ability of a national government to make overarching school funding reforms. Inevitably, some areas of a country will perform better than others. However, typically this happens anyway, and from a perspective of managing risk, it is desirable that the federal government have less power. If a provincial government implements defective school funding policies, at least the damage is limited to the local area where they can easily be held accountable. In contrast, if a federal government implements a similarly flawed approach, the entire country suffers.

Ultimately, the principle of subsidiarity should override the principle of consistency, because local governments are best able to cater for local needs with respect to school funding, and a flawed country-wide approach must be avoided. More localised school funding arrangements also make it easier to implement policies which maximise school choice for parents, such as school vouchers and charter schools.

School Vouchers

A school vouchers system is a way of allocating government funding for schools whereby parents are given a voucher for each child which they can then spend on any school they wish, in the government or non-government sectors. Vouchers maximise school choice for parents and mean government funding is allocated to schools almost entirely on a per student basis.

There are three major pragmatic benefits of a school vouchers system. Firstly, they are simple. The public can easily understand the school funding model, which is not open to complex government funding agreements with schools. There are potentially some additional layers of complexity, such as minimum levels of funding for schools and means-testing the size of the voucher, but overall vouchers are much simpler than most other systems.

Secondly, they are transparent. With vouchers, it is clear exactly how funding is allocated to schools. There is no potential for arbitrary school funding formulas, or opaque agreements between governments and school systems based on historical levels of funding.

Lastly, they are fair. Vouchers treat all schools and all parents equally by allowing them to spend the same amount of government funding on the school of their choice. In particular, vouchers give low socioeconomic status (SES) parents much greater school choice.

In theory, vouchers also provide positive incentives for government and non-government schools to improve, as parents have more school choice. Funding models based on school vouchers have been implemented in several countries around the world, including Sweden, Chile, and some states in the US.

The evidence about the impact of school vouchers on student achievement is strongly disputed, as the effects vary greatly depending on the context and implementation. Overall, according to two recent systematic reviews of the literature, school voucher programmes have often had substantial positive impacts on student achievement, but in some cases the effects have been negative.[5] Some studies have found that a significant benefit of vouchers is improvements in the government school system, as a result of greater competition from non-government schools. However, other studies have found that students perform worse after moving from government schools to non-government schools in voucher programmes, although it appears that these students may eventually catch up with their peers after several years.

---

[5] Dennis Epple, Richard Romano, and Miguel Urquiola, *School Vouchers: A Survey of the Economics Literature* (No. w21523, National Bureau of Economic Research, 2015); Danish Shakeel, Kaitlin Anderson, and Patrick Wolf, *The Participant Effects of Private School Vouchers Across the Globe: A Meta-analytic and Systematic Review* (EDRE Working Paper No. 2016-07, The Department of Education Reform, 2016).

School vouchers are a viable funding model based on the principle of empowering parental choice in education. But there remain some practical implementation issues to be resolved, so as to preserve the positive effects and limit the possible negative effects for students.

Charter Schools

Charter schools are government-funded schools, but autonomous and locally controlled. These schools are essentially privately run government schools, with significantly more flexibility than standard government schools. They enable more school autonomy and choice within the government school system. Charter schools have existed for many years in some US states, and have been introduced more recently as Free Schools in England and Partnership Schools in New Zealand.

Based on the international experiences, charter schools have a small positive effect on overall student achievement, according to a recent meta-analysis of the literature.[6] Further, there is also a large body of evidence that charter schools significantly help low SES students in particular.[7] In theory, charter schools have much more flexibility to cater for the needs of individual students, so it is unsurprising that they seem to greatly benefit disadvantaged students. This means that charter schools are capable of boosting the results of disadvantaged students without requiring considerable increases in government funding. Charter schools have the benefit of improving student achievement, better catering for the needs of disadvantaged students, and increasing parental choice.

Universal Free Public Schooling

Universal free public schooling exists in most OECD countries; that is, all parents are able to send their children to a local government school without any compulsory fee.

In the absence of policies favouring schools choice such as vouchers and charter schools, this results in an inequitable and unfair situation. High-income parents in high SES areas—where government schools tend to perform much better—are able to send their children to government schools for free. In contrast, low-income parents in low SES areas—where government schools tend to perform much worse—have to make significant financial con-

---

[6] Julian Betts and Emily Tang, *A Meta-Analysis of the Literature on the Effect of Charter Schools on Student Achievement* (Society for Research on Educational Effectiveness, 2016).
[7] For a full discussion of recent developments in charter schools and a review of the evidence regarding positive effects for disadvantaged students, see: Trisha Jha and Jennifer Buckingham, *Free to Choose Charter Schools: How charter and For Profit Schools Can Boost Public Education* (The Centre for Independent Studies, 2015).

tributions to send their children to a non-government school if they are (understandably) not satisfied with the quality of the local government school.

The underlying long-term issue is the inconsistent quality of schooling, but in the meantime parents in low SES areas are unfairly disadvantaged. In addition, the unnecessary constraint on government schools—stopping them from receiving compulsory contributions from high-income parents—means much more taxpayer funding than needed is spent on the government school system.

The truth is government schools in rich, metropolitan areas tend to reflect the demographics of their areas, and so they have the capacity to raise funding themselves. With parents contributing directly to their local school, this cuts out the middleman of the government departments of education, and therefore allows for a more efficient flow of school funding.

'Free' public schooling for everyone is an idea without any practical reason to support it. This article of progressive faith should be challenged.

The Way Forward
School funding is important. How much is spent, who spends it, how it is distributed, and the extent of parental choice allowed for by school funding models are all crucial policy questions. Nevertheless, the impact of school funding must not be overstated. The evidence indicates that beyond a certain point of funding, extra money has little or no further positive effect.

In order to generate the largest possible return from school funding, policymakers should advocate decentralising the distribution of funds, and giving local and state government more control, instead of federal governments. This would allow for better allocation of funding, according to local circumstances. On a local level, school vouchers would maximise parental choice outside the government school system, while charter schools would give parents more options within the government school system. Parents are generally in the best position to know what is best for their own children, and school funding policy should reflect this. Empowering local communities and schools is the best way of ensuring education funds are well-spent. Only then can it be hoped that school systems will enable all children to flourish.

DISCIPLINES AND METHODS

Mathematics, Core of the Past and Hope of the Future

James Franklin

Mathematics has always been a core part of western education, from the medieval *quadrivium* to the large amount of arithmetic and algebra still compulsory in high schools. It is an essential part. Its commitment to exactitude and to rigid demonstration balances humanist subjects devoted to appreciation and rhetoric as well as giving the lie to postmodernist insinuations that all "truths" are subject to political negotiation.

In recent decades, the character of mathematics has changed—or rather broadened: it has become the enabling science behind the complexity of contemporary knowledge, from gene interpretation to bank risk. Mathematical understanding is all the more necessary for future jobs, as well as remaining, as ever, a prophylactic against the more corrosive philosophical views emanating from the humanities.

The Ancients and Deductive Proof

In the mid-fifth century BC, the Parthenon was rising over Athens, built according to the best geometrical principles. The construction lines are not visible on it, though on some other Greek temples they are.[1] Among the tragedians, artists, sophists and merchants creating Western civilization in the city below, a number of visitors from out of town brought an interest in what we would now call scientific questions. According to Parmenides of Elea, for example, thinking about the geometry of eclipses is enough for a convincing argument that the earth is round, even for someone fixed in one place on the earth's surface.[2]

A lesser-known genius who visited Athens was a certain Hippocrates of Chios.[3] He came to appreciate that geometry could be organised so that the complicated and less obvious propositions followed with strict logic from the simple and obvious ones. His project was perfected a century or more later in

---

[1] Lothar Haselberger, "The construction plans for the Temple of Apollo at Didyma," *Scientific American* 253, no. 6 (1985): 126-32.
[2] Otto Neugebauer, *A History of Ancient Mathematical Astronomy* (Berlin: Springer, 1975), 576.
[3] Confusingly, not the same person as Hippocrates of Cos, the medical writer after whom the Hippocratic Oath is called.

the *Elements* of Euclid, which was such a success that its predecessors have not survived. But one fragment of Hippocrates's work is left, enough to demonstrate his extraordinary brilliance. Being still at the "bare hands" phase of mathematical development, it can be appreciated by anyone.

The fragment concerns the "quadrature of lunes", that is, finding the area of a crescent-shaped figure as shown in the shaded portion at the top left of the figure:

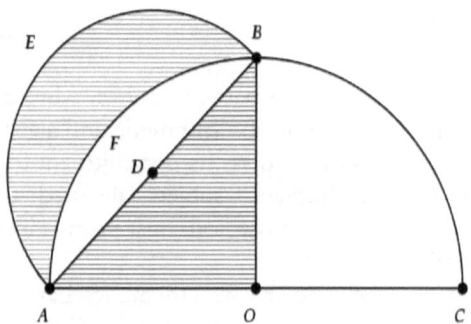

Fig. 1: The Lune of Hippocrates [4]

The lune is bounded by two arcs of circles: the upper one AEB which is half of a circle with diameter ADB, and the lower one AFB which is a quarter of a circle with diameter AOC. Hippocrates proves, amazingly, that the area of the lune is exactly the same as the area of the right-angled triangle AOB (also shaded).

Note that there is no π in the answer, as there is in the formula for the area of a circle: Hippocrates does not use anything about the area of a circle, but proves directly that the two areas, one curved and one straight-sided, are equal. If the radius AO is one unit of length, both shaded areas are exactly half a square unit. The original text of his proof is given in this footnote in case some readers wish to skip it.[5]

---

[4] Michael Hardy, "Lune of Hippocrates", 7 March 2009,. https://upload.wikimedia.org/wikipedia/commons/e/e0/Lune.svg

[5] "He started with, and laid down as the first of the theorems useful for the purpose, the proposition that similar segments of circles have the same ratio to one another as the squares on their bases. And this he proved by first showing that the squares on the diameters have the same ratio as the circles. After proving this, he proceeded to show in what way it was possible to square a lune the outer circumference of which is that of a semicircle. This he effected by circumscribing a semicircle about an isosceles right-angled triangle and a segment of a circle similar to those cut off by the sides. Then, since the segment about the base is equal to the sum of those about the sides, it follows that, when the part of the triangle above the segment about the base is added to both alike, the lune will be equal to the triangle." "Text of Simplicius", translated in Thomas L. Heath, *A Manual of Greek Mathe-*

The Greeks immediately realised there was something special about deductive proof as a way of acquiring knowledge. It is not like measuring a number of lunes and triangles and finding that in all cases the lune equals the triangle in area. Proof somehow gets to a deeper level of reality. It reveals not only what *is* so, but what *must* be so. And the proof allows us not only to know what must be so, but to understand *why* it must be so.

The results are not thereby cut off from physical reality, as if they are about a Platonic realm of ideal forms. If real lunes and triangles are drawn on paper, they are nearly equal in area, and the more perfectly they are drawn, the nearer the drawn shapes approximate the exact parts of real space to which the proof applies, and so the nearer they are equal in area.

There are plenty more exact and provable results where that came from, as laid out in the thirteen books of Euclid's *Elements* and many thousands of mathematical books and papers since. The method of deductive proof generates indefinitely many results. It is just a matter of human interest and energy keeping up with them.

A very simple example shows how the initial and most basic results of mathematics are known.

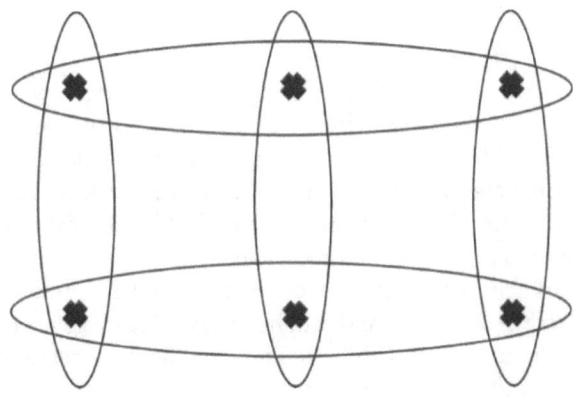

Fig. 2: Why 2 × 3 = 3 × 2

In the figure, the six crosses are arranged both as two rows of 3 and as three columns of 2. Since they are the same six crosses, 2 × 3 = 3 × 2. We can literally see not only *that* 2 × 3 = 3 × 2, but that 2 × 3 *must be* 3 × 2.[6]

Further, we can easily see that the same reasoning applies if we add more rows and columns. If we have m columns and n rows, the same reasoning is

---

matics (Mineola NY: Dover, 2003), 121-132; a more accessible explanation in W.S. Anglin, *Mathematics: A Concise History and Philosophy* (New York: Springer, 1994), 52.
[6] Catherine Legg and James Franklin, "Perceiving necessity," *Pacific Philosophical Quarterly* 98, no. 3 (2017), 320-343.

valid. Therefore $m \times n = n \times m$, for any numbers m and n. So the insight produces an infinite number of truths, all of them understood to be true with certainty. Again, these truths apply directly to the real world of actual crosses written on paper, or of any other objects whatsoever. There is no need for getting out in the wet and observing, but the abstract truths predict what will be observed by anyone who does get out there.[7]

Excited by these possibilities, Aristotle proposed in his *Posterior Analytics* that *all* sciences should follow the model of mathematics, with immediately understood axioms supporting a superstructure of more complex theorems, and proofs explaining why the theorems were true.[8] That did not quite work out. Contrary to Aristotle's hope, in the natural and human sciences observation and measurement are still essential to establishing the truth of theories. Only in mathematics, and in some closely related fields like computer science and just possibly ethics, is proof in the full sense feasible.[9] Thus mathematics remains the ideal training ground for the human faculty of understanding and proof.

Mathematics at the Centre of Western Education
Western education has not lost sight of the point of mathematics and has always made it central to education, despite the fact that it is quite hard to learn and subject to a certain degree of customer resistance.

Medieval liberal tertiary education, the preparation for specialised studies such as theology, law and medicine, was divided into two levels, the *trivium* and the *quadrivium*. The *trivium* consisted of grammar, logic and rhetoric, that is, studies in words and how they work. Then came the *quadrivium*: arithmetic, geometry, music (theory) and astronomy, all of which are mathematics in one form or another.[10] Then the Italian merchant schools of the later Middle Ages made the remarkable discovery that calculation with indefinitely large numbers could be reduced to rules and taught to seven-year-olds.[11] Basic numeracy became widespread along with basic literacy. The new technologies of early modern times found a population able to understand and manipulate them.

---

[7] Briefly in James Franklin, "The mathematical world," *Aeon* 7 Apr 2014 https://aeon.co/essays/aristotle-was-right-about-mathematics-after-all; fully in James Franklin, *An Aristotelian Realist Philosophy of Mathematics: Mathematics as the science of quantity and structure* (Basingstoke: Macmillan, 2014).

[8] Richard D. McKirahan, *Principles and Proofs: Aristotle's theory of demonstrative science* (Princeton: Princeton University Press, 1992).

[9] See Svetlana V. Drachova *et al*, "Teaching mathematical reasoning principles for software correctness and its assessment," *ACM Transactions on Computing Education* 15, no. 3 (2015): article 15; and James Franklin, "On the parallel between mathematics and morals," *Philosophy* 79 (2004): 97-119.

[10] David L. Wagner, ed., *The Seven Liberal Arts in the Middle Ages* (Bloomington, Ind: Indiana University Press, 1983).

[11] Richard W. Hadden, *On the Shoulders of Merchants: Exchange and the mathematical conception of nature in early modern Europe* (Albany NY: SUNY Press, 1994).

There was some backsliding from the humanists of the Renaissance, who preferred words, but the Scientific Revolution of the seventeenth century was and was seen to be based on mathematics and data instead of wordy disputation. Galileo explains:

> If what we are discussing were a point of law or of the humanities, in which neither true nor false exists, one might trust in subtlety of mind and readiness of tongue and in the greater experience of the writers, and expect him who excelled in those things to make his reasoning more plausible, and one might judge it to be the best. But in natural sciences whose conclusions are true and necessary and have nothing to do with human will, one must take care not to place oneself in the defense of error; for here a thousand Demostheneses and a thousand Aristotles would be left in the lurch by every mediocre wit who happened to hit upon the truth for himself.[12]

When the Jesuit missionary Matteo Ricci reached China in 1582, he soon found that the Chinese scholars were particularly impressed with Western mathematical science. The first work translated into Chinese by him and his collaborator Xu Guangqi was the first six books of Euclid's *Elements*. Ricci says in his diary:

> Nothing pleased the Chinese as much as the volume on the Elements of Euclid. This perhaps was due to the fact that no people esteem mathematics as highly as the Chinese, despite their method of teaching, in which they propose all kinds of propositions but without demonstrations. The result of such a system is that anyone is free to exercise his imagination relative to mathematics without offering a definitive proof of anything.[13]

That is quite right about the difference between Western and other mathematics. Non-Western mathematics was in many ways impressive, especially in Babylon, India and China, but it looks more like modern computer science than modern mathematics: a series of recipes for calculating rather than an organised body of proofs of theorems.[14]

In Victorian England, the study of Euclid was presumed suitable for training boys of the upper classes in the intellectual tasks that awaited them

---

[12] Galileo, *Dialogue Concerning the Two Chief World Systems*, trans. S. Drake (2nd ed, Berkeley: University of California Press, 1967), 53-54.

[13] *China in the Sixteenth Century: The Journals of Matthew Ricci*, trans. L.J. Gallagher (New York: Random House, 1953), 476; details in Peter M. Engelfriet, *Euclid in China: The Genesis of First Chinese Translation of Euclid's* Elements *Books I-VI (Jihe yuanben; Beijing, 1607) and its Reception up to 1723* (Leiden: Brill, 1998); typical postmodernist complaints about the resulting "loss of indigenous mathematics" in Sara N. Hottinger, *Inventing the Mathematician: Gender, Race and Our Cultural Understanding of Mathematics* (Albany NY: SUNY Press, 2016), 121-2.

[14] George Gheverghese Joseph, *The Crest of the Peacock: Non-European Roots of Mathematics* (3rd ed, Princeton: Princeton University Press, 2011).

such as governing India. Animated debate proceeded merely as to whether Euclid was best swallowed whole or whether modern re-hashings were easier but not oversimplified; Charles Lutwidge Dodgson (Lewis Carroll)'s book *Euclid and His Modern Rivals* defended teaching straight Euclid.[15]

The upshot of this long process was that mathematics—and mathematics at a substantially high level—has become a compulsory part of education across the board. That has applied not just in Western countries. The Soviet Union, for all its Marxist ideology in the humanities and Lysenkoist delusions in biology, left pure mathematics alone and maintained a very high standard of mathematics education in schools.[16] East Asian countries have surpassed Western ones in school mathematics education, having successfully grafted Western mathematics onto their cultural traditions.[17] Third World countries are doing their best to catch up. The culture of research mathematics is the same worldwide, with the same symbols used everywhere and virtually everything written in English. Mathematics is a universal culture—as international and standardised as air traffic control but impacting vastly more people.

Enemies of Mathematics

Naturally, the enemies of Western civilisation and of rationality have not taken the achievements of mathematics lying down.

The Greeks in Athens in the fifth century BC, multi-talented as they were, invented not only Western civilisation but how to complain about it. The Sophist Gorgias of Leontini, in the course of making a lot of money corrupting the youth of Athens around 420, defended the propositions:

> Nothing exists
> If anything existed, it could not be known
> If anything were known, it could not be communicated.[18]

That just about covers everything, and the postmodernists of the late twentieth century did not have much to add to it (except prolixity, obviously). They found plenty of life left in Gorgias's insights, and recycled them in such forms as:

---

[15] Charles Lutwidge Dodgson, *Euclid and His Modern Rivals* (London: Macmillan, 1879); Rafael Montoito and Antonio Vicente Marafioti Garnica, "Lewis Carroll, Education and the Teaching of Geometry in Victorian England," *História da Educação* 19, no. 45 (2015): 9-27.
[16] Alexander Karp and Bruce R. Vogeli, *Russian Mathematics Education: History and World Significance* (New Jersey: World Scientific, 2010).
[17] Frederick K.S. Leung, Klaus-D. Graf and Francis J. Lopez-Real, *Mathematics Education in Different Cultural Traditions: A Comparative Study of East Asia and the West: The 13th ICMI study* (New York: Springer, 2010).
[18] Bruce McComiskey, "Gorgias, "On Non-Existence": Sextus Empiricus, "Against the Logicians" 1.65-87, translated from the Greek text in Hermann Diels's "Die Fragmente der Vorsokratiker"," *Philosophy & Rhetoric* 30 (1997): 45-49.

1. Doubt whether there is any solid reality out there for science to know (or at least, label "naïve" the assumption that there is such a reality)
2. Maintain that even if there is some sort of reality out there, we cannot know what it is because we are trapped in our own evolutionarily-determined brains/cultural understandings/specific historicities/reactionary educations[19]
3. Allege that language is incapable of communicating any truth about objective reality, as it cannot refer directly to things and their properties

The evils of postmodernism are a well-studied field and need not be rehearsed again.[20] Here we confine ourselves to the case of mathematics. Naturally, the most shameless and foolhardy in the irrationalist camp have been keen to make a name for themselves by trying to knock over this last line of defence. Sokal and Bricmont's exposé of postmodernist absurdities, *Intellectual Impostures,* easily collected a whole chapter of garblings of mathematics from the best French theorists. Gilles Deleuze, one of the most worshipped gurus of "theory", had a special taste for pieces of mathematics (or apparent mathematics), such as:

> The respective independence of variables appears in mathematics when one of them is at a higher power than the first. That is why Hegel shows that variability in the function is not confined to values that can be changed ($2/3$ and $4/6$) or are left undetermined ($a = 2b$) but requires one of the variables to be at a higher power ($y^2/x = P$). For it is then that a relation can be directly determined as differential relation dy/dx, in which the only determination of the value of the variables is that of disappearing or being born, even though it is wrested from infinite speeds...[21]

The writings of the irrationalists about mathematics have had absolutely no impact on mathematicians. Mathematicians have not read one word of any complainers. It has been all water off a duck's back to them because they have remained unaware of and unaffected by the sell-out by the humanities. The production of theorems and the application of mathematics to climate modelling and airline scheduling have proceeded, totally untroubled by any

---

[19] James Franklin, "Stove's Discovery of the Worst Argument in the World," *Philosophy* 77 (2002), 615-24.
[20] One of the earliest and best refutations is Raymond Tallis, *Not Saussure: A Critique of Post-Saussurean Literary Theory* (Basingstoke: Macmillan, 1997). Needless to say it was as ineffective as it was brilliant.
[21] Gilles Deleuze and Félix Guattari, *What is Philosophy?* (New York: Columbia University Press, 1994), 122, in Alan Sokal and Jean Bricmont, *Intellectual Impostures* (London: Profile Books, 1998), 150-1; Australian imitations in James Franklin, *Corrupting the Youth: A History of Philosophy in Australia* (Sydney: Macleay Press, 2003), 368.

doubts as to the fallibility of proof (but subject to the politics of funding, of course).

That's the good news. The bad news is that it is otherwise in mathematics education. There, works like Paul Ernest's *Social Constructivism as a Philosophy of Mathematics* are taken very seriously indeed.[22] It may be that the paper 'Toward a feminist algebra' that was analysed in Gross and Levitt's *Higher Superstition* was somewhat beyond what is typical of the field,[23] but it is not hard to find text still being produced like this extract from *Educational Studies in Mathematics*, 2004:

> The supposed apolitical nature of mathematics is an institutional frame that functions to sustain specific power structures within schools. This paper disrupts the common assumption that mathematics (as a body of knowledge constructed in situated historical moments) is free from entrenched ideological motives. Using narrative inquiry, the paper examines the ways in which novice mathematics teachers negotiate the intersection of curriculum and institutional politics ... [24]

Recent trends may be observed by following up in Google Scholar the 41 works that cite this article, such as 'Criticising with Foucault: towards a guiding framework for socio-political studies in mathematics education', 2016. The research field remains active. And activist.

Mathematics as it is Now

Those outside mathematics, especially those in such distant regions as the humanities, may have missed some important trends in the last century or so. People with a general school education know some very old pure mathematics such as arithmetic, geometry and algebra, have a rough idea of statistics, and have a notion that mathematics of some advanced sort is used in physics, computing and finance. That is not exactly wrong but is a very partial view. The truth is more complex and interesting.

In the mid-century, there appeared a number of disciplines at the edge of mathematics, variously called the "formal" or "mathematical" sciences or sciences of complexity—operations research, systems engineering, control theory, theoretical computer science and others.[25] To take just one example of the kind of thing they do, consider train timetabling. Train speeds, length of stops,

---

[22] Paul Ernest, *Social Constructivism as a Philosophy of Mathematics* (Albany NY: SUNY Press, 1998). (800+ citations on Google Scholar)
[23] Paul R. Gross and Norman Levitt, *Higher Superstition: The Academic Left and Its Quarrels With Science* (Baltimore: Johns Hopkins University Press, 1994), 113-5.
[24] Elizabeth de Freitas, "Plotting Intersections Along the Political Axis: The Interior Voice of Dissenting Mathematics Teachers," *Educational Studies in Mathematics* 55 (2004): 259-274.
[25] James Franklin, "The Formal Sciences Discover the Philosophers' Stone," *Studies in History and Philosophy of Science* 25 (1994): 513-33.

and crew rosters create (quantitative) constraints that train journeys must satisfy, on top of which there are delays and breakdowns of various degrees of predictability. Those constraints must be described mathematically and software must be programmed to timetable the trains, ideally so as to minimise delays. Though developed originally for use in various such applications, these bodies of knowledge are in themselves purely mathematical disciplines (though often now housed in faculties of engineering).

More recently, the situation has changed through the ability of computers to deal with large amounts of data. Where once the strength of computers was in calculation, the focus has moved, as the rise of the phrase "information technology" suggests, to the processing of the flood of data. There are unstoppable streams of data arriving from satellites, from telescopes, from weather buoys, from medical imaging machines, from supermarket scanners, from wire services serving up tick data of all the world's financial transactions. Huge databases await mining and matching. As the science journalist Mitchell Waldrop says, "drink from the firehose of data".[26] Data interpretation tasks that the brain finds easy, like opening the eyes and seeing what's in front of them, remain very challenging for computers. Computer vision is still unreliable on the problem of listing the objects in a natural scene.

While there is plenty of activity in these fields, it is recognised that the capabilities of the hardware and software in storing and accessing the data have raced well ahead of the mathematical algorithms needed to make sense of the data. There is sophisticated technology for recording and displaying Pap smears, say, but for recognising whether they are cancerous, the method of choice is still to have a trained human looking at them—or at least, supervising any results generated automatically. That is the typical situation.

Data mining, interpretation of pathology results, target recognition and the like are all held up because the mathematics of pattern recognition, and statistical methods appropriate to large data sets in general, remain in a grossly primitive state. Surely one of the main directions for future mathematics is to sort that out. The problems to be solved include fraud detection and finding missing planes.[27]

The future of mathematics is hard to predict, but perhaps less so than the future of just about everything else. Mathematics has been going a very long time, and its changes have been expansions rather than revolutions. Mathe-

---

[26] M. Mitchell Waldrop, "Learning to Drink From A Firehose," *Science* 248 (1990): 674-5.

[27] Bart Baesens, Véronique Van Vlasselaer and Wouter Verbeke, *Fraud Analytics Using Descriptive, Predictive and Social Network Techniques: A guide to data science for fraud detection* (Hoboken: Wiley, 2015).; "How Statisticians Found Air France Flight 447 Two Years After It Crashed into the Atlantic," *MIT Technology Review*, May 27, 2014, https://www.technologyreview.com/s/527506/how-statisticians-found-air-france-flight-447-two-years-after-it-crashed-into-atlantic/; Sam Davey, Neil Gordon, Ian Holland, Mark Rutten and Jason Williams, *Bayesian Methods in the Search for MH370* (Singapore: Springer, 2016).

matics does not go back to square one, and there is some sense of what will come next from the pattern of the unsolved problems of today.

Undoubtedly many advances in mathematics in the near term will be simply cracking the problems that seem today to be in the course of yielding. Not long ago speech recognition by computer looked intractable, but the algorithms advanced and it is now, if not perfect, usable enough to answer phones for large organisations. Just now at the cutting edge is the recent sudden improvement in Google Translate arising from a powerful statistical learning algorithm applied to huge corpora of translated texts.[28]

Some problems are a little farther "out there". A big one that is not so far going very well but surely ought to be reasonably solvable is that of extracting causality from data. Among the many amazing things that human infants learn very fast is how to infer what causes what from looking at how things behave. They can manipulate a few close things, but most things can only be observed from a distance, and causality is not something that can be directly observed. Yet infants can work out what causes what and hence predict what will happen next. It is a difficult problem because "correlation does not imply causality".[29] If we could learn the algorithms behind that, we could trawl through medical data to learn the causes of disease. We would be able to determine automatically whether, for example, lower cholesterol is a cause or symptom of lower heart disease. The causes of global warming would be established beyond doubt and we would know what interventions will work.

A different kind of problem lies at, so to speak, the opposite end of the spectrum from big data. It concerns the estimation of "extreme risks"—risks of major disasters that are not exactly like anything that has happened yet, such as terrorist attacks or major quarantine incursions. It is "data-free statistics", in that there are no data, or hardly any, directly relevant to the event to be predicted. In that case one must combine the little data of some relevance (such as the occurrence of somewhat similar events) with expert opinion on possible scenarios. How to use data to keep opinion honest is a challenging problem.[30]

Plenty of problems remain, too, in mathematical finance, the area most popular as an employment destination for maths graduates. It would be good to understand how to apply mathematics to enhance instead of undermine

---

[28] Gideon Lewis-Kraus, "The Great A.I. Awakening," *New York Times Magazine,* Dec 14, 2016, https://www.nytimes.com/2016/12/14/magazine/the-great-ai-awakening.html

[29] Divorce rate in Maine correlates with per capita consumption of margarine, correlation = 99.26% (http://www.tylervigen.com/spurious-correlations)

[30] James Franklin, Scott A. Sisson, Mark A. Burgman and Jennifer K. Martin, "Evaluating Extreme Risks in Invasion Ecology: Learning from Banking Compliance," *Diversity and Distributions* 14 (2008): 581-91.

the stability of the global financial system. Medicine too presents a huge number of problems needing mathematics, in areas like gene expression.[31]

Directions for Mathematics Education
We are used to a stream of reports of falling standards in schools, falling enrolments in advanced maths, and the better performance of our Asian neighbours.[32] The first thing, plainly, is to make sure all students study an appropriate level of mathematics, and do not, for example, ditch mathematics because easier subjects gain higher HSC marks.[33] Efforts to explain the need for mathematics to students and their parents need to continue. It is true, however, that enrolments by the brighter students in university mathematics have held up well in recent years, especially in those courses related to jobs in finance.

Having said that, the mathematics taught needs a few adjustments to be suitable for an intelligent person in the present century.[34] Syllabuses at school and university are dominated by pure mathematics, about numbers and algebraic techniques that are promised to be useful in the "real world" in an indefinite future. It is indeed necessary to study those things, but an exclusive focus on them is both unmotivating and untrue to real mathematics.

The first thing that needs adding is some serious mathematical modelling. Modelling is the process of describing some real-world structure or problem in mathematical terms, so that mathematical techniques can be brought to bear on solving it. It is quite a different skill from pure mathematics. Take a problem like: is it feasible to tow an iceberg from Antarctica to provide fresh water for Adelaide? That does not require solving a set mathematical problem like "Simplify $(x-3)(x^3 + 4x - 7)$" and the skills involved are not the same. It needs a team to model what would need to happen to tow an iceberg and work out what quantitative information is needed—such as the size of icebergs, rates of melting, feasible speeds of towing, Adelaide's water demands—and finding that information. The outcome should be a clearly written report advising what the result is and setting out the reasons clearly.[35]

---

[31] E.g. Ahmet Ay and David N. Arnosti, "Mathematical Modelling of Gene Expression: A Guide for the Perplexed Biologist," *Critical Reviews in Biochemistry and Molecular Biology* 46, no. 2 (2011): 137-151.
[32] Most recently Samantha Hutchinson, "Australia looks to China for Maths, Science Lessons," *The Australian* 11/7/2017; figures in Frank Barrington and Michael Evans, "Participation in Year 12 Mathematics 2004-2014," Australian Mathematical Sciences Institute report, http://amsi.org.au/publications/participation-in-year-12-mathematics-2004-2014/ .
[33] Eryk Bagshaw, "HSC Maths: Students Studying Advanced Maths Stung with Lower Marks in ATAR," *Sydney Morning Herald*, 19/5/2015.
[34] James Franklin, "Mathematics for the Intelligent," *Gazette of the Australian Mathematical Society* 24 (1997): 2-3.
[35] Robert B. Banks, *Towing Icebergs, Falling Dominoes and Other Adventures in Applied Mathematics* (Princeton: Princeton University Press, 1998); UNSW's course 'Mathematical Modelling For Real

Statistics too needs a higher profile in mathematics education, as dealing with data and reaching conclusions from it are now the main uses of mathematics. In fact mathematics syllabuses have been moving in that direction, at both tertiary and secondary levels.[36] However syllabuses have been slower to adapt to the statistical needs of the "big data" that is flooding into data warehouses from the sophisticated hardware collecting it. Extracting meaning from huge datasets in real time is not quite the same task as the one for which classical statistical methods were developed, of extracting the most from small and expensive datasets such as in medicine.

The next thing that needs adding is a course on proof. Although mathematics advertises itself as "teaching you how to think"[37] and, as we have seen, proof is central to the Western mathematical tradition, mathematics degrees rarely include an explicit course on how to prove mathematical results. It is an easy enough skill to pick up but it is not inborn. Here is a simple example:

Prove that the square of every even number is even.

Proof: Let x be an even number (so that the result has generality by applying to *every* even number)
So $x = 2 \times k$ for some whole number k (that is the meaning of "even")
So $x^2 = (2 \times k)^2 = 2 \times 2 \times k^2$ (basic algebra)
which is even (again from the meaning of "even": it is twice some whole number)
Therefore the result is proved: for every even number, its square is even.

Understanding that does not require any stroke of genius: it is a perfectly mechanical application of the definition of "even" and simple algebraic manipulations. Such proof techniques can be and should be taught directly.[38]

Mathematical communication also needs to be taught. Communicating via graphs and diagrams is not the same as communicating via text. Mathematical professionals face the task of communicating their recommendations to people who cannot really understand them, and the challenges of communicating a simplified but sufficiently honest account of the mathematics are considerable. Those employers who habitually complain about the poor communication skills of graduates may want to consider the fact that they are

---

World Systems' is described at https://www.maths.unsw.edu.au/courses/math3041-mathematical-modelling-real-world-systems

[36] NSW Education Standards Authority, Mathematics K-10 syllabus, Statistics and Probability, https://syllabus.nesa.nsw.edu.au/mathematics/mathematics-k10/statistics-and-probability/
[37] Research on this tricky question in Matthew Inglis and Nina Attridge, *Does Mathematical Study Develop Logical Thinking? Testing the Theory of Formal Discipline* (New Jersey: World Scientific, 2017).
[38] James Franklin and Albert Daoud, *Proof in Mathematics: An Introduction* (Sydney: Kew Books, 2010).

acquiring their supply of graduates absolutely free and draw the obvious conclusion.

Mathematics has enormous effects in the "real world", as shown by such headlines as 'The Formula That Killed Wall Street'[39] and the fact that the military has always been an enthusiastic investor in mathematically-based technologies.[40] It follows that education in mathematics should include attention to ethical questions, in the same way as is normal in medical education. The issues for professional mathematicians are much the same as in other information management professions—duty of care, conflict of interest, honesty in drawing and communicating conclusions, confidentiality and whistleblowing, and the like—but the effects of malfeasance can be orders of magnitudes larger than in most professions.[41]

Conclusion

For those who wished to retain their sanity amid the stress of twentieth-century cultural chaos, where was there to escape to? In the humanities world, there was always the past, and many a cultural refugee from various Modernisms recuperated through communion with Monteverdi, or Vermeer, or Jane Austen. But for those who preferred their culture still living and breathing, the most extensive vandal-free space was science and mathematics.

Two regions of science stayed particularly free of any modern nervousness about themselves. One was engineering, for the obvious reason that bridge construction on cultural relativist principles is forbidden by the laws of nature as strictly as by those of man. The other was mathematics.

Mathematics has several advantages as a cultural counterweight to relativisms and scepticisms. Everyone knows something about it—in fact quite a lot about it—so it is not necessary to take the word of experts about everything in it, as it is for, say, quantum physics. Secondly, the truths in it are subject to proof, and what is proved does not become unproved (though it can be proved better).[42] For these reasons mathematics has always been an unfailing support for rationalist views, views which exalt the capacity of the human

---

[39] Felix Salmon, "Recipe For Disaster: The Formula That Killed Wall Street," *Wired* 23/2/2009, https://www.wired.com/2009/02/wp-quant/

[40] Examples in Nicholas Daras, ed, *Applications of Mathematics and Informatics in Military Science* (New York: Springer, 2012).

[41] James Franklin, "A 'Professional issues and ethics in mathematics' course," *Gazette of the Australian Mathematical Society* 32 (2005): 98-100; an Australian case study of the misuse of actuarial information in David Jackson QC, Report of the Special Commission of Inquiry into the Medical Research and Compensation Foundation, 2004, ch. 23
http://www.ir.jameshardie.com.au/jh/asbestos_compensation/special_commission_of_inquiry.jsp.

[42] It is sometimes claimed that non-Euclidean geometries are a counterexample, where Euclid's proofs were "overturned". That is not correct; the case is examined in James Franklin, *An Aristotelian Realist Philosophy of Mathematics: Mathematics as the science of quantity and structure* (Basingstoke: Macmillan, 2014), 160-2.

mind to find out the truth. Conversely, mathematics has been a perennial thorn in the side of opinions that abase human knowledge, and claim it is limited by sense experience, cultural horizons or one's personal education and perspective. Any culture or person that can count to 4 has discovered that 2 + 2 = 4, and should any fear arise of losing a grasp of that truth, resort to counting stones will quickly relieve any anxiety.

The truths of mathematics, unfortunately, cannot defend themselves, as they are not physical things with a causal action on the physical world. Neither ethical nor mathematical truths and ideals can fight tanks, or blizzards of allegations about history or politics (though again, neither can they be liquidated by those enemies). They depend on human minds to attune to them to act on their behalf—to implement those ideals and teach them to the next generation.

Bolstered by the continuing success of mathematics in applications, that makes an education in mathematics the surest way forward to a grasp of eternal verities.

Art Teaching as Part of a Liberal Education

Christopher Allen

Most art education curricula, whether in primary schools, secondary schools or vocational colleges, seem to have been written by people who have no real understanding of art, either as practitioners, historians or critics. Art classes, especially in primary school, are often treated as a kind of playtime, a break from serious academic subjects, and when art is taken a little more seriously, it is either thought of as a form of self-expression or as a way of articulating some kind of social critique.

But pupils are hardly ever taught any discipline of drawing, painting or any other art form that might make expression or articulation possible. Nor are they taught art history, which would allow them to reflect critically on their own practice; instead they are provided with a pre-digested set of ideological messages which they are encouraged to use both as inspiration for their own work and in the interpretation of any works by other artists they are shown.

This essay will begin by asking what role the teaching of art plays in a liberal education, and will then go on to suggest what approaches to the teaching of both art practice and art history, theory and criticism might best serve those ends. It will propose that art practice develops the intellect and the imagination in ways different from but complementary to other disciplines such as mathematics and languages, and that art history expands our understanding of human experience in a way comparable to the study of literature and music.

Art, in its many manifestations, means different things to different countries in the modern world: in Japan, for example, the aesthetic sensibility remains central to cultural life; in Italy, the art and architecture of past centuries is a source of pride even to uncultivated people, and opera remains a kind of popular music; the French take great pride in their literature and cinema, and in Iran such poets as Hafez and Sa'adi are loved by learned and unlearned alike.

In the British tradition, literature has always been richer and more highly regarded than either music or painting and sculpture, and perhaps that is why the English-speaking countries have comparatively little appreciation of the visual arts even today. We have biennales and art fairs, but these contrived and ultimately commercial events themselves betray the lack of a more organic and deeply-rooted culture of art.

Art has no public role today in articulating the shared values of our society; attempts at public art almost always founder in pomposity, bathos or ideological posturing. More recently commercial galleries complain that even the community of private collectors, or art lovers, as they were known even in the Dutch golden age *(kunstliefhebber)* has dwindled in favour of a new set of buyers who are not lovers but merely investors or even speculators. It is such speculation that has driven auction prices to levels that have no relation to aesthetic value. Record prices have become in themselves signs of status. As in all forms of conspicuous consumption, the prestige is greatest when you pay more for less, for the ability to throw money away is regarded as the most convincing demonstration of wealth.

Overlapping with this crude use of art as a symbol of wealth is a more subtle phenomenon: the quasi-religious prestige of contemporary art, fetishised in the spiritual vacuum of the consumer society. Contemporary art museums have taken the place of cathedrals as the would-be sacred edifices of today's cities, deliberately conceived as architecturally extravagant and non-functional to distinguish them from the ruthless utilitarianism of the real world.

But where does this leave art education, and art in education? Over the last century, art academies have gradually lost the sense that they can teach any solid foundations, methods or techniques, and students are largely left to their own devices, trying to second-guess the market and fashion. A tiny fraction of those who attend art schools will succeed, either because of innate talent, luck, or ruthless careerism.

And what about art in schools? A few have a relatively rigorous approach to the teaching of both practice and art history. Most have neither the will, the resources, nor adequately-trained staff to teach art properly. The textbooks produced for primary and secondary art classes in Australia reveal a fundamental lack of orientation, tending to treat art as playtime in primary school and later intent on indoctrinating pupils with the stale ideologies of an earlier generation rather than offering any coherent historical perspective or critical framework.

Why is Art So Poorly Taught in School?

Art curricula—whether the one used in NSW for the last couple of decades or the new National Curriculum which is meant to replace it—appear to have been written by people who have no understanding of the subject. They barely mention Art History and clearly take no interest in it, if they are not actively hostile to both its form and content. But even more surprisingly, they barely speak of any practical applications of art: there is no discussion, for example, of why it might be useful to teach children to draw, or paint, or make pots.

Instead, the emphasis is ideological and yet superficial, with a mishmash of feminist, postcolonial and deconstructive themes. Any coherent historical perspective is considered as an expression of the hegemonic discourse of white male ascendancy and must be demolished. And yet while pupils are ostensibly urged to be critical, in reality they are not encouraged to think for themselves: they do not learn to ask questions but to accept a set of pre-formulated answers.

At the deepest level, the problem is that the authors of these documents, and most of the teachers trained in this spirit, do not understand how art works at all. They conceive of it merely as a medium which can be employed to transmit a social or political message. They do not understand that art is something much more important than that: a way of thinking, a vehicle for the development of human awareness of the world and of self-consciousness.

Art, in all its forms, is in reality a way of thinking that long predates logical, discursive or theoretical reasoning. In some of its forms it may even predate language. But certainly the rational use of language—as we see it emerge in the reasoning of the Presocratic philosophers—is only around 2,500 years old, while art, in the form of storytelling, dance and song, painting and sculpture, is many thousands of years older than that.

Art works not by reasoning in abstract terms, but by reshaping the world in concrete form: ordering events into a story which makes sense of seemingly disparate or disconnected occurrences; fixing appearance as an image and a pattern: defining these things—literally setting limits to them—and giving them meaning in the process. And these operations do not happen merely in the mind, but in the handling of materials, with chalk or charcoal in hand. The painter does not think and then paint, but thinks in paint and while painting a subject.

Of course that is putting it in a simplistic way: an artist may be influenced by philosophical or other ideas, and a painter's thinking may pass through many stages of drawing and studies and critical reflection before his picking up the brush, but the point is that the crucial act of thinking takes place in the handling of materials and the manipulation of the concrete world. A painter may indeed have ideas before setting to work, but even these ideas are anticipations of practice and only possible because of profound familiarity with the act of making.

That is why it is so misleading when curricula imply that a child's 'artwork' has to begin with a 'concept'. A poster designer may begin with a concept, but an artist begins with an interest in a medium, a subject, or both (oil paint or film or ceramics; the human figure, landscape, a narrative subject), and it is only pursuing that thread of interest that can lead eventually to a work endowed with coherence and conviction.

Why is Art a Subject in a Liberal Education?

Clearly, the aim of art teaching in primary and secondary schools is not to train future artists, since only a fraction of graduates even of tertiary art academies succeed in becoming professional practitioners. The justification of teaching art in schools must lie in more general pedagogical benefits.

The aim of a liberal education, in any case, is not to train pupils for any particular trade or profession, but to develop their ability to undertake whatever role or opportunity may await them in an unpredictable future. The argument for teaching art as part of a liberal curriculum is similar to the argument for teaching any other subject whose aim is not directly utilitarian.

When we study mathematics, for example, we learn to think, to reason in a certain kind of way. We quite literally become more intelligent by developing this kind of capacity for complex reasoning. A similar thing happens when we learn Latin or Greek: once again we have to proceed systematically, building up new ways of thinking through different and at first unfamiliar syntactic structures, in the process also becoming far more conscious of the logic of language itself. Mathematics and grammar are indeed the two faces of logic, fundamental building blocks for rational thinking and the beginnings of philosophical reflection. Grammar could in principle be learnt through the study of English and modern languages, but in the debased way these subjects are taught now, it is unlikely that most pupils will end up with much intellectual benefit from them.

Music is another subject that teaches us to think in new ways, different again from those of mathematics or grammar. And this is exactly what art can do too, if it is taught as a discipline and not merely as playtime. It develops new ways of thinking and of imagining the world, different from and yet complementary to those of literature and music.

If each of these—and other—disciplines trains the mind to think in different ways, it is the intersection of such varied modes of thought that forms an intelligent, flexible and original mind. The object is not to train the mind to follow a single pathway, which can become an ever-deepening rut, but to move along many pathways and in multiple directions.

So far I have stressed the formal benefits of the academic disciplines that make up a liberal education, and some, like mathematics, are essentially formal. Others, like science and the humanities, are equally important for their content: a rounded education is not only about training the mind to think in a clear and agile manner, but also furnishes that mind with scientific, historical, literary and art-historical knowledge, which helps us to think more effectively and live better, wiser and more thoughtful lives.

Practical Teaching—Drawing

As anyone with a school-age child knows, art teachers would rather do almost anything than teach drawing. Children bring home a succession of gruesome collages on themes such as Father's Day, and later present their 'experiments' in abstract painting or pop art, or at best a self-portrait based on a photograph. In most cases, their teachers are not equipped to teach drawing, since they were never properly taught themselves. And they were most likely prophylactically indoctrinated with the idea that drawing is after all just copying the world of appearances. Surely it is more creative to distort and express and make things up than merely to copy?

In reality, this is a fallacy, based on a naïve understanding of both drawing and the nature of experiential reality. A photograph can be copied, because it is already a two-dimensional, flat picture. But the world is not something that can be copied; it is not two-dimensional and it is not a picture. Ultimately, it is not even an object or a set of objects but an almost infinitely complex and irreducible field of visual and affective experience. But even at the simplest level, making a drawing involves not copying but translating, transposing our visual experience of a three-dimensional world into a two-dimensional image.

Drawing is therefore among the most complex of intellectual operations, involving both reaching out to a reality beyond the human mind and, in response to what we apprehend, constructing a flat, finite picture that offers some graphic equivalent of that experience, fixing and defining it, as though forming a visual hypothesis about its ultimate nature. And this process is not carried out simply in the head, but with pencil in hand, involving body and mind in a seamless process, the hand becoming a tool of an embodied intelligence.

This is why drawing is the foundation of art teaching. It is the primary way that we engage with the visual world and begin to make something finite and ultimately truly expressive out of the world that we encounter: at the simplest level, merely to draw a few bottles on a table leads us to understand shape and volume, and to discover how the appearance of the world is inseparable from the perspective of the viewing subject.

And most surprising of all, the more clearly defined the project, the more truly individual each pupil's work becomes. When you let young people draw whatever they like, just to 'express themselves', what they produce all looks the same, because it comes from the surface of the self, which is occupied by the flotsam and jetsam of the commercial culture they consume. But when you assign a project with strict guidelines, the effort required seems to drive them deeper within, and what emerges is a range of works reflecting the artistic character or aesthetic sensibility of each pupil.

Practical Teaching—Other Media and Artforms

Drawing is a core subject, a foundation for the various studio disciplines, such as painting, printmaking, ceramics, sculpture, photography, film, and so on. Each of these, in turn, has much to offer as a school subject, but once again only if taught in a methodical way and with a respect for the practice of each craft.

In painting, for example, we learn to think not only in abstract formal terms, but to deal with the phenomena of colour and light. Once again there is no sense in which painting merely copies the world. One of the things that painting teaches us is the profound difference between the colours we see in the world—themselves only ways that our perceptual system has evolved to discriminate between different frequencies of light—and the pigments that can be used to emulate such effects. There is no straightforward equivalence between the colour we see and the pigments we paint with, but we learn to produce combinations and relations of pigments to form a version of the phenomena of the world. It is not even the closeness of the illusion that matters, but rather the coherence of the collection of pigments in relation to the world of experience, once again, the artificial model that we produce is an act of interpretation.

And the understanding of colour is only one aspect of painting, although logically the first step after drawing. But ultimately painting involves many different problems and choices, from the selection of a subject to composition, point of view, colour temperature, tonal range and the expressive handling of brush marks. Similar points could be made about any of the other specific art forms. Sculpture is inseparable from the handling of materials, and the experiences of carving, modelling and constructing involve fundamentally different ways of thinking about the world and about materials. Similarly a film maker learns to think through cinematography, framing and editing as much as through devising a story, casting and directing the performers, selecting sets, costumes and music.

In practice we find that some pupils, like professional artists, are more drawn to one or other art form because it suits their own inherent sensibility and way of thinking about the world. A film maker enjoys the temporal nature of the medium, but also the necessity for collaboration; a painter may prefer solitude and a potter may fall in love with the meditative stillness of the potter's wheel.

Each of these art forms, if taught well, is an opportunity to develop aspects of the mind and the imagination. Ultimately too an even deeper lesson is learnt in the benefits of dedication, focus and concentration. A boy or girl may well find that it is while making work in the studio that they first discover a capacity for true attention, which can be extended to other areas of their studies and indeed to their life. But all these benefits arise in direct proportion to the rigour of the discipline imparted.

Art History and Practice

Art History, as a secondary school subject, is valuable from several points of view, the most obvious of which is as an inspiration and guide to practice, as well as a touchstone of quality. For the first thing that Art History reminds us is that all forms of practice, including art forms themselves, genres and styles, arise under particular social and historical conditions. They were motivated in their time, not arbitrary, connected and not random.

Without the perspective of Art History, schools tend to treat all the art forms, genres and styles of the past as a kind of smorgasbord from which they can pick and choose at will. The result, inevitably, is to produce insipid formalist pastiches unrelated to the deeper concerns that inspired these forms in the first place. With a proper art-historical foundation, it is still possible to employ some of the forms of the past, but the pupil or the artist will do so consciously, and a proper awareness of what they meant originally permits thoughtful reinterpretation.

The other thing that Art History reminds us is that styles, like the social conditions that inspired them, in fact succeeded each other in a certain order. It used to be fashionable to sneer at teaching anything in chronological order, but that sequence is based on an undeniable historical reality: that some things actually did happen before or after others, in a sequence of linear succession that cannot be reversed.

The later forms or styles tend to be influenced by, or responses or reactions to, the ones that preceded them, as for example Neo-Impressionism to Impressionism, or the naturalism of Caravaggio to the mannerism of the mid-sixteenth century. In the longer sweep of history, we cannot understand Cubism and its implied world view, without understanding the Renaissance discovery of objective space, starting with Giotto, and pondering the meaning of that movement, once again in relation to the social environment that gave it birth.

Art History and Other Subjects in Curriculum
More broadly, Art History complements other subjects in a curriculum of liberal studies. This is most obvious in the case of history, where it can give a human face to periods that are primarily being studied from a political, military or economic point of view. To realise that the greatest explosion of modernist art and culture coincided with the tense decade before the outbreak of the Great War, for example, clearly enriches our sense of what was really going on in European society and the European mind on the eve of the catastrophe.

Similarly Art History has clear affinities with the study of English and other literatures: the cultural world that we encounter in the study of 16th century art, for example, can illuminate the reading of Shakespeare, writing at the end of that century and deeply influenced by the example of Italy. Some movements, like Romanticism, express themselves as readily in art as in literature.

Less immediately obvious, no doubt, are the affinities between Art History and Mathematics or the sciences, and yet Geometry and Mathematics are intimately involved both in the geometry of pictorial composition and in the Renaissance theory of Perspective. Even more significantly the emergence of the perspectival view of space in Renaissance painting can be understood as an integral part, or even the first tangible expression, of the new objectivising vision that underpins the birth of modern science.

Conclusion: Art and Culture

As art is generally taught in schools today, its benefits are unpredictable, and depend on the good fortune of a gifted pupil encountering a talented and enthusiastic teacher, a well-resourced school, and the support and inspiration of a cultured family. The purpose of an effective curriculum should be to leave less of this to good luck, but the curricula as they stand—once again speaking mainly from experience of the NSW system—not only fail to give positive guidance and support, but actually embody and thus transmit harmful misunderstandings about the nature of art.

If art is taught well, as I have argued, it can play an important part in a child's education. The practical disciplines, starting with drawing, develop the eye, the intellect and the hand, introducing the young mind to a different way of thinking about and being aware of the world and complementing the kinds of thinking fostered by other academic subjects.

Art History enriches practice with an understanding of the meaning inherent in style and also a sense of standards and quality; in addition it deepens our appreciation of other disciplines, encouraging the pupil to see the various branches of their school studies as offering different perspectives on the world, rather than as entirely separate subjects, each segregated and isolated within its own set of problems and methods.

And finally, the study of art—both the practice of making art and the reading of its history—as is also true of literature or music—gives us access to some of the highest expressions of human culture. These are the books, pictures, sculptures, musical compositions and buildings which are in many ways the most precious inheritance of humanity, for they help us to reflect on what it is to be human and to live our lives with greater insight, joy, compassion and consciousness.

Helping to Regain Lost Ground by Re-vitalizing Music Education

Richard Gill

That I should claim this to be a scholarly article would be, in my view, a claim I could not in all seriousness make or pretend to substantiate. I do not see myself as a member of the company of scholars, who write so well, and from whose writings I derive enormous pleasure and, not infrequently, very useful and helpful information, especially in reference to interpretation of music from 1720 to 1911, the death of Mahler. This article is more in the nature of a little bit of history followed by a call to arms.

While I despair at the current state of the universities and some of the teacher training institutions, I conclude this article by quoting Alexander Pope: "Hope springs eternal in the human breast." My subject, music, is very much about hope, humans and the feelings we have in our hearts, our breasts if you will, and our minds and souls. After all, hope is all we have.

One of my sources, Kenneth Simpson's excellent book of essays entitled *Some Great Music Educators* (1976), refers to the appearance in the United Kingdom of the first edition of *The Handbook of Suggestions for the Consideration of Teachers and Others Concerned in the Work of Public Elementary Schools* (1905). In the preface to this edition the following information is given:

> The only uniformity of practice that the Board of Education desire to see . . . is that each teacher shall think for himself, and work out for himself such methods of teaching as may use his powers to the best advantage and be best suited to the particular needs and conditions of the school.[1]

In 1937 a revised edition appeared which added the following:

> It remains for the teachers themselves to apply and adapt the standards and practice suggested in this volume to the particular circumstances of the schools in which they are at work.[2]

---

[1] Cited in Kenneth Simpson (gen. ed.), *Some Great Music Educators* (Borough Green, Kent: Novello and Company Ltd, 1976), 9.
[2] *Ibid.*

These suggestions obviously carried with them huge responsibilities for the teacher, with the assumption that each teacher was also a practising philosopher who was capable of establishing a methodology based on the formation of an individual philosophy. From this, it is abundantly clear that the autonomy of the teacher was paramount at every level, the teacher being free to devise programmes of work for students based on needs and not on some artificial construct of a government authority.

In Australia in 2017 we have nothing in any of the State systems of education which replicates the circumstances of the United Kingdom in 1905.

We are hampered by the constraints of a national system which requires that children undergo a series of standardised tests in Grades 1,3,5,7 and 9. These tests place the creative teacher in a very difficult position, often stifling the very things children need from such a creative individual, who is in fear of not covering enough exemplars for the style of answer required by the standardised test format set by some faceless and nameless examiner.

For the lazy teacher, the standardised test is a gift. The lazy teachers simply buy books of practice tests which their classes do regularly, and pass off these activities as education. In short, teachers are not autonomous, being accountable to a system imposed on them nationally, ostensibly in the interest of increasing Australian children's' capacities in literacy and numeracy.

In some schools I have visited I hear the Principal and teachers talking about literacy and numeracy as if they are subjects in and of themselves. When it is explained that literacy and numeracy are states or conditions at which one arrives as a result of being educated, the lack of comprehension of this concept from some teachers and Principals is palpable. The anecdotal evidence I have gathered from a huge number of primary school teachers to whom I have spoken regularly as I travel the country doing music education workshops, is, that standardised testing is largely a waste of time.

The reason for the detail in regard to standardised testing is that it is my considered view that this form of activity is crippling the country's education systems and having a profound effect on the teaching of music, dance, visual art and drama, subjects often perceived as frills, or add-ons if there is time. There was a time when music education was considered essential—something far removed from the notion of being a frill or an add-on.

Knowledge of music, and the ability to teach it at a very sophisticated level, were the principal requirements for the appointing of kindergarten teachers in New South Wales. In New South Wales in the early part of the 20th century, through to the early 1950s, kindergarten teachers were required to play the piano to a very high standard. Without this keyboard skill there was no chance an applicant to any training institution such as a Teachers' College or a Kindergarten Training College, would be accepted as a candidate for Kindergarten training. Each teacher trainee was required to demonstrate proficiency in the following musical fields:

(i) using an A tuning fork, sing any major, melodic or harmonic minor scale in solfeggio ascending or descending as required by the examiner;
(ii) play from sight an accompaniment to a nursery rhyme, a folk song and an art song;
(iii) play a hymn from sight and sing any part of the hymn as required by the examiner;
(iv) continue with the hymn and play the bass part while singing the alto, soprano or tenor part, or any other combination of parts as required by the examiner;
(v) improvise at the piano a march, a waltz, a polka and a dance of one's own choice as required by the examiner.

A prospective teacher, found to be lacking in any of these skills, was not given a position.

The point of all of this is that musical competency was considered as the determining factor in appointing a Kindergarten teacher. Music was seen as being fundamental to the life of every Kindergarten child, beginning with singing. This, regrettably, is not the case today. There was a time when the daily life of a kindergarten child began with music. Music was played on the piano by the Kindergarten teacher at the start of each day as an accompaniment for children to march into class. Marching to music was considered an essential skill as it instilled order, a sense of beat or pulse and helped settle the classes.

The march was followed by a session of singing and movement. The movement was often free which balanced the discipline of the morning march and within the movement component of a lesson, children were encouraged to explore the space around them, move freely and react to the music, being reminded constantly to listen to the music as intently as they could.

The songs were essentially nursery rhymes and simple folk songs, again accompanied at the piano by the teacher. The children sang these songs unconducted and relied on the strength of the teacher as a musician to hold the class together. This required high intensity listening on the part of the class, a result of which was a sharpened listening focus from the children, an increase in children's concentration and an ability to focus on a specific task for an extended period of time together with rhythmic independence and a heightened sense of ensemble.

Once the children had learned a number of songs and games, the process of teaching music reading and writing began. All successful music reading was taught on the principle of sound before symbol. Teachers who tried to teach reading as an independent activity, not based on real music, simply failed at the task. In New South Wales the fixed-doh principle was employed. In fixed-doh, C is always doh, D is always re, and so on. The moveable doh system of Tonic Sol Fa where any note can be doh was introduced by Englishman, John

Curwen (1816-1880) and then later taken up by Hungary's Zoltan Kodaly.[3] Kindergarten teachers were aware of a handbook of Solfeggio, as it was called, compiled by a music educator, Joseph Bradley (1857-1935). In this manual for teachers, published in 1919, there is a series of exercises, songs and the like, with which the average Conservatorium undergraduate student, in my experience, would struggle today.

Joseph Bradley taught at the then New South Wales State Conservatorium of Music under the directorship of Henry Verbrugghen. He conducted the Royal Philharmonic Society in 1908, the year of his arrival in Sydney from England, and then later the first Sydney Symphony Orchestra, established by an almost unknown and uncelebrated musician, George Plummer. This orchestra survived until 1914, the outbreak of World War One. This background information is important information in relation to the position of a music educator.

All reports describe Bradley as an outstanding musician at every level and a hugely gifted conductor. That he would concern himself also with music education is a concept completely alien to most professional conductors these days. Many of them pay lip-service to education in music but few will ever dirty their hands by conducting a concert for children, often perceived as a sub-standard activity and beneath their dignity.

It is important to make reference to these events of the past as this is a part of our musical heritage which has almost disappeared. There was clearly a time when music education was paramount within the State system and taken seriously by the community as a whole. Aspects of this interest in music generally in the community would have been reflected in a very informal way when families gathered for a meal and then sang around a piano as a form of entertainment, a form now almost extinct I would imagine, in most parts of Australia.

Once music became universally available, through the emergence of the radio and the record industry, listening to examples of music became part of every teacher's directed listening activities. Children followed the themes of the recorded music, as written on the blackboard by the teacher, learning to sing the themes and clap the rhythms. This clapping of the rhythmic material was later translated to percussion instruments, and many kindergarten teachers took the trouble to create percussion charts to accompany recorded music. Indeed, the onetime City of Sydney Eisteddfod had an Infants School Percussion section to which there was a massive subscription. This activity had implications for the reading of music, which was seen as a logical and natural development in a child's music education.

---

[3] Simpson, *op. cit.*, chs IV and IX.

As a result of these activities, children developed extraordinary musical memories and were able to identify dozens and dozens of songs from the sounding of the first two or three notes. This repertoire stayed with them for life, and is often, in the case of adults with dementia, the only aspect of early life many of them are able to recall—such is the power of music.

This capacity to remember dozens and dozens of songs and the associated activity with each song had an immediate impact on the way in which children learned to read, write, spell, count and perform simple tasks in the subjects of English and Arithmetic. This concept, the effect of music on learning generally, is now being examined by neuroscientists the world over.

Although the effect of music on the brain, and indeed on all learning, has become quite recently the subject of a huge number of research papers, the perception that music had this quality was never really discussed by teachers, as music was seen to be good in its own right and needed no further justification. However, teachers often noted that the students who were the top performers in many subjects were also the top music performers. This was, quite simply, an observation of little or no consequence.

So what do we do now to restore music to every state school and see that every child has access to a qualified music teacher who is a trained specialist? An examination of the current system, nationally, is essential.

In 2017, Queensland leads the way in music education and has done so for some time. The employment of specialist teachers in music and physical education in Queensland has had a profound impact on education in that state. Along with a very highly developed instrumental instruction programme, Queensland continues to be a source of inspiration to the rest of the country. While the other states employ a variety of music practitioners, none of the states to my knowledge has a policy which indicates that every child in a state school should have access to a properly trained specialist music teacher who works in a classroom and provides music education to every child in the school.

So, what is meant by the words 'music education'? In my mind, it is very clear. All music education begins with singing and movement, together with the use of simple classroom percussion instruments leading to improvisation. The reason for teaching music to children is so that children can make their own music.

Children should sing a wide variety of songs and play an equally wide variety of musical games, including nursery rhymes, folk songs, composed songs, popular songs and so on. The songs should be of two types. Type A is for fun and because the children just like to sing the song. Type B is also for fun, but contains concepts of pitch, rhythm, dynamics and tempo which will be encountered later in a formal way. Both types of songs and the associated activities provide children with material and vocabulary for improvisation which is fundamental to the way in which children understand how music works.

As stated previously, movement is an integral part of singing in the early years as is the playing of simple percussion instruments. This is an approach to music education which existed in New South Wales in the early part of the twentieth century which we need to regain.

From the song material, teachers undertake the business of teaching music reading and writing. When a child becomes musically literate the whole world of notated music opens up to them and they begin their journey of musical independence. It is not dissimilar to teaching children how to read. Once they are fluent readers they have access to some of the most wonderful imaginations and ideas in the world from antiquity to the present.

All of this teaching should be sequential and dictated by the teacher's understanding of where the children sit musically. If the children have a large repertoire of music, as they go through the process of reading and writing, they begin to make observations about similarities and differences in pitch, rhythm, dynamics and the like within the repertoire. This process of analysis and observation is fundamental to comprehension.

In some benighted areas of education today, it is seen as a badge of honour for so-called music teachers to stand up at seminars and say: 'I can't read or write music but I have been teaching music for years'. This is often greeted with applause from those who share that view. Many Jazz musicians, for example, have not been music readers but have had phenomenal musical ears and an inherent ability with an instrument. Indeed, in fifty-five years of teaching I have found students who have incredible facility on an instrument by dint of hard work and devotion to practising, who later undertake courses of reading. Recently, I encountered a rock and roll musician who was bemoaning the fact that he had never learned to read. It takes him five times as long to learn a tune as any other member in his band, all of whom are readers.

Any self-proclaimed non-reader with whom I have worked at a music workshop has been unable to take part in most of the activities because of a fundamental lack of musical skills. These people are not music teachers—they are highly paid baby-sitters and should be required to leave the service. It would be insupportable in the teaching of science for a teacher to claim that he or she knew nothing of Physics, Chemistry or Biology but has been teaching these subjects for years.

So how do we rebuild and regain? In order to start re-building and regaining lost ground I have begun a training program for classroom teachers known as the National Music Teacher Mentoring Program, NMTMP. With strong financial support from the current Federal Government and equally strong support from a private donor, the program was launched in 2014 and sits under the auspices of the Australian Youth Orchestra, a national body able to receive Federal money.

The NMTMP works on the principle of a mentor teacher who is a music teacher, working with two classroom teachers in an attempt to provide the classroom teachers with enough skills to enable them to introduce music to children in Kindergarten to Grade 2. It entails the teachers working collaboratively and sharing ideas generously and frequently. Participating teachers observe mentor teachers working, and then mentors watch the participating teachers work. Following these lessons are evaluations and planning sessions. The teachers are autonomous and devise their own curricula. The only conditions imposed on them are that the children must sing, they must move, they must play simple percussion instruments and improvise. How this is done is based on the teachers' assessments of where their charges are musically.

The program, which has been thoroughly evaluated by Professor Margaret Barrett and her team at The University of Queensland's Creative Collaboratorium, has been proven to be hugely successful. At the time of writing, the program now exists in New South Wales, Queensland, in collaboration with Good to Great Schools, South Australia, which has an exemplary version of the program, Victoria, Tasmania and Western Australia. The NMTMP had a short stay in the Northern Territory with great success, but administrative changes caused a hiatus that we will soon fix with our collaboration with the Good to Great Schools, which has outreach in the Northern Territory.

The weakness in the program is that it is, in reality, a band-aid approach. We need to be able to convince State Governments that what every private school child has in the form of access to a specialist music teacher, every state school child should also have. We need to convince universities to become serious about teacher training and check the credentials of the people they admit to their courses. They also need to send their lecturers into the field as practising teachers so that the students to whom they lecture can see them putting their words into practice.

Some school Principals tell me that they have a music programme in the form of a band. A school band is not a music programme; it's a band program. A music program includes every child. We know that music is good: that is why we teach it. We know also that to understand music, children must make their own music—another reason for teaching music and in truth the principal reason for teaching music.

We know that we teach music because it is abstract, it goes to the heart, the mind, the soul and the very fibre of a human being, and is capable of providing profound emotional reactions. We know all this and many people all around the world know all this. However, in Australia, there are still many people in positions of authority who don't know any of this or don't want to know.

I see it as one of my jobs to change their minds, and bring them around to see reason, which some of the greatest educators in the world can already see. Hope springs eternal in the human breast, including mine.

A Plea for Narrowness

Jeremy Bell

Liberal Education and the Study of 'Great Books'
Liberal education is education 'for its own sake'. It is in some sense an end in itself, not a mere means to other ends. The study of the liberal arts (including the pure sciences) may have professional and other 'practical' benefits, but its *raison d'être* is not solely or primarily instrumental—or so I shall assume.[1]

Some of its advocates argue that a liberal education should consist chiefly in the study of classic texts or 'great books'. They favour some variant on the Great Books curriculum pioneered early last century by John Erskine, Mortimer Adler, Robert Hutchins and others. Rare outside the United States (and virtually non-existent in Australia), Great Books programs have come in for heavy criticism in recent decades. They are charged with an objectionably narrow focus on the work of 'dead, white males' and they are alleged to encourage an unscholarly disregard for the historical context of the 'great books'.[2] I am inclined to think these criticisms grossly exaggerated. However, it is not my goal in this essay either to defend existing Great Books programs or to propose improvements in them. It is rather to make a case for the inclusion in any undergraduate or postgraduate humanities program of a substantial number of courses of the kind taught in Great Books programs, i.e., courses devoted to the close reading of a small number of complete, classic texts. As a teacher of philosophy, I wish more particularly to make a case for the inclusion of such courses in undergraduate and postgraduate philosophy programs.

The general format of a close reading course in philosophy is straightforward. One or two classic texts are selected for study, e.g. Spinoza's *Ethics* or a couple of thematically related Platonic dialogues. By the end of the course, students are to have read every assigned text in its entirety. In each session, the instructor guides students through a section of text, with careful attention

---

[1] 'This process of training, by which the intellect, instead of being formed or sacrificed to some particular or accidental purpose, some specific trade or profession, or study or science, is disciplined for its own sake, for the perception of its own proper object, and for its own highest culture, is called Liberal Education.' John Henry Newman, *The Idea of a University*, ed. Frank M. Turner (New Haven & London: Yale University Press, 1996), Discourse VII, 109.

[2] For a very different and (I think) more interesting critique of Great Books programs from a 'conservative' perspective, see Patrick Deneen, 'Why the Great Books Aren't the Answer', *Minding the Campus*, 31 March 2010 http://www.mindingthecampus.org/2010/03/why_the_great_books_arent_the/

to detail. Extra-textual information (e.g. historical or biographical material) is introduced only for the sake of aiding comprehension of the text and is kept to a minimum. In order to leave students as much time as possible to read and reread the primary text(s) slowly and thoughtfully, assigned secondary scholarship is likewise kept to a minimum. The basic intention of the course is to treat each text studied as a serious and enduringly relevant essay in philosophical thinking, not merely as a source of information about the 'history of ideas'.

Courses of this kind, especially on pre-modern texts, are relatively uncommon in Australian tertiary institutions. One understandable objection to close reading courses in philosophy at the undergraduate level is that they are unduly narrow. While it may be appropriate for doctoral students and professional scholars to engage in prolonged, intensive study of complete classic texts, the case is surely different—so the objection runs—when teaching philosophy to beginners. What undergraduates need and want is, instead, exposure to a broad range of texts, ideas and arguments. I have called this essay 'a plea for narrowness' in acknowledgment of the force of this objection.

My conviction of the enormous value of courses based on the close reading of one or two classic texts is due in large part to their role in my own intellectual formation. I had the good fortune to take a number of such courses during my doctoral studies with the Committee on Social Thought at the University of Chicago, and they were by far the most satisfying and memorable that I have ever experienced. Well attended by undergraduates as well as postgraduates, they were for most of us an inspiration and a joy. That philosophy students at Australian universities often have little or no opportunity to take such courses seems to me a shame and, indeed, an injustice.

Learning How to Read
The most basic benefit of taking a close reading course is that one can learn to read better. Learning to read better is not the same as acquiring increased facility in comprehending complex material. A first-year undergraduate will certainly have much greater trouble making sense of the *Critique of Pure Reason* than a Masters student used to abstruse philosophical argumentation and with a prior grounding in epistemology, but this need not mean that the Masters student is a better reader. To be a good reader is to be in the habit of attending carefully and patiently to everything present in a text, which is in truth a difficult habit to acquire. It is difficult partly because most of us are neither original thinkers nor great writers and, consequently, we tend to underestimate the meticulous craftsmanship that has gone into a classic text. It is also difficult because we are all, to a greater or lesser extent, apt to read into a text what we expect or wish to find in it. More generally, we are all apt to hear the things we expect or wish to hear, rather than the things people actually say.

The book of Genesis (a staple of Great Books curricula) provides a striking illustration of this familiar but important truth in its narrative of what Christian tradition calls the Fall of Man. When the serpent first addresses Eve (Genesis 3:1), he asks her why God has commanded her and her husband not to eat the fruit of any of the trees in paradise, despite presumably knowing full well that it is only the tree of the knowledge of good and evil whose fruit God has forbidden them (2:16-17). The serpent thus begins his work of temptation by tacitly inviting Eve to misconstrue the literal sense of God's words. She rightly replies that it is the fruit of only one tree that God has commanded her and Adam not to eat—but she then adds that God has also commanded them not even to touch this fruit (3:2-3). This addition is apparently her own invention, since no such commandment is recorded elsewhere in Genesis. Though Eve has rejected the outlandish distortion of God's words suggested by the serpent, she has substituted for it a milder and more plausible distortion of her own. Quite possibly she has done so because the serpent's suggestion has had its intended effect: it has prompted her to reflect on God's severity, and to magnify it. If, as the context seems to indicate, her seemingly innocuous distortion of God's commandment was her first step towards disobedience, it cannot have been truly innocuous. One might almost go so far as to say that the Fall of Man was due in part to a failure to listen properly.

We need not be Jewish or Christian believers to appreciate the psychological acuteness of this narrative. Our natural propensity to 'filter' what we hear and see (or remember hearing and seeing) on the basis of our own inclinations and prejudices is a major cause of our difficulties both in establishing and fostering relationships with our fellow human beings and in expanding our knowledge and understanding of the world we inhabit. A key priority for educators is to help students to recognize and resist this propensity. Close reading courses on philosophical classics have several advantages over standard philosophy courses in this regard:

(1) Firstly, and most obviously, they are expressly devoted to the task of reading an author with the utmost possible care. Students are constantly encouraged to read slowly and thoughtfully—and, moreover, to reread what they have already read. In addition, they are required to read a classic text from beginning to end, rather than merely reading excerpts. Reading (fragments of) a text only once and hurriedly all but guarantees that one will misunderstand it or, at best, understand it only in part. To misunderstand a text is to substitute for the author's own thought some figment of one's own imagination. And what one is prone to imagine the author thinks will, inevitably, in some way reflect one's own inclinations and prejudices. Fast, careless reading thus tends to imprison the reader in his or her own pre-existing worldview. A close reading course is designed to make it possible for a student to be genuinely touched by the worldview of another. It trains students to cultivate the steadfast attentiveness that is indispensable for good reading—and for good listening.

It is much more difficult to practise such attentiveness in philosophy courses of the kind most commonly taught at Australian universities. In a standard philosophy course, a large selection of (often incomplete) texts are assigned, none of which is normally studied for longer than a week or two. Little class time is spent on close reading. Students are not encouraged to engage in such reading out of class and, in any case, they rarely have the time to do so, given the volume of assigned material. A predictable consequence is that they very often acquire only a garbled understanding of what they read.

This is especially likely in the case of texts written hundreds or thousands of years ago. The terminology and style of older texts is often unfamiliar to students, and thinkers of past centuries naturally wrote in the first instance for their contemporaries, whose shared assumptions were not always the same as ours. Moreover, students of philosophy who cut their teeth largely on Anglophone philosophy of the last century, as do most students at Australian universities, will likely come to have certain expectations of philosophical texts. In particular, they will come to expect all serious philosophical writing to have the kind of rigour characteristic of analytic philosophy. The analytic philosopher tries to make his argumentation as 'clear and distinct' as he can. Key terms are laboriously analysed, presuppositions are made explicit, premises of arguments are fastidiously elaborated, and the logical structure of arguments is formally identified (and sometimes formally represented by means of mathematical symbolism). Technical jargon is common. Even apparently straightforward concepts and claims are painstakingly spelt out.

If a student is accustomed to analytic philosophy, her first impression of many older philosophical texts will probably be that they are simply deficient in philosophical rigour. Many thinkers who wrote before the twentieth century did not attempt exhaustive elaborations of their ideas and arguments. In part, this was due to their confidence in the intelligence and assiduity of at least some of their readers. After presenting arguments for the existence of void in *De Rerum Natura*, Lucretius says that 'these little traces are enough for a keen intellect, and by their means you are able to discover the rest on your own'.[3] He was disinclined to spoon-feed readers with 'keen intellects'.

Some past philosophers not only eschewed spoon-feeding, but deliberately opted for a highly condensed or even elliptical presentation of their thinking. Speaking through his Zarathustra, Nietzsche compared his aphorisms to mountain peaks, implying that the scaling of these peaks—the prolonged and arduous thinking required both to formulate the aphorisms and, on the reader's part, to understand them—is not openly presented in his books, but only indicated.[4] Elsewhere he warned that, easy as they are to read quickly, his

---

[3] Lucretius, *De Rerum Natura*, Book I, 402-3; *On the Nature of Things*, trans. Walter Englert (Newburyport, MA: Focus Publishing, 2003), 11.

[4] Friedrich Nietzsche, *Thus Spake Zarathustra*, 'Of Reading and Writing'; trans. R. J. Hollingdale (Pen-

books can only be understood if read slowly.⁵ He apparently felt he had good reason to leave much of his thinking implicit.

Aphorists like Nietzsche are not alone in purposefully leaving things unelaborated. Rousseau claimed that, when composing his *Discourse on the Arts and Sciences*, he often 'went to great trouble to try and condense into a single sentence, a single line, a single word tossed off as if by chance, the result of a long chain of reflections'.⁶ Put differently, he went to great trouble *not* to be explicit about all facets of his thinking. He added, with remarkable frankness, that a majority of his readers 'must often have found my discourses poorly structured and almost entirely disjointed, for want of perceiving the trunk of which I showed them only the branches'.

Tantalizing and provoking readers into thinking for themselves by showing only the 'peaks' or 'branches' of one's thought is more than a dispensable pedagogical device. The choice to write in this way arguably reflects, at bottom, a certain view of the world, or at any rate of human life, that is at odds with characteristically modern presuppositions. The rise of modern, mathematical natural science and its phenomenal successes over the last three or four centuries have encouraged the hope that a mathematically precise study of human things (history, ethics, politics, etc.) might also be possible. The modern disciplines of economics and sociology were fruits of this hope. To the extent that human things can indeed be treated with mathematical precision, they can be treated with the clarity and distinctness to which analytic philosophy aspires.

It is far from obvious, however, that human life in its full richness is susceptible of such treatment. Sceptics of this possibility who nonetheless take mathematical natural science as their model for all genuinely 'scientific' investigation will tend to regard the humanities with more or less undisguised contempt. An alternative, characteristically pre-modern view finds its classic expression in a famous passage early in Aristotle's *Nicomachean Ethics*, where the Stagyrite warns that 'precision ought not to be sought in the same way in all kinds of discourse'.⁷ When discussing such topics as the noble, the just and the good—in short, the human things—'one ought to be content…to point out the truth roughly and in outline'. The disarming gentleness and prosaic

---

guin: 1969), 67.

⁵ '[M]y earlier writings…are, indeed, not easy to penetrate.' *On the Genealogy of Morals*, Preface, trans. Walter Kaufman & R.J. Hollingdale (New York: Vintage Books, 1989), 22. Nietzsche goes on to say that an aphorism 'has not been 'deciphered' when it has simply been read; rather, one has then to begin its *exegesis*, for which is required an art of exegesis' (23).

⁶ Jean-Jacques Rousseau, "Preface of a Second Letter to Bordes", in *The Discourses and Other Early Political Writings*, ed. and trans. Victor Gourevitch (Cambridge: Cambridge University Press, 1997), 110.

⁷ Aristotle, *Nicomachean Ethics*, 1094b 18-20; trans. Joe Sachs (Newburyport, MA: Focus Publishing, 2002), 2.

sobriety of this remark may lead us to overlook its radical implications. If the study of human life is unavoidably 'rough' and 'imprecise', then man and his most vital concerns are fundamentally elusive. The 'proper study of mankind' is somehow doomed to frustration. Moreover, since man is in some sense only a part of a bigger whole ('Nature', the cosmos, Creation, the universe) it seems to follow that this whole is likewise fundamentally elusive.[8] If philosophy is the search for knowledge of all things, then it too is doomed to frustration. For this very reason, earlier philosophers who declined the attempt to present an exhaustive, clear and distinct account of things are likelier to have been faithful to the phenomena than their contemporary scientific counterparts. Furthermore, their decision to give only attenuated presentations of their thought would serve a profoundly important pedagogical function: it would have a discouraging and hence sobering effect on readers over-zealous for systematicity and completeness.

(2) The preference of some past philosophers for a condensed or elliptical presentation of their thought would be reason enough to read their works more slowly than one might read the works of Paul Grice or Donald Davidson. A further and no less important reason is that, unlike contemporary writers, past philosophers were by no means averse to making purposefully misleading statements.[9] In his introduction to the *Guide for the Perplexed*, Maimonides expressly declares that his treatise contains 'contradictory or contrary statements' and he provides the reader with general guidelines for interpreting them.[10] Other philosophers were not so open about their willingness to mislead. I shall take an example from a thinker renowned for his unapologetic straightforwardness, Thomas Hobbes.

Readers of Hobbes' *Leviathan* will get the impression that he believes in the natural equality of all human beings. His depiction of the 'state of nature' in Part I, Chapter 13 seemingly begins with the assertion that men are naturally equal (or nearly so) 'in the faculties of the body, and mind'.[11] Two chapters later he flatly declares that, 'in the condition of mere nature... (as has been shewn before,) all men are equal' (102). Yet on closer examination it is clear that this declaration cannot be taken at face value. Hobbes' precise claim at the beginning of Chapter 13 is not that all men are naturally equal, but that

---

[8] It is usually supposed that, while Aristotle did not regard ethics and politics as exact sciences, he took a more optimistic view of the natural sciences. But consider what he says at the start of Book II, Ch.12 of *De Caelo* (291b24-28). For a broader discussion of this question, see David Bolotin, *An Approach to Aristotle's Physics* (New York: SUNY Press, 1997).

[9] This admittedly controversial thesis is most famously associated with Leo Strauss. The *locus classicus* of his theory of 'esoteric writing' is *Persecution and the Art of Writing* (Chicago & London: Chicago University Press, 1988).

[10] M. Maimonides, *Guide for the Perplexed*, Vol.I, Introduction; trans. Shlomo Pines (Chicago and London: University of Chicago Press, 1963), 17-20.

[11] Thomas Hobbes, *Leviathan*, ed. J. C. A. Gaskin (Oxford: Oxford University Press, 1996), 82.

the natural differences between them are 'not so considerable, as that one man can thereupon claim to himself any benefit, to which another may not pretend, as well as he' (82). And he begins his defence of this claim by speaking of natural *inequality*, averring that 'as to strength of body, the weakest has strength enough to kill the strongest, either by secret machination, or by confederacy with others'. In other words, natural physical inequality is real—and perhaps great—but supposedly irrelevant when men are in competition.

Hobbes then says that, as to the natural 'faculties of mind', he finds 'yet a greater equality amongst men'. For 'prudence, is but experience; which equal time, equally bestows on all men, in those things they equally apply themselves to'. Prudence, we should note, is only one of the natural 'intellectual virtues' he has previously recognized, and his more nuanced discussion of this virtue in Chapter 8 does not lend support to the claim that all men share in it equally. On the contrary, Chapter 8 as a whole seems to tell against the claim that men are equal (or nearly so) in *any* of the natural intellectual virtues.[12] But even if we disregard Chapter 8, we have cause to take with a grain of salt the claim in Chapter 13 that men are naturally equal as to 'faculties of mind'. If readers find this claim incredible, Hobbes says, this is because they share with nearly all other human beings a natural proclivity to think themselves wiser than most. But, he continues, this near-universal conviction of intellectual superiority 'proveth rather that men are in that point equal, than unequal', for 'there is not ordinarily a greater sign of the equal distribution of anything, than that every man is contented with his share'. This is nothing but a wry joke, a variation on a similar witticism found in Montaigne and Descartes.[13] Men have what Hobbes calls a 'vain conceit' of their wisdom, imagining themselves to have more than almost anyone else, and each is accordingly 'contented with his share'—from which Hobbes purports to conclude that wisdom is equally distributed!

There is good reason to wonder whether Hobbes' professed belief in the natural physical and mental equality of men is entirely serious. Yet, if it is not, what is its significance? An answer is suggested by what Hobbes says in Chap-

---

[12] In this chapter, Hobbes does not simply identify 'prudence' and 'experience', but rather says (more plausibly) that prudence *dependeth on* much experience', as well as on 'memory of the like things, and their consequences heretofore'. The crude identification of prudence and experience enables him, in Ch.13, to sidestep the question of whether men are naturally equal in their capacity to learn from experience. While he also does not directly address this question in Ch.8, he does say there that there are differences in men's 'natural wit' (of which prudence is one species), which in turn are partly attributable to differences in men's bodily constitutions. He does not say or imply here that these natural differences are negligible.

[13] Descartes' apparently earnest use of it is found in Part I of the *Discourse on Method*. According to Richard Kennington, it is an old French proverb. Richard Kennington, "Descartes's *Discourse on Method*", in *On Modern Origins: Essays in Early Modern Philosophy*, ed. Pamela Kraus & Frank Hunt (Lanham & Oxford: Lexington Books, 2004), 107.

ter 15, shortly after his flat, unqualified declaration of the natural equality of men:

> If nature therefore have made men equal, that equality is to be acknowledged: or if nature have made men unequal, yet because men that think themselves equal, will not enter into conditions of peace, but upon equal terms, such equality must be admitted. (102)

He here introduces an unexpected note of tentativeness, abandoning his earlier categorical statement of natural equality for a merely conditional one ('*if* nature therefore have made men equal…*'*). More importantly, he also intimates that, even supposing that men are in fact naturally *unequal*, it is politically necessary to *say* that they are naturally equal. He solemnly lays it down as a 'law of nature', a basic moral precept, that '*every man*'—including, of course, himself—'*acknowledge another for his equal by nature*'. His understanding of the requirements of political society compels him to affirm something that he possibly does not believe, and in support of which he has provided what he presumably knows are less than watertight arguments.

Students taking a standard philosophy course whose weekly readings include Chapters 13 and 15 from Part I of *Leviathan* will almost certainly entertain no doubt that Hobbes seriously and unqualifiedly endorses the thesis of the natural equality of all human beings. The discreet indications that his true position is not nearly so straightforward might go entirely unnoticed. They might be noticed and cause a student passing, fruitless bemusement. Perhaps most likely, they might be noticed and taken to show only that Hobbes was muddle-headed or careless. In this last case, one effect of hasty reading will be to leave a student disinclined to attempt any more detailed engagement with Hobbes' writings. In all three cases, students will be left with a distorted understanding of Hobbes' thought. Moreover, they will have learned nothing from him. The proposition that all human beings are (in some sense) 'equal' is—partly thanks to Hobbes' influence—one of the fundamental tenets of contemporary liberalism. Many contemporary students will unthinkingly accept it and perhaps even regard it as unquestionable. ('We hold these truths to be self-evident …') They will then have been denied an opportunity to discover that one of its seeming champions at the dawn of liberal modernity was perhaps unpersuaded of its truth, a discovery which in turn might have prompted them for the first time to examine the proposition seriously. In short, hasty reading will have reinforced their pre-existing world view and made it impossible for them to learn from a great mind.

(3) The purpose of a close reading course is, very simply, to read and learn from a given text or texts. By contrast, the purpose of most philosophy courses is either to clarify one's thinking about some specific philosophical question or cluster of related questions, or else to learn about the history of thought. It follows that, when reading classic texts for such courses, one's

guiding interest is not the texts themselves but the philosophical problems or historical themes on which the texts are supposed to shed light.

For instance, in a course in political philosophy one might read Plato's *Republic*, or (much more likely) excerpts therefrom. One would approach the text with such questions in mind as 'what is justice?', 'what is the best regime?' and 'is censorship necessary in a well-governed city?' One would compare what Plato's Socrates has to say on these questions with what Aristotle, Hobbes, Mill and others have to say on them. One would pay little, if any, attention to the Myth of Er or to Socrates' discussion of such topics as poetry and the Forms. Literary and dramatic features of the text would probably be disregarded.

In a course devoted to the close reading of the *Republic*, on the other hand, one would approach the text with one question above all in mind: 'what does Plato's *Republic* have to teach me?' With *this* as one's guiding question, it would be necessary to attend diligently to everything in the text and not to assume in advance that any of Plato's choices are arbitrary or trivial. One would ask why he has written a dialogue rather than a treatise, and one would be sensitive to the ways in which the character of each participant is revealed as the dialogue proceeds. The curious fact that four out of the eleven *dramatis personae* say nothing at all throughout the dialogue would be noted, and its possible significance considered. The better-known elements of the subject-matter would be properly contextualised. (Thus, whereas many readers of the dialogue take for granted that the notoriously 'authoritarian' arrangements described by Socrates represent Plato's view of the simply best political arrangements, Socrates expressly states at 372e that the 'true' or 'healthy' city is one in which citizens lead austere and honest lives, without 'guardians' or philosopher-kings. The 'city in speech' that he goes on to describe so memorably and shockingly is a kind of 'feverish', unhealthy city.[14]) One would attend to the dramatic context in which Socrates says certain things. One would, for instance, compare the context (470e) in which he apparently suggests that the 'city in speech' would be a Greek city with the later context (499c-d) in which he acknowledges that an actual city identical to the 'city in speech' could exist among non-Greeks. Rather than focussing exclusively on this topic or that, one would reflect on every topic canvassed by the participants.

To be sure, it is natural and appropriate when reading any text to be guided at least initially by questions and concerns of one's own. Nonetheless, reading a classic text in the hope of learning anything that the author may have to teach is importantly different from reading it exclusively in order to better one's knowledge or understanding of some specific topic. By compelling students to read (excerpts from) classic texts in the second way, standard

---

[14] Plato, *Republic*, trans. Allan Bloom (New York: Basic Books, 2016), 49.

philosophy courses inevitably tend to discourage them from approaching these texts with truly open-minded willingness to learn. They tend, in other words, to foster a subtly self-centred attitude to reading these texts.

Conclusion: Narrowness and Depth
My proposal is that every student of philosophy should have the opportunity to take at least one close reading course in the subject. Indeed, I am inclined to think that at least one such course should be mandatory for every undergraduate philosophy major. Provided it is well taught, there is no better way for students to improve their reading skills and to come to appreciate the real depth and power of the greatest works of philosophy.

Close reading courses are admittedly narrow in scope. Given the choice between a course on Plato's *Republic* and a standard philosophy course (say, an 'Introduction to Ancient Philosophy') in which the *Republic* is one of a number of texts studied, many undergraduates would unhesitatingly pick the latter. Why settle for less, when one can get more? An easy answer is that this means sacrificing depth for breadth, which some students, of course, might deem a fair exchange. The truth is, however, that there is a serious risk of losing significantly more than one gains. As I have sought to show, the over-hasty study of older philosophical texts will often leave students with notions about their content that are not merely superficial, but grossly distorted. Moreover, philosophy of its very nature resists swift absorption. In this respect it is importantly different from other subjects, such as history. A history course that moves swiftly from topic to topic, providing an avowedly superficial overview of a period, will with any luck leave students with a basic knowledge of major names, places and events. Those who wish to do so can then extend and deepen this knowledge through further study. By contrast, a philosophy course that covers a broad selection of texts or arguments, touching briefly on each, may leave students with no real philosophic understanding at all, but only familiarity with a list of evocative slogans. The most interesting and important philosophical problems cannot, as a rule, be adequately understood and impressed on one's memory unless they are studied carefully, patiently and with no felt need to hurry.

A student who takes an 'Introduction to Ancient Philosophy' will no doubt become acquainted with 'Plato's Theory of Forms'. That is, he will learn about a doctrine, commonly attributed to Plato, according to which the everyday objects we see and touch 'participate in' unchanging Forms. He will also learn that Plato's student Aristotle vigorously criticised this doctrine. But will he acquire any authentic understanding of the philosophical motivations for the doctrine or of the arguments that Aristotle marshalled against it? Will he acquire a real sense of the deep interest and bewildering difficulty of what would eventually be called 'the problem of universals'? Perhaps s/he will— but it is to be feared that s/ he will instead emerge from the course with little more than an assortment of stale and uninteresting platitudes, together with a sneaking suspicion that Plato was a fool.

The difficulty in instilling real understanding of philosophical ideas and arguments in courses that cover a wide range of material is partially obscured by the fact that much of what is often taught in first-year philosophy courses is of a mainly *negative* character. Gettier's counter-examples to the claim that knowledge is justified true belief, Descartes' hyperbolic doubt and Hume's attack on the idea of necessary connection are all standard fare in first-year philosophy, and none of them is especially difficult to grasp—but this is largely due to their lack of positive content. It is easier to tear down than to build up; and it is easier to understand a sceptical challenge to common sense than to follow an attempted ascent from untutored common sense to philosophical insight.

This, then, is the basis of my plea for 'narrowness'. Breadth is no substitute for depth in philosophy. If, as teachers, we wish our students to become seriously engaged with philosophy, we should offer them close reading courses in philosophical classics.

Reclaiming 'English'

Barry Spurr

The Problem

Either 'English' is a discipline, or it isn't. If it is to command respect in any university environment worthy of the name—and it is a fair point to argue that such environments no longer exist, the idea of the university having been so traduced in our time—then it is only insofar as English can claim recognisable disciplinary status and characteristics that it will, or deserves, to survive.[1] Either it makes challenging discipline-specific demands on its students, as other university disciplines do—anatomy, chemical engineering, law, and so on—or it disintegrates into a smorgasbord of the current staff-members' cultural-studies preoccupations and orthodoxies, promising 'not an education in how the world really works based on reason, logic, and rational analysis; [but] an indoctrination in how academic ideologues with a one-trick agenda demand it should work'[2]; of inevitably uninformed student choice, confronted by that ideological potpourri[3]; and with unstructured progression and unrigorous assessment.

---

[1] Frank Furedi, *What's Happened To The University? A Sociological Explanation of its Infantilisation* (Abingdon: Routledge, 2017); Camille Paglia, 'Universities are an absolute wreck right now': https://www.youtube.com/watch?v=B553na_skKI (accessed 8/8/2017); Michael Wilding: 'Universities no longer function as repositories of the accumulated history and culture of our society but as moneymaking institutions offering contemporary career courses. University libraries should preserve printed books': http://www.theaustralian.com.au/higher-education/university-libraries-should-preserve-printed-books/news-story/ce4635593ea79db5a53d2cad584d31a8 (accessed 24/8/17). Brendan O'Neill, 'Universities are now factories of conformism'. 'Students are the new masters – and the result is campus tyranny': https://www.spectator.co.uk/2017/08/students-have-become-the-new-masters-and-the-result-is-campus-tyranny (accessed 28/8/17); Alison Wolf, 'Degrees of failure': https://www.prospectmagazine.co.uk/magazine/degrees-of-failure-do-universities-actually-do-any-good (accessed 4/9/17). Roger Scruton, 'Universities' war against truth': https://life.spectator.co.uk/2016/06/universities-war-against-truth (accessed 20/9/17); Ross Gittins: 'We've turned our unis into aimless, money-grubbing exploiters of students' http://www.smh.com.au/business/comment-and-analysis/weve-turned-our-unis-into-aimless-moneygrubbing-exploiters-of-students-20170916-gyiv0e.html (accessed 17/9/17); And many more books and articles along the same lines which, at least to date, appear to be making no impression on the institutions they are critiquing.

[2] Jeremy Sammut, 'What's Happened to the University?', 29 September, 2017: https://www.cis.org.au/commentary/articles/whats-happened-to-the-university (accessed 3/10/17).

[3] In today's university English Departments, Bruce Bawer notes, students have been 'trained to parrot jargon, to regurgitate bullet points about Western imperialism, colonialism and capitalism and to

Defining the disciplinary character of English and identifying what the essential elements of the discipline are is not rocket science, yet all would be stridently contested and rejected today, and the very word 'discipline' is on the nose. It indicates an authoritative approach, the word 'authoritative' now customarily and wilfully confused with the negative 'authoritarian' by those who would dispose of educational disciplines, while ruthlessly and comprehensively enforcing their own authority in the process. As with studies such as anatomy and the varieties of engineering, it was once obvious what kinds of aptitudes the serious, committed student would bring to the study of English, from school or earlier university work, and the training and essential mastery that would be required for successful progress to graduation in the subsequent tertiary study of it.

The preliminary requirement is obvious, as Bruce Bawer notes: "Once upon a time students had majored in English because they loved reading".[4] Given that assumed aptitude, the knowledge that has to be mastered, and that is not negotiable, as one proceeds in the study of English, is a four-fold matter of:

1. the acquisition of a working historical knowledge of the periods in which texts in English were written, from the late Middle Ages to the present;
2. familiarity with the variety of literary forms, themes and subjects which authors have initiated and developed, through the centuries and, where relevant, with their origins in earlier literature, especially the Classical sources;
3. the nurturing of scholarly and literary-critical skills to bring to bear on the free and independent discussion, analysis and evaluation of texts; and
4. the refining of grammatically-correct, etymologically-informed, lucid, articulate and compelling expression in both written and oral communication to describe and discuss the wide range of literary texts in English at an appropriate level of accuracy, subtlety and persuasiveness that might be expected of a tertiary-educated graduate in the Humanities.

All of these crucial aspects of the discipline have been deliberately undermined and eroded to the point, today, of disappearance, stripping 'English' of

---

think that this is what it means to be educated.... They've been trained to reduce the rich complexities and ambiguities of human life to simple formulas about oppressors and oppressed, capitalists and workers, western imperialists and their non-Western victims'. *The Victims' Revolution: The Rise of the Identity Studies and the Closing of the Liberal Mind* (New York: HarperCollins, 2012), 3.
[4] Bawer, 7.

the very features that gave the subject at least some standing and respectability in the wider scholarly community and the intellectual world, at large.

Such is the triumph of postmodernism in Humanities departments, in today's universities, that reclaiming traditional disciplinarity is now all but unimaginable. What Keith Windschuttle has described as the 'postmodern ascendancy' is so pervasive that colleagues who may argue for those traditional principles are regarded not as peers whose different politics and perspectives may be tolerated, but as people operating with such a deeply flawed set of assumptions that they would be better off in institutions for the feeble minded.[5] The leftist position at universities, especially in Humanities faculties, has become progressively normative to the point, now, where anyone who fails to toe the Marxist-Feminist party line is regarded (at the very least) as an eccentric aberration.[6] In striking contrast, writing exactly fifty years ago, in 1967, a distinguished literary scholar could refer, in passing, to what would have been simply taken for granted then: the 'exchange of ideas through discussion and debate which has always been the most valuable part of a university education'.[7] If you were to make this statement today, you would, perfectly justifiably, be a laughing-stock. There can be no discussion, let alone exchange or debate where only the 'correct' interpretation of such as race-gender-class orthodoxy is tolerated and a mere querying of the dogmatic position is regarded as intolerable and even, for staff, grounds for reprimand, dismissal and Orwellian vaporisation.

With regard to the first disciplinary requirement for English, Michael Wilding (now an Emeritus Professor of the discipline) has observed:

> One of the most worrying aspects of the post-modern, and of current institutional practice in the universities, in particular in departments of history and literature, is the surrender of history; even more than that, the rejection of history, the denial of history.[8]

How can you read a text by an author from, say, the sixteenth or seventeenth century (and any self-respecting Department of English will be teaching numerous texts from those centuries, the era of Shakespeare and Milton) with-

---

[5] *The Killing of History: How Literary Critics and Social Theorists Are Murdering Our Past* (San Francisco: Encounter Books, 1996),130.

[6] Some years ago, it was reported that an applicant for promotion in such a Faculty, was confronted at the promotion committee interview by a female professor: 'Your c.v. seems to indicate that you are a conservative', she said. The applicant, wondering how best to respond to this serious – and true - allegation, replied. 'Well, perhaps, a radical conservative'. 'That's even worse', snapped the professor, as the committee nodded in agreement.

[7] Michael Meyer, *Ibsen* (1967; new edn. Stroud: Sutton Publishing, 2004), 38. The beginning of the end of the traditional understanding of the idea of a university can be dated from the campus riots of the next year, 1968.

[8] *Growing Wild* (North Melbourne: Australian Scholarly Publishing, 2016), 219.

out at least elementary knowledge of the society and culture of the time and how the biography of a chosen writer resonates with that culture—in celebration of it, probing and querying of it, even subversion of it? As Elizabeth Bishop insisted, 'the only real way to understand poetry is to know the life and beliefs of the poet'[9] and these are grounded in the history and culture of the writer's times. The religious poetry of John Donne and John Milton, for example, expresses their (very different) interpretations of Christian theology and spirituality in what was not only a profoundly theocentric age but a time of vigorous religious debate and controversy. Lacking at least some understanding of those heartfelt convictions and the historical contexts and circumstances in which they arose, and without sufficient respect for them to suspend any problems of disbelief in our anthropocentric, post-(even, anti-)Christian age, you read in utter ignorance and devoid of empathy. So, your enjoyment of (and what of substance you might derive, thereby, from) those works of genius is severely compromised.

Further, any given 'present', in historical ages and periods, cannot be understood without knowledge of the past (especially, the immediately preceding epoch) which has brought it about, often in the way of a spirited reaction. The fervour of Romanticism cannot be explained, let alone fully appreciated unless its rejection of the principles of the foregoing Age of Reason is understood. So, that age has to be surveyed also. In literature, in all its forms, writers draw upon what has gone before, in thought and in forms of writing, and concentrate it, extend it, overturn it and reject it—and it is only through an understanding of what they have appropriated from the historical past and how they, in their own historical times, were formed by those *mores*, that we are able to respond intelligently to what they have written and are equipped to delve into and probe those expressions with confidence and conviction. You cannot read Alexander Pope's *Rape of the Lock* intelligently if you have not read *Paradise Lost*, from the previous century, on which it draws in detail for its satirical brilliance. So a graduate in English (and certainly anyone who presumes to teach the subject to others) needs to have had sustained exposure to each of the several periods of the writing of literature in English and the major, representative works of those periods. That English graduates today can (indeed, usually) emerge, even with first class degrees, without having read, for example, either *Paradise Lost* or *The Rape of the Lock* or any text at all from the entire eighteenth century (for instance) indicates the ludicrous depths to which the discipline has been driven, with regard to this requirement of the historical sense and the great works of its heritage.

Developing this sense—as with the other, formerly non-negotiable demands of the discipline—is hard work; disciplines (worthy of the name) re-

---

[9] Quoted in John Drury, *Music at Midnight: The Life and Poetry of George Herbert* (Chicago: University of Chicago Press, 2014), 322 – where Bishop's point is abundantly demonstrated.

quire concentrated, sustained application and much drudgery—and, as anyone genuinely committed to a discipline knows, it is a lifetime's labour. One's school and undergraduate university experience provide just an introduction, with some helpful tools and training, but, if rightly presented, can offer a sufficiently rigorous sampling of the ongoing challenges posed by the discipline. Surrender the requirement of a thorough historical survey as the basis of English and students are left in the risibly diminished position of being able only to respond with any confidence to literary texts that were written in or near their own time and place, and which reflect that present and their circumstances back to them, confining them to the prison of the present and, worse, of themselves. Hence, the current obsession with relevance—that students cannot be expected to submit themselves to world pictures and interpretations of human existence and experience that do not connect with their own lives or conform to their own opinions, and lose themselves in:

> Words of the fragrant portals, dimly-starred,
> And of ourselves and of our origins,
> In ghostlier demarcations, keener sounds.[10]

This is accentuated by the nonsense of readers as (somehow or other) 'composers' of the texts that they are reading; that they should take a kind of ownership of the text, instead of being drawn out, in order to lose—and rediscover—themselves in the widest possible range of human experience which literary expression, in all its imaginative richness, affords. This ideologically-driven procedure (that we must expunge anything from a curriculum of study that confronts and contradicts the mainstream views of today or so transform and misread texts from the past in order to bring them into lockstep with 'correct' thought) contradicts the two Latin words which combine as the root of 'education'—to train or mould ('educare'), and to lead out ('educere'). Ironically, the supposedly enabling and self-affirming requirement of relevance inhibits the wise understanding and interpretation 'of ourselves and of our origins', which is the only criterion of relevance worth anything to anybody.

The only way we can comprehend what is happening to us now, is to be able to compare and contrast it with what has happened at other times; once we allow the sense of history to be removed, then the possibility of any narrative of our present is vastly reduced.[11]

In the dystopic future imagined by Ray Bradbury in *Fahrenheit 451*, where book-burning has achieved the desired outcome of everybody having the

---

[10] Wallace Stevens, 'The Idea of Order at Key West':
https://www.poetryfoundation.org/poems/43431/the-idea-of-order-at-key-west (accessed 25/8/17).
[11] Wilding, *Growing Wild*, 219.

same 'correct' opinion as everybody else—or, better, no opinion at all—principal book-burner, fire-captain Beatty announces, exultingly:

> Each man the image of every other; then all are happy, for there are no mountains to make them cower, to judge themselves against. So! A book is a loaded gun in the house next door. Burn it! Take the shot from the weapon. Breach each man's mind. Who knows who might be the target of the well-read man? Me? I won't stomach them for a minute…. Coloured people don't like *Little Black Sambo*. Burn it. White people don't feel good about *Uncle Tom's Cabin*. Burn it…. Burn them all, burn everything.[12]

His Professor of Poetry, old Faber, had been 'thrown out upon the world forty years ago when the last liberal arts college shut'. Terrified of the fiery Thought Police, he dares to carry, surreptitiously concealed on his person, a book of poetry and to the inquirer who would know about books, Montag, he responds, 'I talk the *meaning* of things, I sit here and *know* I am alive'.[13] Faber bitterly regrets that he had not spoken out, years before, against intellectual totalitarianism:

> I saw the way things were going a long time back. I said nothing. I'm one of the innocents who could have spoken up and out when no one would listen to the 'guilty', but I did not speak and thus became guilty myself. And when finally they set the structure to burn the books, I grunted a few times and subsided for there were no others grunting and yelling with me. Now it's too late.[14]

One of the most effective ways in which books have been destroyed in our day is to submit them to 'theory'. Its rise, over the past half-century, however half-baked, uninformed and ill-digested by students utterly untrained, philosophically, to perceive its inadequacies and flaws, has been a godsend for those unwilling or intellectually incapable of doing the disciplinary hard yards (copious reading, in particular) which the development of such as the historical sense requires. As Windschuttle explains, in relation to History (but it is equally true of English):

> Tackling the major issues of human experience no longer requires the hard work of steeping yourself in the writings of all those practitioners of your discipline who have gone before you, and then putting in the even harder slog of doing your own original research. Instead, all you need do is take a small selection of the more prominent and familiar authors, label them in terms used by the currently fashionable theoretical guru, add some linguistic speculations about the

---

[12] *Fahrenheit 451* (1954; London: Harper, 2008), 77-8.
[13] Bradbury, 98.
[14] Bradbury, 106-7.

textuality of everything, and then wait for the self-same guru or his acolytes to recognise your genius and lavish you with hyperbole.[15]

Each of the four disciplinary points I have mentioned places considerable demands on teachers and students, but challenging students with formidable requirements in learning is today unacceptable, as it may make them feel 'unsupported' (to be 'supportive' being the ultimate litmus test of the good teacher). The demanding teacher, on the contrary, refusing to indulge delinquency, absenteeism, idleness and ignorance, and calling students to account, could find himself hauled before a committee to answer a complaint of harassment or discrimination from a student-victim; or discover, when the student evaluations come in at semester's end, that he has been scored a failure (the student's assessment and excoriation—'this is the worst lecturer I have ever had', and so on—being protected by anonymity) because he has failed to make students feel comfortable and safe in the womb-classroom.[16] With this infantile culture of endless affirmation now securely in place from young people's earliest schooldays (where to 'fail' is the unspeakable four-letter word) through to university, laziness and stupidity flourish like bacteria, and the dumbing-down of learning and its challenging requirements, if it is to amount to anything worth doing, continues apace.

Indicative of the loss of nerve and conviction about what 'English' is and should be at university-level study is the constant re-structuring and revision of the syllabus and curriculum—inevitably so, when there is no consensus about what the discipline is (apart from assisting in bringing about the Marxist-Feminist utopia), or should be insisting upon. Wilding (whose active university experience of English stretched from the 1950s to the end of the twentieth century) sees such constant change and fiddling as a deliberate ploy for 'demoralizing and degrading' the discipline.[17] The source of the damage, incredibly, is to be found within English Departments themselves—a self-defeating disciplinary suicide identified by Professor of English, Simon Haines:

> What has been hardest of all to fathom [in the destruction of the Humanities] is the decades-long war of attrition carried out against the study of poetry and other literary genres, especially the English poetry and literature of the past, by other

---

[15] Windschuttle, 129.
[16] Professor Richard Dawkins: 'A university is not a "safe space". If you need a safe space, leave, go home, hug your teddy & suck your thumb until ready for university.'
http://www.economist.com/news/international/21699903-young-westerners-are-less-keen-their-parents-free-speech-dont-be-so-offensive (9/6/16).
[17] Wilding, *Growing Wild*, 282.

academics in the humanities – most of all, incredibly, within English departments themselves.[18]

Examples of the pervasive and deeply-embedded process of the eroding of English are abundantly available. Let us take just three from current secondary school students' work, at one private and two state selective high schools, all of high renown, in Sydney. The first is from Year 11. The text set for close study (supposedly) is Joseph Conrad's *Heart of Darkness*. This is a popular choice at schools and universities, for two main reasons: as a novella, it is short (no-one should expect teachers and students of English now to read *long* works of literature) and it is politically acceptable, as it presents a critique of Western colonisation in Africa, so no-one should feel challenged, confronted or unsafe in reading it. One's correct beliefs can be reassuringly preserved and further solidified. No trigger warnings required! Carefully written, it provides much scope for detailed literary analysis, of such as its descriptive passages, of its characterisations of Marlow and Kurtz, of various dramatic encounters that occur, and the author's skilful use of imagery and symbolism—introduced in the metaphor in its very title. Sufficient, you would think, for several classroom periods of stimulating study, analysis and discussion, led by a teacher committed to the discipline, over a couple of weeks in Year 11 English. But that is by no means enough. Indeed, it turns out to be utterly beside the point. Instead, the text has to be studied not only in tandem with Francis Ford Coppola's *Apocalypse Now*—his bloated, four-hour-long indictment of the American involvement in Vietnam, where a few aspects of Conrad's story-line, and a couple of names and some key phrases are appropriated from *Heart of Darkness*—but subordinated to it.

So the first step of this particular version of the eroding process of the discipline of English is under way: what Coppola has taken from Conrad—and what he has done with what Conrad has given us—becomes the focus of classroom study. Then—and, by this stage, the reading of a literary text has flown out of the English classroom entirely, and landed in historical and cultural studies—in the students' assignment, they are asked to describe how the appropriation of Conrad's work in the film has exposed and denounced the wickedness of 'American imperialistic policies'. We need to remember that this exercise is designed for a class of students (aged about 16) who have (inevitably, by this stage in their education) only a patchy exposure to literature in English—some, for example, would have studied no poetry at all, poetry being the least susceptible of literary forms to binding on the Procrustean bed

---

[18] Simon Haines, "On Professing Poetry in Australia in the 21st Century", in Catherine Runcie, ed., *The Free Mind: Essays and Poems in Honour of Barry Spurr* (Sydney: Edwin H. Lowe,, 2016), 101.

of ideologically-driven socio-historical cultural studies.[19] These youngsters are still in the early stages of learning the tools of critical reading of texts of a degree of complexity, such as Conrad's (set in a historical and cultural period of which they know next to nothing) and expressing and assessing what they have found in lucid prose. The pedagogical approach to them at this formative stage of their education in the discipline of English is clear. They need to have painstakingly revealed to them an appreciation of how the author's prose mastery works and to contextualise the book in its own cultural and historical settings and with reference to Conrad's life and corpus. This is the 'texture' of a book, to which Bradbury's Professor Faber refers:

> Do you know why books… are so important? Because they have quality. And what does the word quality mean? To me it means *texture*. This book has *pores*. It has features. This book can go under the microscope. You'd find life under the glass, streaming past in infinite profusion. The more pores, the more truthfully recorded details of life per square inch you can get on a sheet or paper, the more 'literary' you are. That's *my* definition, anyway. *Telling detail*. Fresh detail. The good writers touch life often.[20]

Books are, in other words, as John Milton insisted:

> not absolutely dead things, but do contain a potency of life in them to be as active as that soul was whose progeny they are; nay, they do preserve as in a vial the purest efficacy and extraction of that living intellect that bred them. I know they are as lively, and as vigorously productive, as those fabulous dragon's teeth: and being sown up and down, may chance to spring up armed men…. as good almost kill a man as kill a good book: who kills a man kills a reasonable creature, God's image; but he who destroys a good book, kills reason itself, kills the image of God, as it were, in the eye.[21]

Anyone who believes in literature knows all this, and if you do not believe in literature, you have no business teaching it. Sending a class off to watch a film from an entirely different historical and cultural setting from Conrad's

---

[19] Some years ago I was contacted by a student from Melbourne who had just completed the highest level of English in the VCE, the Victorian equivalent of the New South Wales HSC. She was coming to Sydney to read English but was concerned about a lacuna in her background. She had studied no poetry. I commented that, surely, as she had taken the highest level of English in her final year at school some poetry would have been required. She responded that it was on the syllabus, but only optional, like everything else, and her school had decided not to teach it. Worse, she had studied no poetry at all in the previous years of high school – none, in fact, since primary school. I reassured her that, in spite of this appalling betrayal by her teachers and the syllabus, given her excellent results she obviously had the intellectual capacity to study poetry and I encouraged her to proceed with her enrolment.
[20] Bradbury, 108.
[21] *Areopagitica* (1644): http://oll.libertyfund.org/quote/97 (accessed 3/10/17).

text and then to do an assignment on the damnable political foreign policy of the United States of America, about which, furthermore, it is assumed that students will submit the 'correct' judgement, is an evasion of what the teaching of English requires.

Certainly, the relationship between texts and filmic versions of them is a fascinating and important area of study, but to be pursued at the university postgraduate level, when students have read very widely in literature (one might once have assumed) and (equally) seen sufficient films to have both the skills and the breadth of learning to embark on this complex interdisciplinary venture. But to impose this on school children and undergraduates is simply a method of deflecting attention from the hard and necessary disciplinary work of grappling with the close reading of a text; but, far worse—and this is more sinister and related to much else that is happening in the destruction of English, especially at universities—it reveals a discarding of the belief in the worth and integrity of literary texts themselves and the value of the study and appreciation of them as such. A novel is not of sufficient interest in itself. We must find a film to validate its existence and, further, find within both book and film a political message that conforms to current ideology to justify and validate our reading and viewing of both.

At the second of our schools, the following topic was set for an essay: 'Shakespeare represents a patriarchal society in which the voices of women are suppressed'. Again, the correct response is assumed. Woe betide the pupil who contradicted this nonsensical statement—about the era, no less, of the superbly unsuppressed and articulate Virgin Queen, and, verily, named after her: the Elizabethan Age! Or the student who turned her attention away from the feminist theory of silenced victimhood and focused, instead, in close textual analysis on the voices of the host of wondrously loquacious, outspoken women in Shakespeare's plays. An essay I read, from the class, had this as a typical sentence: 'Shakespeare advocates the conventional Elizabethan virtue that females are, and always have been, muted'—presenting Shakespeare as an advocate, no less, of the silenced woman. It would be risible if it were not so despicable. Let us briefly consider three of Shakespeare's allegedly muted women. Here is Portia, in *The Merchant of Venice* giving voice in—what is more—the most famous speech in the play, as memorable as any speech any man makes in Shakespeare's works:

> The quality of mercy is not strained.
> It droppeth as the gentle rain from heaven
> Upon the place beneath. It is twice blessed:
> It blesseth him that gives and him that takes.
> 'Tis mightiest in the mightiest. It becomes
> The thronèd monarch better than his crown.
> His scepter shows the force of temporal power,
> The attribute to awe and majesty

> Wherein doth sit the dread and fear of kings,
> But mercy is above this sceptered sway.
> It is enthronèd in the hearts of kings.
> It is an attribute to God himself.... (IV, I, 173-84)

If this is a suppressed voice, then let us hear more of such silenced, non-speech!

Here is Miranda, in *The Tempest*, outspokenly rebuking the book-burning savage Caliban (of which we have his modern counterparts in our schools and universities):

> Abhorred slave,
> Which any print of goodness wilt not take,
> Being capable of all ill! I pitied thee,
> Took pains to make thee speak, taught thee each hour
> One thing or other. (1.ii.354-8)

A non-speaker teaches another to speak. Caliban responds to her, saying that 'you taught me language', acknowledging her instruction. And then there is forthright Desdemona, supposedly one of the women silenced by the wicked patriarchy, who says that she will 'trumpet' her voice, no less, 'to the world' (1.iii.249) and resolutely confronts her own patriarch, senator Brabantio, with her bold choice of the forbidden Othello as lover:

> But here's my husband,
> And so much duty as my mother showed
> To you, preferring you before her father,
> So much I challenge that I may profess
> Due to the Moor my lord. (1.iii.184-88)

This is a woman *silenced* by patriarchy? And Desdemona's confident rebuking of that constituency could be multiplied a hundredfold in the splendid female characters in Shakespeare's plays. At the tragedy's end, Desdemona's voice is indeed finally silenced, at her death. The ideologues would have their students believe—and insist on them replicating the belief—that this silencing is what Shakespeare is advocating, rather than bemoaning (which are the demonstrable facts of the case). But the last matter ideologues are interested in, as the history of the Thought Police has shown repeatedly, is evidence and the truth. They have turned English Studies into what Les Murray has called 'Lying Studies' and their students into liars, thereby.[22] But that is by no means the

---

[22] In Justin Norrie, 'Alas, poor students'. Les Murray: 'They could call it Lying Studies, because it prepares kids to talk the bullshit': http://www.smh.com.au/news/national/alas-poor-students-8230/2005/08/14/1123957949797.html (accessed 16/8/17).

end of their wretched strategy. In the case of Shakespeare, they have set out to destroy the respect and admiration that this universal genius and his works (and that of many others) should nurture in readers, and which, especially, should be cultivated in young readers, by consigning him to that sole constituency of the human race, the white male, which it is now acceptable to denounce and repudiate with whatever hate speech and mendacious libel you care to cook up.

For the final example, here are the set texts for a term's study this year in 'English' in Year 11 at our third school: the film, *Selma*, about the American civil rights movement; speeches by Martin Luther King, Barack Obama and the Australian Indigenous leader, Stan Grant; and the film *Matrix*. No novel, no poem, no play; nothing from earlier than the latter half of the twentieth century and nothing from the source of all literatures in English, the British Isles. This is a subject degraded into cultural studies, where the appraisal of the 'texts', furthermore, has to be along approved Party lines. What kind of English teacher, we may ask, would want to preside over an entire term's work in English in Year 11 that included not a single poem (for example) from the entirety of literature in English, from Chaucer to Les Murray, in the precious periods allocated to English in a preposterously overcrowded curriculum? The answer is not far to seek: the kind of English teacher with the kind of training and indoctrination now provided by Departments of English and Education in our universities.

Wherever you look in the teaching of English today you find evidence not merely of a discipline in its death throes, but a corpse in decomposition.

The Solution
This is as clear, as it is formidable. On any realistic assessment of what has been inflicted on education over the last fifty years, and especially in the Humanities, it is next to impossible to imagine the reclaiming of disciplines such as English as disciplines. But as the saying goes, it is impossible, and it must be done. What is urgently required is a radical intervention at a decisive point in the otherwise ongoing downward spiralling of the destruction of English which has been in dismal process for nearly half a century. The character and quality of teacher recruitment, training and education would seem to be an obvious point for such an intervention.

All teachers of English at high school level should be required to have an Honours degree in the subject—that is, four years study of it, with a final year devoted solely to that study, after three years of English as a 'major' in their degree. For university entry for such a degree for teachers there should be a minimum cut-off point of an ATAR of 90, so that instead of the dregs of matriculants for and graduates with Arts degrees becoming teachers, we move (and it would be a revolutionary change) to recruiting teachers of English exclusively from the upper echelons of Humanities students.[23]

Further, as part of their degree, would-be teachers should be required to take at least one European language as a major study, both for the literary and linguistic skills (obviously pertinent to English, too) that such a study would develop and refine.

Within Departments of English, where the teachers-to-be are studying, there needs to be a recovery (similarly radical) of the traditional disciplinary procedures of devoting, in the course of the mandated four-year Honours degree in the subject for teachers, equal time and attention to the several historical periods and great texts, from the late Middle Ages, to the present. Moreover, this would entail a closely-monitored curriculum whereby equal time is spent on poetry, the novel, non-fictional prose and drama. An historically-based core course, supplemented by a range of optional courses extending and intensifying that core study, would be the ideal arrangement—so, for example, the reading of seventeenth-century literature could be supplemented by a special study of the Metaphysical poets or of Milton or of Restoration drama.

So that future teachers may be exposed to the assessment regime to which their own students will be submitting, there should be an equal balance, through the four-year course, between essay-writing and closed-book examination assessment, and with a short thesis and an oral (*viva voce*) component in the Honours year.

Without a recovery of a strenuous and rigorous disciplinary approach, along lines such as these, there is no realistic prospect of reclaiming English as a worthy discipline in our schools and universities, and the ongoing, ideologically-driven destruction of the subject will continue, to the point where it has disappeared entirely.

---

[23] This is a modest – perhaps, too modest – requirement, when it is remembered that the ATARs for professional degrees such as Medicine and Law are customarily in the high 90s. Does not the education of young people by highly-qualified teachers matter as much to a society as the intellectual quality of people providing medical care and legal advice?

The Role of Appreciation in Literary Study: its Centrality and Presuppositions

David Brooks

Many attempts have been made by writers on art and poetry to define beauty in the abstract, to express it in the most general terms, to find some universal formula for it. The value of these attempts has most often been in the suggestive and penetrating things said by the way. Such discussions help us very little to enjoy what has been well done in art or poetry, to discriminate between what is more and what is less excellent in them, or to use words like beauty, excellence, art, poetry, with a more precise meaning than they would otherwise have. . . .

"To see the object as in itself it really is", has been justly said to be the aim of all true criticism whatever; and in aesthetic criticism the first step towards seeing one's object as it really is, is to know one's own impression as it really is, to discriminate it, to realise it distinctly. . . .What is this song or picture, this engaging personality presented in life or in a book, to *me*? What effect does it really produce on me? . . . .And he who experiences these impressions strongly, and drives directly at the discrimination and analysis of them, has no need to trouble himself with the abstract question what beauty is in itself, or what its exact relation to truth or experience—metaphysical questions, as unprofitable as metaphysical questions elsewhere. He may pass them all by as being, answerable or not, of no interest to him.

Walter Pater, Preface to *The Renaissance: Studies in Art and Poetry* (4th ed., 1893)[1]

Pater was writing at a time when he could believe that at least a large section of the educated class still took for granted that beauty is objectively real, and that the taste and judgment of a discriminating critic have a claim to universal validity. Even though the natural sciences had become very powerful by the end of the nineteenth century, and positivism had already lodged its claim to be the only valid philosophy corresponding to the natural sciences, the influence of positivism in elevating the sciences over the humanities was still countered by philosophical idealism, a strong force in both Britain and the United States of America. Pater evidently felt that the objectivity of beauty

---

[1] Walter Pater, *The Renaissance: Studies in Art and Poetry* (Mineola, New York: Dover Publications Inc., 2005 [republication of 4th edn, 1893]), 1-2.

and the validity of the critic's taste did not need to be defended, or that if they did, the truth of these notions would be manifest in any piece of good criticism on particular instances of beauty or works of art.

We no longer live in the same cultural world as Pater. Since he wrote, positivism has come to dominate the general climate of opinion. Politicians, the media, and people in general take for granted the positivist assumptions that only the natural sciences provide us with genuine knowledge, or, more weakly, that the methods of the natural sciences ought to be regarded as models for inquiry in all other fields. Within this conceptual framework beauty cannot even be assumed to exist, except as an illusion projected by an individual's likings (or the likings of a group). Positivism has thus given rise to subjectivism in aesthetics. From the standpoint of subjectivism, anybody's opinion is as good as anybody else's. The implications are that objective beauty can no longer be studied, and that criticism is merely a sophisticated game for a self-indulgent, leisured class. Romanticism, which still pervades our cultural climate of opinion, unwittingly supports positivism, by its tendency to reject reason in its desire to dignify imagination and feeling.[2]

Within the last half century the academic world has responded to this situation by various theoretical manoeuvres. Literary works have been transformed into texts, inscribed in codes that need to be deciphered.[3] Literature has been reduced to language, but to a language that is radically incoherent, and continually threatening to unmake itself.[4] Literary works have been regarded as the intersection of pre-existing 'discourses', the collective linguistic habits of particular social groups or activities.[5] Or, literary works have been seen as constructed within, and disclosing particular ideologies, whether those ideologies are regarded as just sets of ideas and values, or as sets of ideas involving a 'false consciousness'.[6] The assumed subjectivity of taste has itself

---

[2] As positivism has not been a strong influence in the philosophy of science for decades, it is reasonable to suppose that popular positivism and subjectivism are due to social factors: probably the immense prestige of natural science itself, increased by the never-ending supply of technological applications, especially in the field of consumer goods, a false notion of egalitarianism, and the needs of mass-marketing ("the customer is always right"). There is a large element of collective self-deception in the popular subjectivism with regard to beauty. The film, media, cosmetics and plastic surgery industries invest billions of dollars each year into the production and distribution of images of beauty, on the assumption that hundreds of millions of people world-wide will find those images beautiful. And they do. Perhaps we should adopt a Capital Investment Criterion of Truth in aesthetics.

[3] See Terence Hawkes, *Structuralism and Semiotics* (London: Methuen and Co. Ltd, 1977); Catherine Belsey, *Critical Practice* (London and New York: Methuen and Co. Ltd, 1980).

[4] See Christopher Norris, *Deconstruction: Theory and Practice* (London and New York: Methuen and Co. Ltd, 1982); Jonathan Culler, *On Deconstruction: Theory and Criticism after Structuralism* (London: Routledge and Kegan Paul plc, 1983).

[5] See Antony Easthope, *Poetry as Discourse* (London and New York: Methuen and Co. Ltd, 1983).

[6] See Belsey, *Critical Practice;* Terry Eagleton, *Criticism and Ideology: A Study in Marxist Literary Theory* (London: Verso, 1978); Terry Threadgold, E. A. Grosz, Gunther Kress and M. A. K. Halliday eds, *Semiotics Ideology Language*, Sydney Studies in Society and Culture 3 (Sydney, 1986). The malign influ-

become an object of sociological inquiry.[7] In general, academic criticism has become 'political', and a certain kind of cultural politics has reduced aesthetics and the arts to species of ideology.[8] In these ways a revolution has occurred in the academic study of 'literature', renamed 'textuality'. My essay is intended as a contribution to the counter-revolution.[9]

Pater was correct to believe in the objective reality of beauty, and the universal validity of discriminating taste. He was correct to hold that the critic must 'realise' the work in his own imagination before analysing his own impressions of it. But he was mistaken in thinking that aesthetics and any kind of theory could be dispensed with. At least, he was wrong for the times that lay ahead of his own lifetime. When the critical projects of American New Criticism and of F.R. Leavis and his disciples were effectively complete by the middle of the twentieth century, academics were bound to look around for new things to do. Since the New Critics and the Leavisites failed to enter the domain of theory to defend their activities from hostile forces, the opportunity was presented for those academics unsympathetic to a traditional kind of criticism to import from France theories and methods that rejected entirely the aesthetic nature of literary criticism, and that substituted the theories and methods described above.[10] The common feature of these new theories is a

---

ence of positivism is seen in the pseudo-scientific discourse associated with structuralist, semiotic and post-structuralist trends.
[7] See Pierre Bourdieu, *Distinction: A Social Critique of the Judgment of Taste* (London: Routledge Classics, 2010).
[8] See Terry Eagleton, *The Ideology of the Aesthetic* (Oxford: Basil Blackwell Ltd, 1990). I have criticised Eagleton's views in "Eagleton on Aesthetics and Ideology", *Literature and Aesthetics: The Journal of the Sydney Society of Literature and Aesthetics* 5 (October 1995): 7-21.
[9] During the last forty years or so there have been many critiques of structuralism and post-structuralism. I will cite only the following, written from a variety of standpoints: Fredric Jameson, *The Prison-House of Language: A Critical Account of Structuralism and Russian Formalism* (Princeton, NJ: Princeton University Press, 1972); Perry Anderson, *In the Tracks of Historical Materialism: The Wellek Library Lectures* (London: Verso, 1983); J. G. Merquior, *From Prague to Paris: A Critique of Structuralist and Post-structuralist Thought* (London and New York: Verso, 1986); Kate Soper, *Humanism and Anti-Humanism* (La Salle, Illinois: Open Court, 1986); John M. Ellis, *Against Deconstruction* (Princeton, New Jersey: Princeton University Press, 1989);Bernard Bergonzi, *Exploding English: Criticism, Theory, Culture* (Oxford: Clarendon Press, 1990); Richard Freadman and Seumas Miller, *Re-Thinking Theory: A Critique of Contemporary Literary Theory and an Alternative Account* (Cambridge: Cambridge University Press, 1992).; Patrick Grant, *Literature and Personal Values* (London: The Macmillan Press Ltd, 1992); Hugh Mercer Curtler, *Rediscovering Values: Coming to Terms with Postmodernism* (Armonk, New York and London: M. E. Sharpe Inc., 1997). The most acute study of the social conditions in which postmodernism emerged is, in my view, by the Marxist historian Perry Anderson. See his *The Origins of Postmodernity* (London and New York: Verso, 1998).
[10] Perhaps not quite fair to the New Critics or to Leavis himself. The original New Critics produced some theoretical work, mostly in the 1930s, 40s, and 50s, especially in relation to rhetoric and poetic language. But this was well before the structuralist onslaught. René Wellek and Austin Warren published a wide-ranging textbook *Theory of Literature*, which went through three editions between 1949 and 1963. It discussed critical trends up to about 1950, but it did not lead to any new theoretical work, as theory was generally regarded as exotic and superfluous. Leavis seemed belatedly to realise

tendency to use literary works as raw material for the propagation of the theories, rather than using the resources of a theory to inform criticism, so that the works themselves may be appreciated.

We do need theory, and more than ever before. But the theory that we need must be a justification of Pater's assumptions regarding the objectivity of beauty and the validity of taste. Fortunately, the intellectual resources for such theory already exist, and have existed for up to two centuries. It is just that the English-speaking world has been largely indifferent to them.

In this essay I have no original ideas to present. I only wish to clarify and justify what has been in the past the common wisdom. But what is true and important needs to be endlessly repeated, if the contemporary climate of opinion is hostile to it. The old rule applies, in theory as in war: if one does not occupy a terrain, one can be sure that one's opponents will occupy it.

Appreciation and Literary Study

My topic, then, can be posed as the question: can the appreciation and criticism of literary works be, to any degree, objective?

But, before we try to answer that question, it may be asked: is there anything that can be called "appreciation"? Why distinguish appreciation from criticism? And why choose such an old-fashioned term, which seems to suggest the most amateurish and naive kind of intellectual activity? Surely, appreciation went out with the Edwardian Age, and has been exiled ever since I.A. Richards' work in the 1920s? Richards takes his subject-matter as *criticism*.[11]

I propose that we restore the term 'appreciation' to its rightful place at the centre of the whole vocabulary of literary study. I do so for two reasons. First, it captures the two sides of the mental process that occurs when we read. On one side we have cognition, the apprehension of the work, both in

---

that something more was necessary than the criticism of individual works and authors, and in his *Living Principle* (1975) set out briefly the essence of the existence of the literary work in language. But the discussion is in the form of hints, and it is buried in a rambling account of matters concerning life, knowledge and philosophy, in which nothing is really clarified, or rendered cogent. By this time the importation of French doctrines had begun. Leavis again set out his position, in the same desultory manner, in the essay 'Thought, meaning and sensibility: the problem of value judgment', written for his *Valuation in Criticism and Other Essays* (Cambridge: Cambridge University Press, 1986). From 1955 to 1992 Wellek published his monumental *A History of Modern Criticism, 1750-1950*, in eight volumes. Its title indicates the *terminus ad quem* of its subject-matter. He did, however, discuss structuralism and other critical trends from a humanist point of view in his *The Attack on Literature and Other Essays* (Chapel Hill, NC: University of North Carolina Press, 1982). Wellek discusses New Criticism in his *American Criticism 1900-1950* (London: Jonathan Cape Ltd, 1986), volume six of *A History of Modern Criticism 1750-1950* (1955-92). See also F. R. Leavis, *The Living Principle: 'English' as a Discipline of Thought* (London: Chatto and Windus Ltd, 1975), 19-69, esp. 35-36; *Valuation in Criticism*, 278-279, 285-297.

[11] I. A. Richards, *Principles of Literary Criticism* (London: Routledge and Kegan Paul Ltd, 1967; first published 1924, 2nd edn 1926); *Practical Criticism: A Study of Literary Judgment* (London: Routledge and Kegan Paul Ltd, 1964; first published 1929).

its parts and as a whole, both form and content, and on the other side we have emotional responses. Some of these emotional responses pertain to the recreation of the work, and others to our spontaneous valuations of the work, and to our pleasure in it. But when we read, these two sides are in activity together. They are in immediate unity. 'Appreciation' thus captures the fact that knowing and being affected by the work are not two processes, externally related. They are two aspects of one process.

Second, appreciation in this sense is not *thought*. Appreciation occurs prior to thought. It is spontaneous and intuitive. Criticism, by contrast, is thought. For a century academic critics have written as if we read for the sake of criticism. The work presents itself as an object of analysis, and on the basis of the analysis carried out in thought, we write criticism, as thought. This is true for both early twentieth century criticism, and for the various kinds of textual study calling themselves criticism, of the last fifty years. But it is a mistake. We read to enjoy the work, to become aware of its insights and power, and to be affected by it. All this occurs prior to thought, although our consciousness of the work may be deepened or refined by thought. But that deepening and refinement belong to our intuitive apprehension of the work, even if they have been stimulated by thought.

This prior, spontaneous, intuitive experience of the work needs a name, and 'appreciation' is obviously appropriate.

So, how can appreciation be objective? What is the relation between appreciation and criticism? To open up these issues it will be desirable to offer some preliminary remarks on the objectivity of beauty.[12]

The Objectivity of Beauty

The appreciation of literary works, as of artworks generally, belongs with the appreciation of beauty, since all these forms of appreciation are intuitive. A brief account of our relation to beauty, then, will provide a context for our account of literary appreciation.[13]

---

[12] In his essay 'Thought, meaning and sensibility: the problem of value judgment' Leavis dissociates the terms "aesthetic" and "beauty" from a serious concern with literature. For the "intuitions that science ignores" he prefers the term "vital". I think the mutual exclusiveness of this distinction is misguided. If natural beauty, the arts and literature all have common qualities as well as their own distinctive qualities, then we need to know the common qualities as well as those that are specific. In general, if our knowledge of anything is to be strongly based, then we need to know about genera as well as about species. By widening, knowledge can be deepened. See *Valuation in Criticism*, 291.

[13] For my own account of beauty I am primarily indebted to Francis J. Kovach, who is one of the few modern philosophers to defend the objectivity of beauty. I am also indebted to the aesthetics of George Santayana. Santayana is a subjectivist, but his analyses of aesthetic experience are acute. See Francis J. Kovach, *Philosophy of Beauty* (Norman: University of Oklahoma Press, 1974); George Santayana, *The Sense of Beauty: Being the Outline of Aesthetic Theory* (New York: Dover Publications Inc., 1955 [first published 1896]). Kovach discusses the intuitiveness of aesthetic cognition on pp. 309-311 of his study.

First, it is crucial to insist that the objectivity of beauty cannot be demonstrated, it can only be experienced. The only argument for the objectivity of beauty is the overwhelming experience of it. In such an experience one knows that one is in the presence of something that one has *found*, not something that one has conjured up by desire, or established by the power of one's own decision. This is the only argument for the objectivity of beauty, but it is sufficient—at least, for those who have had the experience.

All other arguments for the objectivity of beauty are really arguments against its subjectivity. Most of such arguments can be divided into two kinds: (1) arguments against the *a priori* assumption of primary and secondary qualities; (2) reasons to explain why people disagree over matters of beauty.

The assumption of the distinction between the primary and secondary qualities of bodies, associated with two thinkers of the seventeenth century, the physicist Robert Boyle and the philosopher John Locke, removes not only beauty but colours and sounds and all sensory phenomena, except size, shape, motion, rest, number and solidity, from the real properties of bodies.[14] This is a metaphysical question that aesthetics need not concern itself with, since aesthetics is only concerned with the forms and contents of our experience. Within our experience, the beauty of beautiful objects is just as real as their shapes, colours, sounds, and other sensory qualities. To claim that the beauty of objects is somehow ontologically different from the other qualities of objects perceived in sense-perception would be to set up some metaphysical theory against what experience actually tells us. Even if the doctrine of primary and secondary qualities could be proved true, it would make no difference to our experience, since within our experience we would still have to distinguish between objective and subjective.[15]

The reasons why people disagree about beauty are many and various. They include incapacity, indifference, doctrinal preconceptions, prejudice, ulterior motives, and so on. These are causes why some people cannot acknowledge the real beauty of some object. Such causes commonly cannot be overcome in practice, but they do not affect the objectivity of beauty. Of more interest are the tastes of individuals and groups, which have been formed under the influence of particular abilities or of the particular interests of social groups or of whole societies. Such tastes enable people to discern rightly particular styles of beauty, but inhibit them from appreciating other styles of beauty. Whether such limited tastes can be overcome in practice is a contingent matter.[16]

---

[14] Strictly speaking, secondary qualities are sensations in us caused by powers in a body in virtue of its primary qualities. See John Locke, *An Essay Concerning Human Understanding* [1690], Book II, ch. 8; 2 vols (London: J. M. Dent & Sons Ltd, rev. edn 1965), vol. 1, 102-111.

[15] See Kovach, *Philosophy of Beauty*, 77-81.

[16] *Ibid.*, 101-136. Kovach lists 36 reasons for aesthetic disagreement.

The Definition and Essence of Beauty

There is no reason not to accept the traditional definition of beauty as being that which, when contemplated, arouses delight.[17] The definition captures the facts that the contemplation of beauty is an experience removed from the context of our practical ends, and that the object of the experience pleases for its own sake. What the conditions are for such an experience, I will discuss below.

The essence of the beauty of material objects is primarily constituted by formal relations, specifically by integrity or wholeness, the proportionality or suitability of parts, and unity.[18] Together, these qualities constitute the traditional aesthetic notion of unity in variety.[19] The species of this genus are symmetry, harmony, balance, and so on.[20] That these qualities are the principal constituents of beauty can only be known from experience.

However, even some of the material objects of Nature, as well as artworks, also have a source of beauty in their content. A brilliant full moon shining against the darkness of a clear night sky is beautiful not only because of its perfectly circular shape, but also because of its radiance. A champion racehorse stretching out to leave its rivals in its wake is beautiful for its outstanding vitality and energy as well as for its physical form.[21]

That such characteristics are sources of beauty can only be known from experience. But we can know why both unity in variety and such characteristics of content are sources of beauty by examining our experience. The starting-point of that examination must be disinterestedness.

Disinterestedness as a Condition for the Appreciation of Beauty

Disinterestedness is the subjective counterpart to the objectivity of beauty, and as such is the principal condition for the appreciation of beauty.[22] This

---

[17] *Ibid.*, 7, 24, 29, 58-59, 61, 146 and n. 28, 269 and nn. 28-30.

[18] *Ibid.*, 184-215.

[19] Cf. Alexander Pope, *Windsor Forest* (London, 1713), ll. 7-16; Francis Hutcheson, *An Inquiry into the Original of Our Ideas of Beauty and Virtue*, 2nd edn (London, 1726), sec. 6, p. 82; S. T. Coleridge, 'On the Principles of Genial Criticism' [1814] in *Biographia Literaria*, 2 vols, ed. J. Shawcross (Oxford: Oxford University Press, 1907), vol. II, 232; Santayana, *Sense of Beauty*, 61-69. I think Roger Scruton is wrong to dismiss the notion of unity in variety. He prefers the notion of what is fitting. But, it is fittingness that makes an integrated whole out of distinct parts. See Roger Scruton, *Beauty: A Very Short Introduction* (Oxford: Oxford University Press, 2011), 162-163.

[20] For the tradition stemming from Pythagoras and Plato that beauty depends on precise mathematical ratios, see Dan Pedoe, *Geometry and the Visual Arts* (New York: Dover Publications Inc., 1983 [first published 1976]); John Powell, *How Music Works* (London: Particular Books, 2010).

[21] See Santayana, *Sense of Beauty*, Part II 'The Materials of Beauty', 35-51. Plotinus recognises beauty of content in the sun, the stars, gold, the virtues of the soul, and so on, but he interprets it as the manifestation of the divine Idea, in which all beautiful things participate. See *Enneads* VI ('Beauty'); tr. Stephen MacKenna ([no place of publication]: CreateSpace, 2012), 36-42.

[22] Kovach, *Philosophy of Beauty*, 281-285, 297.

thesis depends on three presuppositions. One is that we can distinguish between taking a practical interest in an object, and taking, as we might say, a 'disinterested interest' in the object. The second is that we take pleasure in the exercise of our faculties, when our faculties have their appropriate objects. The third is that human beings are capable of both interested and disinterested emotions.

This third presupposition might sound strange, but experience tells us that it is true—unless we are hopelessly cynical.[23] It must be considered a fundamental axiom of not only aesthetics, but of ethics and logic, and indeed all intellectual inquiry (whether involving intuition or discursive thought).

On the basis of these presuppositions we can say that we can take pleasure in the exercise of our faculties, when those faculties have their appropriate objects, both when we have some practical end in view and when we do not, that is, when we are exercising our faculties for their own sake. In the case where we have a practical end, our pleasure is double: we feel pleasure in the exercise of our faculties, and we feel pleasure in anticipating and reaching the attainment of our end. In the case where we have no practical end our pleasure is single, consisting in simply the exercise of our faculties.

This disinterested pleasure in the exercise of our faculties is the basis for aesthetic delight and the recognition of beauty. In our practical life human reason is continually involved in finding identities in multiplicity, or unities in variety. To survive in the world we must be able to distinguish between order and chaos, and we must find an order within chaos, no matter how hidden it may be. Practical life depends entirely on this search, whether it be in ordinary life or in the natural sciences, and whether it be carried out by intuition or by any of the varieties of discursive thought. Similarly, in practical life we have an interest in the powers of natural objects, including those of ourselves. Those powers, such as light or energy, also demand our rational attention.

But, we can exercise our faculties for discerning unities in variety, and natural powers even when we have no practical end. This is what happens when we experience beauty. We may be unconscious that we are experiencing unity in variety, but our faculty for it is aroused, and we feel delight. In the case of natural powers, we will be aware of what causes delight in us. But in both cases, the beauty is intuited, and immediately fills our mind with delight.

As this capacity is essential to human reason, we must suppose that anyone is capable of experiencing beauty. Or, at least, this will be so in principle, but in practice there may be particular difficulties or obstacles. Some beauty may be too complex for one individual's capacity. Or, since the instances of

---

[23] The humanistic psychologist Abraham Maslow recognises disinterested emotions in his *Toward a Psychology of Being* [2nd edn 1968]; (Floyd, VA: Sublime Books, 2014), 38-39. This reference is to section 8 of the essay 'Deficiency Motivation and Growth Motivation' in Part II of the book.

particular beauty must be infinite, so that there are infinite styles of beauty, some groups may be unfamiliar with a particular style of beauty, and led astray by their preconceptions. Or, extraneous factors, such as religious or moral prejudice, may interfere with a disinterested appreciation. Or, indeed, some philosophers may be so convinced that beauty is "in the eye of the beholder", and so, unimportant, that they do not bother to look for it.

We arrive at the general principle that the appreciation of beauty is related to our common human nature, with the proviso that there must be no obstacles to a disinterested exercise of our human faculty. The corollary of this principle is that the appreciation of beauty is a *choice*. Disinterestedness is a choice. We can choose whether to open ourselves to beauty or not. But, a choice, if it is to be rational, must be founded in truth—in this case, the truth of the objectivity of beauty.

Beauty in Art

In artworks there are two possible sources of beauty: formal relations, and some content that is representational or expressive. The relations between these two constituents may vary, according to the kind of art. In one kind of art, form is subordinated to representation/expression, as in history painting or portraiture. In another kind of art, representation is subordinated to form, as in some Postimpressionist painting. In some artworks representation and expression seem to disappear altogether, so that only formal relations are presented, as in some Baroque music, or abstract painting.

Thus, the appeal of artworks is constituted by the delight in a work's formality, or a delighted response to the work's representation/expression, because what is presented is such as to arouse a common human interest. These two kinds of appeal may be mixed and interrelated, according to the kind of artwork. The emotions aroused by the work's representation/ expression will be disinterested, provided that the beholder or listener is prepared to be disinterested.

With literary works we generally expect that the formal aspect of a work will be strictly subordinated to the presentation of its content. This is because the medium of a literary work, namely, language, is inseparable from the communication of meaning, and does not have the capacity to make its sound characteristics of much intrinsic interest. In literary works the sound characteristics are used in combination with the sense-meaning to create emphasis and tone, the expression of feeling, and the suggestion of sensations. We tend to regard poems that seem to subordinate representation to form, such as Edgar Allan Poe's 'The Raven', as misguided, if amusing, curiosities.

The Literary Work

A literary work is a formal arrangement of words to present what is of common interest in human experience, that is, those matters of character, passion, desire, purpose, and social relationships that make up human life, and manifest human nature.

Thus, in literary works, (i) form is generally subordinated to content, and (ii) the content of literary works is made up of life-experiences, or, more precisely, those life-experiences that bear upon human happiness and misery, well-being and its absence, and all matters in which human beings find good and evil. In practical life such experiences are of practical interest. In literary works they are of 'disinterested interest'.

Literary works are suited to this kind of presentation because their medium, language, if developed, is an unusually powerful means of expression. In real life we may suffer, but be unable to articulate our suffering adequately, because our command of language is poor, or because we are so emotionally moved that we cannot control our expression. By contrast, in a literary work an imaginative writer may command such power of expression that the whole complex of a character's situation, thoughts, feelings and sensations is brought before us for our emotionally involved apprehension. Othello's mind, in his jealousy, is filled with pain, uncertainty, rage, and horrible images of Desdemona and Cassio. A real-life Othello might only produce screams, oaths, and broken phrases. Shakespeare gives to Othello an expression of such complexity and power that his whole situation becomes an inexhaustible object for our contemplation and reflection. This is expression raised to a higher power, as it were.[24]

What makes this possible is an imaginative writer's capacity to unify complex processes of cognition with the creation of images, and their emotional accompaniments. When we speak of the 'expression of emotion', we are not being accurate. Emotion is only one element in what we call the 'Expression'. What is being presented is not only emotion, but both the contents of the character's psyche, and his sense of his objective situation. The usual name for this capacity of a creative writer is Imagination. Imagination, thus, involves understanding and insight, thought, imagery, emotion, and external perception. The imaginative writer presents something *concrete*, whereas the thinker abstracts. The thinker connects abstractions in series, whereas the imaginative writer presents something endlessly complex all at once.

Typification

Literary works that we hold to be good have the power to interest varieties of readers across temporal, national and other social boundaries (race, class, religious affiliation, and so on)—at least, if those readers are willing to be disinterested. Such works appeal to, and presuppose a common human nature.

---

[24] That the power of expression admits of a very wide range of degrees is obvious every night in the sports news, when a brilliant footballer player, who has had a superb match, is almost inarticulate when asked to discuss it by an interviewer. But his business is not with the power of expression.

This kind of general appeal is said to have its source in the work's 'typification'. All that this term means is that the work is such as to arouse common human interests, in a disinterested way, so that social differences can be suspended in the work's appreciation.[25]

Such typification can occur at different levels of interest, and in different modes (comic, tragic, elegiac, satiric, and so on). At its most existentially and emotionally profound, the typification of a work such as *Hamlet* will engage our interest in some of the most basic and most emotionally demanding of human situations, and thus exhibit for us, in depth, what it is to be human. In *Hamlet* we are presented with love, grief, rage, horror, despair, the demands of conscience, the burdens of duty, the pains of love, the agony of doubt, the anguish of failure, the demoralisation of the self from demands too great to be met, the weariness of life. The great writer presents such things not as ideas but as situations, concretely imagined, to be lived through.

But such typification requires a character that exists at multiple levels, and in many relationships. *Hamlet* is able to present us with these existentially challenging situations because Hamlet is so multi-faceted a character. He has his individual habits of behaviour and expression, a particular temperament, a particular set of abilities and dispositions, characteristic virtues and vices, strengths and weaknesses, a set of manners, a view of life, tendencies to particular passions in particular circumstances, a code of conduct, a set of ideals, characteristics of age, sex, and class, social relations with family, friends, enemies, equals, superiors, inferiors, with those who are loved, and those who are hated, those who are admired, and those who are despised, and so on and so on. It is through the exhibition of all these traits and relations that we become aware of what is at stake in Hamlet's life at the most fundamental level. But we see that it is at stake also at the higher levels, in the most trivial of incidents. Everything in the play demands our engaged interest.

All this comes about through the power of the imagination to create something concrete for intuitive apprehension, in contrast to the power of the intellect to analyse and synthesise abstract concepts for a reflective and discursive consideration.[26]

---

[25] See Wilhelm Dilthey, 'The Typical in Poetry', section 3 of 'The Imagination of the Poet: Elements for a Poetics' (1887); also, the sections 'Life' and 'The Poetic Imagination' in 'Goethe and the Poetic Imagination' (1910); both monographs are contained in *Poetry and Experience*, vol. V (1985) of Wilhelm Dilthey, *Selected Works*, 6 vols, ed. Rudolf A. Makkreel and Frithjof Rodi (Princeton, NJ: Princeton University Press, 1985-).

[26] "Only have the courage to give yourself up to your impressions, allow yourself to be delighted, moved, elevated, nay, instructed and inspired for something great; but do not imagine all is vanity, if it is not abstract thought and idea." Goethe to Eckermann, 6 May 1827, in *Conversations of Goethe with Eckermann*, trans. by John Oxenford (London: George Bell and Sons, 1909), 258. Cited in Dilthey, *Poetry and Experience*, 137.

Art and Entertainment

The distinction between art and entertainment must be insisted on, because it is founded in a real, and most important difference. It is true that a literary work can be both, but before we consider the combination, it is essential to be clear about the difference.

A literary work that is art presents a situation, founded in truth, and in common human interests, that we can imagine our way into, not by the arbitrary workings of our own fantasies, but under the discipline of the forms in which the situation is presented. Such a literary work stimulates both the cognizing and emotionally affective sides of our imagination, and leaves a permanent impression. In doing so, it modifies, in some cases slightly, in other cases extensively, our understanding of and attitude towards the world and to ourselves.

The effect of entertainment is more superficial and ephemeral. No human situation is explored in much depth. We are moved by transitory stimuli, but they leave no strong impression, and do not change our view of anything. Because of their stimuli entertainments may be immensely pleasurable, and we may repeat the experience many times because we know we will experience the pleasure again. But this is not art.

This does not mean that there are no standards of excellence in entertainment. There certainly are. The differences between high-class action-movies with serious actors, and 'high production values', and C- or D-class movies with wooden acting, perfunctory direction, a mindless script, an inappropriate musical score, and heavy-handed editing, are real.

Nor am I saying that there is no place for entertainment. There certainly is, since in a society still given to overwork, and continual stress, sources of relaxation are vital. But art and entertainment are two different things. The difference is essential for the issue of objectivism and subjectivism. The subjectivist view allows unthinking people to conflate the two categories and assert that Shakespeare is no better than the latest soap-opera. Some people like one thing, others like another. It is important, therefore, to insist that literature as art has real powers that entertainment does not have. The possession of these powers by literary works of art is something objectively real.

Having clarified the differences between art and entertainment, we can now consider their combination. It is striking that until the late nineteenth century such combinations were very common, if not predominant: for example, the works of Homer, Greek tragedy and comedy, *Beowulf*, Chaucer's *Canterbury Tales*, most of the plays of Shakespeare and of his contemporaries, Dryden's political satires, Swift's *Gulliver's Travels*, Fielding's *Tom Jones*, and, most blatantly, the novels of Dickens.

One may well refuse to call *King Lear* entertainment, but the other great tragedies were undoubtedly entertainment for Shakespeare's audiences. [27] However, they were also—and more importantly *sub specie aeternitatis*—works of art. *Twelfth Night* is perhaps the most revealing case. The plot of *Twelfth Night* is outrageously incredible and preposterous. It is for that very reason immense fun in the theatre. What lifts *Twelfth Night* above the level of absurd farce is the poetry. The poetry is of such intensity and power that the emotions of Viola, Orsino and Olivia have the same vividness for us as the emotions of characters in a tragedy. The same is true for the prose that allows Malvolio to move from being just a ridiculous fool to a figure of pathos, and even someone too formidable for a comedy. *Twelfth Night* is a classic because of what Dryden would have called "the writing".[28] There is no complex psychology, there are only simple passions. But those passions are presented with all the power of a great poet.

What enables much of the literature before the late nineteenth century to be entertainment is that their stories have the simplicity of their sources in myth, legend, and folk-tale. But a great literary artist can take the commonplace material and transfigure it by verbal art. It is the triumph of 'treatment' over 'matter', but in the process the truth of the human psyche is vividly presented.

We can now sum up:

1) Insofar as a literary work of art has the formal relations of integrity, proportionality, and unity, such that they present powerfully a situation of common human interest, it possesses beauty.

2) Insofar as a literary work of art embodies insight into a human situation, it possesses truth.[29]

---

[27] Cf. T. S. Eliot's famous comment on the "thriller interest" in *Hamlet, Macbeth,* and *Othello*. See *Selected Essays*, 3rd enlarged edn (London: Faber and Faber Ltd, 1951), 81 and n. 1.

[28] See "An Account of the Ensuing Poem [*Annus Mirabilis*], in a Letter to the Honourable Sir Robert Howard" (1667) in John Dryden, *Of Dramatic Poesy and Other Critical Essays*, 2 vols, ed. George Watson (London: J. M. Dent & Sons Ltd, 1962), vol. 1, 96-102.

[29] Dilthey, *Poetry and Experience*, 83-84. For discussions of truth in the arts and literature, see John Hospers, *Meaning and Truth in the Arts* (Chapel Hill: The University of North Carolina Press, 1946); Peter Lamarque, *The Philosophy of Literature* Oxford: Blackwell Publishing, 2009). Structuralism has become associated with anti-realism. It is argued that because of the patterns in the structures and functions of language literary works cannot represent or express anything truthfully. This is a blatant *non-sequitur*, as it confuses the means of representation with what is represented. However, once realism is rejected, structuralism itself is abandoned, and we pass to a post-structuralist doctrine, according to which literary works are recast as instances of ideology or discourse or textuality. These are to be 'interrogated' or deconstructed with the help of Althusser's theory of ideology, Lacan's psychoanalysis, Foucault's theory of discourse, or Derrida's deconstruction. By this stage the nature of

3) Insofar as a literary work of art extends our understanding of the possibilities of human good and evil, it possesses goodness.

The Platonic triad of Beauty, Truth and Goodness has not become irrelevant, merely because we are living in the twenty-first century.

The Epistemology of Literary Appreciation

Epistemology or the theory of knowledge is the branch of philosophy that investigates how we come to know anything.

If we are to consider whether appreciation can be objective, then we need to examine how we 'appropriate' a literary work, how it becomes an object for us, and how its doing so involves our entering into a relation with it. But the epistemology of literary appreciation has two peculiarities: (i) we have to recreate the work in our imagination before it can be said to be an object of knowledge; (ii) our mental relation to the work involves not only knowing, but feeling, both the cognitive and the affective sides of the mind being indispensable both to the recreation of the work, and to our response to it.

A preliminary caution: the term 'objective' in popular usage is ambiguous. It ought to mean 'belonging to the object'. However, when people use the term, they generally mean 'known with certainty to belong to the object'. This shifts the meaning of the term from the object to the subjective conditions of knowledge, and general agreement becomes the criterion of objectivity. Thus, the colour of litmus paper is considered objective, because distinguishing pink from blue is such a simple act of sense-perception that everyone will agree about it, except the blind. By contrast, whether one concert musician is more skilled than another is a matter that only expert listeners can judge. In this situation, people will say that the matter is one of opinion, that everyone will have a preference, and that the matter is subjective. In reality, which of the two musicians has the greater skill is just as much an objective question as whether the litmus paper turns pink or blue. But most people will not recognize that, and will take cover behind subjectivism to protect their proprietary right to the dignity of their own preferences. This ambiguity leaves any complex matter in ethics or aesthetics obscured in confusion.

My approach to the epistemology of appreciation is that of the Romantic hermeneutics of Wilhelm Dilthey (1833-1911), which was based on the hermeneutic theory of Friedrich Schleiermacher (1768-1834). Neither of these thinkers has had the influence on literary study in the English-speaking world that they deserve. But this tradition merits more respect, because it takes seri-

---

a literary work and of literary appreciation has altogether disappeared, to be replaced by partisan critiques of desire and power, or 'playful' destruction of the text. See Hawkes, *Structuralism and Semiotics*, 86; Belsey, *Critical Practice*, 4-14, and *passim*.

ously the nature of the existence of the literary work in language, and the nature of language as the interface between the physical and mental worlds.[30]

How does a literary work exist? In language. How does language exist? More, especially, how does written language exist? Language is a system of signs with both physical and mental aspects. A word is a sound or a written mark that is understood as having a meaning by human beings. Consequently, a word does not function as a word unless it is understood by some human beings. The sound that is taken by human beings for a word is in itself merely a physical event. Similarly, a written mark that human beings take for a word is merely a material object, a scratch on a stone, an inky mark on paper, or a black mark on a computer screen. None of these marks becomes a word unless human beings understand them as such, and so are able to share the meaning that is to be communicated from one mind to another.[31]

Since literary works are structures of language, they exist as actualities only when they are understood by human beings. Until understanding occurs, a literary work is merely a potentiality waiting to be realised.

But the literary work does have its own identity that has been given to it by its author. It may have all sorts of emergent characteristics that its author did not consciously put into the work. But these emergent characteristics will be present as potentialities because they depend on the characteristics put into the work by the author's act of composition.

---

[30] See Friedrich Schleiermacher, *Hermeneutics and Criticism and Other Writings*, ed. Andrew Bowie (Cambridge: Cambridge University Press, 1998). For Dilthey's hermeneutics and associated doctrines, see the following volumes in the Princeton *Selected Works*: volume II, *Understanding the Human World* (2010); volume III, *The Formation of the Historical World in the Human Sciences* (2002); volume IV, *Hermeneutics and the Study of History* (1996). See also the pieces "The Imagination of the Poet: Elements for a Poetics" (1887), "Fragments for a Poetics" (1907-1908), and "Goethe and the Poetic Imagination" (1910) in volume V, *Poetry and Experience* (1985). For discussions, see Richard E. Palmer, *Hermeneutics: Interpretation Theory in Schleiermacher, Dilthey, Heidegger, and Gadamer* (Evanston: Northwestern University Press, 1969); H. A. Hodges, *The Philosophy of Wilhelm Dilthey* (London: Routledge & Kegan Paul Ltd, 1952); Wellek, *History of Modern Criticism*, vol. 4 (New Haven and London: Yale UP, 1965), 320-335; Rudolf A. Makkreel, *Dilthey: Philosopher of the Human Studies* (Princeton: Princeton University Press, 1975; with afterword, 1992). Robert Holub discusses Schleiermacher and Dilthey in his essay 'Hermeneutics', pp. 255-288 of Raman Selden ed., *From Formalism to Poststructuralism* (Cambridge: Cambridge University Press, 1995), vol. 8 of *The Cambridge History of Literary Criticism*, gen. eds P. Brooks, H. B. Nisbet and Claude Rawson (Cambridge: Cambridge University Press, 1989-). (Wellek is unsympathetic to Dilthey's poetics.)

[31] See Dilthey, "The Rise of Hermeneutics" (1900) in *Hermeneutics and the Study of History*, 235-258; also, "The Understanding of Other Persons and their Manifestations of Life" in *The Formation of the Historical World in the Human Sciences*, 226-247. See also Hodges, 116-159. For this idea in English-speaking literary criticism and theory, see Richards, *Principles*, 90-91; F. R. Leavis, *The Common Pursuit* (Harmondsworth, Middlesex: Penguin Books Ltd, 1976 [first published 1952]), 212-213; Leavis, *Living Principle*, 35; Leavis, *Valuation in Criticism*, 278-279, 285; Wellek, *Theory of Literature*, 142-157. For phenomenological theory, see Roman Ingarden, *The Literary Work of Art: An Investigation on the Borderlines of Ontology, Logic, and Theory of Literature*, tr. George G. Grabowicz (Evanston: Northwestern University Press, 1973); Roman Ingarden, *The Cognition of the Literary Work of Art*, tr. Ruth Ann Crowley and Kenneth R. Olson (Evanston: Northwestern University Press, 1973).

From this account we can draw the following conclusions:

1. A literary work has its own identity, which can be understood or misunderstood. Both success and failure are possible in relation to understanding.[32]

2. Emergent characteristics also fall under the categories of understanding and misunderstanding. Either these emergent characteristics truly depend on the work's basic identity or they do not.

3. Within the scope of valid understanding, disagreements can occur as to the meanings of a work, but only because a work is objectively ambiguous, or because a work is commonly a highly complex structure, presenting multiple aspects, or because the scope of emergent characteristics is infinite, *not* because there is something irrational or chaotic in language. If language were really subject to such irrationality, communication between human beings would not be possible, and the human species would never have survived.

4. If disagreements as to the understanding of literary works occur, what is needed is a more powerful discipline of interpretation (and, as we shall see, response), not the abandonment of the task of interpretation from a lack of serious interest in the task.

Re-living

A literary work, then, has to be recreated or realised in a reader's imagination. This process has been called by Dilthey re-living or re-experiencing. The allusion to life and experience in these terms points to the fact that what the reader has to recreate is not only the sense-meaning of the words, but sound patterns, movement, rhythm, and tempo, and thereby emotion, tone, attitude, the suggestion of sensation, and so on. The presupposition of this process is that the mental contents that the author has put into the words can be aroused in the reader's mind by the words, provided that the principles of valid interpretation are observed.[33]

---

[32] See E. D. Hirsch, Jr., *Validity in Interpretation* (New Haven and London: Yale University Press, 1967); Dilthey, 'The Rise of Hermeneutics'.
[33] See references for Dilthey's hermeneutics in notes 28 and 29, and references for F. R. Leavis in note 29. See also Richards, *Practical Criticism*.

The reader's task is to revive all the mental contents latent in the words in his own imagination. While this may be a highly complex and difficult task (depending on the difficulty of the work), the task is not arbitrary. On the basis of the sense-meaning, which is the simplest element to understand, the reader can proceed to integrate the formal characteristics of the work, its sound patterns, movement, figures of speech, and so on, until the flow of feelings, the transitions between attitudes, the purposes expressed in the words, and so forth, emerge. They emerge, if they do, because the reader has succeeded in integrating the sense-meaning of the words with the words' formal characteristics.[34]

This whole process of recreation depends on three things. First, it depends on a knowledge of vocabulary and grammar, and of idioms and of what departures from the usual forms of expression are possible and what are not. Second, it depends on what Schleiermacher called the 'hermeneutic circle', the principle of moving back and forth within a text between parts and whole, at all levels, on the assumption that the meaning of any element depends on its relations to other elements with which it forms a coherent structure.[35] Third, it depends on the capacity of the human mind to reproduce the feelings of another from the linguistic forms in which those feelings have been expressed. This capacity, empathy, is essential to human communication, and so vital to the survival of that most social of species, the human race.[36]

---

[34] Prose has a degree of formal element, as well as verse. In some cases, the formality is very pronounced, as in the prose of such authors as Sir Thomas Browne, Milton, Gibbon, Carlyle and others. The more simple and straightforward prose of most novels is self-effacing, and functions to express the writer's imaginative grasp of characters, feelings and situations. Since the Prague School of linguistics, it has been recognised that an unusual concentration of linguistic forms and functions attracts attention to itself, thereby constituting what we call the 'poetic' use of language. This 'poetry' offers a special beauty of its own, distinct from, albeit related to the meanings of the language. It is ironical that this very beauty of language is immediately converted into an object of structuralist analysis, and everybody is now too embarrassed to say, "Aren't these lines beautiful?" In positivist fashion, a 'science of the text' displaces the appreciation of poetic beauty. See Hawkes, *Structuralism and Semiotics*, 75-82.

[35] Schleiermacher, *Hermeneutics and Criticism*, 24, 27, and *passim*; Dilthey, "Rise of Hermeneutics", section 4. See also Palmer, *Hermeneutics*, 87-88, 118-121; Hodges, 138.

[36] Dilthey, "Rise of Hermeneutics"; "Transposition, Re-creating, and Re-experiencing" in *The Formation of the Historical World in the Human Sciences*, 234-237. English-speaking philosophers tend to be suspicious of intuition and empathy as allegedly non-rational. See Makkreel, *Dilthey*, 252, and n. 5. Dilthey holds both that, insofar as understanding requires reliving, there is a non-rational element in understanding, and that, nonetheless, understanding is capable of objective validity. See "Exegesis or Interpretation" in *The Formation of the Historical World in the Human Sciences*, 237-241. Contemporary neuroscience takes the cognitive claims of empathy seriously. See Daniel Goleman, *Emotional Intelligence: Why It Can Matter More than IQ* (London, Berlin and New York: Bloomsbury Publishing Plc, 1996); Simon Baron-Cohen, *The Essential Difference* (London: Penguin Books Ltd, 2004); Iain McGilchrist, *The Master and His Emissary: The Divided Brain and the Making of the Western World* (New Haven and London: Yale University Press, 2009).

The criterion of success in understanding turns out to be unity in variety, the same principle that informs our experience of beauty. The literary work or any other linguistic text has been apprehended as a unity, and an integrated whole, with every word playing its suitable role. If the literary work is not a unity, for whatever reason, then this will be discovered in the bafflement of the attempted process of integration.

If this task of understanding is carried out relatively easily, then it proceeds as intuition. There is no need to think discursively. However, if the reader's understanding is baffled at any point, then the reader's mind must shift into reflection. He may ask himself questions, look for answers, try out hypotheses, and so on, until he has a flash of illumination, and the reader's mind is back in intuition. The essential nature of the appreciation of a literary work is, then, intuition. Reflection is ancillary.

The Role of Sensibility in Understanding

I said above that as we integrate the sense-meaning of the words of a work with the work's formal characteristics, feelings, tone, suggestions, and so on 'emerge'. I also said that if difficulties of understanding arise, we can 'try out hypotheses'. It is important to note that such hypotheses may be of two kinds. They may be a different sense-meaning which we conceive in *thought*. Or, they may be a new movement in our imaginary sensation, as we try to get the combination of words to sound differently or move differently. When we have got the elements of the words' meanings integrated with the forms of the words, then we feel in our own sensibility the feelings expressed in the words. In this way, sensibility is essential to our understanding.

Thus, we need to emphasise that in the 'understanding' of a literary work both the cognitive and the affective sides of the mind are involved. This is a kind of knowing that is very different from the knowing that takes place in the natural sciences, or in our ordinary experience with material objects. It is not a matter of observation, reasoning, and more observation. It is a combination of intuition (supplemented by reflection, if necessary), of imaginary sensation, and of feeling.

The result of this process of understanding is not just the knowledge of an object, but the recreation and possession of the work in our own minds. This understanding is both cognitive and creative. In this process of understanding, the various powers of the mind, which are naturally free-ranging, are disciplined both by the linguistic forms of the work, and by the rules of interpretation, including the hermeneutic circle. This is a real discipline, but it is primarily a discipline of imagination, intuition and sensibility, and only secondarily a discipline of thought. We shall meet an essential discipline of thought later, but not yet.

Sensibility and Response

But our experience of a literary work has further dimensions. Sensibility is involved in a second way. Since literary works commonly depict human behaviour that is good or evil, our perception of what kind of behaviour is present to us is not just a matter of a classification of an object, it involves our own response. Is a certain character's act admirable or contemptible? Lovable or tiresome? Justifiable or unjustifiable?

While we are still reading in the mode of intuition, we will have spontaneous emotional reactions that will depend on our previous experience of life. In this way our understanding of the work will involve this obviously subjective component. Must we leave this as an alien subjective element within our otherwise objective understanding of the work? Or can we remove the arbitrariness of our response, so that we can consider our response as at least claiming to be universally valid?

Before I consider this issue, there is another similar matter to bring forward. That is evaluation. It will be best to consider the justifications for our response and our evaluations together.

Evaluation

What I wish to argue here is that the evaluation of a literary work is in the first instance an element in our direct experience of it. At first, at least, it is not something extra or external.[37]

What happens is that as we read, and understand the work in the ways described above, we respond spontaneously with our sensibility not only to what is depicted in the work, but also to the work itself. These spontaneous feelings are feelings of valuation. Because we will have experienced other works, we will have built up over time implicit and unconscious standards concerning the truthfulness and power of literary works. These are not two kinds of standards, one for truthfulness and one for power. A literary work, if it is to be excellent, must present us with something truthful and of human importance, and it must do so powerfully. The relation of formal characteristics to content serves to present the author's insight into his material, and to present it with appropriate vividness, the appropriateness being determined by the intrinsic importance of what is being presented. We therefore spontaneously form unconsciously in our minds standards of what is powerfully true.

When we experience a new work, and as we proceed in our understanding of it, including our response to its contents, we spontaneously have feelings of valuation toward the work itself. We cannot help feeling that the work is excellent, or good, or fair, or weak, or dreadful. All this happens before we

---

[37] Dilthey, 'Rise of Hermeneutics' in *Hermeneutics and the Study of History*, 255-256. Cf. Leavis, *Common Pursuit*, 212-213; *Living Principle*, 35-36; *Valuation in Criticism*, 278-279.

begin to think about the work. Once again, we are proceeding at the level of intuition and sensibility.

Having read the work, we can re-read other works with which to compare the new one. As we do this, we may find that our feelings of valuation are confirmed, or they may be modified so that we feel a higher or lower valuation for the work, or our feelings of valuation for the earlier works may be similarly modified.

As with understanding, we may pass from intuition to reflection, if we are puzzled as to why we feel that one work is superior to another. Such puzzlement may prompt us to think and analyse, and try to locate in thought the nature of the various works' merits. Greater depth of emotion? Greater range of character? Greater command of verbal form? And so on. But our feelings of valuation come first. Any thinking that we do is an attempt to be true to our feelings. We are thus engaged here both in a discipline of sensibility (truth to the relative merits of works, as felt), and a discipline of thought (truth to our feelings, as articulated in thought).

We can conclude that in literary experience (as in aesthetic experience generally) cognition is immediately united with valuation. These are not two externally related processes. They are one process with diverse aspects. In literary experience we have a quite different relation between cognition and valuation from that in the natural sciences. Literary study cannot be a value-free science. In literary experience cognition of the object and valuation of the object can be united, because the feeling of valuation is itself a kind of cognition, a cognition of the relative excellence of any given work in the context of other works.

But these valuations of truth and power themselves presuppose common human interests and a common human nature that provide the basis for comparisons between works. So, are there common human interests? Is there a common human nature?

Common Human Interests and Common Human Nature

Common human interests are grounded in a common human nature. All human beings have a range of needs: some material (food, drink, sleep, shelter, exercise, sex, security), some social (respect, love, friendship, comradeship, belonging generally), and some relating to individual development. These needs are supported by corresponding abilities, and are manifested in desires. When frustrated, desires turn into passions (rage, grief, fear, despair . . .). In addition, society has its needs for stability, harmony, and integration, which impose obligations on individuals. Such obligations, in the form of virtues, are also necessary for the individuals' own development and integration. Needless to say, all these needs can conflict with one another, depending on circumstances, but they can all still be identified.[38]

Although social institutions, customs, and codes of conduct change historically as a result of changes in technology, wealth and power, the common human interests can be discovered working their way out across historical periods and national boundaries. Jane Austen's social world may be very different from ours, but we can still identify courage, cowardice, justice, injustice, self-control, self-indulgence, and so on, and respond with the appropriate sympathy or antipathy, approval or disapproval. To this extent, cultural relativism is a straw man.

But do we have the capacity to appropriate mentally the literary works of different periods and societies? Can we avoid misunderstanding and erroneous valuations, arising from obstacles due to historical differences?

Assuming that we have acquired sufficient information to navigate another society, we only need generic abilities to appropriate that society's works. For making out the sense of works we only need a familiarity with the language. For recreating the formal characteristics—sound, movement, rhythm and so on—we only need sensitivity. For difficulties of understanding, our imagination, if well-informed, and well-exercised, will produce 'leaps' and flashes of insight. None of these mental powers depends on historical conditions.

Given the generic powers of understanding and sensibility, we must assume that the human truthfulness of a work, and its artistic power of presentation can be apprehended and responded to, across historical periods and societal boundaries. This has been abundantly verified in experience for millennia. The exercise of our generic powers is only impeded by historically created obstacles such as censorship, or religious prohibitions, or misguided literary prejudices.

However, some disagreements among readers are due to differences of psychological make-up. Human beings not only have a common human nature, they are divided into various psychological types by temperament and abilities. Since we feel pleasure in the exercise of our abilities, and the expression of our temperament, different groups of this kind will form different tastes. In this sense a taste is simply the pleasure felt in the exercise of a particular power. So, some people will enjoy watching football, and others will enjoy going to the opera. These likes and dislikes are real and valid, but have nothing to do with the merits of literary works or other works of art. A foot-

---

[38] I have broadly followed Maslow's hierarchy of needs. I have added society's needs, and the virtues. See Abraham Maslow, "A Theory of Human Motivation", *Psychological Review* 50(4) (1943), 370-396; *Toward A Psychology of Being* [2nd edn 1968]; (Floyd, VA: Sublime Books, 2014); *Motivation and Personality*, 3rd edn rev. Robert Frager, James Fadiman, Cynthia McReynolds, and Ruth Cox, ([no place of publication]: Pearson Education Inc., 1987).

ball fan may despise poetry because it is outside the range of his faculties, but, equally, an aesthete may fail to recognise any excellence in sport. Both are prejudiced. Neither is making a genuine judgment. These kinds of tastes are legitimate for entertainment. But art requires that we make allowance for the limitations of our individual constitution, and attempt to respond on the basis of our common human nature. But that is our choice. Whether we do or not, the merits of particular works of art remain what they are.

A corollary of the notion of a common human nature is that some emotional responses are *natural*. This is a very unfashionable idea, but it is fundamental to trans-historical understanding, as well as to human sociality in general. For example, an act of service tends to arouse gratitude in its beneficiary, other things being equal. Or, a show of friendliness tends to arouse a friendly response, other things being equal. Or, a disinterested act of courage tends to elicit admiration, other things being equal. The key phrase is 'other things being equal'. These responses will occur, provided that they are not overridden by some other passions, interests or prejudices. In *King Lear*, Edmund is ungrateful to his father Gloucester who loves him. Edmund's behaviour is described in the play as 'unnatural', and it is. We are right to feel disapproval of Edmund, but the correctness of our feeling depends on an essential tendency of our common human nature. There are basic features in human nature that are beyond 'social constructionism'. The general principle is that our common human nature will manifest itself in responses that correspond to stimuli, provided that contingent passions, interests or prejudices do not override them. Whether they do or not depends on choice and rational self-control. This must be an axiom of any humanism.[39]

It is true that there are cases where a difference in world-view between two societies is too great to be overcome. The most striking example that I have ever found is the homecoming of Odysseus in Homer's *Odyssey*. Odysseus kills all the suitors of his wife, who have pillaged his house and property. This seems inevitable in Odysseus' world, as the only possible form of justice. But he also feels betrayed by his servants. So, he hangs the offending maidservants in the courtyard, and mutilates and disembowels the swineherd Melanthios, cutting off his nose and ears, hands and feet, and genitals. Melanthios' offence had merely been insulting Odysseus, when he had not recognised Odysseus. To us the punishments must seem out of proportion to the offence and barbaric, but evidently not to Homer. In such a case, we can

---

[39] I do not mean to say that a common human nature is merely a matter of feeling. Clearly, reason, will and feeling need to be integrated in a mature personality. By the standards of such integration some feelings will need to be moderated or overridden in particular circumstances. But every society will require such integration and maturity, even if specific values, codes and customs vary according to material and social conditions, and degree of cultural development. Such variability does not subject us to arbitrariness and irrationality. It does not make behaviour in other societies or periods unintelligible, or incapable of arousing an appropriate response, at least not generally.

still acknowledge the power of Homer's art, but our emotional response is baffled. I am inclined to say that this incident exhibits the distorting effect of unbridled power on natural human tendencies, and the dangers of aristocratic government. But I recognize that this is a 'bourgeois' sentiment.[40]

Setting aside exceptions, we can say that we can respond to literary works from our common human nature because they appeal to common human interests, provided this process is not hindered by obstacles. It is up to us to see that it is not. To that end we must approach literary appreciation with disinterestedness, seriousness, and open-mindedness. On these conditions, there is nothing to prevent us from engaging in the "common pursuit of true judgment".[41]

We can also conclude that we can discover some works to have more of permanent human interest, at a high level, than others. We are justified in regarding them as 'classics', and as constituting a canon, in the sense of being works of permanent interest and value, although not in the sense of being models for all future production.

Appreciation: its Centrality

So far we have remained in the mode of intuition and sensibility, and any shift into reflection has been ancillary, with a view to returning to intuition. This mode of apprehending, responding to, and valuing literary works may be called *appreciation*. Appreciation in this sense is an immediate unity of cognition and feeling.

But we cannot remain in the mode of appreciation. We must move into the mode of *thought*, and for two reasons. First, for our own sake, if we wish to relate our current appreciation of one literary work with our previous experience of other works, or with anything else whatever in human life that is relevant, we must use thought, since it is only by thought that we can move between a plurality of particular experiences and realities. Second, we must make the transition to thought so that we can share our intuitive apprehension and response to a work with others. The social dimension of all study of the arts is essential, since works of art are complex, multi-faceted entities, whose adequate appreciation may require the contribution of many persons.

Thus, moving into the mode of thought, we enter the domain of *criticism*. It is essential to distinguish appreciation and criticism because they are processes that call on two completely different sets of mental powers, which require training in two completely different ways.

---

[40] Homer, *The Odyssey*, xxii, 419-477.
[41] See T. S. Eliot, 'The Function of Criticism' in *Selected Essays*, 3rd enlarged edn (London: Faber and Faber Ltd, 1951), 25; Leavis, *Common Pursuit*, v.

Intuition and sensibility, the powers of appreciation, require repeated practice in noticing with care and with mental flexibility, and practice in feeling with disinterestedness, strength, and refinement.

Critical thought requires a sincere and diligent attempt to be true to one's intuitions and feelings, to find conceptual equivalents for these, which state neither too little, nor too much. This translation of appreciation into criticism is a real discipline of thought, not only because of the usual requirement of discursive thinking for logical coherence and consistency, but also, and more especially, because the vocabulary of ordinary language is crude and impoverished in comparison with the richness, variety, and subtlety of intuitions and feelings, especially those constituting the appreciation of something as complex as a literary work. This need to compel (persuade, help?) language to express or at least suggest the contents of intuition and sensibility is a respect in which the thinking in literary criticism differs from the thinking in the natural sciences, and in practical life.

Thus, *both* appreciation (as immediate experience) and criticism (as thought) differ from the kinds of experience and thought associated with the natural sciences and practical life. These differences need to be insisted on in an age still dominated by positivism.

We can now conclude, that appreciation is central to literary study, in that it, and only it, can provide the basis for literary criticism. Anything that purports to be criticism that is not founded in appreciation is liable to go astray, to become arbitrary and irrelevant, and to take our investigations away from the literature.

Criticism's Distinct Contribution
While the above is true, there is a peculiarity of criticism as thought which distinguishes it from appreciation, although it can deepen understanding and heighten valuation.

Appreciation is directly focused on trains of images, meanings, feelings, and suggestions. Their unity as the presentation of, say, an action, or a speech is recreated in the reader's mind unconsciously. But, in a literary work, especially a significant one, there is a massive substructure hidden beneath the words. This substructure may be the character of a dramatic personage as complex as Hamlet, or it may be a shifting pattern of social relationships, as between Coriolanus and the plebeians, or between Coriolanus and his mother.

It is one of the tasks of criticism to elicit that substructure. This must mean that the critic will be obliged to introduce all sorts of concepts that are never mentioned in the literary work. For a long time nobody objected when literary scholars such as Bradley analysed the characters of Shakespeare's tragedies, because to understand characters seemed (rightly) to be the natural thing to do. But concepts taken from, say, historical materialism or psychoanalysis have been more controversial. Assuming that the concepts from such sources are not problematical in themselves, the criteria for their application must be relevance and accuracy. These can only be determined in relation to what appreciation has already told us, and they must not go beyond the evidence presented by appreciation.

Moreover, such concepts should be applied to illuminate the work. The work should not be used as raw material for the propagation of the theory from which the concepts are drawn, or of any political ideology associated with the theory. There is a real difference of direction and goal here.

Eliciting this substructure means, in a sense, constructing something out of the words of the work. But the aim of such construction should be to elicit what is really there, what is really implied by the words. This effort of construction by critical thought, therefore, need not call in question the objectivity of the criticism.

Such application of concepts can deepen understanding of what is being represented or expressed, and so heighten our valuation of a work. But the essential work of valuation remains what we feel in appreciation, since it is only in appreciation that we actually experience the power of the work.

From appreciation and criticism so performed we can move in different directions. We can investigate literary history in all its varieties. We can construct theories to clarify appreciation, criticism, literary history, the relationship of literature to collective mentalities, the history of ideas, the history of social institutions, and so on. But all this activity depends on critical thought, and critical thought depends on appreciation. Appreciation is thus central.

Presuppositions

It would take too long, and be too tedious to repeat here all the presuppositions for the centrality of appreciation for literary study, which have been mentioned in this essay. The most important are the following:

- Beauty is objectively real.
- Beauty is an object of intuition.
- Disinterestedness is required for the apprehension and appreciation of beauty.
- Human beings are capable of disinterested, as well as interested emotions.
- Disinterestedness is a choice.
- There are many potential obstacles to the recognition of beauty. Some can be overcome.
- Delight in a literary work's representation/expression is aroused by common human interests.
- Common human interests arise out of a common human nature.

- Works of art and literature have real powers that must be objectively known and valued.
- Expression can be performed at multiple levels, from excellence down to incompetence.
- Literary works, as existing in language, must be recreated in the reader's imagination.
- A literary work, having its own identity, can be understood or misunderstood.
- Human beings can communicate successfully through language.
- Human beings can empathize with one another through expressive signs.
- The essential nature of the apprehension and appreciation of a literary work consists in intuition and sensibility.
- Appreciation is a discipline of intuition and sensibility.
- Valuation of a work is primarily feeling, but feeling that is cognitive.
- It is possible to transcend individual characteristics and characteristics of psychological type, and respond from one's common human nature.
- There are natural emotional responses, but they can be overridden by passion, interest or prejudice.
- Criticism is a discipline of thought, but it depends on appreciation.
- The creation of literary works, and literary appreciation/criticism are activities, dependent on specific abilities, that are capable of degrees of achievement and of failure.

We can now make a deduction. The appreciation of literature depends on disinterestedness, and, we may add, seriousness and open-mindedness. The appreciation of literature also invokes a common human nature. But disinterestedness, seriousness and open-mindedness, and belief in a common human nature are the essential constituents of 'liberal humanism'. 'Liberality' of mind is precisely the disinterestedness, seriousness and open-mindedness needed for any objective inquiry. 'Humanism' presupposes a common human nature. If all literary study, including criticism, depends on appreciation, then all literary study presupposes liberal humanism. Liberal humanism is not a rival of other styles of criticism. It is the precondition for any kind of criticism. How could it be otherwise?[42]

Concluding Remarks

I began this essay with a quotation from Pater. I did so because, when we have investigated the nature of literary works, and of literary appreciation, we discover that we are still engaged in the same tasks as those of Pater—and of Dr Johnson, Coleridge, Arnold, T.S. Eliot, and F.R. Leavis. We should honour the ancestors, and remember where we belong.

Do we want to educate our children to recognise that beauty is real, and that great art and literature can change one's understanding and appreciation of life? Or do we want them to believe that in ethics and aesthetics there is no objective truth, and that everything is a matter of opinion?

We can choose. But we must live with the consequences.

---

[42] The development of our powers of intuition and sensibility cannot be the *aim* of literary study, since the aim of such study is to enjoy literary works. The development of intuition and sensibility is a beneficial by-product of literary study that enables us to enjoy the works more successfully. Similarly, the extension of the bounds of our moral imagination (Shelley) is a beneficial by-product which may improve our relations with other human beings. But it is not the aim of literary study. Moreover, it is not a substitute for a moral education, a training of the will. Virtues are habits that must be acquired by deliberate effort in the real world. As Parson Yorick discovered, having a compassionate sensibility is by no means the same thing as acting generously. See Laurence Sterne, *A Sentimental Journey Through France and Italy* (London, 1768).

The Cultivation of Memory: Developing Memory Habits in the 21st Century Classroom

Natalie Kennedy

The disparity between the high quality of student work, and their ability to respond to complex questions in class discussions sparked a deep curiosity in me as a teacher. Why was this such a noticeable trend? Why did students reluctantly answer questions, caveman-like, with fragmented phrases and thread-bare vocabulary? Why was there no force, persuasion or beauty in their articulated thinking? Had they become a product of their age: outsourcing their knowledge and their memory to Google?

All of that "trivia" could be accessed at a click of a button, so why bother trying to store it themselves? One can tell, though, when a speaker or writer has done a quote-dump from Google—it just doesn't ring true. The quote or piece of dialogue stolen from a novel summary that is drudged up on-line and pasted into a thoughtless collage of ideas just doesn't have the conviction of authenticity. English pedagogues can't keep calling forth from the empty heads and hearts of their students something that is rich, powerful and beautiful, if we don't first show them how to furnish their minds and hearts with literary treasures. The cultivation of the memory and the power of recall will be the vehicle that will deliver a change to this paucity of thought and discussion within the classroom.

In English class, my top students often remember their speeches and quotations for their assessment. However, after these assessments are finished, the lines echo in the distant horizon of their minds, and then are lost. Strayer and Norsworthy state that "there is no sharp distinction between habit and memory."[1] Students' recall power, therefore, becomes dependent on their "power of retention, number of associations, [and] organization of ideas."[2] Elements like "repetition, attention, interest, and vividness of impression" are the bedrock elements needed for the development of this "brute memory."[3] If we want our students to have recall of the complex vocabulary, elegant phrasing, quotes that provoke and delight them, and paradoxes that befuddle

---

[1] George D. Strayer and Naomi Norsworthy, *How to Teach*, 1917. EBook. (Project Gutenberg, 2016.) 92, accessed via http://www.loyalbooks.com
[2] *Ibid.*, 93.
[3] *Ibid.*, 93-4.

them, *beyond* the classroom and assessment paradigms, we must instruct them how to cultivate their long-term memory. It is profound in its simplicity. The act of penning our thoughts down on paper along with the immortal thoughts of great minds, is the first step in the cultivation of our memory.

Like a priest who is grieved by the parishioner's confession of sin, I sadly have had a string of students over the years confess that they haven't *actually read* the set novel. Relieved, post-purge, they would then boast that chapter summaries were quite efficient at giving them the fodder for the assessment, and their good result testified to that. In the harsh but true words of William Franklin Webster, people are often "too lazy to think, [and] too indolent to read."[4] Maybe the student's diet of second-hand, pre-digested versions of the primary texts is at fault, though. The dreaded text book or chapter summaries are the middle men, the fragmented and unrecognisable snippets of the original source presented as an acceptable substitute. The student has cultivated a dependence on feeding only upon other people's ideas, summaries, and selections about the primary text. The problem with this approach is that it assumes there is one way to react to the primary text, and it is entirely *impersonal*. There is no time given for the student to reflect and ruminate. In the discipline of English, students actually need to read the novel and *personally* respond to it.

The first thing I did to encourage students to read the novel was to get rid of chapter questions. I required my students to do reflection entries for each chapter instead. They could comment briefly on plot points, topics for further research and other questions that were raised by the passage, along with descriptions, interesting phrases and figurative devices that *appealed* to *them*. They were also encouraged to write on stick-it notes within the novel or play. This is an adaptation of *making a book your own*, where Mortimer Adler states that "full ownership of a book only comes when you have made it a part of yourself", via the act of writing within the pages of it.[5] Mortimer goes on to state that the act of writing down one's reaction to the text also "helps you to remember the thoughts of the author."[6] These marginalia are a useful didactic tool for the student, and can also be a fascinating window of insight into the minds of great luminaries and laypeople alike. Mark O'Connell mused in *The New Yorker* that the rising popularity of marginalia is due to the increasing self-awareness of people's reading practices.[7] Encouraging students to take an interest in the practice of marginalia will also highlight that there

---

[4] William Franklin Webster, *English Composition and Literature*, 1900 (London: Forgotten Books, 2015), 240.
[5] M.J. Adler & C. Van Doren, *How to Read a Book*, 1972 (New York: Simon and Schuster, 2014), 49.
[6] *Ibid.*
[7] Mark O'Connell. "The Marginal Obsession with Marginalia", *The New Yorker*, January 26, 2012. 1. Accessed June 20, 2017. http://www.newyorker.com/books/page-turner/the-marginal-obsession-with-marginalia

are reading practices and tools that can be employed when approaching a text. However, the magic of marginalia can become a problem in the school context: students' marginalia are seen in prosaic terms as wanton damage to school property. English teachers might have to persuade students to buy their own copies of the text, if the full benefits of this practice are to be experienced. Writing within the pages of a book allows the student to see that there can be a conversation between them and the author of a text. This creates a more intimate and relational bond that has the potential to leave a greater impression upon their memories. It also leaves forensic evidence for the suspicious teacher that the pupil has indeed read the novel!

We must help students decide what elements will be retained only for assessment, and what elements they would like to take with them in life. Organisation of these ideas will be the first step. They will need one book for vocabulary and one journal or "common place" book to record quotes, descriptive prose and their impressions of novels, plays and films that moved them especially. Author Ryan Holiday states:

> A commonplace book is a central resource or depository for ideas, quotes, anecdotes, observations and information you come across during your life and didactic pursuits. The purpose of the book is to record and organize these gems for later use in your life, in your business, in your writing, speaking or whatever it is that you do.[8]

I have seen such an improvement in students' engagement levels when they begin their own common place book. They begin to realise that when they search and find buried treasure within the literary works studied, they now have a vessel that will contain them and go with them on life's journey. The sense of going beyond the frameworks of assessment, and engaging in didactic practices that are intrinsically personal makes maintaining a common place book a rich and rewarding task for the student. Keeping a common place book invites them to sit with a text, mull it over, chew upon it, write within it, and then select which elements they will place inside. This sifting process hones their discernment and builds a stronger association within their memory. They will then begin to notice a shift; other writer's words and sentiments start to become a part of how they think, and in turn become a part of who they are. Like anything worth having, though, effort and discipline are required.

I was at the beach recently, and feeling sapped of energy. I sat on the sand and in awe and wonder was struck by the beauty of the ocean. As I went to offer up praises in my mind about it, I drew a blank! If only I had been

---

[8] Ryan Holiday, "How and Why to Keep a Common Place Book" *Ryan Holiday*, January, 24, 2014. 1. Accessed June 29, 2017. https://ryanholiday.net/how-and-why-to-keep-a-commonplace-book

able to recall John Keats' poem *On the Sea* where he encourages me to feast my eyes "upon the wideness of the Sea."[9] Out, out beyond, as I watched the ships that disappeared on the horizon—that feeling of anticipation might have been diagnosed as nothing more than my thoughts of adventure or longing for an unuttered dream, leaving the shore upon the ship's bow:

> For that strip of sapphire sea
> Set against the sky
> Far horizons means to me—
> And the ships go by
> Framed between the empty sky
> And the yellow sands,
> While my freed thoughts follow them
> Out to other lands.[10]

I could have enjoyed kindred spirit Lucy Maud Montgomery's phrasing that "the sea is a beautiful, sinuous thing!" in her poem *The Sea Spirit*.[11] In the crowd on the beach that day, I would not have felt alone in my contemplations and adoration of the sea. Others have sat and waxed lyrical about how the sea reawakens them from their brooding contemplations:

> It keeps eternal whisperings around
> Desolate shores, and with its mighty swell
> Gluts twice ten thousand caverns, till the spell
> Of Hecate leaves them their old shadowy sound.
> Often 'tis in such gentle temper found,
> That scarcely will the very smallest shell
> Be moved for days from where it sometime fell,
> When last the winds of heaven were unbound.
> Oh ye! who have your eyeballs vexed and tired,
> Feast them upon the wideness of the sea;
> Oh ye! whose ears are dinned with uproar rude,
> Or fed too much with cloying melody—
> Sit ye near some old cavern's mouth, and brood
> Until ye start, as if the sea nymphs quired![12]

---

[9] John Keats, "On the Sea", in *The Selected Poetry of Keats* (New York: Mentor, Plume and Meridian Books, 1966), 90.
[10] Dorothea Mackellar, "The Open Sea" in *Sunday Times*, Sydney, Sun 19 December 1909, 9. Accessed August 8, 2017 http://www.trove.nla.gov.au
[11] Lucy M. Montgomery, *The Watchman and Other Poems* (Toronto: McClelland, Goodchild & Stewart, 1916), 31. Accessed 25 June, 2017 http://www.digital.library.upenn.edu>montgomery
[12] John Keats, "On the Sea", 90.

Most importantly, their words that day would have saved me from my own vacuity at the moment. If I could have uttered those lines or even fragments of those lines, it would have caused my own to flow. In that solitary moment, rather than feeling mute in my musings, I could have been transported to another shore at a different time and seen the ocean through *other* eyes. I love the ocean, but my devotion to it was hampered that day by a lack of discipline. I was chastised by the experience and knew again the value of entering poems that I love, for later recall, into my common place book.

If a student (or teacher) simply writes down the quotation in their common place book and never re-visits it, there may not be a strong enough connection for recall. They must at various intervals throughout the year re-read their common place book. This return to their memory will help them to learn *anew* what they loved, and to know again why they fell in love with it in the first place. If students are given opportunities throughout the year to share these musings with others in conversation, their memory and recall will become stronger.

Many students will purchase a common place book that is rather cumbersome to carry around during their day to day activities. In order for them practically to maintain a relationship with their common place book they must also have a pocket notebook on them; this task is often seen as easier for handbag-carrying individuals and hipsters, though. Often keeping a diary or journal has been misrepresented as a "feminine pursuit," leaving some male students cold. It becomes necessary then to remind our male students that history is full of great male politicians, writers, artists, comedians, doctors, architects, soldiers, priests, businessmen, professors and famous philosophers, who have carried upon their person a note book. In the *Methodist Review* Pastor Ackerman succinctly expounded upon the value of a common place book and a pocket notebook:

> Have upon your study table, always accessible, a good-sized substantially bound blank book. Whenever a germinant thought comes seize your pen and write it down. Such thoughts will come out of your special course of literary reading, out of your cursory scanning of current fiction, even out of the five-minute glance given to the morning paper, out of nowhere and from anywhere. Thought-compelling suggestions entirely foreign to the sermon on which you are just now engaged will frequently send you to your treasure book, and without any damage to present preparation you will scribble down a page of matter that will set you on fire at some future day just when you are in need of inspiration and help. Have also a special vest-pocket notebook and let nothing escape you.[13]

---

[13] G.K. Ackermann, "The Growing of a Sermon," *The Methodist Review*, Vol 89, (New York: Eaton and Mains, 1907), 729. Accessed July, 10, 2017 https://hdl.handle.net/2027/coo.31924057400966

Maintaining a common place book and carrying a pocket notebook will furnish the student's memories with clarity and force. This method will also help to sharpen their abilities to actively listen and observe people, places, and ideas.

Grenville Kleiser suggests that one of the most important things that should be put to memory for recall are words. Not just any word or phrase but the mastery of using the "choice word, the correct phrase", which in turn may "reach the heart, and awake the soul."[14] The reciprocity between thought and language is clear. Kleiser suggests that "what we think molds the words we use, and the words we use react upon our thoughts. Hence a study of words is a study of ideas, and a stimulant to deep and original thinking."[15] According to the Reverend Jonathan Swift, it is the common speaker who only has "one set of ideas, and one set of words to clothe them in."[16] This is not a supercilious snark, but rather a desperate wake-up call to the diligent student who desires to communicate *precisely*. Further to this thread of thought is George Orwell's alarming dystopian vision in *1984* of the narrowing of vocabulary as a way of controlling the way people think. Language engineer Syme delightedly admits to Winston that:

> We're destroying words—scores of them, hundreds of them, every day. We're cutting the language down to the bone. Don't you see that the whole aim of Newspeak is to narrow the range of thought? In the end we shall make thoughtcrime literally impossible, because there will be no words in which to express it...Every year fewer and fewer words, and the range of consciousness always a little smaller.[17]

The learning of complex, powerful and beautiful words and phrases not only becomes the genesis for a student's thinking, but a weapon to protect them against ignorance and subjugation.

When it comes to filling the students' toolkit with words, a more concerted effort is required in order to gain mastery. Just as people wear many different hats, so too students need to recognise that words function in different forms. Many students who are familiar with, and who can confidently use, the verb *reciprocate*, struggle to recognise it in its noun form, *reciprocity*. They can identify the verb *desire*, but rarely use it in the adjectival form *desirous*. I require students to look up different **forms** of the word, and record them in their vocabulary book. I have encouraged students to try and remember trickier

---

[14] Glenville Kleiser, *Fifteen Thousand Useful Phrases*, (New York: Funk & Wagnalls Company, 1919.), 12. Kindle edition.
[15] *Ibid.*, 21-22.
[16] Jonathan Swift, "Thoughts on Various Subjects", *The Works of the Rev. Jonathan Swift*, volume 5. 5. http://en.wikisource.org/wiki/The_Works_of_the_Rev._Johnathan_Swift/Volume_5/
[17] George Orwell, *1984*, (London: the Penguin Group), 55.

words by creating a visual image as a prompt. This is simply one form of a mnemonic device that can assist students in remembering their word study. Bramwell encourages students of vocabulary that once they have "learnt how a word is made and have pinned an image of it in [their] mind, [they] will never forget it. And the system will help [them] to look at other hard words fearlessly, break them down and tame them, then use them properly and effectively whenever [they] want to."[18]

Unfortunately, vocabulary lists within units of work are often only treated in isolation and are never taken beyond looking at the word and a definition. This is problematic as words do not exist in isolation, they are synergistically understood within phrasing. I began instructing my students to start with identifying two-word phrases rather than single vocabulary words from their novels. William Franklin Webster in the classic book *English Composition and Literature* states that:

> ...the knowledge of words that the student derives from the dictionary is not sufficient... [it is] only by studying them in combination with other words [that] the influence of one word upon another may be noted. [19]

Students will begin to see that words influence other words and, at times, can change in the presence of others—as friends, enemies and lovers being in close proximity do. Words are no longer seen as static isolated units but as fluid, organic agents of power. From Charles Dickens' *A Tale of Two Cities* and *Little Dorrit*, they could take down "insensate brutality", not "insensate" on its own; "base insinuation", not "insinuation;" "addled jumble", not "addled"—these simple pairings point to the connotation of the key words' meaning.

As they progress with this approach, they can begin to look for different *types* of phrasing. Kleiser's book *Fifteen Thousand Useful Phrases* provides the student with "a mint of phrases at their command from which to draw when in need of the golden mean for expressing thought." The language praxis found in this book will help students "to correct careless diction and slovenly speech, and lead to the art of speaking and writing correctly; for, after all, accuracy in the use of words is more a matter of habit than theory."[20] A focus on prepositional phrasing can also double up as a grammar lesson—students can study his list of prepositional phrases containing of, by, in, into, to and with. The following is a small selection of prepositional phrases using "of,"

---

[18] David Bramwell, *The Mellifluous Book of Hard Words* (Bath: Crombie Jardine Publishing Limited, 2008.), 2.
[19] William Franklin Webster, *English Composition and Literature,* 1900 (London: Forgotten Books, 2015), 238.
[20] Glenville Kleiser, *Fifteen Thousand Useful Phrases,* (New York: Funk & Wagnalls Company, 1919), Kindle edition, 12.

"by," "in," "into," "to," and "with" from Kleiser's *Fifteen Thousand Useful Phrases:*

> Abatement of misery; accretions of time; beggared of faith; buoyancy of youth; laxity of mind; luxuriance of expression; obduracy of mind; period of lassitude; rectitude of soul; tenacity of execution; vagrancy of thought; animated by victory; condemned by posterity; disgusted by servility; embarrassed by timidity; fortified by faith; inculcated by practise; narrowed by custom; prompted by coquetry; unadorned by artifice; vitalized by thought; affable in manner; barren in intellect; cumbrous in style; experienced in duplicity; indulge in reverie; kept in abeyance; languish in obscurity; petulant in expression; wallow in idolatry; waver in purpose; bring into disrepute; chill into apathy; claim to perpetuity; degenerate into monotony; deaf to entreaty; electrify into activity; excite to pity; goaded into action; incursions into controversy; inveigled into dispute; impervious to suggestion; lapse into pedantry; ripened into love; repugnant to justice; snubbed into quiescence; withdraw into solitude; ascertain with exactness; behave with servility; cling with tenacity; echo with merriment; endure with fortitude; imbued with courage; move with alacrity; quiver with anxiety; relate with zest; and suffuse with spirituality.[21]

Kleiser also provides literary expressions and striking similes for the student to study:

> A brave but turbulent aristocracy; a face as pale as wax; a curious vexation fretted her; a mighty wind, like a leviathan, ploughed the brine; bartering the higher aspirations in life; buffeted by all the winds of passion; cruel as death; deep shame and rankling remorse; essay a flight of folly; fatally and indissolubly untied; fluid as thought; guilty of girlish sentimentality; he airily lampooned their most cherished prejudices; her thoughts outstripped her erring feet; his brow grew knit and gloomy; her lips parted in a keen expectancy; his constraint was excruciating.[22]

As students become familiar with some of these phrases they begin to exercise discernment—which phrasing is familiar but not clichéd? Simple yet effective? Or trite and uninteresting? They will begin to notice the particularities of a speaker's or author's *turn of phrasing* and begin to judge the effectiveness of the compositions. As their critical faculty becomes stronger, they might notice weak phrasing and, like Paris' servant, in Shakespeare's *Troilus and Cressida*, be emboldened to say, "there's a stewed phrase indeed!" (an English teacher's fantasy perhaps?) They will also become increasingly confident not to use stale and trite phrases which can only be credited to those with little study and understanding. Ultimately, "there is no better way in which to de-

---

[21] *Ibid.*, 515-615.
[22] *Ibid.*, 653-706.

velop the mental qualities of clearness, accuracy, and precision, and to improve and enlarge the intellectual powers generally, than by regular and painstaking study of judiciously selected phrases and literary expressions."[23]

Ultimately the strengthening of memory is a complex process. As educators we should model good practices that develop a strong, powerful recall. As we speak in front of our students, we should be drawing easily from our store of literary treasures and sharing this love. Smith warns, though, that "our ultimate love/desire is shaped by practices, not ideas that are merely communicated to us."[24] We must then learn to cultivate these memory-forming habits ourselves if we have any genuine power to pass these habits along to our students. Glass states that "we are creatures of habit, and our habits are forming themselves all the time. If we do not take care to form good habits, the bad ones establish themselves without effort, just as desirable plants require care while weeds thrive in untended soil."[25] So developing a strong recall of quotes, ideas, words, and phrasing will require effort and consistency. Smith articulates that this sort of education is a "constellation of practices, rituals, and routines that inculcates a particular vision of the good life by inscribing or infusing that vision into the heart by means of material, embodied practices."[26] The repeated rhythms of these simple practices help to form the *love*. In turn, there arises a stronger connection to the ideas, and recall becomes a natural by-product. The very simple process of pen to paper becomes one of the greatest tools for the student in developing cogent, persuasive, beautiful and original thinking. Finally, the common place book and vocabulary book become the palpable symbols of what one's heart and mind love, value and *want* to remember.

---

[23] *Ibid.*, 15.
[24] J.K.A, Smith, *Desiring the Kingdom: Worship, Worldview and Cultural Formation*, (Grand Rapids: Baker Academic, MI: 2009), 27.
[25] Karen Glass, *Consider This: Charlotte Mason and the Classical Tradition, (*Karen Glass Net Publishing: United States.), 67.
[26] Smith, *Desiring the Kingdom: Worship, Worldview and Cultural Formation*, 26.

The Spirituality of Time: Bridging the History Gap in the Postmodern Classroom

Sarah Williams

> Time past and time future
> What might have been and what has been
> Point to one end, which is always present.[1]

As a historian time is my trade. Yet, it has only been in the last few years that I have begun to consider *time* as a subject in itself and to *question the ways of thinking* that my subject teaches, and the underlying practices and values of historical pursuit. How do our perceptions of time influence the way in which we understand ourselves? Does time have a pedagogy? What does it mean to have a historical consciousness, and why does such a consciousness matter?

It is my students who are provoking these questions. They grapple with the subject matter of history like any other generation of students, but *their* questions are distinct and profoundly existential both in character and form. The challenge I face in the classroom is no longer simply a matter of intellectually convincing my students that history is relevant to their lives. I am faced with the much deeper challenge of engaging a generation for whom time has lost its fundamental shape and meaning. The postmodern mindset has elevated the present moment to such an extent that it has flattened out the contours of the past and obscured the future landscape. My students see the present as the only valid epistemological starting point for academic as well as personal reflection. The *Now* has become a philosophical end and a political commitment in its own right. *Now* is a point beyond which the postmodern imagination is ill-equipped but also unwilling to go. This essay aims to contextualize the postmodern perception of time and, more importantly, to suggest ways of moving beyond the endemic presentism that such a perception engenders.

In January 1964 Bob Dylan released his third album entitled *The Times They Are a Changing*. The title track of this album addressed the generation to which Dylan's parents belonged, the generation for whom civil rights, eman-

---

[1] T.S. Eliot, *Burnt Norton, I,* in *Four Quartets* [1943]. *Collected Poems of T.S. Eliot* (London & Boston: Faber & Faber,1963), 190.

cipation, liberalization were alien. In this song Dylan appropriates the language of the Sermon on the Mount to argue that the past must be understood as an impediment to progress, and sweeping away its effects a necessary prelude to the rise of a new kind of future. The present, Dylan argues, must be freed to stand on its own, cut loose from all deference to past. Nearly six decades later what we find in Western culture is a history gap. This history gap involves a loss of historical knowledge, but far more crucially, it represents a way of understanding the past and the present as juxtaposed and antithetical categories.

We are familiar with the effects of late twentieth and early twenty-first century globalisation in lifting our bodies out of geographical and social places of belonging, but we are less aware of the ways in which globalisation also lifts our sense of identity out of time.[2] As postmoderns, we treat with skepticism any identity-forming stories handed down from one generation to the next. Identity creation is no longer connected to our situation in time or to the larger story of time—past, present or future. Instead, identity formation is linked tightly to the present moment in time. In advanced capitalist societies we form identity through the acquisition of symbolic tokens, objects and images all of which clothe us with a self and distinguish us in the eyes of others. Crucially, these symbolic tokens are inherently linked to the present or—to put it more crudely—they are inherently linked to the market. The objects and images we acquire to construct our identities are in many cases literally designed for obsolescence. Indeed most consumer markets depend on perpetual obsolescence for their ongoing vitality. Closely mimicking consumerism, postmodern identities are fluid and shifting. They are timed rather than timeless. As Walter Brueggemann writes:

> Our consumer culture is organized against history. There is a depreciation of memory and a ridicule of hope, which means that everything must be held in the now.[3]

The interweaving of postmodern identity culture with the present moment is direct and practical, but it is also philosophical in form. The idea that *I am what I choose to be* upon which postmodern consumerism depends, contains a distinct temporality. In the hyper-subjectivity of the last five to seven years, the sacred right of the individual to define and create who he or she is has also come to mean freedom from the givenness of one's past and the socio-political and linguistic heritage bequeathed to the present by that past. Being male or being female, for example, are increasingly understood as iden-

---

[2] For further detail on dislocation of persons from place, see Anthony Giddens, *Run Away World* (London: Profile Books, 2002).
[3] Walter Brueggemann, *The Prophetic Imagination*, 2nd ed. (Minneapolis: Fortress, 2001), 4.

tity categories imposed upon the individual by certain historic readings of the body from which the individual must be allowed to escape, should they wish to do so. Within this framework gender categories have no inherent meaning beyond the meaning brought to them by the individual. Freedom from the idea that history—my history, your history, our history—tells me, and you, what and who we are, is increasingly seen not just as desirable but also as a right to be upheld in law.

This assertion of the postmodern self as the only valid site for the formation of human identity changes the way in which history is understood and studied. From this perspective history is viewed as a regressive anti-world devoid of wisdom and from which we have necessarily progressed. Moreover, the past can only be studied by applying a methodology that begins and ends with the self-referential individual. As a teacher, what I face in practice in the classroom is a virulent and endemic form of presentism. Today's perspective is imposed on the past as the only legitimate form of interpretation in ways that are ideologically informed and politically defined. Before I can even begin to develop my student's historical knowledge I must demonstrate the importance of distinguishing *then* from *now;* the past from present-day agendas.

In a homily delivered at the Vatican on Pentecost Sunday, 2014 Pope Francis addressed the want of historical sensitivity among the current generation as a spiritual problem. This generation, he argued, are 'without memory' and as a result they have become 'prisoners of the moment', unable to read or to treasure their history in the light of 'salvation history'. Francis's version of salvation history is contentious. For the majority of postmoderns it is an example of the kind of grand interpretative story of time from which the current generation must escape. But in focusing primarily on the rights and wrongs of Francis's version of history it is easy to overlook the insight that his words offer into the dilemma of the postmodern classroom. Strong though the word *prisoner* may be, it carries the necessary metaphorical weight to communicate the extremity of the problem. Without history the postmodern generation is stripped of the ability to contextualize the moment within a wider evaluative framework. Without this wider framework we do not notice the differences and the contrasts between our age and ages past and we lose the capacity to understand ourselves and distinguish meaningful action from irrelevance. If the self-referential vantage point of the present is treated as a normative position from which to view reality, we become unable to identify the assumptions and cultural presuppositions in which we are saturated. This is a form of imprisonment.

Historically, Christianity has provided Western culture with the ability to contextualize time by establishing a fundamental distinction between finitude and infinitude, *now* than *then*. A quintessential description of finitude is found, for example, in the biblical passage from Isaiah, chapter 40:

> All men are like grass, and all their glory is like the flowers of the field. The grass withers and the flowers fall, because the breath of the Lord blows on them. Surely the people are grass. The grass withers and the flowers fall but the word of our God stands forever. [4]

These images echo loudly throughout the literature of the ages. Set within a chapter that begins equally famously with the words, "Comfort, comfort my people, says your God", this image of finitude creates a paradox within which and through which time itself is explained. The finitude of skin and bones, flowers falling and withering is placed alongside the eternal 'word of our God'. The proximity of the one to the other—man's fleeting temporality to 'the word'—reverses the natural order of futility and despair, and points instead to hope and, crucially, to the meaning of time in an ultimate sense. For the theologian, the pronoun *our* before God shapes an interpretation of time.[5] The 'word' of which Isaiah speaks is relational, personal and immediate whilst at the same time remaining transcendent and infinite. God the infinite stands both in contrast to and in dynamic relationship with the transitory glory of man. He stands above time, but he also stands within time to uphold it.

The phrase, the 'word of our God', points ultimately to the *logos* Christ, who in time, dignified time with infinite meaning through the Incarnation. Within the Christian tradition transcendence and immanence are interwoven in the life, death and resurrection of Christ. The introduction during the ninth-century of BC and AD as designations of time was far more complex than simply a carving up of time into units or periods of centuries. These categories arose out of a re-imagining and re-arranging of time around what was understood to be the pivotal and defining moment of the Incarnation from which the meaning of all time is derived. As Henri de Lubac wrote, 'Christianity is not one of the great things of history but history is one of the great things of Christianity'.[6] This is the 'salvation history' that Pope Francis is talking about in his homily.

In re-imagining time in this way Christianity challenged the idea of time as an endless cycle that moves relentlessly on and on and round and round, and bequeathed instead a chronological perception of time in which the unfolding of divine purpose happens in sequence, each moment waiting for the next, with clear eschatological direction towards which all of history moves from beginning to end. Traditionally, it has been this perception of time that has given definition to our understanding of the minutiae of individual histor-

---

[4] New International Version, Isaiah 40 vv 6-8.
[5] See, for example, Colin E. Gunton, *The One the Three and the Many: God, Creation and the Culture of Modernity*, The Bampton Lectures 1992 (Cambridge UK: Cambridge University Press, 1993; reprinted 1996).
[6] Henri de Lubac, *Paradoxes of Faith*, trans. P. Simon et al., (San Francisco: Ignatius Press, 1987), 98.

ical events, and lent a moral complexion to the way in which we imagine the relationship between actions in the present and consequences in the future. This concept of 'salvation history' is personified in the New Testament Letter to the Hebrews. Here, time is depicted as a crowded amphitheatre where the shouts of the faithful, who have passed from the present into eternal time, urge those currently running the race of life to remain fixed on the existential orientating point of history; the person of Christ himself.

> Therefore, since we are surrounded by such a great host of witnesses ....let us fix our eyes on Jesus the author and perfector of our faith, who for the joy set before him endured the cross...Consider him who endured such opposition from sinful men so that you will not grow weary and lose heart.[7]

The present state of 'running the race' is given direction and meaning precisely because it is fleeting and finite, but also transfigured by an overarching eternal reality. It is the immanent presence of the transcendent in the mundane that provides the moral framework for the interpretation of human action. As we run the race of life in the present, we avoid becoming like Caliban in Shakespeare's *Tempest,* distracted by 'trinkets' and 'sparkling things', because they are seen plainly to be a temporary distraction from the underlying meaning of the larger story. The causal relationship between events is in this way invested with theological meaning, and momentary things are endowed with overall moral significance. As Rowan Williams puts it in his useful book *Why Study the Past?*:

> The action of God is allowed to appear in the telling of such a story as that which holds together apparent contradictions and drives us to deeper levels of consistency.[8]

Given the profound and enduring impact of Christianity on perceptions of time, it is perhaps unsurprising that in the wake of the 'secular revolution', Western culture is struggling to find an encompassing sense of meaning after having eradicated a vision of the eternal from the cultural imagination.[9] To avoid the pitfalls of endemic presentism, what we lack in the postmodern classroom is a spirituality of time. As a history teacher, challenging contempo-

---

[7] New International Version, Hebrews 12 vv 1-3.
[8] Rowan Williams, *Why Study the Past? The Quest for the Historical Church* (Grand Rapids, MI: Eardmans, 2005), 9.
[9] Most historians agree that the 'secular revolution' began in the 1960s. See, for example, Callum Brown, *The Death of Christian Britain: understanding secularization 1800-2000* (London: Routledge, 2001); Stephen Bruce, *God is Dead: Secularisation in the West* (Oxford: Oxford University Press, 2002); Hugh McLeod, *The Religious Crisis of the 1960s* (Oxford: Oxford University Press, 2007); Charles Taylor, *A Secular Age?* (Cambridge MA; Belknap, Harvard, 2007).

rary perceptions of time is perhaps the most important contribution I can make to society. Indeed, in a climate where all the humanities are under threat, such a contribution may not only be useful but also essential. For this task, *time* continues to offer us its own pedagogy or—as I would like to suggest in this chapter—its own spirituality.

Time teaches us finitude. Defined as the state of having limits or bounds, finitude is an increasingly counter-cultural lesson. In a society that hides physical death and insures to the hilt against the unfortunate effects of time, limitation of any kind is problematic. Cultivating an awareness of finitude, specifically of the limited nature of our own existence in time, and thus our perspective on time, is vital both at an individual and a societal level. Of course, we learn finitude first, of course at a deeply personal level, in our bones and on our skin, in birth and death, through the perennials in the garden, the cyclical rhythms of light and dark, warmth and cold. However, we are rarely encouraged to reflect on own fragile movement through time, to raise larger questions about the wisdom of using *now* as the sole reference point from which to derive a larger sense of meaning. Our marriage to the present can leave the individual without an adequate framework within which to situate their experience. We are so embedded in the present that we have no ability to see beyond it, or to critique its immediate values and assumptions as themselves finite and relative. Our view of the human person, for instance, is so closely bound to the moment within the value system of consumerism that it blinds us from seeing the recent historical development of these ideas. Inducted, day-by-day, into the consumerist liturgies of the present moment, as Jamie Smith's book *Desiring the Kingdom* so helpfully describes, we are told at every turn that our choices are unlimited and, moreover, that to be authentic these choices must be realized in the now.[10] We are, therefore, ill-prepared for the confusion and suffering that come when we discover that in fact our choices are limited, and economic growth is in fact impossible. We have little ability to critique, as a historically constructed contextual definition, the idea of the individual as an autonomous unit that chooses, obtains and acquires what it desires, as the essential element of what it means to be human.

Furthermore, we lose the capacity to see that the interweaving of personhood with the ideal of unlimited choice actually makes us less rather than more able to live with the choices we have made. Instant gratification shrinks our ability to live with unfulfilled desire, and at a societal level it reduces our capacity to chart a strategic pathway through the present to bring about substantive political and economic change in the future. The full weight of technology compounds this tendency, squeezing us all the more into the instant. It is not simply that immediacy has become a functional possibility. Far more

---

[10] James K.A.Smith, *Desiring the Kingdom: Worship, Worldview and Cultural Formation* (Grand Rapids: Baker Academic, 2009).

insidious is the transformation of social expectation and mentality that this possibility brings. Longing, yearning and waiting are seen as problematic states of being that are antithetical to the core thrust of postmodernity. The fact that longing, yearning and waiting are *time* words is of crucial importance to the argument of this chapter. These words—that the fourteenth-century mystics loved but that we postmoderns find so troubling—underline the point that our perceptions *of* time shape our capacity to live *with* time.

An awareness of finitude is equally important for the culture as a whole. The capacity to identify the unique characteristics of a given moment in time plays a crucial part in developing cultural and political identity. Without a sense of where we have come from, we are stripped of our ability to create a coherent cultural identity. Philosopher Charles Taylor describes the protracted existential dilemma of the twenty-first-century-self as a profound and explicit identity crisis. He defines the cultural identity crisis that we find ourselves in as 'an acute form of disorientation which people express in terms of not knowing who they are'.[11] Taylor links this shift in cultural mood to a loss of 'horizon' in which people's sense of the cosmos and their place within it as a meaningful and ordered whole has become profoundly dissipated. Without a sense of our location in time our identity is impeded, and with it our sense of social, cultural and political direction. Identity is the foundation of moral conduct and political action. It is the starting point for institutional and social design, and it forms the substance of our vision of the common good. Without a cultural memory we are cut adrift like a ship without a compass, and we become, as nineteenth- century historian Lord Acton said, 'tossed around by the wind unable to fix our position'.[12]

Cultivating an awareness of our finitude can also re-position us as learners, and re-shape our every-day classroom practices. Time is of the essence in a history lesson, but it is often flattened into nothing more than a time-line of dates. We place great store in students remembering and regurgitating dates, but far less attention is paid to helping students imagine other periods in which time itself was understood differently. What was it like, for example, to live in a culture in which waiting for things formed an integral part of human consciousness and the socio-political conditions of life—waiting for letters, for the harvest, for an army to muster, for an epidemic to lift?

Waiting is not only something we can point to and observe in the classroom. It is also a capacity that we can foster. Patience is not a postmodern virtue. Consequently, we must teach patience rather than assume it. Driven by the pressing demand for speed, the executive summary and the sound bite

---

[11] Charles Taylor, *Sources of the Self: The Making of the Modern Identity* (Cambridge, M.A.: Harvard University Press, 1989), 29.

[12] John Emerich Edward Dalberg Acton, from a lecture delivered at Cambridge, June 11, 1895. Reprinted in *Lectures on Modern History* (London: MacMillan Co., 1906) 4.

become the nub or crux of the matter, rather than any body of research that might stand behind them. In an educational setting where rapid knowledge acquisition is encouraged, reading *much* is often explicitly or implicitly prized over and above reading *well*. Glancing at a topic replaces dwelling in the material and doing the hard, patient work of struggling to understand. We forget, as art historian Jennifer Roberts points out in an article on the importance of immersive attention, access to knowledge is not necessarily synonymous with learning itself. 'What turns access into learning is time and strategic patience.'[13] I can help students to imagine other times in part by reminding them, through the pace and depth of learning, that history is as much about our awareness of time and our sensitivity to the passage of time, as it is about remembering dates.

If, as a history teacher, time is my trade, then how I treat time in the classroom matters. Ultimately, my treatment of time within the classroom setting will reflect and model, wittingly or unwittingly, my overall understanding of the meaning and purpose of education. I can employ time as a unit in which to wield an unremitting pressure to acquire new and ever expanding quantities of knowledge about the past. To do so is to fuel the appetite for ownership and control of information, and reinforce the belief that education is nothing more than knowledge acquisition for the purpose of securing identity credentials.[14] Alternatively, I can invite students to contemplate and consider what they can learn with their own limited vantage point from other moments in time. I can establish an active dialogue between our own moment in history and previous moments in time, in which students are drawn beyond their endemic presentism, as they practice the humble skill of listening. History as a discipline requires us to withhold the imposition of a conclusion until such time as we have listened respectfully to evidence. It is a slow and meticulous task to recover and reconstruct the past accurately and empirically. It takes careful attention to minute detail to get as close as possible to the primary material, and to avoid wrenching this material out of its setting, and fitting it into a brief summary. Working to listen and understand will always involve a delay and this delay can provide its own lesson. To listen well is to respect the particularity—the finitude—of every era, including our own. It is to resist imposing ourselves onto the past, as though all people imagined the world as we do. Inevitably, observers can never shed their perspective entirely, but the crucial question is: are we listening? When the study of history becomes an exercise in listening to cultures qualitatively different from our own, it can offer a powerful antidote to the hubris engendered by endemic presentism. Humble listening is, I would like to suggest, a spiritual quality with

---

[13] Jennifer Roberts, http://harvardmagazine.com/2013/11/the-power-of-patience

[14] For additional reflection on this point, see Paul J. Griffiths, *The Vice of Curiosity: An Essay on Intellectual Appetite* (Winnipeg: CUM Press, 2006).

which we can re-enchant the teaching of history.

> The only wisdom we can hope to acquire
> Is the wisdom of humility: humility is endless.[15]

---

[15] T.S. Eliot, *East Coker, II,* in *Four Quartets* [1943]. *Collected Poems of T.S.Eliot* (London & Boston: Faber & Faber, 1963), 199.

"Latin is for the Elite"...and other Zombie Myths

Sarah Lawrence

For some years I worked at a large, independent bookshop in a capital city in Australia.[1] I was hired (in part) for my knowledge of Latin and it was customary for my colleagues to refer customers to me when questions about Latin or Ancient Greek arose. One morning a customer discovered that I was currently teaching her nephew Latin at one of the universities in that capital city. Her immediate, not unexpected, question was "Where did you go to school?" I replied that I had attended Armidale High School (one of two large, public high schools in a country town at that time of around 22,000 residents). Her response, delivered with enthusiasm and warmth, was: "I love stories like that! It's so heartwarming! Did you see the story in the paper this morning about the Afghani refugee who came to Australia with nothing and is now doing medicine?" For the record, I am the child of two primary-school teachers; I grew up in a loving, stable household in which few things were more highly valued than reading and education. I am also white-skinned, heterosexual and able-bodied. Some years before this incident, I vividly recall one of my beloved Latin lecturers declaring in class, "Latin is for the elite." When I responded that I was deeply uncomfortable with that sentiment, he advised me, "Better stick to Ancient History then." What I did not realise at the time, however, was that my own background of privilege and comfort apparently did not qualify me for membership of the Latin-learning elite.

At some point in the past two thousand years the language (literally) of the plebs became a hallmark of the patrician class.[2] This has not been helped by the tendency of Classicists to retreat to two interrelated positions when the position of Ancient Greek or Latin in the curriculum is challenged: the first, that these subjects should be studied purely because they are the 'foundations of Western Civilisation', and the second, that the value of Classics is in their very elitism (frequently described in terms of 'rigour' or 'standards') and that this in itself justifies their survival as the premise of an elite class of students

---

[1] A 'zombie myth' is a belief that persists despite substantial evidence to the contrary: it refuses to die.
[2] The process of this transformation in the microcosm of USA history is elegantly set out by Stanley M. Burstein, "The Classics and the American Republic," *The History Teacher* 30 (1996): 29-44.

and scholars.³ I would argue that both defences fail to really engage with what Classics has to offer and with the students that will ensure our discipline survives.

The place of the study of 'Western Civilisation' in education has been kicked back and forth like jury composition at Rome during the first century BCE, and voices on either side of the debate are loud and highly partisan. This paper is concerned, however, not with the inherent value of studying Western Civilisation but, instead, with the way it has been used as an argument for studying Greek and Latin.⁴ Firstly, it should be acknowledged that the definition of 'Western Civilisation' is not static: for around a thousand years, the study of 'Western Civilisation' did not actually include Ancient Greek, for instance, and the introduction of Greek language study at Oxford prompted vigorous student protests against this threat to the canon.⁵ Likewise, Egypt is included in some definitions of 'Western Civilisation', and not in others.⁶ The fundamental line of this argument for the teaching of Greek and Latin nevertheless remains largely clear: exposure to Greek and Latin texts, preferably in the original language, is important because the languages allow us to appreciate the historical foundations and intellectual structures of 'Western Civilisation'. Daniel Walker Howe, the emeritus Harold Vyvyan Harmsworth Professor of American History at Oxford University, voiced this view when he noted that, in their interaction with Native Americans, "...the missionaries were introducing native people to all aspects of Western civilisation... and they considered classical learning basic to that project."⁷ By the end of the article Walker makes his approval of the underlying assumptions of the missionary project clear: ". . . the march of civilisation has paralleled the vi-

---

³ Christopher Stray, "'Thucydides or Grote?' Classical Disputes and Disputed Classics in Nineteenth Century Cambridge," *TaPhA* 127 (1997): 363-371 is a good example of the latter approach.
⁴ The passionate adherence to this argument by some of its defenders can be seen clearly in the vitriolic response of Stephen J. Willett to a presidential address to the American Psychological Association (now renamed as the Society for Classical Studies) by James O'Donnell suggesting that, as Willett interprets the speech, "we should abandon the notion that Greece and Rome are the foundation of the West or even that the West exists as some sort of coherent cultural identity." Stephen J. Willett, "Postmodernist Classics," *Academic Questions* (Spring, 2004): 59. Willett goes on to attack O'Donnell's scholarship on an academic level (ibid. 59-60), refers to O'Donnell's speech as being written in "full schizophrenic mode" (ibid. 63), containing "absurdity" (*Ibid*), describes O'Donnell as holding "membership in the Grand Academy of Lagado" (*Ibid*.) and notes that O'Donnell's "English rarely indulges much logical clarity, swinging as it does from hyperbole to opacity, from cliché to aphorism, from clotted reference to sharp imperative." (*Ibid*. 64)
⁵ Bernard Knox, *The Oldest Dead White European Males: And other reflections on the Classics*, (New York: W.W.Norton & Co., 1993) 17. It is also true that the traditional study of Western Civilisation includes only a sliver of that civilisation both in terms of gender, ethnicity and social diversity – as Knox notes himself (12-3, 41, 49-52).
⁶ See Robin H. Wood, "Teaching the Classics in the Middle Grades," *Phi Delta Kappan* (September, 1998): 72-4 for an instance of the former understanding and Knox, *Oldest Dead*, 67 for the latter.
⁷ Daniel Walker Howe, "Classical Education in America," *Wilson Quarterly* (Spring, 2011): 31.

brancy of Classical schools."⁸ The argument seems to be that civilisation is fundamentally Western in character; that Western civilisation is fundamentally good; and that the teaching of Classics is a fundamental aspect of the model.⁹

This, I would argue, is not amongst the many effective arguments for studying Latin and Greek. There are two major and connected difficulties with the position: firstly, the argument fails to address the changing and diverse world in which we live; secondly, it aligns the Classics with very particular political ideals; both of these things threaten to exclude students who might otherwise be interested in studying Latin or Greek. In Australia, as is the case in most nations in the West, we do not live in a society composed only of people of European descent, and that homogenous society is very much the audience frequently envisaged in the 'Western Civilisation' argument.¹⁰ This assumption is clear when Robin H. Wood (a teacher at Far Brook Elementary School in the USA at the time of writing her article) notes, as a rationale for studying the classical world ("the historical periods that together form the underlying basis of what we know as Western Civilisation") in schools, "children at Far Brook are able to begin connecting **their** present with **their** distant past."¹¹ Far Brook is a school that currently prides itself on its diversity; this quality is presented front and centre on the school's website and supported with several pieces of documentation.¹² Wood assumes, however, that the student body will uniformly view the history of Egypt, Greece and Rome as "their" history. Although the Italian journalist and author Italo

---

⁸ Howe, "Classical Education," 36. Howe concludes his article by stating that "the neglect of classics in our education curriculum has been a loss for our civilisation".

⁹ Bernard Knox draws a similar link between the classics, 'civilisation' and the Western tradition, arguing that the Greeks "invented" democracy, philosophy, national literature, "political theory, rhetoric, biology, zoology, the atomic theory – one could go on", prior to the point at which "any modern Western nation" moved in that direction: Knox, *Oldest Dead,* 67. In these comments Knox seems to deliberately limit the competition to Western states, which is just as well, given the history of Vedic literature (c.1500-200 BCE) in India, for instance, the invention of the decimal system in the 14th Century BCE in China, or the writings on logic and optics amongst other things under the influence of the Mohists in China from the 5th century BCE.

¹⁰ Sean Gurd, "Out of Athens: The New Ancient Greeks. By Page DuBois. Cambridge, M.A: Harvard University Press. 2010," *Phoenix* 65 (2011): 168. Note Arlene Fromchuck's comments on the increasingly "polyglot" nature of New York City by the early eighties: Arlene R. Fromchuck, 'The Measurable Benefits of Teaching English through Latin in Elementary School' *The Classical World* 78 (1984): 25.

¹¹ Wood, "Teaching the Classics," 72 and 74; my emphasis. See the same assumption at a much earlier point in the 20th Century when the student body was presumably much more homogeneous: T. W. Valentine, "The Correlation of English and Latin Teaching in High School," *The High School Journal* 12 (1929): 313: "Not only the bones of our language, but also our literature, our institutions, our architecture, our art, our religion, our philosophy, our thought-forms, all come to us...through ancient Rome."

¹² "Diversity in race, ethnicity, gender, socio-economic level, sexual orientation, family structure, and religion provides us with a vibrant community in which to learn about the array of perspectives and experiences that enrich our world." *Far Brook School Diversity Statement*, viewed 15th of February, 2018, https://www.farbrook.org/uploaded/Diversity/Far_Brook_School_Diversity_Statement.pdf

Calvino notes that even for Europeans the connection with Classic literature is generally personal, rather than historical, and quite dependent on one's geographical location within Europe, Wood's comments speak to a belief that Greek, Roman and Egyptian history is automatically the history of her students.[13] This could be read as an attempt to create a shared sense of history (albeit a narrow and Western version of history) for a diverse group of students from any background, or it could be read as assuming that the student body is European in descent and that a direct line runs from the Ancient Mediterranean to the inhabitants of the West today.

Unfortunately, this language of cultural descent tends to be used in such a way by its proponents that it is tied to a very white model of both ancient and modern society; as Bernard Knox, the first director of the Centre for Hellenic Studies based in Washington D.C., tellingly asserts of the Ancient Greeks: "they were undoubtedly white, or, to be exact, a sort of Mediterranean olive colour."[14] We may feel that the idea that Greeks and Romans were white is an attitude of the past, yet Professor Mary Beard attracted a great deal of controversy and abuse in mid-2017 for confirming that a citizen family in Roman Britain may well have included a member who was 'African' in appearance.[15] Also in 2017, Sarah Bond, an Assistant Professor of Classics at the University of Iowa, received a barrage of online threats after suggesting that the popular, and frequently unchallenged, perception that Greek and Roman statues were white tends to create an inaccurate association between white skin tone and ideals of beauty and heroism in the Classical world.[16] There is apparently still eagerness in many quarters to make Greek and Roman paradigms of a white-skinned ideal of Western Civilisation that does not actually reflect the historical reality of these societies, but does fit into a model of the past that links Classical antiquity directly with the white inhabitants of western nations. This tends to suggest that the study of Western Civilisation is one that should make certain students feel pride in their history and leave others as awed external spectators.

If we base our argument for the teaching and learning of Latin and Greek on a historical connection to the foundations of Western society, we risk inadvertently excluding potential students of Latin or Greek who fall outside of

---

[13] Italo Calvino, *Why Read the Classics?* trans. Martin McLaughlin (London: Jonathan Cape, 1999) 3-5.
[14] Knox, *Oldest Dead*, 26. Cartledge, while critically examining this difficulty in Classics refers explicitly to "white classical culture": Paul Cartledge, "Why/How Does Classics Matter?" *The Arts and Humanities in Higher Education* 4 (2005): 194.
[15] Mary Beard, "Roman Britain in Black and White," *Times Literary Supplement* August 3, 2017 https://www.the-tls.co.uk/roman-britain-black-white/ viewed 2nd of March, 2018.
[16] Colleen Flaherty, "Threats for What She Didn't Say," *Inside Higher Ed* June 19, 2017, Viewed 2nd of March, 2018. https://www.insidehighered.com/news/2017/06/19/classicist-finds-herself-target-online-threats-after-article-ancient-statues

the aegis of European descent and power.[17] As Paul Cartledge, the A.G. Leventis Professor of Greek Culture emeritus at Cambridge University, notes regarding Derek Walcott's *Omeros* and its links to Homeric epics: "Homer was the preferred literature of the very white men who were responsible ultimately for enslaving his African ancestors."[18] The risk of inadvertent exclusion is heightened because, to be frank, Classics has 'form': colonial forces have in the past deliberately excluded those who were darker than "a Mediterranean olive colour" from learning Latin.[19] Likewise, Classics in the modern world has been a discipline that was taught on strict lines of social class demarcation[20] and deliberately excluded women.[21] By 1995 a long study of 34,000 academics in America already revealed an increasing belief that "diversity and multiculturalism" should be central tenets of university education.[22] To cite just one group excluded from the traditional and accepted history of Western Civilisation: people of colour have noted how important it is to have history programmes that include experiences other than the mainstream European, including the honest history of slavery as more than a background to economic growth and decline.[23] Because the experience of the poor and slaves, the experience of women, the experience of those outside of the social paradigms of Greek and Roman thought and society are not necessarily part of the traditional history of Western Civilisation, a commitment to diversity fre-

---

[17] George Parsons, "Clio's Language War: Ancient and Modern Historians at Macquarie University in the 1970s," *History Australia* 5 (2008): 79.5. Note that in Parson's account of the conflict between Modern and Ancient History at Macquarie University the expansion of Ancient History into Classical languages was conceived to be directly at the expense of "non-European traditions" such as "Australian, Asian, Pacific and American History" as well as 'History from Below': 79.8, 11.

[18] Cartledge, "Why/How Does Classics Matter?" 194. Cartledge goes on to speak of Walcott's interaction with Homer almost in terms of a kind of cultural bondage: "...white classical culture's deep and unavoidable hold over him...He can't live with it, yet it seems he can't live without it either."

[19] As under the apartheid regime in South Africa, for instance: Sally Macewen, "Using Diversity to Teach Classics," *The Classical World*, 96 (2003): 416.

[20] As Howe indicates when he speaks of the association between Latin and "gentility" and "refinement" and hence its appeal to the "newly commercial middle-class" after the industrial revolution: Howe, "Classical Education," 33. In Australia by the early 70s Classical languages were associated with "the 'cultural cringe', which has so bedevilled the nation" and were regarded as an act of obeisance to "a limited section of the Australian society who can afford such studies." Parsons, "Clio's Language War," 79.5.

[21] Burstein, "The Classics and the American Republic," 40; Laurie J. Churchill, "Is There a Woman in This Textbook? Feminist Pedagogy and Elementary Latin" in *When Dead Tongues Speak: Teaching Beginning Greek and Latin,* ed. John Gruber-Miller, (New York: Oxford University Press, 2006) 87.

[22] Denise K. Magner, "Fewer Professors believe Western Culture Should be the Cornerstone of the College Curriculum," *Chronicle of Higher Education* (September 15, 1996): A12.

[23] Reni Eddo-Lodge, *Why I'm no Longer Talking to White People about Race* (London: Bloomsbury Circus, 2017) 2-1. In contrast, Sean Gurd terms Classics: "a good example of a discipline that is out of touch with...the real and ongoing struggle of most of the world": Gurd, "Out of Athens," 169.

quently goes hand in hand with a decreasing emphasis on Western Civilisation in the curriculum and, with it, subjects like the Classics.[24]

The value of studying Western Civilisation is also frequently connected to a belief in the inherent authority and superiority of the West in contrast with the rest of the world. Donald Kagan, a very influential scholar and Sterling Professor Emeritus of Classics and History at Yale University, articulated this clearly in an article for the *Intercollegiate Review* titled 'Why We Should study the History of Western Civilisation':

> No fair-minded person can deny that, whatever its other characteristics, the West has created institutions of government and law that provide unprecedented freedom for its people and a body of natural scientific knowledge and technological achievement that together make possible a level of health and material prosperity undreamed of in earlier times and unknown outside the West and the areas it has influenced.[25]

Daniel Walker Howe throughout his account of Classical education in America, while he acknowledges the difficulty of the originally exclusive nature of classical education,[26] does not question the values he argues are embodied in that education. Indeed, he accepts the ongoing moral authority of the Classical idea of virtue and vice so completely that he can only explain the decreasing popularity of Classics by referring to a "declining confidence in human reason and virtue" and a rising "moral relativism" that have sabotaged the "standards" embodied by Greek and Roman authors.[27] These are the authors, we must remember, who uniformly accepted slavery as an institution; who saw women as eternally immature, and who believed that torture was an essential part of the legal process. And yet a failure to study the history of Western Civilisation is often seen as presenting a considerable risk to our values:

> Unless we as a people regain an understanding of what has made our civilization such a remarkable human achievement, such a bountiful source of blessings,

---

[24] Magner, "Fewer Professors," A13.
[25] Donald Kagan, "Why We Should Study the History of Western Civilisation," *Intercollegiate Review* Fall, 2017, viewed 2nd of March, 2018, https://home.isi.org/why-we-should-study-history-western-civilization-0.
[26] Howe, "Classical Education," 31-2: he notes those educated were "by and large, white males" but notes that Latin was being taught in women's colleges, to some free black boys and to Native Americans by the 1850s.
[27] Howe, "Classical Education," 36. Cf. Burstein, "The Classics and the American Republic," 40-2, on the interaction of Latin and Greek studies with the changing nature of American values and identity.

such an exception in a world largely marked by poverty and oppression, we are likely to soon lose its breathtaking advantages.[28]

The moral high ground is depicted here as unquestionably belonging to the West, and once again this is explicitly put into contrast with the history and contemporary identity of non-Western states and their peoples.

Given the increasing diversity of societies around the world, 'Western Civilisation' as an area of study, and the subjects associated with Western Civilisation, sometimes come to be regarded as both exclusive and inherently politically conservative as a result of arguments like those put above.[29] As early as 1971 academics in Australia were arguing that Classics and Ancient History "perpetuated the ruling class…and were not democratic" because they did not connect to the reality of modern Australian society.[30] The most frustrating aspect of this situation is that, as a discipline, Classics can easily include far more than the white, "man's club" view of Greece and Rome if we are willing to let go of our reliance on the 'Western Civilisation' argument.[31] The nature of Rome as a state and the nature of the Hellenistic world allow significant scope for engaging with societies, which were diverse, complex and fluid.[32] Likewise, Gary Kates, Professor of History at Pomona College, USA, made a plea in 1989 for people to remember that there is easily as much inspiration for radicalism in the Greek and Roman world as there is for conservative and traditionalist ideology.[33] As John Heath, Chair of Classics at Santa Clara University, has inadvertently demonstrated both within his controversial article attacking what he sees as the current two-tiered model of classical studies in American universities, and via the varied responses his article drew from other scholars, there is more than enough ground in classical literature and history to house the most radical and the most conservative political and his-

---

[28] Thomas K. Lindsay, "Who Needs to Study Western Civilisation? We Do," *Huffpost* 12/12/2012, viewed 2nd of March, 2018, https://www.huffingtonpost.com/thomas-lindsay-phd/who-needs-to-study-wester_b_2271142.html.

[29] Gary Kates, "The Classics of Western Civilisation do not belong to Conservatives alone," *The Chronicle of Higher Education* (July 5, 1989): B1; Karl Galinsky, "Classics Beyond Crisis," *The Classical World* 84 (1991): 448; Gurd, "Out of Athens," 168. Gurd describes Classics, in terms of methodology and cultural politics, as "one of the more conservative in the contemporary academy." He also notes that Classicists need to reflect on the fact that so many in our discipline tolerate "a belief that 'the Classics' stand for something like the ideals of western civilisation, when the rest of the academy is busily disabusing students and the general public of the value of precisely…the categories of 'the ideal' and 'western civilisation'."

[30] Parsons, "Clio's Language War," 79.11.

[31] Knox, *Oldest Dead*, 12.

[32] Galinsky, "Classics Beyond Crisis," 450.

[33] Kates, "Classics of Western Civilisation," B1-2. See too Cartledge, "Why/How Does Classics Matter?" 192 on *Iphigeneia in Aulis*.

toriographical views.³⁴ If we as Classicists hitch our subjects to the 'Western Civilisation' train, however, we run a serious risk of alienating potential students at a time when we need them most.

It is not only a question of ensuring we do not shut out students from non-Western backgrounds or with more liberal political ideals; we must also be aware of the risk of shutting out students of any background who are not 'elite'—a problematic term that will be discussed further below. Robert Ball and J.D. Ellsworth, both professors emeriti in Classics at the University of Hawaii, note that the argument arose that Latin played an essential role in the development of "intellectual discipline" because, by the nineteenth century, it was harder to make a case that Latin was practically useful.³⁵ Aptitude in Latin and Greek has historically been given a special status in terms of its intellectual value; thus Howe records that in American universities of the mid nineteenth century skill in Greek and Latin translation and composition was regarded as "a measure of general intelligence".³⁶ This attitude was carried on at an official institutional level for well over 100 years: it was not until the 1960s that knowledge of Greek and Latin was revoked as an entry requirement for Oxford and Cambridge Universities.³⁷ While the structural use of Greek and Latin as *de facto* IQ tests is now much less of an issue, defenders of the languages have continued to invoke the spectre of intellectual elitism. This frequently takes the form of an attempt to wrestle control of the very meaning of the term 'elite'. At one end of the spectrum, Karl Galinsky, Floyd A. Cailloux Centennial Professor in Classics at the University of Texas in Austin, notes that "elitism" can be used in a variety of ways, and not purely to indicate social status.³⁸ At the other, Daniel Walker Howe comments plaintively "in 20ᵗʰ Century America, elitism came to seem like an accusation one needed to deny."³⁹ Both scholars suggest in slightly different ways that (intellectual) elitism is a good and valuable thing. Ball and Ellsworth, in response to the suggestion from other classicists that our discipline should stop worrying

---

³⁴ J. Heath et al., 'Self-Promotion and the 'Crisis' in Classics: With Responses' *The Classical World* 89 (1995): 4.
³⁵ Robert J. Ball & J. D. Ellsworth, "Against Teaching Composition in Classical Languages," *The Classical Journal* 85 (1989): 55. See too Howe, "Classical Education," 31 on the teaching of Latin in the USA in the nineteenth century, and Frank Jones at the beginning of the twentieth century in the United Kingdom: Frank Jones, "The Teaching of Latin in Grammar Schools," *The Classical Review* 22 (1908): 33.
³⁶ Howe, "Classical Education," 32.
³⁷ Cartledge, "Why/How Does Classics Matter?" 186. Note too the traces of the same attitude in the close association between a programme that is "increasingly rigorous academically" and the introduction of Latin roots for English vocabulary in Wood, "Teaching the Classics," 74. Interestingly, Harvard and Yale Universities removed the entry requirement of Latin and Greek proficiency in the late 1800s: Frank Donoghue, "Can the Humanities Survive the Twenty-first Century?" *The Chronicle of Higher Education* (Washington, September 5, 2010): NA.
³⁸ Galinsky, "Classics Beyond Crisis," 445.
³⁹ Howe, "Classical Education," 36.

about our association with elitism, argue passionately that Classics must do everything it can to distance itself from elitism, social or otherwise.[40] There are two separate points to address here: firstly, exactly what we mean by elitism when it comes to Classics and secondly, the question of whether Latin and Greek do indeed represent a particularly difficult and rewarding intellectual activity, and are in that sense elite. Once again, I am primarily interested in these ideas insofar as they function as arguments for encouraging the study of Classical languages.

Ball and Ellsworth have controversially suggested that Classicists have a tendency to refer to the "pursuit of excellence" when what is meant is often straightforward elitism in a negative, exclusive sense and there is evidence to support their point of view.[41] For example, when the doctor, medical writer and journalist Tony Smith critically examined his own experience as a student in the United Kingdom of the mid twentieth century, he framed the realm of Greek and Latin as an intellectually "elite interest": "the academic high flyers were put under pressure to join the classical stream". Seamlessly and silently, however, the article shifts to refer to a sense of the elite social status, rather than the academic skills, of those students studying Latin. Smith goes on to comment that university degrees concerned with more practical arts, such as architecture or medicine, were viewed as being "suitable for the second rate, the children of artisans and a few eccentrics." This is clearly a reference to class, not capacity.[42] The situation becomes even murkier when we consider the way that access to particular kinds of educational experiences can influence the performance of students, irrespective of their natural talent or intellect. The use of proficiency in Greek and Latin as a measure of intellectual capacity for the purpose of university admission, for example, rested on an uncomfortable assumption about the connection between an individual's suitability for university education and their access to Classical Languages within the school system.[43] This is unfortunately not a problem that has disappeared with IQ tests and the 11+ examinations used in the past to stream school students in the United Kingdom. In 2013 Lee Baker, at that time a Classics student and volunteer Latin teacher in Glasgow, warned that the shortage of trained Latin teachers in Scotland, together with the inability of state schools to hire teachers outside of the government approved professional accreditation, meant that "Classical education is fast becoming a discipline for the pri-

---

[40] Robert J. Ball & J. D. Ellsworth, "Flushing out the Dinosaurs: Against Teaching Composition II," *The Classical Journal* 88 (1992): 56.

[41] Ball & Ellsworth, "Against Teaching Composition," 56 and Ball & Ellsworth, "Flushing out the Dinosaurs," 56.

[42] Tony Smith, "The Death of the Classics," *British Medical Journal* 309 (1994): 1587.

[43] Something that Paul Cartledge fails to recognise when he calls the revocation of this requirement a change "by no means for the better" in an otherwise sensitive and self-aware article on the future of Classical languages: Cartledge, "Why/How Does Classics Matter?" 186.

vate sector", despite the fact that there was still marked enthusiasm for Latin and Greek amongst students in the state system.[44] Unfortunately, the current limited profile of Greek and Latin in the state school system in both the United Kingdom and Australia can be used to support the view that only a select few students are really capable of excelling in our discipline. Personally, I have heard at least one Classicist say publically that they believe the reason final year examination results in Latin have improved over the years in Australia is that the subject is basically no longer taught at country schools and state schools, as though the students of those institutions are naturally of a poorer quality than their urban, affluent or, in the case of selective schools, carefully chosen, counterparts. We must be wary of making an argument in defence of our discipline that conflates the alleged intellectual rigour of Classical languages with actual social or economic privilege.

We should be especially wary because it is very hard to make a case that Latin and Greek represent a higher form of intellectual activity than many other languages or, indeed, other disciplines. Certainly Greek and Latin are almost fully inflected (that is, the forms of nouns, adjectives and verbs change to reveal their function in a sentence) and this presents particular challenges in terms of memorisation and sentence word order. Classical Greek also uses a different alphabet and one must learn to handle accentuation. Consider in comparison, however, Mandarin Chinese and its 7000 or so intricate characters. Then there is the fact that meaning in spoken and written Mandarin is further modified through four different tones. This one example demonstrates why, while I think that scholars like the Professor and Chair of Classics at Howard University Molly Levine have articulated the intellectual and spiritual benefits of learning Latin in a truly inspiring way, I cannot in good conscience argue that these benefits are unique to Latin.[45]

Latin and Greek certainly provide excellent intellectual discipline when diligently studied, but we cannot rest on the assumption that our discipline is unusual, or elite, in this respect. A factor that might make one believe otherwise in the Australian system is the way in which Latin and Classical Greek are 'scaled' in the Higher School Certificate so that the student's raw mark is

---

[44] Lee Baker, "Disappearance of Classics in Education," *Times Education Supplement Scotland* London, Iss. 2332 (Aug. 30, 2013): 14; see also Sue Blundell, "Gender and the Classics Curriculum: A Survey," *Arts & Humanities in Higher Education* 8 (2009): 153. In some cases, as South Africa, there is almost no Latin left in the secondary system: M. Dircksen, "Reassessing Latin Pedagogy: A Proposed Model for South African Learners," *Akroterion* 61 (2016): 68.

[45] Molly Levine, "Oracles of a Quadragenarian Latin Teacher," *The Classical World* 100 (2006): 50-2. Mathematics, too, comes to mind as a discipline that can provide similar stimulus and discipline across a range of learning areas as demonstrated by Susan Jane Colley's innovative programme: Susan Jane Colley, "What is Mathematics and Why Won't it Go Away?" *PRIMUS* 21 (2011): 211-24. Studies undertaken by Thorndike in the 1920s and by Haag and Stern in 2003 have suggested that no substantive contribution to intelligence or reasoning can be demonstrated in students who study Latin: Lisa R. Holliday, "The Benefits of Latin?" *Educational Research Quarterly* 36 (2012): 5.

transposed to a higher grade for the purpose of calculating their overall Australian Tertiary Admission Rank (ATAR).[46] If one scrutinises past and present student ideas of scaling, there is a popular belief that it reflects the comparative difficulty of a unit of study.[47] This isn't the case; rather, scaling reflects the academic performance of the candidature that took that unit across the full spectrum of their studies[48] and in New South Wales, all government secondary schools that currently teach Latin (for instance) are academically selective.[49] The scaling of Classical Greek and Latin does not indicate that the subjects are difficult in themselves; it indicates that only a small number of highly achieving and/or very well resourced students are currently able to enrol in Latin and Classical Greek.

Leaving aside any moral concerns or anxiety about social justice, it is obviously not in our interests for Classical languages to be regarded as the province of only the socially and intellectually elite, and, as such, exclusive. As Heath has argued in response to ideological disputes in Classics that he regards as elitist in every sense, it does not matter what we are teaching, if we are standing in front of an empty room.[50] Scholars of many different stripes and over many decades are in agreement that the future of Latin and Greek as subjects in the tertiary and secondary education systems is crucially dependent on opening the discipline up, and inviting people in.[51] Inclusivity can be directly linked to student numbers; after being historically excluded from the discipline altogether, the number of women enrolled to study Classics in the

---

[46] The Higher School Certificate is the matriculation examination that concludes secondary education in the Australian school system in New South Wales, and immediately precedes tertiary study, should the student wish to go on.

[47] For example: "the markup reflects the difficulty of the subject." – 'Chavi'; "The whole point of scaling is to make things equal though, because from what I've heard from others, to get a 30 in Latin is just as hard as it is to get a 40 in any other subject. I wouldn't be so quick to judge before you've actually done the subject yourself." – 'Shinny', viewed 19th of February, 2018, https://atarnotes.com/forum/index.php?topic=33958.0

[48] NSW Vice-Chancellor's Committee – Technical Committee on Scaling, *Report on the Scaling of 2016 NSW Higher School Certificate*, (Sydney: UAC, 2017) 7.

[49] Including: Baulkham Hills High School, St George School for Girls, North Sydney Boys High School, North Sydney Girls High School, Sydney Boys High School and Sydney Girls High school. For further perspective, 'continuers' language courses, designed for those who have studied the language for four years previously, consistently scale more highly than 'beginners' language courses – though many people will find the first two years of studying a new language more challenging than the next two.

[50] Heath et al., "Self-Promotion," 12.

[51] Marie Cleary, "Tribune: A new job for the Classicist," *The Classical World* 72 (1978): 71-2; Arlene R. Fromchuck, "Nobis Cura Futuri: Teaching Latin in the 80s," *The Classical Journal* 80 (1986): 249; Ball & Ellsworth, "Against Teaching Composition," 55, 61; Galinsky, "Classics Beyond Crisis," 451; Ball & Ellsworth, "Flushing out the Dinosaurs," 56; Ronald Mellor, 'Response' in, Heath et al., "Self-Promotion," 40; Richard F. Thomas, 'Response' in Heath et al., "Self-Promotion," 89 (1995): 51; Cartledge, 'Why/How Does Classics Matter?" 169.

United Kingdom overtook men by 2009.[52] This point is equally relevant in terms of the reputation of the unusual, intimidating difficulty—and thus rigour—of Latin and Greek. Classical languages certainly can be challenging but, crucially, they do not have to be, if we are committed to teaching the students in front of us, rather than a very narrow selection of 'ideal' students from another age.

If we do indeed want numbers to grow in Latin and Greek, if we want these areas to be secure in themselves, instead of being dependent on a larger ideological struggle about the value of studies in Western Civilisation, it means genuine changes for Classical languages. This is especially true in a tertiary context where there is still a chance to capture new hearts and minds from all kinds of backgrounds.[53] The central motivation of Ball and Ellsworth's two articles campaigning against the teaching of Latin composition (that is, the translation of substantial passages from English into Latin in the 'style' of particular ancient authors) is that this kind of old fashioned exercise offers nothing essential and is not justifiable in pedagogical terms, but, via its difficulty and association with humiliation, risks discouraging students from learning Latin.[54] Instead they passionately argue that we must teach the students of today with methodology appropriate for contemporary classrooms.[55] Importantly, this does not mean that the material needs to be 'dumbed down'; it means that we need to work harder as teachers to meet the students at least halfway[56] and develop appropriate educational goals. It might not be possible—for instance—for students who have not previously studied any Classical language and have little knowledge of formal grammar on entering our subjects to read large amounts of un-adapted Latin or Greek in their first year.[57] Rethinking our goals for first year isn't defeat; it's sensible pedagogy if we want to retain students into second year who have a strong enough foundation upon which to build further knowledge confidently. Even at the beginning of the twentieth century, teachers of Latin were aware that what was lauded as "discipline" in the learning of the Latin grammar, was often just

---

[52] Blundell, "Gender and the Classics Curriculum," 141. However, there is still considerable distance to go in terms of real gender equity in the field: Churchill, "Is There a Woman," 87-90.

[53] Particularly as regards the 'grammar-translation' method of teaching which has held sway in Greek and Latin since the 19th century: Dircksen, "Reassessing Latin Pedagogy," 59-61, 67-8.

[54] Ball & Ellsworth, "Against Teaching Composition," 56-8; Ball & Ellsworth, "Flushing out the Dinosaurs," 56; 59.

[55] Ball & Ellsworth, "Against Teaching Composition," 61; Ball & Ellsworth, "Flushing out the Dinosaurs," 56. Lisa R. Holliday suggests that at least some of the measurable benefit of studying Latin is closely tied to the way in which the Latin is taught: Holliday, "The Benefits of Latin?" 9-10.

[56] Martha G. Abbott and Sally Davis, "Hyperreality and the Study of Latin: Living in a Fairy Tale World," *The Modern Language Journal* 80 (1996): 86. Abbott and Davis argue that this is already happening in secondary school classrooms and must make greater inroads into tertiary education.

[57] Daniel P. Carpenter, "Reassessing the Goal of Latin Pedagogy," *The Classical Journal* 95 (2000): 391-2.

plain "drudgery", especially for those students who were not naturally talented.[58] As Arlene R. Fromchuck, a Classicist and teacher for many years at Brooklyn College, observed in 1986, the greater diversity of our students in terms of educational background and prior learning is a natural aspect of the democratisation of education and a challenge that we should—and must—meet if we wish to remain relevant as a discipline.[59] For Fromchuck, this meant thinking of new ways in which Latin could be taught and could be valuable for new cohorts of students in, and from, the state school system.[60] It is notable that Arlene R. Fromchuck's legacy as a Latinist was not one of watering down the classics, but of spreading their power.[61]

It is worth putting in the effort to make these kinds of changes because it can be demonstrated that Latin and Greek are valuable on their own terms, outside of the literature and society of the Ancient world. The results of a number of studies suggest that Latin has particularly impressive measurable benefits for the comprehension of English language and for vocabulary skills.[62] I would argue that this is a particularly excellent reason for committing to teaching and supporting Greek and Latin, because it is often the students with the least academic confidence, the least familial background in English language and the least success or experience in formal education, who can be shown to have the most to gain from studying the Classics. The majority of evidence here relates to the study of Latin, and to programmes carefully designed by Latin teachers not for "the more successful students, but for the 'underachievers'", and aimed at building both academic confidence and English literacy.[63] When Latin was integrated into remedial classes designed to improve English language usage, for instance, Fromchuck was also able to show that the programme that included Latin supported markedly higher ongoing achievement for students in university writing assessments than other programmes.[64]

---

[58] Jones, "Teaching of Latin," 34.
[59] Fromchuck, "Nobis Cura Futuri," 249.
[60] Fromchuck, "Nobis Cura Futuri," 249.
[61] Paid Death Notice, *New York Times*, August 3rd, 1999: "Her colleagues in the Brooklyn College Classics Department lament the passing of Arlene Fromchuck, whose inspired teaching influenced generations of students for over three decades. She was a true champion of liberal education."
[62] Fromchuck, "Measurable Benefits," 26-8. Students in the Latin programme consistently demonstrated as much as 38% improvement on the government administered California Achievement Test. The link between Latin instruction and English literacy was also supported by Lisa R. Holliday's critical synthesis of studies on the effect of Latin learning on various core competencies: Holliday, "The Benefits of Latin?" 7-8, 10.
[63] Harry C. Avery, "Conference on the Teaching of Latin in Inner City Schools," *The Modern Languages Journal* 54 (1970): 425.
[64] Fromchuck, "Nobis Cura Futuri," 249. Also, Rudolph Masciantonio, "Paraclassicists: A Means for Expanding the Teaching of Latin at the School Level," *The Classical World* 77 (1984): 168. T. W. Valentine advocated the potential of Latin teaching as a way to reinforce English reading, spelling and vocabulary nearly sixty years earlier: Valentine, "Correlation of English and Latin Teaching," 311.

More recently, the teaching of Latin in extremely diverse, socio-economically disadvantaged state schools in the United States has been linked to improved SAT scores and increased college admissions.[65] The baton has been taken up in the United Kingdom by the Iris Project, which teaches Latin in diverse, often underprivileged, urban primary schools in order to support English literacy.[66] The role of Latin in supporting English literacy has particular potential given the undeniable importance of clear and effective English usage. It has been powerfully argued that though cultural diversity in terms of language and expression is something to be both treasured and celebrated, we cannot pretend that the "gatekeeping" points (such as applications for jobs or tertiary admission) where students will be required to show command of 'standard' English do not exist.[67] Nevertheless, the question of just whose standard is entailed in 'standard' English is complex, political and fraught.[68] Difficulties around Aboriginal literacy rates in Australia are a good example of this issue: in contemporary Australia it is clear that proficiency in 'standard English' is necessary in order to access a wide range of social and economic benefits, but learning 'standard English' is also closely linked to a history of white power and oppression and a loss of Aboriginal identity.[69] One possible strategy is to teach grammar (with minimal initial reference to English) via something like Latin purely because, as a dead language, it is not the language of a contemporary, or recent, oppressor. Yet, because of the historical development of English, Latin is an excellent means of supporting vocabulary and recognition of linguistic patterns in English.[70] This means that while some of the ways that learning Latin helps support English literacy might be available through learning any foreign language,[71] Latin has a definite, useful, edge. It is also potentially exciting: it is the language of gladiators and the Colosseum after all, and, as teachers have found via the Iris Project in the UK and in programmes in America, Latin is also unusual enough as a subject to be exciting and to disarm some of the received suspicion students may feel about the

---

[65] Ron Janoff, "The Elite Meets the Street: Teaching Latin in a Nonselective Brooklyn Charter School," *The Classical World* 107 (2014): 261-2.
[66] http://irisproject.org.uk/ viewed 27th of February 2018. Lorna Hardwick cites the Iris project as a model for future roles and succes for Classics: Lorna Hardwick, 'Editor's Postscript: Thoughts for the Future' *Arts and Humanities in Higher Education* 8 (2009): 218.
[67] Lisa D. Delpit, "The Silenced Dialogue: Power and Pedagogy in Educating Other People's Children," *Harvard Educational Review* 58 (1988): 292-3. See too David Corson, 'Social dialect, the semantic barrier, and access to curricular knowledge' *Language in Society* 12 (1983): 213-222; esp. 218.
[68] e.g. L.M. Christensen, "Teaching Standard English: Whose Standard?" *The English Journal* 79 (1990): 26-40.
[69] Margaret Zeegers, Wayne Muir & Zheng Lin, "The Primacy of the Mother Tongue: Aboriginal Literacy and Non-Standard English," *The Australian Journal of Indigenous Education* 32 (2003): 53 and 55.
[70] David Corson, "Social dialect, the semantic barrier, and access to curricular knowledge," *Language in Society* 12 (1983): 222.
[71] Holliday, "The Benefits of Latin?" 8.

education system.⁷² For diverse school communities, Latin also has the great point in its favour that it is also no-one's home language; therefore it creates a reasonably level playing field on which students can build new skills and knowledge. Of course, if we link Latin too closely to the study of Western Civilisation, understood in Kagan's terms of its inherent superiority to other cultures and intellectual traditions, we lose some of the benefits that Latin currently offers for students who may be resistant to, or intimidated by, the associations of 'correct' English grammar.

The potential for Latin's new life is well embodied by the example of the students at the Williamsburg Charter High School (WCHS) in Brooklyn. The students, 70% of whom were Latino (largely from the Dominican Republic) and 80% of whom were classified as being below the poverty line, were on average two years behind their expected level of educational achievement.⁷³ Neither elite socially nor educationally, these students would never traditionally have been given the option to study Latin. More than this, these students mostly came from a geographical region that had inherited Spanish language as a result of colonisation, not as a symbol of their European descent and personal connection to the past glories of Greece and Rome. Yet, because the school hired a consultant, Dr. Ron Janoff, who understood that the curriculum needed to meet the needs of the students in front of him, who knew that this meant giving students an opportunity for "real success" on an academic level within a Latin programme that was shaped to take every advantage of the strengths the students had, WCHS was boasting a Latin cohort of 1200 students by 2012.⁷⁴ Quite a lot of the programme revolved around ensuring that students experienced small triumphs, moments of achievement and proficiency that had often been sorely lacking in their previous educational experience.⁷⁵ For instance, because the students, many of whom spoke Spanish, found Latin relatively easy to pronounce, Janoff put a great deal of emphasis on oral/aural interaction in the early stages. As the students advanced, 'living Latin' pedagogy based on modern language immersion methods was introduced to further build on these strengths.⁷⁶ Students were also engaged on a creative level, as instructors asked them to design charts to represent conjugations of Latin verbs and noun declensions using models taken from Roman

---

⁷² http://irisproject.org.uk/index.php/literacy-through-latin/89-literacy-through-latin-wins-eu-language-label-2013 Viewed 2nd of March, 2018. Janoff, "The Elite," 260. Janoff makes the point that the students at WCHS were unlikely to have encountered others who had studied Latin.
⁷³ Janoff, "The Elite," 259.
⁷⁴ Janoff, "The Elite," 260-1. Students from the school who had studied three years and took the Comprehensive Latin Examination run by the Office of State Assessment also maintained an 80% pass rate.
⁷⁵ Janoff, "The Elite," 260.
⁷⁶ Janoff, "The Elite," 260. The argument is sometimes made that these skills (embedded in a 'living Latin' pedagogical approach) are particularly effective levellers of the educational playing field: M. Dircksen, "Reassessing Latin Pedagogy," 65.

inscriptions and graffiti.[77] The founder of the school, and the teachers he employed, were successfully able to make the argument to the students that Latin was worth studying for its own sake, not because of its role as a foundation language of Western Civilisation, not because it was a symbol of elitism of any kind, but because it was fun, exciting and useful for students who didn't have many past reasons to feel positive about education.[78]

A similar story can be traced with younger students in the progress of the Iris Project in the United Kingdom. Teachers (usually volunteers) have gone to great lengths to show the students that Latin is fun by using a range of interactive, kinetic and creative activities, such as drama and art activites, planning Roman menus and working with physical puzzle pieces to learn about inflection. As a result of this, the students are as excited about the classes, as their teachers are about the gains in literacy involved, and the Iris Project Literacy through Latin project continues to expand.[79] This is not to argue that this kind of English language support is the most important or primary purpose of Latin in 2018; Latin and Greek will always be most attractive to those students and scholars who work in Ancient world studies.[80] It is to say, however, that there are compelling arguments for students, even outside of these areas, to consider studying Classical Languages, and for institutions at both secondary and tertiary level, and also perhaps primary school level, to continue to teach them.

As the extensive body of literature referenced in this chapter should have made clear, Classics is not an unreflective discipline. For some decades now scholars have identified the need for Classics programmes to be as egalitarian as possible, and have levelled critiques at perceived weaknesses of historical teaching practice that they believe tend towards 'elitism'.[81] Ball and Ellsworth, for example, have condemned the teaching of Latin composition as an exercise designed "to humiliate and eliminate the less capable students"[82] and Heath has argued that too great a focus on philology or theory in classes at the expense of creative and innovative pedagogy demonstrates "disdain (for) the average student".[83] Still more scholars have opened Classics out in the best possible ways, teaching thoughtful, exciting programmes, developing a role for Latin in supporting literacy, and working with high school teachers to

---

[77] Janoff, "The Elite," 261.
[78] Janoff "The Elite," 259. The founder, Eddie Calderon-Melendez, believed that his own study of Latin had been crucial to his ability to write English effectively.
[79] http://irisproject.org.uk/index.php/the-iris-project/iris-project-history viewed 2nd of March, 2018.
[80] Patrick O'Sullivan & Judith Maitland, "Greek and Latin Teaching in Australian and New Zealand Universities: A 2005 Survey," *Antichthon* 41 (2007): 109.
[81] Ball & Ellsworth, "Against Teaching Composition," 54-62; Ball & Ellsworth, "Flushing out the Dinosaurs," 55-65; Heath et al., "Self-Promotion," 3-52.
[82] Ball & Ellsworth, "Against Teaching Composition," 56.
[83] Heath et al., "Self-Promotion," 14.

expand our impact in the school system.[84] Now more than ever it is time to abandon arguments for the classics which revolve around the value of Western Civilisation and the supposed peculiar intellectual qualities of our languages. If we teach the students of today, and trust in the value of Classical languages on their own terms, Latin and Greek, unlike the myth of elitism that continues to cling to them, have the potential to be alive and well for many years to come.

To end as I began: the study of Latin took me from Armidale High School to the University of Sydney and Yale University; it has taken me to Cape Town, Munich, Turin and London, amongst other places, and introduced me to people all over Australia and the world. More importantly, however, it has given me the privilege of teaching new generations of Latinists every year and watching as their love of Latin, and their understanding of their own language, grow with each trimester. I am also fortunate enough to teach at an institution where students can study online and where we have a large percentage of mature age students, supported with governmental fee remission. I work hard to resist assumptions about what students do and do not know, and I proudly use every tool in my arsenal, including diagrams, terrible drawings, interactive whiteboards, live-streamed interactive online classes, colour coding, analogy, songs by *James*, quotes from *Blackadder*, even––at a pinch—pronoun pictionary, to try to make the complex, clear and the intimidating, exciting. In this way, Latin becomes more accessible for those who would never have been able to study it in any other fashion: full time carers, people who are incarcerated, people who left school before their final year, and people whose bodies have betrayed them and left them isolated. And every year there are people just like me: young men and women from state schools in country towns who have been attracted to the mystery, excitement and scholarly community of those who are passionate about Latin and Greek. Some go on to research, some go out to teach, and some leave after a year, knowing they have achieved something substantial, and able to control English grammar and language with increased confidence. In every case, I hope that we have worked together to make Latin a little bit less elite.

---

[84] See Fromchuck, "Nobis Cura Futuri," 249-252 for a remarkably humble and inspiring example of this activity.

Bridging the Wandering Islands: Education and Connectivity. Some Personal Observations

Ivan Francis Head

For many years, as an academic, I have interviewed eighteen-year-old students in transition to University. I have always been reminded of what I did not know when I finished high school, what I had tried to begin to think about at age seventeen (the age for Year 12 graduation in Western Australia), and what I thought I knew or took for granted. Forty seven years later I can still sense some of my own bewilderment in the experiential gap between Year 12 and University.

I have had transition conversations with students for twenty seven years. For the last twenty three years, this has been mostly with a cohort well within the top ten percent by ATAR in the Higher School Certificate in New South Wales, or very well placed in the International Baccalaureate.[1] Many have been with students who finish this part of their education within the top two percent. Some candidates' rankings are not at this level, and so I also watch diligently for students who have not yet flourished, but may do so in the future. Not everyone wakes up at the same time or rate. I gain a sense of what has been taught and not been taught, and of islands or archipelagos of learning in an ocean of the as yet unknown.

The poet A.D. Hope began *The Wandering Islands* with these lines:

> You cannot build bridges between the wandering islands;
> The Mind has no neighbours . . .[2]

In at least one sense I disagree with a reading of the poet at this point. I have found that to some real extent it is possible to build or find such a bridge in a conversational interview, though I acknowledge that this immediately places me amongst those who stress the indelibly personal in an educational process. I would say that what I do in conversation cannot be replicated by 'tick-box' form, that could then be marked and graded by a further AI (artificial intelli-

---

[1] Australian Tertiary Admission Rank, the principal criterion for university entry at undergraduate level, indicating a student's position relative to all students of their year in high school.
[2] A.D. Hope, "The Wandering Islands", in A.D. Hope, *The Wandering Islands* (Sydney: Edwards & Shaw, 1955).

gence) machine and given a programmed admission score. One could write a thesis on how closely a brilliantly designed Interview Test by multiple choice could replicate functional outcomes here, but at the end of the day, the phenomenological and personal core, the relationship in community, would be stripped away, and the collegiate realities of nascent friendships would vanish. In this sense, my experience has been to assume the validity of something like J.H. Newman's views on collegiate learning and university life.[3]

A.D. Hope might be referring to the person thinking, or to what is being thought about. I have become very interested in the larger neighbourhood of the mind, in the sense of 'the better curriculum'—what is included in a useful sum of learning, what is learned, that covers not everything, but is sufficient for a *cosmion* to emerge in the young adult's mind.[4]

One stands in silence before the sum of what would be included in universal knowledge, or even the idea that there is such a domain. One does not speculate too much about what could be objectified in the sum of books, or in all data stored online in the largest and total 'cloud', say that of Google or Amazon.[5] Even then, the phenomenological and personal dimension distributed amongst the sum of 'all knowing minds' is not really or actually included in this vast resource.

I do not intend to discuss it here, but I am interested in the theoretical question whether there are limits to what can be known, and how, if there are, what this implies about a realm that may simply remain unknowable to a human being, even one possessed of the sum of human capacities. I *am* interested here in a working sample that provides holistic, or working, small-scale access (*cosmion*) into the larger body of knowledge, which may become a lifelong pursuit in some way.[6]

It is from within some such setting of connectivity or systematic body of knowledge and inquiry that I presume students will have begun the study of small but significant 'islands of meaning' in their journey to Year 12. To some extent, it is beginning with what Isaiah Berlin calls 'the foxes' of multiple and interesting ideas and events that for a time remain fascinating and worthy of study in their isolation or individual 'brilliance', worth studying as stand-alone

---

[3] J.H. Newman, *The Idea of a University* (1852), and in various writings on the Oratory ideal.
[4] *cosmion* – 'A little world', as in Short Eric Voegelin Glossary, http://watershade.net/ev/ev-glossary.html 21/10/2017
[5] Karl Popper posited this idea of knowledge objectified in books in *The Open Society and its Enemies*. It suggests that the book is a potential conversation, an opportunity to discuss ideas and arguments at one remove only from the living person. See Karl Popper, *The Open Society and its Enemies*, 2 vols, 5th ed., (London: Routledge & Kegan Paul Ltd, 1966; first published 1945).
[6] At another level I am interested in how a knowing mind rich in subjectivity can arise in a realm in which in one sense it may be the only 'mind'. 'I' raises the question, how can a designing mind arise in a universe where it is the only thing capable of design? This is not Paley repeated; but it is related to the question of the arising of difference and differentiation in a universe where ultimately all 'stuff' is of the same kind.

units.⁷ Some of these will have begun to be encountered by the age of eighteen and the end of secondary school. Many may not appear until University, or perhaps never. I distinctly remember thinking in my PhD studies that I wished that I had read the book then in front of me at least ten years earlier, because of its implications for a systematic approach to a different reading of Gospel texts.⁸

Leo Tolstoy's 'How Much Land Does a Man Need?' (1886) and Jack London's 'To Build a Fire' (1908) are both brilliant, stand-alone short stories that illuminate a wider ethos or *cosmion*. In a way they are parabolic, and disclose the larger universe. They come with 'bridge attached'. The same can be said of Nicholas Monsarrat's novel *The Cruel Sea* (1951), in which the British corvette captain depth charges an area in which merchant seamen from a torpedoed convoy ship are afloat and struggling to survive. He depth charges the area because his new technology ASDIC operator believes a 'ping' is from the lurking submarine, but later they realise it is from the freighter sinking into the depths below. There is a multiple challenge in what is described: ethical and existential, and about the character of war, and in the context of a conflict that generates historical and political inquiry into contemporary realities. All of these convey existential realities via their embodiment of a wisdom that can still provoke an experiential response in the student, or prepare them in some ways for some of what life may lead them to, or throw at them (even in Heidegger's sense of 'thrownness' or *Geworfenheit*).⁹ Those meta-or bridging themes in these works could be listed as avarice, personal enmeshment, *libido dominandi*, and death (Tolstoy), futility, risk and existential vulnerability (London), and ethics, mistakes, negligence, warfare and modern history (Monsarrat). Thus, the works build bridges to larger themes, or signpost trajectories for further exploration.

I did not encounter any of these three texts until after my first University studies, and had not read them by age eighteen. But I have met a few students of that age who have begun to synthesise an intentional or singular worldview or *Weltanschauung*, or are striving for a singular big idea or vision of life. Berlin used the metaphor of hedgehog for this larger task. It is hard to be a philosopher at eighteen. To some extent one always breathes the spirit of the

---

⁷ πόλλ' οἶδ' ἀλώπηξ, ἀλλ' ἐχῖνος ἓν μέγα. A fox knows many things, but a hedgehog one important thing. *The Hedgehog and the Fox* was first published, in the UK, in 1953, by Weidenfeld and Nicolson.
⁸ It was D.F. Strauss, *The Life of Jesus Critically Examined,* translated from the 4th German edition by George Eliot (London: Swan Sonnenschein & Co., New York: Macmillan and Co., 1898).
⁹ There is another sense of thrownness in the earlier cultural trajectory, and it involves the Greek word from which our word ball (something thrown) derives. The two terms are *symbol* and *diabol*. On this reading a symbol is a word or event (a liturgy?) that unites and connects, while a diabol is the diabolic that literally throws apart and disconnects. In this sense, a bad curriculum 'throws apart' and disintegrates the human person. It is not the same as deconstruction, for there is a difference between taking things apart into components, and throwing something away so as to smash it.

age in which one is emerging (perhaps in a cohort by decade), and does not overly question it, or know how to question it at the time.

It took me some time into a life at University to begin to hear the claim in Philosophy that 'the point of doing philosophy is to protect you from other people's philosophies', or to move to a point where one re-affirms the content of a philosophy (a metaphysic, even) that is more than a defensive methodology.[10] Hume stated (*Enquiry Concerning Human Understanding*), the strong case for non-assent to 'content claims'[11], and while that may be the great defensive masterstroke against humbug, ideology, fundamentalisms, or utopian dreams of many kinds, it might also close the mind to what is in fact possible. Something very unlikely on the surface may prove to the contrarian, a counterfactual of great price or value.

Most, in preparation for entry to university in Sydney, or more widely in a globalised educational market recruiting talent, are focused on isolated or singular units of learning. To some extent, it is someone's canon, something generated by a curriculum committee, as it must be. Some 'islands' will have been truly explored and mastered, and the student's drive for more is palpable. At the same time, a few questions in conversation will tell you where the present frontiers of learning lie, and whether the student is working in depth on any topic. Of course, that student's frontier of learning may be beyond my own in a topic, and the student will be asked to tell me as much of that as I can connect to, out of interest, and as a bridge builder.

A student of Chinese language may have wider knowledge of Chinese history and culture. A question about the Taiping Rebellion is always fruitful, not only as confined to 'events in the mid nineteenth century', but perhaps to see if curiosity drives the student. The bridge from there into studies of Empire, and of psychological and religious drives to utopian thinking is connective, and leads to further singular insights. That mid-nineteenth century set of events unleashed powerful forces in this world, in the name of a transcendent order. Millions lost lives. Most students are fascinated by the phrases 'God's Chinese Son' or 'Jesus's Chinese Brother', and almost all will not have heard them before. Most Western students have no idea of the scale of that conflict. Bridges from here to serious economic and political theory, and to the value of the human person lie close at hand, and key words like Buddhism, Tao, Marx and Mao also lie close at hand, as do the 'neighbourhood words' Korea and Japan.

Utopian thinking and symbols of transcendent order have their own history in the West. It is good to try to place some of them in a curriculum for

---

[10] I attribute the phrase to Julius Kovesi, author of *Moral Notions*, 1967.

[11] 'I should not believe such a story were it told me by Cato.' He notes that this was proverbial in Roman times. David Hume, *An Enquiry Concerning Human Understanding and Concerning the Principles of Morals* (Oxford: Clarendon Press, 1982 [1777]) X. I. 89.

scrutiny—lest forms of them sneak up on our own times, and pass for good or strong or benign leadership. Some of this could happen in Studies in Religion, or Ancient History, or in Modern History. Some of the themes cannot be confined to one unit or area of study. Mohammed, the Buddha and Jesus are hard to confine to isolated and disconnected singularities, and diachronicity and synchronicity are required. By this I mean that 'through-time' recurrences, and cross-cultural parallels are needed, for as the saying goes, 'what goes around comes around', and we tend to access these figures through the history of interpretation, even when we stress primary resources.

Within the modern history syllabus, the 'Third Reich' is not properly confined to a study of the nineteen thirties. Nor is the symbol 'Kingdom of Heaven' simply a first century symbol. Joachim of Fiore and his 'Age of the Spirit' are hard to constrain within the thirteenth century.

Year 12 is perhaps too early to look for *mastery* of a grand narrative, or master theme that may connect or bridge the wandering islands of 'learning by units'. Some may say that the very idea of a grand narrative or master theme is a delusion at any age, but I think most who teach and think, have some such master themes, even if they are assumptions about progress, the general endurance of societies, or the superiority and adequacy of human reason post-Enlightenment. The gender conflicts in recent educational debates may be indicative of a background conflict at the level of master narrative or theory, or of new insights in biology, or of claims at the level of presupposition and theory, or of concern over 'who sets a curriculum and chooses the texts'. In the background of any concerns about curriculum at the moment will lie anxieties about actual wars in progress, and the possible dismantling of Syria and Iraq and Afghanistan. At the least, the curriculum opportunity is to try to follow the bridge and trajectory to other 'mid-points', such as the carve-up of the Ottoman Empire after World War One.

Amongst the poets, an early reading of Eliot, Yeats or Auden may provoke a sense of that connective and disclosing vision within the modernity of the West. 'Leda and the Swan' is not too far from the Infancy Narratives of St Matthew and St Luke for the astute student and the good teacher to cross a bridge. 'Sailing to Byzantium' and 'The Second Coming' lie in that same bow of diachronicity and recurrence that connects a culture to its origins, and enables the human condition to be interrogated in questions that are both old and new and contemporary. One raises the question of death and immortality, the other the end of the age and the dualities within the possibilities of the human story, as a negative messiah appears 'from below', as Girard might put it. Auden's 'The Shield of Achilles' spans three thousand years on a page, and in some ways does more readily for the student what the more compact and dense Eliot does. So it seems to me.

For completion, the bridges or ships to the wandering islands of mythology, can at least be signposted. One can go back to Germany in the nineteen thirties, to the work of the great scholar, Rudolf Bultmann, or read the reworked myths of Tolkien, or think about Zeus and Europa, or ponder what lies in the name of that church in Rome, "Santa Maria sopra Minerva". Most students are arrested by Yeats's expressions 'What rough beast slouches towards Jerusalem?' and 'the centre cannot hold'. For much of its history, Europe, or Christendom, was immersed in the idea that the myth of the Virgin Mother had a literal dimension to it, and at the least, the bridges from that point into the world of wider myth can be signposted and evaluated. At some point in a university curriculum, demythologisation and re-mythologisation can enter the inquiry. A careful handling of Yeats's great poem 'Leda and the Swan' can lead not only to a study of history, but into the almost taboo or potentially difficult subject of sexual malpractice[12], given that in this poem-myth, the deity itself assumes an animal form to impregnate a woman. It is not far to the Feuerbachian question of how the human mind imagines the form of the deity, and what can inform that process by way of best practice. One of the great contributions of female New Testament scholars has been to ask the question systematically, 'Where are the women in this story?' Their absence may also be telling.[13]

I could say that within the West, there will be one or more master narratives or first order assumptions already sitting in the background of units of study. Some units of study will disclose the idea that Christianity was a master idea or dominant 'myth' for Europe, and that there has been something called an 'Enlightenment'. Others presume that empires *must* give way to national-political units (since they have), and that this has led automatically to an ethically superior way for peoples to organise themselves. A ladder theory of succession or of progress is always lurking and resists criticism, unless perhaps the very city one lives in has been obliterated in pursuit of a good cause. Some associate a notion of nationalism with democracy in a naïve way, and think that anything claiming the use of those names will be, or has been, 'good for us', regardless of outcomes.

Coup d'états are often seen to be good things for 'the people', since they move a society on from corrupt leadership. An unelected general may be a hero for deposing an unelected monarch, or a villain for deposing an elected government. The American Revolution expressed the powerful Lockean idea that a government tending to absolutism may in some cases be removed by the people, and the British in general absorbed the idea that Charles I did lose his head by some process of law, notwithstanding the fate of the lawyers in the Restoration.[14] In much the same way, assumptions that a republic must of necessity succeed a monarchy may often be informed by factors not always

---

[12] I note the controversy over the poem 'Mango' in the 2017 HSC paper.
[13] I simply mention the work of Elisabeth Schüssler Fiorenza.
[14] See Geoffrey Robertson, *The Tyrannicide Brief* (London: Chatto & Windus, 2005).

transparently at the table of debate, but which tend to be in conformity with the spirit of the age. The unthinkable can become normative thought very quickly. Australia was formally part of the British Empire during two World Wars. But now, the pro-imperial mentalities of our forebears are hard for many to imagine. Reminding a student that AIF stood for Australian Imperial Force, and not for Australian Infantry Force, is occasionally helpful.

Some larger and connective questions are about forms of human utopia or order, the locus of a millennium or thousand year reign of perfection, and the extent to which any human activity may relate to that, aspire to it, seek to enter it or bring it about, or to display in some way its stated or presumed core values. Economics, technology, communications and ecology become interrelated disciplines here, as well as the traditional master theme of theology, as we consider various human futures that emerge through time, and become the actualities we live with. It is in this domain that a better understanding of North Korea may emerge.

At the level of personal utopia, the old Funeral Service still says at every funeral that "we leave the departed in the sure and certain hope of the resurrection of the dead"; and elsewhere in that book a collect petitions that "we may lead quiet and godly lives"—expressing the presumption that elements of normality in the human city or village are to be valued highly.[15]

For me, the point is how expertise in any one discipline bridges to conversation with experts in another, and whether it is possible for a polymath or *intermath* to be competent to sustain validity in an interdisciplinary exercise, and find coherences in some way. Learning must happen this way. Perhaps curriculum can embrace genuine interdisciplinary knowledge, and a hint of a grand narrative, or a viable trajectory which is contemporary both in science and the humanities (not a new or nostalgic medievalism in disguise), so that we can see ourselves in some ways mirrored in the past.

Many sciences invite interdisciplinary competencies. Gravity waves, dark matter and the edge of the Universe invite the imagination to participate. Embryonic stem cell research is inherently interdisciplinary. IVF invites knowledge in the microbiology of the human species, in genetics specifically, in fertility and embryology in particular, in the study of hormones, and in ethics and theology—not to mention the question of a biological basis for any gender theory or opinion.[16] The rise of genomic studies, via 'coding' that is partly linguistic and partly mathematical, is amazing. It has been a challenge to find the diversity of competencies needed in this area in one person, and a

---

[15] The reference is to the *Book of Common Prayer* and its Funeral Services.

[16] One has to read Robert Jansen, *Getting Pregnant: a compassionate resource to overcoming infertility and avoiding miscarriage* (Allen and Unwin, 2003). In particular the section on Intersex is a fundamental text, and must be read in particular by those committed to a uniform binary simplicity 'for all God's children'.

boon to find groups of people who may connect the wandering islands in one coherent discourse. It has also been an area where strong opposition to the venture exists, and where embryonic stem cell research may be forbidden. Discussions of 'soul' are needed too, and of the incredibly subtle issue of the rise of differentiation during the process of the development of the embryo into the human person, from sets of stem cells that are in some ways 'the same', or the same at some nano level.[17] How does organic difference arise within a set of things that are organically the same? Is that a philosophical or a biological or a metaphysical question, or all three?

Leo Tolstoy's short story 'How Much land Does a Man Need?' (1886) springs to mind as a challenge to interdisciplinary knowledge, and the need for generalists to know something about quite a lot of things. In Tolstoy's story, the aspirational protagonist (tempted by the *diabolos*, sitting by the stove to keep warm) over-reaches, and cannot circumscribe in a day the land that his heart desires to possess. In the effort to have it all, in one final burst of energy, he expires, and the Deceiver arranges his burial in the tiny plot reserved for him in the cemetery. His story makes its point of a life 'thrown away'. Both the wise and the fool will end in the same place. The story leads into a consideration of the issues of the quest for knowledge, of reasonable limits for an individual's life, and of the novel value of genuine collaboration in a non-competitive pursuit of knowledge.[18]

In relation to Tolstoy's subject of death, a proper study of the cultures of East and West must raise the question whether death, the end of every human life (unless magic *telomeres* emerge), has been de-absolutised from *within* the historical process. Different religious faiths address the same theme differently. The actual or literal claims about the character of this claimed intrusion of a transcendence, or resolution from within the stream of existence, must be considered dispassionately as part of a complete curriculum. The Tolstoy story could be used as a provocation. I did not seriously study wider Faith traditions until finding a brilliant program in Classical Indian Thought at Melbourne University in 1977, by when I was twenty-four. HSC Studies in Religion now attempts that study before the age of eighteen.

---

[17] I found the perspective of Eric Voegelin helpful here. He links 'soul' to anamnetic memories, those first primordial experiences that one remembers forever, and that establish lived continuity with childhood. These are one's first memories, to which one can return at any time in 'vivid colour' and immediacy. There is a connection to the 'memory' of a complete culture or society, and thus to some extent to symbolic heritage or even 'liturgy'. Some liturgies are real, some are confected and manufactured. Some enhance participation in a truth, some do not. See Eric Voegelin, *Anamnesis* (Columbia, MO: University of Missouri Press, 1990).

[18] On a different level, I am reminded of a conversation I had years ago with one of the first Australian women to graduate from Cambridge, who told me that *The Cruel Sea* was banned from the curriculum in her school, not because of the evils of war, but because the words "venereal disease" occurred in the text, and it was deemed improper for young ladies even to see the words. Wrong call on many levels.

Catholic, Orthodox and Reformation claims for the universality of truth claims are still part of a global educational venture, and cannot be sidelined, or ignored. Whether the eighteen-year-old is exposed to the study of Greek, Roman or other myths, an education will traverse the question of the literal virgin mother, the tension between Dionysus and Christ, and stories of the empty tomb, acting as a sign of something, for which the word resurrection is needed, as the first step in addressing an event with transcendent dimensions. *Pneuma* in various guises, whether holy or otherwise, is also on the agenda. The Christ question may even be retro-encountered through a detailed study of Nietzsche. But that's not likely to happen in year 12. However, I have discussed Nietzsche with some Year 12 leavers.

I have met eighteen-year-olds whose capacity for connective thinking along a trajectory has already emerged from within foundational units. A student was thinking about a fellow student's untimely death from cancer. He raised the topic with me via his study of Homer, in the Greek, and Achilles' use of the word Θῦμος (*thumos*), with its translation as life-breath— suggesting the inviolability of Achilles' last *thumos* as it passes with integrity from his mouth. Such a student will have a foundation on which to engage nineteenth-century romanticism or postmodern nihilism, and to ask whether there can be a buoyant vision for humanity in a cosmos where the good do still die young, and if so, what that might be, and whether it can it be embraced. One might make individual studies of Sylvia Plath or of Beckett, and these might do some good. However, if they lead only to a vision of a modern wasteland emerging in the twentieth century, and to nothing more, then the resulting map may not be adequately sign-posted or to scale.

In some ways, I can understand the contemporary University of Sydney trying to market itself with the slogans that read: *unlearn truth, unlearn medicine, unlearn career path, unlearn criminal, a lesson in unlearning, unlearn classroom, unlearn drought, unlearn threat* and *unlearn love*. It is clear that the eighteen-year-old will encounter much that is new at University. But I am not sure that 'unlearn' is the best term to use retrospectively of the journey that the university bounds. One could market by just omitting the prefix *un*.

Critical thinking at University has always involved a close and serious study of the ways in which genuine knowledge has been achieved in the human past. Few will have believed that the modern scientist, researcher or scholar in any field assumes that we know already all that needs to be, or can be, known. Few if any will think that their aim is to defend truth and knowledge from advancement or obsolescence by placing it in the chiller of set-thought, and turning down the dial to zero degrees Kelvin. One must however acknowledge the new media of the IT and AI realms, and contemplate MOOCs and on-line learning, and the desire to relegate books from their prominent place.[19] Whether all this is part of the actuarialisation and commodification of learning, of falsely linking all learning to economic outcomes or wealth creation, remains to be seen, since we all may be too close to it to evaluate it.[20]

University learning, when freed from dogmatisms, has always been a key promoter of critical thinking, and the study of how the new is discovered and validated. For decades, students studied Popper, Lakatos, Kuhn and Feyerabend, and learned how 'phlogiston' became redundant, along with its equivalents in other fields. An hypothesis of demons is no longer needed to diagnose or treat epilepsy. Some 'soulless and possessed' people, dismissed by Luther, are now recognised as a problematic phenotype. It is now commonplace to know that empirical observation will be theory-laden to some real extent, and that testing and disproving are essential to the task of finding the better approximation to the truth of the matter. Perhaps it should just be said plainly that truth is more than a *method* of critical scepticism, and that it may also be a discovered content that can be life-changing, or that can found a newer and better world—with a real cure for cancers, or a capacity to slow and even halt aging by rejuvenating *telomeres*, or the study of genetics in embryology, or indeed the study of Homer in the original language, or the Letters of St Paul, in a milieu where one finds oneself thinking in *koine* and not sixteenth-century English. Nano science is not simply pursued as a method, but as a way to new content and truths.

Deconstructing knowledge or deconstructing learning might have methodological merit. *Reconstruction*, and closer discernment of truths will be as valuable; just as a re-mythologisation might supplant the demythologisations of those theologies dominant in the mid twentieth century.

Some questions put to the student leaving secondary school invite genuine synthetic capacities. I think of the colourful question that I have tried: "Do you think Australian society is like a secular ornament on a religious tree, or, is Christianity in Australia a religious ornament on a secular tree?" The question can be answered in a simple manner, or with more complexity. It illustrates the role of the schematic linking of units of knowledge with the background structures which create coherence across individual topics. To sharpen the question and answer it, one would need precise legal and historical and theological and philosophical knowledge about a Federated Australia, knowledge dating back into British history and our Federal and Colonial past. A sense of 'the vibe' will only take us so far.

I sometimes think that Year 12 students have been given a handful of pieces of a thousand or a ten thousand-piece jigsaw puzzle, pieces picked ran-

---

[19] Courses of learning freely available on the Internet.
[20] One has to read Ha-Joon Chang, *23 things they don't tell you about capitalism* (London: Allen Lane, 2010).

domly from a scattered pile. Sometimes the pieces may belong to a different puzzle picture. But how are they to be re-assembled into a larger coherency. Can the student ever know from which larger picture the scattered pieces have come?

It might be that in Year 12 one poet has been studied, and that might mean as few as three to five poems. The poet might be 'famous' locally, but otherwise unknown. Some have studied none. Within the Modern History syllabus, in the domain headed 'personality', one individual will have been chosen for detailed study. It is interesting to talk with lots of young people who have all made a study of Albert Speer. Perhaps the catchment of schools for my intake is too limited, and in fairness, one cannot study properly all twenty-seven people named as a 'personality'. Perhaps in the end, it is very much in the spirit of the age to describe these figures as personalities. 'Personality' used to be found in reference to 'show business' which at its more entrepreneurial and studio-driven, invented personalities and their fame, as part of a complex psycho-marketing of desire and fantasy to the paying cinema goer. From being a sub-set of character, personality has become the principal category—without remark by the student.

Having the fiftieth discussion with candidates about Albert Speer is a bit like the fiftieth discussion with someone about Mary Shelley's *Frankenstein,* or perhaps that well-worn film *Blade Runner*. Some students choose Ho Chi Minh, or even more rarely Douglas McArthur. I have met a few who chose Che Guevara. I never met a year 12 student who had made a study of Winston Churchill, or could think why he might have been on the list of twenty-seven names. I never met anyone who chose Chifley, Evatt or Menzies, though each is on the list. I add that some capacity to evaluate and distinguish between human types is needed, lest one think that all twenty-seven were western liberals, some being dressed in exotic costume.

It could be possible, but very challenging, to add Franco to the list. A trajectory- or bridging-approach could just manage that, though the task of studying him would be as challenging as a study of the generals of the South in the American Civil War, or of Cecil Rhodes.

I am pondering the puzzle of how one connects 'the wandering islands' at this point, and how one can place anything like a canonical burden on the one individual chosen for detailed study, in what might well be the one and only formal study of history that a student may undertake in the course of a lifetime. Clearly, the rest of a course will address at least some of that. Will knowing a bit about Albert Speer carry the burden of giving to the student the experience of what it is like to study an individual *historically*, that is, in the midst of the at times mysterious and much larger social process that we call history? In the end, of course, we may want to do more for the eighteen-year-olds than send them out into the world armed with a little of Plath, Beckett and Speer as mentors, plus some Physics, Chemistry and Mathematics, to be supplemented by the study of Commerce and a few background pieces in 'method', which may not be sufficiently robust in the encounter with the philosophies of others.

Students who select Douglas MacArthur as a 'personality' could discuss policy conflict over the use of atomic weapons in the 1950s during the Korean War. But, mostly, they do not. Very few MacArthur students seem to have heard of General Curtis LeMay, or know much about the technology of the B-29, and its development as the greatest airplane of the age. Very few see a trajectory from there to the Cuba crisis. Few if any students offer a comment on the oddity of Ho Chi Minh imbibing from the European well of Marxism as a source for his nationalist movement.

Great discussions do arise by asking whether Dr Frankenstein did a good thing by abandoning the creation of a female monster, that was to keep company with the male monster he had made. Usually this leads to a discussion of single-sex education, and occasionally to a discussion of *A Vindication of the Rights of Woman,* a foundational text for feminism by Mary Shelley's mother, Mary Wollstonecraft. Major highways linking the islands are well established. It is great to ask young men whether they think *Romeo and Juliet* might be studied differently, if young men and women were in the same seminar for at least part of the teaching week.

Connectivity was seen in conversations about *Blade Runner,* which as a movie was often said to be in a separate realm of discourse from that of the original 1966 story by Philip K. Dick, *Do Androids Dream of Electric Sheep?* Some students were aware of Dick's preoccupation with the possibilities of altered states of consciousness as a result of his using a dental narcotic following work on his teeth. Conversations ensued about the differences between brilliantly imitative but programmed AI, and the reflective self-aware givenness of the human mind. Dick remains one of the interesting 'personalities', to the extent that one follows his 'off-syllabus' life. A bridge to Coleridge and the role of opiates in nineteenth-century pharmaceutical medicine can follow, and one can jump back to Marx at that point.

I have never met a student who was studying the Nobel Prize winner, Winston Churchill. But I can always ask the question why he is not studied, given his historical significance. There is no one right answer to that question. But any thoughtful answer will be useful. The trajectory to Gallipoli also calls out for study.[21]

---

[21] A key text worth studying for its own sake is 'Shall we all Commit Suicide', published in *Nash's Pall Mall Journal* for September 1924, in which Churchill invites the reader to imagine devastating bombs as small as oranges, and wire- or ray-guided weapons of mass destruction. See https://www.winstonchurchill.org/publications/finest-hour/finest-hour-094/shall-we-all-commit-suicide cited 26th October 2017.

It would be a harder task to ask whether there is any kind of criterion by which a student might conclude that the twenty-seven men and women on the list of personalities are, or are not, *interchangeable equivalents*. Is this even possible? Are they all, for instance, variations on the theme of a western liberal intellectual tradition, even when their field of activity is elsewhere? Is the concept or assumption one of a universal or global human type? Or, does the list include examples of men and women impelled by variations of the drive to create utopian societies (whether in this world or beyond), who in their own situation are driven to find the energy to lead and 'transform', or to generate a movement for good or ill—however that might be measured and by whom.

Popper, writing at the end of World War Two, thought it was a special kind of mistake to think that God was revealed in history.[22] He said that for the most part, history was a tale of the crushing and destruction of the ordinary person, vanishing unknown or forgotten. He thought it a kind of blasphemy to assert that God could be revealed in, or as the sum of that domain. This issue does raise the question of moral evaluation within history, or the ambivalence of historical events which involve loss of life. The documentary *The Fog of War* (2003), about the life of Robert S. McNamara, is one key resource that can extend a trajectory from Coventry to Dresden to Hiroshima to Vietnam and beyond.[23]

Tolstoy's experience in the Crimean War informs *War and Peace,* and connects to the Napoleonic war with Russia of 1805. Once one touches Napoleon, one may try to reach forward through Franco-European and Franco-German relationships to 1946, and also try to reach back to the Thirty Years War of 1618-1648. But then one goes a little further, and reaches the question of the Reformation, and of the Papacy, and of the character of the Christian Ecclesia, both in its Catholic and Orthodox forms—and then it is on to 'rats, lice and history', the Black Death, and dynastic wars within Christendom. One sidesteps into another main pathway of war, that between the competing *oikumenes* of Islam and Christianity, and all of a sudden some primary and elementary theology is needed to cope with the 'new' thing of Mohammed.

One might even end up wondering what Jesus could have meant in the Lord's Prayer by asking for God's Kingdom to come. Or, one might detour into Joachim of Fiore, whose metastatic expectations led him to announce that the Age of the Holy Spirit would begin in 1260, and see the withering away of all external forms of authority, supplanted by Spirit-led men and women.

---

[22] He makes this claim in *The Open Society and its Enemies*. See vol. I, pp. 8-10, and vol. II, pp. 271-275.

[23] http://www.npr.org/templates/story/story.php?storyId=106318407 cited 26th September 2017.

One simply has to stop here and note that these considerations are far from the story of the whole world. They omit the Middle East and the East; they make their own centred assumptions; and they are limited in scope and extent. Niall Ferguson's sharp title *Civilization: The West and the Rest* serves a purpose by indicating that five hundred years of global dominance does not equal permanent status in the long-term. Peoples and nations rise and fall through time, and presumed permanence can vanish 'overnight', as it were. His further study *The Great Degeneration: How Institutions Decay and Economies Die* explores that theme.[24] The Chinese Empire was vulnerable in the 1850s, but ascendant in the 2010s, for instance. No 'deep-freeze' view of global history is sustainable. I spent three years in a graduate Divinity program in an ecumenical Christian institution. Between 1976 and 1978 it was as if Islam were asleep, and 'off-radar', and had been so for a very long time.

The following topics might be my life-long project in connectivity, rather than a year 12 curriculum. It is compatible with a comprehensive kind of civic theology that may yet have a simpler and singular form of expression. These are ongoing questions that interest me.

1) Does history have a form or structure or narrative, and what are the candidates?
2) Do specific motifs shape the study of human experience through time, and what are they?
3) If there is such a thing as western civilization, when was it most exemplified, in what form and by what means? How civilized was it?
4) Consider the history of warfare—locally, nationally, imperially, universally. If it has a history, what future might it have?
5) Is the motif of progress helpful?
6) Consider incremental, revolutionary and apocalyptic change in the study of history.
7) Should we exhibit Malthusian angst today?
8) Is there a comprehensive economic narrative?
9) The fact of human mortality, and intimations of immortality.
10) The motif of the Kingdom or Rule of God, and the modalities by which global faiths appropriate forms of that symbolic order.
11) A Messianic age, and the age of the Spirit.
12) The promise and the failures of Empire as an ideal.
13) The Nation as basic.
14) Mimetic Rivalry and Violent Desire.
15) Advocacy and Democracy and the Individual.
16) Incarnation and Image. Competing Revelations.
17) Periodization, Ladder theories and the ranking of Faith Traditions.
18) Cultural Relativism.

---

[24] Niall Ferguson, *Civilization: The West and the Rest* (London: Allen Lane, 2011); *The Great Degeneration: How Institutions Decay and Economies Die* (London: Allen Lane, 2012).

19) Male and Female, and the Construction of Gender.
20) Poetry, Historical Recurrence, Tradition and Innovation. Auden, Eliot and Yeats.

The simpler form behind these lies in the question of the Incarnation. As I began to consider in my thesis, this question invites a tracking from the role of Mary as the *Theotokos* through the meta-rational Resurrection, and into human participation in the gift of the Spirit of Christ. [25] That is the great *symbalo* of the West and East, and of the Christian mission in the world, the contrary to forms of *dia-balo*, of personal and cultural disintegration. Whether faith in an ecclesia that carries this message can be sustained is another question, and one for which history at times speaks like the Sibyl. That is not reducible to a secular curriculum.

This essay has a personal dimension to it. I have recently reduced my personal library by about sixty percent. I conducted the exercise on criteria that became clearer to me as the process went on. Here, in broad terms is what survived, and exemplifies for me the possibility that the wandering islands form a linked archipelago. The working library contains a connective core around the following.

I have holdings in philosophy from Aristotle to the present, with anthologies, histories and individual works of key thinkers. I read Leibniz for pleasure and his genius. I have imbibed Hume's insights about being very careful about what is believable. I read Feuerbach to locate myself amongst images that can still be affirmed. I read Kant to affirm the non-Kantian power in the icon that can help one to traverse safely, if imaginatively, beyond the limits of cognition. I look at Derrida to think of Augustine and the outsiders, and to be pushed towards poetry and humour. I read Eric Voegelin, the greatest twentieth-century synthesiser in the history of ideas, who grasped the necessity of the study of human types. In his sense, not all 'personalities' are friendly. His studies of the totalitarian type are second to none. I have his *New Science of Politics* and refer to his *Order and History*. [26]

I read gender studies from the eighteenth century onwards: Mary Wollstonecraft through Mary Shelley to Simone de Beauvoir, Camille Paglia, Germaine Greer and, locally, Anne Summers. Wollstonecraft said most things first and most things well. She is the fountainhead. One is also always helped to ask, when reading a biblical text, 'Where are the women in this story?'

---

[25] *The God-bearer.*
[26] Eric Voegelin, *The New Science of Politics: An Introduction* (Chicago: University of Chicago Press, 1952); Eric Voegelin, *Order and History*, vols 14-18 of *Collected Works of Eric Voegelin*, 34 vols (Columbia, MO: University of Missouri Press, 1995-2006). The five volumes of *Order and History* were originally published between 1956 and 1987.

I read via official documents (Catechism. Encyclicals, Papal Letters such as *Salvifici Doloris*, and exemplary representatives). I read von Balthasar on Lay and Clerical Types. I prefer J.H. Newman as a great synthetic and connective thinker from the nineteenth century, and his Oratory has programmatic potential still. That derives from the great and little known sixteenth-century figure St Philip Neri, whose personal synthesis of intellect and faith remains to my mind of greater significance than the teaching of Martin Luther, though without the visible consequence. Materials on Henry VIII and the Tudors and Stuarts got fairly heavily culled, but remain vital for an understanding of Englishness. I hold the Anglican *Book of Homilies* from the sixteenth century, and also read Foxe's *Book of Martyrs* in a sixteenth century edition, when I can get access to it.

I value highly the insights of René Girard, and keep and use his texts, both for an anthropologically informed reading of the New Testament and of surrounding texts, and for insights into modern European history, and its collapse into major conflict at key points. I am interested in Girard's working theory of apocalypse from below and via a critique of von Clausewitz's *On War*. Norman Davies' *Europe*, S.S. Montefiore's, *Jerusalem: The Biography*, Diarmaid McCulloch's *The Reformation: A History*, and Eamon Duffy's *The Stripping of the Altars*—these are among the keep shelves.[27]

I have retained commentaries on key books of the New Testament, preferencing those on St Mark, the major letters of St Paul, and Matthew and Luke's first two chapters, which comprise what are sometimes called the 'infancy narratives'. Josephus is very helpful. I like the works of G. Theissen, including the historical novel *The Shadow of the Galilean*[28]. One cannot ignore Bultmann, but for all his brilliance on the first century, he is a man from a difficult time and place in the mid twentieth century, whose vast historical knowledge of detail became detached from his theological synthesis. He is far more sceptical than David Hume.

I keep *The Norton Anthology of Theory and Criticism*, and *The Norton Anthology of World Religions*.[29] This pair of two volume works is a micro-library of excellence in itself. I again locate the works of Eric Voegelin here, beginning with his *New Science of Politics*, but including his unique and under-used *Order and*

---

[27] Norman Davies, *Europe: A History* (Oxford: Oxford University Press, 1996); Simon Sebag Montefiore, *Jerusalem: The Biography* (London: Weidenfeld and Nicolson, 2011); Diarmaid McCulloch, *The Reformation: A History* (New York: Viking Penguin, 2004); Eamon Duffy, *The Stripping of the Altars* (New Haven: Yale University Press, 1992).

[28] Gerd Theissen, *The Shadow of the Galilean*, tr. John Bowden (Minneapolis, MN: Fortress Press, 1987).

[29] *The Norton Anthology of Theory and Criticism*, 2nd edn (New York: W.W. Norton & Co., Inc., 2010); *The Norton Anthology of World Religions*, ed. Jack Miles et al., 2 vols (New York: W.W. Norton & Co., Inc., 2014).

History, which I would like (with Tolstoy's cautionary short story in mind) to own.

I stress the high value of the complete works of Elie Kedouri, beginning with his *Nationalism*.[30] He remains one of the greater twentieth-century minds whose 'connective' knowledge of the Middle East and of European history endures, and his work cannot be left on the shelf. It may seem a strange addition, but I think the writings of the Nobel Prize Winner Winston Churchill belong here, and decisions not to read him may be based on unexamined assumptions or prejudice. England is too often the 'familiar forgotten' in our studies.

I preference English Language poetry from Great Britain and North America, with an emphasis on the twentieth century, with Eliot, Auden, Yeats and Spender, and Anthologies. I tend to read poets from World War One to the present. Within Australian poetry I preference Murray, Hart, Harwood, Wright, Kinsella, McAuley, Hewitt and Anthologies.

Poetry, contrary to Hope's comment in *The Wandering Isles*, can be, at its best, the great connector, the creator of linked archipelagos, peninsulas and continents. Auden's 'The Shield of Achilles' is one such brilliant example, and it is where the mind finds its neighbour.

---

[30] Elie Kedouri, *Nationalism*, 2nd edn rev. (London, Hutchinson University Library, 1960).

Contributors

Christopher Allen

Christopher Allen is an art critic and historian who graduated from the University of Sydney, has worked at the Collège de France in Paris, and the National Art School, and is currently Senior Master in Academic Extension at Sydney Grammar School. He is the author of *Art in Australia from Colonisation to Postmodernism*, *French Painting in the Golden Age*, and several other books. His most recent, *Jeffrey Smart: Unpublished Paintings 1940-2007* was published in April 2008. He was art critic of the *Financial Review* from 2005-2008 and since 2008 has been national art critic for *The Australian*.

Jeremy Bell

Jeremy Bell completed a B.A. and an M.Phil. at the University of Sydney. In 2006 he was awarded a General Sir John Monash Award to support his doctoral studies with the Committee on Social Thought at the University of Chicago. In 2015 he defended his dissertation on Elizabeth Anscombe's philosophy of mind. In the same year he began teaching at Campion College, Sydney, where he now lectures in philosophy, theology, history and literature.

Chris Berg

Chris Berg is a Senior Research Fellow at the RMIT Blockchain Innovation Hub, a Senior Fellow with the Institute of Public Affairs, and an Academic Fellow with the Australian Taxpayers' Alliance. Dr Berg is one of Australia's most prominent voices for free markets and individual liberty, and a leading authority on over-regulation, economic freedom and civil liberties. He is the author of six books including *The Libertarian Alternative*, *In Defence of Freedom of Speech: From Ancient Greece to Andrew Bolt*, and *Against Public Broadcasting: Why we Should Privatise the ABC and How to Do It*.

David Brooks

David Brooks B.A., B.Phil. is a graduate of the Universities of London and Oxford. At Oxford he specialised in English literature of the Augustan period. He has taught at the University of Dundee and the University of Sydney. He is editor of *Lyrics & Satires of John Wilmot, Earl of Rochester* and co-editor of *Running Wild: Essays, Fictions and Memoirs Presented to Michael Wilding*. His interests are in Renaissance and Augustan English literature, and in literary and critical theory. He has published on Shakespeare, Dryden, Rochester, Defoe, and I. A. Richards, on Marxian critical theory and aesthetics, and on issues in literary hermeneutics. He recently contributed an essay on Shakespeare's *Coriolanus* to *The Free Mind: Essays and Poems in Honour of Barry Spurr*. He is now retired and an independent scholar.

Bella d'Abrera

Bella d'Abrera is the Director of the *Foundations of Western Civilisation Program* at the Institute of Public Affairs. She has a BA in History and Spanish from Monash University, an MA in Spanish from the University of St Andrews and a PhD in History from the University of Cambridge. She is the author of a number of academic works such as *The Tribunal of Zaragoza and Crypto-Judaism, 1484-1515* (2009), which was based on an examination of 120 court trials from the Inquisition, and the charges levelled against Spain's *conversos* or Christians of Jewish descent. She has also authored a number of books on the English Reformation. She specialises in education and skills, faith and society and culture, ideas and liberty and Western Civilisation. Dr d'Abrera appears frequently in the media and is a regular contributor to *The Australian*, *The Daily Telegraph*, *The Herald Sun* and *The Spectator Australia*. She is passionate about educating young Australians in the legacy of Western Civilisation, its values and its institutions.

David Daintree

David Daintree AM KHS was born in Sydney. He is a graduate of the universities of New England, Cambridge and Tasmania. He was Senior Classics Master at St Peter's College Adelaide, Principal of Jane Franklin Hall (University of Tasmania), Rector of St John's College (University of Sydney) and President of Campion College Australia. He served as a Student Ombudsman in the University of Tasmania. He has been a visiting professor at the Universities of Siena and Venice, and at St John's College in the University of Manitoba. He regularly teaches intensive short courses in Latin, with a particular focus on literature of the late antique and medieval periods. He is currently Director of the Christopher Dawson Centre for Cultural Studies in Hobart.

Kevin Donnelly

Kevin Donnelly AM (BA, DipEd, MEd, PhD) is a Senior Research Fellow at the Australian Catholic University and Director of Education Standards Institute. Kevin is one of Australia's leading conservative education commentators and has written extensively on the importance of a liberal education and the significance of Western civilisation and Australia's Judeo-Christian heritage and on-going traditions. Books published include *Why our Schools are Failing, Dumbing Down* and *The Culture of Freedom*. Kevin co-chaired the 2014 review of the Australian National Curriculum and in 2016 he was made a Member of the Order of Australia for services to the school curriculum.

James Franklin

James Franklin is Professor in the School of Mathematics and Statistics at the University of New South Wales. He is the author of *Corrupting the Youth: A History of Philosophy in Australia; The Science of Conjecture; What Science Knows; An Aristotelian Realist Philosophy of Mathematics,* and other books. As editor of the *Journal of the Australian Catholic Historical Society* he has worked to preserve the Catholic heritage of Australia. He has opposed postmodernist currents in academia and argued that science faculties have better defended the quest for truth than humanities faculties.

David Furse-Roberts

David Furse-Roberts is a Research Fellow at the Menzies Research Centre where he has recently edited *Menzies: The Forgotten Speeches*. He is also editor of a collection of speeches by John Howard, *Howard: The Art of Persuasion: Selected Speeches 1995-2016* (2018). David holds a PhD from the University of New South Wales and the University of Edinburgh where he completed his dissertation on humanitarian social reform in Victorian Britain. He has published articles in publications such as *Quadrant* and *Spectator* and has presented conference papers in Australia, the United Kingdom and the United States.

Richard Gill

Richard Gill AO, founding Music Director and Conductor Emeritus of Victorian Opera, is one of Australia's most admired conductors and music educators. He has been Artistic Director of the Education Program for the Sydney Symphony Orchestra, Artistic Director of OzOpera, Artistic Director and Chief Conductor of the Canberra Symphony Orchestra, and Artistic Advisor for the Musica Viva Education program. He is the Founder and Director of the National Music Teacher Mentoring Program, Music Director of the Sydney Chamber Choir, and the inaugural *King & Wood Mallesons Conservatorium Chair in Music Education* at the Conservatorium High School, Sydney.

Simon Haines

Simon Haines is CEO of the Ramsay Centre for Western Civilisation in Sydney. He is also Professor of English at The Chinese University of Hong Kong and a founding Fellow of the Hong Kong Academy of the Humanities. He is the author or editor of five books including the prizewinning *Reader in European Romanticism* and *Poetry and Philosophy from Homer to Rousseau*, as well as articles, book chapters and papers on subjects including Shakespeare and recognition, Romantic poetry, the modern self, and time in philosophy and art. He is co-editor with Alexa Alice Joubin and Tom Bishop of *The Shakespearean International Yearbook 17: Shakespeare and Value* (2018).

Ivan Francis Head

Ivan Head studied Philosophy at the University of Western Australia and at Melbourne University, and Divinity with the Melbourne College of Divinity. He completed a PhD at Glasgow entitled *How Miraculous Can We Consider Jesus To Have Been? A Study in the History of Interpretation*. At the end of 2017 he retired from St Paul's College in the University of Sydney after twenty-three years as Warden. A second book of poetry *The Magpie Sermons: Poems 2005-2017* was published recently. He has published articles on the authorship and date and place of Mark's Gospel, on violence and the reign of Henry VIII, on St Phillip Neri as the alternative to Luther's reform, on the use of Girardian theory to gain insight into post-Napoleonic Europe, and on the implications of asking whether embryos may enter into resurrection life.

Blaise Joseph

Blaise Joseph is an Education Policy Analyst at The Centre for Independent Studies in Sydney. He has been specialising in policy relating to education funding in Australia. He is author of the research reports *The Fantasy of Gonski Funding: The Ongoing Battle Over School Spending* and *Getting the Most Out of Gonski 2.0: The Evidence Base for School Investments*. He completed a Bachelor of Commerce, with a Co-op Scholarship, and a Master of Teaching from the University of New South Wales. He has had experience in both government and private sectors. Blaise is also a former secondary school teacher.

Natalie Kennedy

Natalie Kennedy is the Head of English and Languages Senior School at Northside Christian College where she has been teaching since 2003. She is currently studying her Master of Education at Christian Heritage College, where she intends to specialise in English literature and rhetoric. Natalie has a passion for Shakespeare, poetry, classic literature and vocabulary building. Her favourite pastime is finding antique books that teach explicit instruction about composition and the integration of textual control with clarity of thinking. One of her favourite teaching units involves exploring the dystopian genre of films and novels. She feels that great poems, plays, books and films have the potential to transform the way we see ourselves and the world. Being an English teacher for her is a powerful privilege which she never takes for granted.

Sarah Lawrence

Sarah Lawrence studied Latin and Ancient History at the University of New England before completing a PhD at the University of Sydney. After some years teaching in the secondary school system, Sarah was appointed as the Charles Tesoriero Lecturer in Latin at the University of New England. Sarah is a passionate teacher and researcher with particular interests in Valerius Maximus, Seneca the Elder and the question of 'race' in the Roman world.

Matthew Lesh

Matthew Lesh is a Research Fellow at the Institute of Public Affairs. He has been published extensively in the Australian media, and spoken on radio and television, about intellectual freedom at Australia's universities. In 2016, he completed Australia's first Free Speech on Campus audit, which assessed university policies and actions. Matthew holds a Bachelor of Arts (Degree with Honours), from the University of Melbourne, and an MSc in Public Policy and Administration from the London School of Economics. Before joining the IPA, he worked for state and federal parliamentarians and in digital communications, as well as founding a mobile application development start-up. He is the author of *Democracy in Divided Australia* (2018).

Greg Melleuish

Greg Melleuish is Professor of Occidental Studies in the School of Humanities and Social Inquiry at the University of Wollongong where he teaches Ancient History, Political Theory and Australian Politics. In 2014 he did a review of the History section of the Australian National Curriculum. He has written widely on a range of areas including education, history of political ideas and philosophy of history. His most recent book is *Despotic State or Free Individual*.

Catherine A. Runcie

Catherine A. Runcie was a Senior Lecturer in English at the University of Sydney from 1969 to 2004, and previously taught at the University of Toronto. Her teaching and research have been in fields of 19th century literature and thought, literary theory, film adaptation and aesthetics. She was Foundation President of The Sydney Society of Literature and Aesthetics (1990-1998) and Co-Foundation Editor of the journal *Literature & Aesthetics* (1990-1998). She was a visiting scholar at the Shanghai Institute of Foreign Languages in 1981, where she lectured on literary theory and the relation of literature and art in cross-cultural movements, and the Xi'an Institute of Foreign Languages in 1993, where she lectured on modernism. She was co-editor of the Festschrift *Matters of the Mind. Poems, Essays and Interviews in Honour of Leonie Kramer* (2001). She was editor of the Festschrift *The Free Mind. Essays and Poems in Honour of Barry Spurr* (2016).

Karl Schmude

Karl Schmude has combined a long career in librarianship and universities with freelance writing for Australian and international journals on subjects of religion and culture. He is the author of various booklets, including a biographical study of the historian Christopher Dawson (2014). He served as University Librarian at the University of New England from 1984 to 2000, and was subsequently a co-founder of Australia's first liberal arts institution of higher education, Campion College Australia.

Steven Schwartz

Steven Schwartz AM has been the Chairman of the Board of the Australian Curriculum, Assessment and Reporting Authority (ACARA), a Senior Fellow of the Centre for Independent Studies, and an Honorary Fellow of The University of Melbourne. He is the former Vice-Chancellor of three universities: Macquarie (Sydney), Brunel (London) and Murdoch (Perth). Emeritus Professor Schwartz is the author of 13 books and numerous articles on education, psychology and health and presently continues as a Senior Fellow with the CIS and Honorary Senior Fellow at the University of Melbourne.

Barry Spurr

Barry Spurr was a member of the English Department at Sydney University for forty years and was Australia's first Professor of Poetry and Poetics. He is the author of numerous books and articles, and is an authority on the life and work of T.S. Eliot. He was the Inaugural University of Sydney Fellow in English at Sydney Grammar School, and was elected a Fellow of the Australian College of Educators in 2007 "in recognition of an outstanding contribution to education". A Festschrift, *The Free Mind: Essays and Poems in Honour of Barry Spurr* was published in 2016.

Sarah C. Williams

Sarah Williams BA, MA, DPhil (Oxford) is a specialist in the field of nineteenth- and twentieth-century cultural history. She trained as an historian at the University of Oxford, where she subsequently taught as Fellow and Tutor in Modern History at Harris Manchester College, Lecturer at Trinity College and Praelector at Lincoln College. In 2005 Dr Williams moved with her family to Vancouver, Canada, where she is Research Professor in the History of Christianity at Regent College. Her research interests lie in cultural history, historical theory and methodology, the relationship between popular religion and political philosophy, pedagogy and the history of gender and sexuality.

Index

1

1984   49, 234

A

A Tale of Two Cities   235
A Vindication of the Rights of Woman   275
abolition of slavery   50
Aboriginal literacy   260
acculturation   96
Acemoglu, Daron   94
Ackerman, G.K.   233
acquiescence   7
ad hominem   132
Adler, Mortimer   178, 230
aesthetic sensibility   163, 167
aesthetics   203–4, 207, 209
agonistic   13
Amazon   265
Ambrose   59
American New Criticism   204
American Revolution   269
amour courtois   49
analytic philosophy   181–82
Anders, George   35
Angelicum Academy   40
anomie   5
Apocalypse Now   196
Apple   35
Apple, Michael W.   61
appreciation   205–6, 208–10, 212, 215–16, 219, 224–28
appropriate educational goals   258
architecture   52, 163
Aristotle   29, 59, 75, 152, 182, 186, 187
Armidale High School   247, 263
Arnold, Matthew   33, 55, 56, 58, 70, 228
art
   as a way of thinking   165, 168
   as concrete form   165
   as playtime   163–64, 166
   British tradition   163
   in school curriculum   163–70
   predating rational use of language   165
art academies   164, 166
art history   163, 164, 169, 170
artificial intelligence   265
arts faculties
   liberal arts   24, 37, 52
astronomy   27, 35, 152
Auden, W.H.   3, 268
Austen, Jane   47, 222
Australian Association for the Teaching of English (AATE)   65
Australian Broadcasting Corporation (ABC)   132
Australian Council of Deans of Education (ACDE)   68
Australian Curriculum, Assessment and Reporting Authority (ACARA)   66, 72
Australian Historical Association (AHA)   91, 95
Australian Human Rights Centre   82
Australian Human Rights Commission   134
Australian Imperial Force (AIF)   270
Australian Teachers' Federation   62
Australian Tertiary Admission Rank (ATAR)   76, 200, 257, 264
Australian Youth Orchestra   176
authoritarian   186, 190

B

Bacon, Francis   4, 6
Baker, Lee   255

Ball, Robert	254, 255, 258, 262
Banpo	1
Barcan, Alan	54, 59–60
Barrett, Lisa	83
Barrett, Margaret	177
Barrie, Stephen	59
Battles, Matthew	43
Baudrillard, Jean	64
Bawer, Bruce	190
Beard, Mary	250
Benedikt, Allison	131, 136, 139
Bennett, Alan	131
Beowulf	213
Berlin, Isaiah	265, 266
Bernard of Chartres	43
Bessant, Bob	108, 114
Bible	29–30
Bill of Rights	52
Bishop Berkeley	48
Bishop, Elizabeth	192
Blackadder	263
Blackburn Report	73
Blade Runner	274–75
Bloom, Allan	59–60
Bond University	37
Bond, Sarah	250
Bourdieu, Pierre	61
Bowles, Samuel	61
Boyle, Robert	207
Bradbury, Ray	193
Bradley, A.C.	225
Bradley, Joseph	174
Bricmont, Jean	13, 155
British History Subjects	98
Brooklyn College	259
Brotherhood, Recreation and Outreach Society (BroSoc)	83
Brueggemann, Walter	239
Bruner, Jerome S.	67, 70
Bultmann, Rudolf	269, 279
Burnard, Trevor	95

C

Cailloux, Floyd A.	254
Caliban	4–5, 6–8, 199, 242
Calvino, Italo	250
Campion College	29, 32, 41–42
Canberra University College	108
canon	
in curricula	29–30, 91, 95, 224
Canterbury Tales	213
capitalism	10–11, 48, 59, 61, 63, 78, 100
Caplan, Bryan	38
Caravaggio	169
Carr, Andrew	100
Cartledge, Paul	251
causality	158
censorship	78, 85, 87–88, 222
Centre for Hellenic Studies	250
change the date campaign	99
charter schools	144, 146–47
Chesterton, G.K.	25, 30
Chifley, Ben	109, 119
child-centred learning	55, 66–70
Christianity	34–35, 59, 240–42
Churchill, Winston	8, 91, 274
Cicero	59
cinematography	168
citizenship	32–33, 103, 106, 114–15
civilisation	
modern	104
Clark, Anna	66
Clark, Gregory	92
classical beauty	250
Classical Greek	41, 256
classical liberal	80, 89
Cleese, John	50
close reading	178–81, 185–87
cloud	265
Coase, Ronald	93
codes	203
cognition	205, 211, 221, 224
Coleridge, Samuel Taylor	228
Collins, Cherry	67
Colombo Plan	111
colonialism	48, 60, 86
colonisation	196
Committee on Social Thought	179
common human interest	210, 211–14, 221–24, 227
common human nature	210, 211, 221–24, 227–28
common place book	231, 233, 237
common pursuit of true judgment	224
Commons, John R.	93
competency based learning	71
conspicuous consumption	164

Constant, Benjamin 126
constructivism 69
consumerism 49, 239, 243
Coriolanus 225
cosmion 265
criminology 25
criticism 205–6
Crittenden, Brian 54, 64
Crotty, Martin 95
crucial aspects of English studies 190
cultural amnesia 40, 46
cultural relativism 15, 64, 222
cultural studies 50, 196, 200

D

Dante 30, 41, 47
David, Paul A. 94
Davidson, Donald 183
Davies, Norman 279
Dawkins, Richard 30
Dawson, Christopher 33–35, 46
de Beauvoir, Simone 278
de Lubac, Henri 241
de Tocqueville, Alexis 126
Deakin, Alfred 102
decadence 49–50
decentralising school funding 143
deconstruction and reconstruction of knowledge 273
deductive proof 149–51
Deleuze, Gilles 5, 15, 155
dementia and music 175
democracy 47, 48, 50, 79, 93, 107, 119, 126
democratisation of education 259
demythologisation 269, 273
Department of Education (Victoria) 58, 69
Derrida, Jacques 5, 15, 64, 278
Descartes, René 184, 188
diachronicity 268
Dick, Philip K. 275
Dickens, Charles 213, 235
digital natives 55, 70
Dilthey, Wilhelm 215, 217
diminishing marginal to school spending 141–42
discipulus 120

disinterestedness 208–12, 223–25, 226–28
dispossession 99
diversity
   students 251, 259
diversity and multiculturalism 251
Do Androids Dream of Electric Sheep? 275
Dodgson, Charles Lutwidge (Lewis Carroll) 154
Donne, John 192
Dr Frankenstein 275
drawing
   as a complex intellectual operation 165, 167
   as a foundational subject 167
   as experiential reality 167
Drummond, Henry 102
Dryden, John 213
Duffy, Eamon 279
Dutch golden age *(kunstliefhebber)* 164
Dutschke, Rudi 59
Dylan, Bob 238
dystopian vision 234

E

educational hub in Asia 111
egalitarianism in schooling philosophy 135–36
Eisner, Michael 36
Eliot, T.S. 57, 70, 75, 228, 268
elite schools 132
elitism in education 247–58, 261–63
Ellsworth, J.D. 254–55, 258, 262
endemic presentism 238, 242, 245
endogenous critics 48–49
Engels, Friedrich 61
Englishness 279
Enlightenment 11, 47, 55, 76, 77, 79, 98, 106, 269
entertainment 213–14
epistemology 215–16
equality and inequality 183–85
equality of opportunity 134
Ernest, Paul 156
Erskine, John 178
ethics 209
Euclid 150, 153

Euripides	74
evaluation	220
Evergreen State College	84
evil	28, 49, 50
exogenous critics	48
export income	44
Extra-textual information	179

F

facilitators	55, 70
faith	34, 35, 42
falsehood	3, 4, 7, 10
Far Brook Elementary School	249
Farrago	86
Federation University	98
Ferguson, Niall	97, 277
fetishised art	164
Feuerbach, Andreas	278
Feyerabend, Paul	273
finitude	240, 243, 244
Finkel, Alan	6
Finn, B.	72
First Fleet	99
flexibility of enquiry	45
Flinders University	110
Forgotten People broadcast	100
formality in art	210
Forsyth, Hannah	54
Foucault, Michel	5, 15, 64
France, Anatole	21
Frankenstein	274
Frankfurt School	59
Freire, Paulo	61, 65
French Revolution	98
Fromchuck, Arlene R.	259
Fukuyama, Francis	50
Furedi, Frank	64

G

Galileo	153
Galinsky, Karl	254
gender categories	240
gender studies	40, 86, 97, 278
Genesis	179
genocidal imperialism	48
geography	35

geometry	27, 35, 149, 152
Gettier, Edmund	188
Gibbons, James Anthony	58
Gillard, Julia	101
Gintis, Herbert	61
Giotto	169
Girard, René	268, 279
globalisation	16, 35, 239
Gödel's Theorem	12
Goethe	47, 48
Gonski, David	136
Good to Great Schools	177
Google	229, 265
Google Scholar	156
Google Translate	158
Gorgias of Leontini	154
Gove, Michael	59
grammar	35, 121, 166, 218, 258, 260
Gramsci, Antonio	59, 61
grand narrative	11, 13, 66, 268, 270
Grant, Stan	200
Great Books	29, 40, 178, 179
Greer, Germaine	278
Gregorian, Vartan	45
Grenville College	102
Grey, Carmody	39
Grice, Paul	183
Gross, Paul R.	156
Group of Eight	88
Guattari, Félix	16
Guevara, Che	274
Gulliver's Travels	213

H

Haidt, Jonathan	83
Haines, Simon	195
Hamlet	212
Hannan, Bill	63
Heart of Darkness	196
Heath, John	253, 257, 262
Hegel, Georg Wilhelm Friedrich	11, 50
hermeneutic circle	218, 219
hermeneutics	215
Heterodox Academy	90
Higher School Certificate (NSW)	128, 256
Hippocrates of Chios	149
Hirsch Jr, E.D.	58, 73
historical consciousness	238

History as a discipline	245
history gap	239
history of ideas	179, 226, 278
history teaching	40, 41, 66, 92, 96
Ho Chi Minh	274
Holiday, Ryan	231
Holt, John	68
Homer	29, 47, 223, 251, 272
Hope, A.D.	264
Howard, John	77, 117
Howe, Daniel Walker	254
Hu Zhuanglin	3, 5
Hughes, Billy	119
human plasticity	120–21, 123, 126
humanism	11, 16, 34, 80, 105, 227
Humboldt	122
Hume, David	12, 188, 267, 278, 279
Humffray Street State School	102
Hutchins, Robert	178

I

IBM	26
identity formation	239
identity politics	4, 9, 25, 78, 83, 87, 131
Identity politics	76, 80
ideology	49, 61, 78, 79, 154, 198, 204, 226, 253, 267
idols	4
imagination	212, 215, 217, 219, 222
Imagination	211
immersive attention	245
Incarnation	241, 278
Inclusivity	257
indoctrination	74, 81, 189, 200
Industrial Revolution	98, 99
industrialism	10
Infancy Narratives	268
Institute of Public Affairs	82, 87, 92
institutional economics	93
integrity	208, 214
International Baccalaureate	264
intersectionality	80
intuition	209, 219–21, 224
intuitive apprehension	206, 212, 224
Iris Project	260, 262
Isaiah	240

J

Janoff, Ron	261
Jerome, Jerome K.	102
Joachim of Fiore	268, 276
Jobs, Steve	35
Johnson, Samuel	48, 228
Jones, Barry	26
Jones, Benjamin	100
Jones, David Albert	59

K

Kagan, Donald	252, 261
Kates, Gary	253
Keats, John	232
Kedouri, Elie	280
Kemp, David	106
Kimball, Roger	59
kindergarten teacher	172–74
King Jr, Martin Luther	80, 200
King Lear	214, 223
Kirner, Joan	62
Kleiser, Grenville	234
Knowles, David	40
Kramer, Leonie	107
Kubrick, Stanley	22
Kuhn, Thomas	273

L

La Trobe University	110
La Trobe University Student Union	86
Lacan, Jacques	5, 15
Lakatos, Imre	273
language games	11–15
language immersion	261
Latin	
English literacy	260
Lawler, Peter Augustine	32
Leavis, F.R.	204, 228
LeMay, Curtis	275
Leviathan	183, 185
Levine, Molly	256
Levitt, Norman	156
Lewis, C.S.	42
liberal arts	27, 29, 32–46, 52, 178, 194, 287

liberal humanism	80, 227
Liberal Party	84, 101, 114
liberalism	17, 101, 106, 107, 117
libertarian	89, 137
literary history	226
Little Dorrit	235
living Latin	261
Livingstone, Richard	105
Locke, John	106, 207
logic	27, 52, 209
London School of Economics	85
London, Jack	266
Lord Acton	244
LSE Student Union	85
Lucretius	30, 181
Lukianoff, Greg	83
Luria, A.D.	125
Luther, Martin	279
Lyotard, Jean-François	10–18, 64

M

Macintyre, Stuart	66
Macquarie University	110
Magna Carta	66
mandated thinking	7
Manent, Pierre	123
marginalia	230
Marks, Gary	64
Marx, Karl	78
Marxism	15, 17
master theme	268
mathematical irrationalists	155
mathematical sciences and sciences of complexity	156
Mayer, E.	72
McArthur, Douglas	274
McCulloch, Diarmaid	279
McNamara, Robert S.	276
Melleuish, Greg	66, 102, 107, 117
metaphysics	207
Methodist Review	233
Middle Ages	27, 34, 98, 152, 201
Middlebury College	84
Mill, John Stuart	77, 123, 186
Millar, Carly	91, 95
Milton, John	30, 192, 197
Mirabella, Sophie	84
misogyny	49, 60

Mission Australia	86
Mitchell Institute	71
modernity	10, 27, 34, 268
Monash Student Association	88
Monash University	110
Monsarrat, Nicholas	266
Montaigne, Michel	184
Montefiore, S.S.	279
Montgomery, Lucy Maud	232
Murray Committee	101, 109
Murray, Charles	84
Murray, David	36
Murray, Keith	109
Murray, Les	199
music	35, 52, 58, 152, 163, 166
music teachers	175, 177
Myth of Er	186

N

NAPLAN (National Assessment Program—Literacy and Numeracy)	133, 139
National Music Teacher Mentoring Program (NMTMP)	176
National Union of Students	81, 82
natural sciences	202, 209, 219, 221, 225
negative messiah	268
Neil, A.S.	68
new sociology of education movement	55, 59
New Zealand Curriculum Framework	68
Newman, John Henry	55, 265, 279
Nietzsche, Friedrich	181
Norsworthy, Naomi	229
North, Douglass	93
Notre Dame University	98
Novum Organum	4

O

O'Connell, Mark	230
Oakeshott, M.	56
Obama, Barack	200
objective equality	134
objectivity of beauty	206, 208
Odyssey	223
Olson, Mancur	93

On the Sea	232
Organization for Economic Cooperation and Development (OECD)	141–44
originality	33, 122
Orwell, George	234
Othello	211

P

Paglia, Camille	278
Paradise Lost	192
Parmenides of Elea	149
Parthenon	47, 149
Pater, Walter	202–5
patience in teaching	244
patriarchy	7, 199
Peel, Mark	66, 91, 95–97
Pera, Marcello	63
perceptions of time	238, 242
personalised learning	55, 69
Phillip, Arthur	99
physics	6
Pinker, Stephen	135
Planck, Max	48
Plath, Sylvia	272
Plato	29, 47, 59, 75, 186–88
Plotinus	122
Plowden Report	68
Plummer, George	174
Poe, Edgar Allan	210
political correctness	17
Pope Francis	240
Pope, Alexander	171, 192
Popper, Karl	273, 276
positivism	11, 202–3
Postman, Neil	39, 54, 56
postmodern mindset	238
postmodern nihilism	272
postmodern self	240
postmodernity	9, 244
power relationships	64, 74, 80
prepositional phrasing	235
Programme for International Student Assessment (PISA)	141
proportional allocation	137
proportionality	208, 214
public debate	78, 106, 119, 120, 129
pure learning	101, 103, 108, 111, 117

Q

quadrature of lunes	150
quadrivium	27, 35, 152
quantum physics	6, 48, 161

R

racism	48, 60, 80, 86
Rape of the Lock	192
Ravitch, Diane	39
Reagan, Ronald	17
re-experiencing	217
Reformation	55, 98
re-mythologisation	269, 273
rhetoric	27, 35, 121, 129, 132
Ricci, Matteo	153
Rigby, Brittney	82
Roberts, Jennifer	245
Robinson, James A.	94
Romanticism	169, 203, 272
Romeo and Juliet	275
Rosewarne, Lauren	86
Rousseau, Jean-Jacques	49, 182
Russian Revolution	98
Rylands, Leanne	6

S

salvation history	240–42
Santa Clara University	253
Sartre, Jean-Paul	15
scepticism	11, 26, 48, 161
Schama, Simon	1
Schleiermacher, Friedrich	215, 218
school choice	144
school funding	
accountability	143
Canada	144
Japan	144
low socioeconomic status (SES) parents	145
low-hanging fruit principle	141
Spain	144
school vouchers	139, 145, 146
Schrödinger, Erwin	48
science	11, 13, 15, 28, 35, 37, 58, 64, 81
Scruton, Roger	5

sculpture	167
secular revolution	242
seminar	3–4
Sendziuk, Paul	95
Seneca	127
Senior, John	40
sensibility	219–21, 224–25
Shakespeare, William	24, 47, 198, 213
Shelley, Mary	274, 275, 278
Sherrington, Geoffrey	54
Simmons, Michelle	6
Simpson, Kenneth	171
Smith, Jamie	243
Smith, Tony	255
Snow, C.P.	37
social	139
social class	137, 251
Socrates	75, 131, 186
Sokal, Alan	13, 155
Sophocles	74
Speer, Albert	274
Spengler, Oswald	49
St John's College	37
St Paul	49
St Philip Neri	279
St. Augustine	49–50, 59
standardised tests	133, 138, 172
Stanger, Allison	84
Steinbeck, John	33
Strayer, George D.	229
Stross, Randall	35
student mental health	86
Summerhill school	68
Summers, Anne	278
Sutherland, Rory	38
Sweller, John	73
Swift, Jonathan	213, 234
synchronicity	268

T

Taiping Rebellion	267
Taylor, Charles	244
Tertiary Education Quality and Standard Agency	89
Thatcher, Margaret	17
The Cruel Sea	266
The History Boys	131
The Matrix	200
The Merchant of Venice	198
The Raven	210
The Stanford Daily	48
The Tempest	4, 199
Theissen, Gerd	279
Thomas Aquinas College	37
Tolstoy, Leo	266, 271, 276
Tom Jones	213
trigger warnings	76, 86, 88
trivium	27, 35, 152
Troilus and Cressida	236
truth	2–8
Twelfth Night	214

U

unity in variety	208–10, 219
universal truth	11, 60, 64, 79, 272
university library	42, 45
University of Bologna	1
University of California, Berkeley	84
University of Chicago	87, 179
University of Melbourne	38, 84, 86, 95
University of Melbourne Student Union	82
University of New England	25, 87, 110
University of New South Wales	37, 82
University of Newcastle	110
University of Notre Dame Australia	37
University of Sydney	3, 79, 84, 88, 263
Unlearn marketing campaign	5, 79, 272
University of Sydney Union	82
University of the Third Age	31
utilitarianism	124, 164
utilitarianism in education	32, 34, 38, 55, 57, 71, 74, 108, 130, 137, 166

V

Veblen, Theodore	93
Verbrugghen, Henry	174
victimhood	14, 78, 80, 82, 198
Victoria University	71
Victorian Certificate of Education (VCE)	62
Victorian Committee for English in Technical Schools	67

Victorian Secondary Teachers Association	62
violence in public debate	78, 83, 84
Virgil	29, 41
virtue	123
vocabulary in classroom learning	234
vocational education	29, 32–34, 36, 37–39, 57, 103, 108, 131
Voegelin, Eric	278

W

Waldrop, Mitchell	157
War and Peace	276
Webster, William Franklin	230, 235
Weinstein, Bret	84
Wesley College	102
Western Australia Curriculum Council	65
Wheaton College	37
white supremacy	48, 51, 80
Wilde, Oscar	4, 49
Wilding, Michael	191, 195
William and Mary College	37
Williams, Raymond	61
Williams, Rowan	242
Williamsburg Charter High School	261
Wilson, Bruce	69
Windschuttle, Keith	191, 194
Wollstonecraft, Mary	275, 278
Wood, Robin H.	249

X

Xu Guangqi	153

Y

Yates, Lyn	67
Yeats, W.B.	31, 268, 269
Yiannopoulos, Milo	84
Young, M.F.D.	61

www.ingramcontent.com/pod-product-compliance
Lightning Source LLC
Chambersburg PA
CBHW021804220426
43662CB00006B/172